One Hundred Years
of
Catholic Social Thought

One Hundred Years of Catholic Social Thought

Celebration and Challenge

Edited by
John A. Coleman, S.J.

ORBIS BOOKS

Maryknoll, New York 10545

Second Printing, August 1991

The Catholic Foreign Mission Society of America (Maryknoll) recruits and trains people for overseas missionary service. Through Orbis Books, Maryknoll aims to foster the international dialogue that is essential to mission. The books published, however, reflect the opinions of their authors and are not meant to represent the official position of the society.

ORBIS/ISBN 0-88344-745-2

For Ralph Lane, Jr.
colleague and friend,
without whose generosity
this book could never have appeared

CONTENTS

viii   Contents

Introduction

A Tradition Celebrated, Reevaluated, and Applied

JOHN A. COLEMAN, S.J.

The essays in this volume were originally commissioned as background papers for a conference to be held at the University of San Francisco, June 25-29, 1991, to commemorate the hundredth anniversary of *Rerum Novarum*. The conference aims to bring together a little more than a hundred theologians, bishops, social activists, representatives of unions and corporate America, community organizers, politicians, and economists to help make the tradition of Catholic social thought come alive in new ways as it enters its second century.

The conference will focus heavily on process. For the bulk of its sessions, the participants will divide into six work groups of about a dozen persons each to convene around the three substantive topics of the family, work, and peace. This will represent the major challenge of the conference; that is, where should Catholic social thought go next in these three areas? Each group will choose a focused challenge theme in each of these three areas of family, work, and peace. Then, on the basis of discussion of these background papers, each group will be asked to produce a written document, a kind of mini-pastoral or encyclical that applies the tradition to our contemporary American context. My hope is that readers of this volume will approach these essays in the same spirit. Rather than merely to react passively to the written material, the reader is challenged to ask just where, in this last decade in twentieth-century America, Catholic social thought should develop, address new issues and contexts, and explore new byways in the areas of family, work, and peace.

On this occasion of the centenary of Pope Leo XIII's groundbreaking social encyclical on the rights of labor we want to *celebrate*, *reevaluate* and

1

bring forward this tradition of Catholic social teaching for our own time and country.

A CELEBRATION

We celebrate *Rerum Novarum* as the starting point of an important, indeed precious, tradition of Catholic social thought on the economy, politics, world order, and peace, which has served as a serious alternative and corrective to secular liberal and socialist understandings. At the forefront of that tradition stands the radical primacy of human dignity and human solidarity as correctives to mere technocratic understandings of the economy and politics. We celebrate a tradition that honors and respects social science and the rightful autonomy of the secular and does not avoid hard data, yet refuses to tolerate a kind of silly secularization which would segregate economics, politics, and issues of world order from deeper moral evaluation and human probing about what these do to, for, and with people.

To be sure, Catholic social thought is much older than one hundred years. Its roots go back to the life and words of Jesus. Jesus came "to bring good news to the poor, liberty to captives, new sight to the blind" (Lk 4) and identified himself, in the unforgettable image of the last judgment in Matthew 25, with the hungry, the homeless, the stranger, "the least of these." There are important social and political images and orientations in the New Testament itself: Mark 12:13's "Render to Caesar what belongs to Caesar . . . and to God what belongs to God"; and Peter's decisive reaction in Acts 5:29, "Obedience to God comes before obedience to humans." Catholic social thought finds roots, as well, in the early patristic insistence of Clement of Alexandria, Basil the Great, and Ambrose that caring for the poor was the same as caring for Christ himself, and that alms to the poor was not a matter of charity but justice. Thus, Ambrose could say: "Not from your own do you bestow upon the poor man, but you make return from what is his. For what has been given as common for the use of all, you appropriate to yourself alone. The earth belongs to all, not to the rich. . . . Therefore, you are paying a debt and you are not bestowing what is not due."[1]

For centuries Catholics contemplated the deeper meaning of Pope Gelasius' famous fifth-century formulation of a doctrine of two parallel swords, the temporal and the spiritual, and Augustine's construal of the relation between the two cities, the human city and the city of God.

Medieval theologians, on their part, discussed the morality of tyranicide and the liceity of sedition, measured the conditions for a just war, and worked for "the truce of God" to end wars. The medieval casuists espoused a doctrine of a just price. Thomas Aquinas, in his famous treatise on law in the *Summa Theologicae,* reminded earlier Christians that "law has as its first and foremost purpose the ordering of the common good."[2] For Thomas, the ruler was not above the law but bound by a deeper law of justice. Later Catholic thinkers such as Suarez and Vittorio forged the rudiments of a modern framework of international law. In that sense we could almost as well entitle our volume *Two Thousand Years of Catholic Social Thinking.*

Again, popes before Leo XIII addressed the social question. Gregory XVI's *Mirari Vos* and Pius IX's *Quanta Cura* and *The Syllabus of Errors* spoke to changes wrought by the French Revolution and the new bourgeois liberties and doctrines of the separation of church and state. The modern papal encyclical tradition really dates from 1740 with Pope Benedict XIV. In hindsight we find it fashionable to see these earlier papal social judgments as one-sidedly reactionary. Yet we do well to reconsider and reevaluate the wisdom in these earlier, pre-Leonine, papal no's to modern liberalism.

These popes spoke a loud no to an excessive individualism which broke up a larger solidarity; a decided no to schemes to privatize religion and keep it entirely within the sacristy; no to an espousal of a liberty of rights that allowed no clear corresponding duties; a resounding no to positivism in law and political science and economics, which would divorce the economy and polity (as impersonal and technocratic mechanisms) from moral scrutiny and human measure; a strong no to a theory of civil rights that thought economic rights, in Jeremy Bentham's terms, were "nonsense on stilts."

Recently Michael Schuck has persuasively shown a coherence to this Roman Catholic papal social teaching reaching from 1740 to the present.[3] Popes before Leo XIII abjured monarchical encroachments on the freedom of the church and rejected civil violence against secular states. They addressed family life and practices that threatened marriage and adolescent education. They condemned theft and immoral business practices such as excessive usury. *Mirari Vos* responded to Jeremy Bentham's utilitarian calculus for the social good of the greatest number. Gregory XVI retorted, "Every law condemns deliberately doing evil simply because there is some hope that good may result." Pre-Leonine popes set themselves against the social contract theory and unbridled capitalist market economies. Schuck argues that we lose something when we arbitrarily assign *Rerum Novarum* as the first of the social encyclicals: "By limiting analysis to a conventionally designated set of 'social' encyclicals, previous commentators have missed other letters of social relevance which aid interpretation of papal social thought as a whole."[4]

Schuck also notes:

On one level, the discussions are dissimilar: pre-Leonine period encyclicals portray the world as a nourishing, yet dangerous pasture; Leonine period letters picture the world as a benign, cosmic hierarchy of being; post-Leonine period texts view the world as a temporal context wherein God and humanity journey together. Yet despite these shifting viewpoints, the popes collectively construe the world as a medium of God's ubiquity. Whether pictured as a pasture, a cosmos, or unmarked path, the world is imbued with God's presence. Monica Hellwig discusses this characteristically Roman Catholic perspective when she says: "There is no realm whatsoever outside the dominion of that God." She continues "Neither politics nor economics, neither national interests nor international affairs, neither technology nor commerce, neither aesthetics nor productivity, can ultimately be a law unto itself." As a result, the popes uniformly criticize world views inspired by atheistic naturalism and dialectical materialism.[5]

The unity and coherence of this corpus of papal encyclicals, dating from 1740, argues Schuck, lie neither in Thomistic natural law theory (absent in the pre-Leonine corpus) nor in images of human dignity (not strong before the 1940s). Rather they are based in a view of the world as pregnant with the presence of God; in an understanding of the objectivity of moral values and deep concern for protecting the family, religion, and God's purposes for creation; in a sense of unity between the secular and the sacred, their nexus in God's ubiquitous presence.

Still, by common consent *Rerum Novarum* inaugurated a special new beginning for Catholic social thought and, thus, represents a kind of *magna carta* for modern social Catholicism. Popes subsequent to Leo—frequently on the very anniversary of the promulgation of *Rerum Novarum*—have updated, revised, or revisited its analysis in the light of changing economic and political conditions. Pius XI addressed the new reality of worldwide economic depression and economic monopoly in *Quadragesimo Anno* (1931); John XXIII reviewed new economic conditions in a postwar, postcolonial welfare state in *Mater et Magistra* (1961); Pope Paul VI turned to the North-South issues of development and threatened violent revolution in the Third World in *Populorum Progressio* (1967). No pope of this century has so widely written on or addressed social questions, from nuclear proliferation to ecology, as Pope John Paul II, whose two major social encyclicals, *Laborem Exercens* (1981) and *Sollicitudo Rei Socialis* (1987) bid fair to be viewed by history as ground-breaking renewals of this century-old tradition.

Inspired by this important papal enunciation of social Catholicism, regional and national conferences of bishops in Canada, the United States, Brazil, Germany, France, Chile, Peru, and the Philippines have attempted to apply this Catholic social thought to their own contexts and nations—addressing land reform, nuclear proliferation, refugee problems, unemployment, national economic policies for growth, the national debt of third-world countries, human rights abuse, revolution.

We celebrate the hundredth anniversary of *Rerum Novarum* because we believe that social Catholicism represents a serious and often distinguished tradition of investigation into the social significance of the modern nation-state, economy, and the conditions of interdependence among nations which foster or impede war and human and integral development. In celebrating its anniversary we celebrate the many Catholic peace and justice movements this tradition has spawned and which have added to the tradition of caring service, effective advocacy, and creative action: from *Le Sillon* in France; Antigonish with its cooperative movement in Canada; Mondragon (the worker-owned corporations) in Spain; human rights commissions in Brazil and Chile; the Christian Democratic Parties in Belgium and Holland; The Catholic Worker Movement, The Campaign for Human Development, Catholic community organizing, the Catholic labor schools and interracial work in the United States; Solidarity in Poland. These represent the very best commentary we can find on this tradition. In celebrating them, we recall a tradition whose cornerstone remains a serious option for the poor, for peace, for justice, and for human dignity.

Speaking of these movements for justice, the United States bishops in their 1991 pastoral message, *A Century of Social Teaching: A Common Heritage, a Continuing Challenge,* state:

> Across this country and around the world, the church's social ministry is a story of growing vitality and strength, of remarkable compassion, courage and creativity. It is the everyday reality of providing homeless and hungry people decent shelter and needed help, of giving pregnant women and their unborn children lifegiving alternatives, of offering refugees welcome and so much more. It is believers advocating in the public arena for human life wherever it is threatened, for the rights of workers and for economic justice, for peace and freedom around the world and for "liberty and justice" for all here at home. It is empowering and helping poor and vulnerable people realize their dignity in inner cities, rural communities and in lands far away. It is the everyday commitment and tradition of countless people, parishes and programs and of local networks and national structures—a tradition of caring service, effective advocacy and creative action. At the heart of this commitment is a set of principles, a body of thought and a call to action called Catholic social teaching.

The authors in this volume represent a decided tilt or bias toward Catholic progressivism, the Catholic left, and solidarity movements for justice in the church. We do not shirk from this choice. Others can celebrate the tradition in their own way. We know that Catholic social thought has never been an exclusive monopoly of the Catholic progressives in any sense, nor should it be. We agree with the United States bishops, who stated in their 1991 pastoral commemorating *Rerum Novarum* that "as we celebrate this century of social teaching, it is important to remember who calls us to this task and why we pursue it. Our work for social justice is first and foremost a work of faith, a profoundly religious task. It is Jesus who calls us to this mission, not any political or ideological agenda."

Still, progressive Catholic movements for justice have been in the forefront, for a century, of commenting on, enacting, and giving flesh to this

Catholic charter for their existence. They have been its main expositors and promulgators, and we celebrate this too. The balance we seek in this volume and in the conference is less one among the various ideological poles within social Catholicism than in the make-up of the authors and participants: bishops, pastors, economists, theologians, ethicists, community organizers, representatives of labor, business, and politics—pastors, practitioners, and theorists with a stake in bringing forward this tradition into the twenty-first century.

AN EVOLVING TRADITION OPEN TO HISTORY
AND NEW DATA

Catholic social teaching uses norms of judgment and standards for the orientation of action derived from the gospel and human experience. But the teaching itself has evolved through history and learned from some of its mistakes (such as the romance with corporatism in the earlier part of this century; shifts in the understanding of private property as proposed by Leo XIII; a reversal by John XXIII of Pius XII's opposition to worker co-ownership and co-determination schemes). Catholic social teaching has been inductive in its methodology and remains concerned about reading the signs of the times. It is an arena, preeminently, of the development of doctrine.

Just as the popes themselves have reevaluated the tradition over the years, the authors in this volume were challenged to do the same. They were asked not merely to celebrate the tradition as it already exists, but to evaluate it for any *lacunae* or blind spots, and to point to areas of change already achieved and those which still need to be incorporated into the tradition. They were asked to inspect both the conceptions in the teaching and the structural imagination needed to implement its vision. Clearly, ecology stands out as one major new issue for the tradition to appropriate. The present pope has begun to move the tradition forward in this area, to include with human dignity, justice, and solidarity the new notion of the sustainability of creation in evaluating the economy.

Finally, we made a decided choice to keep the focus on the context of the United States. This decision came not from any triumphalism on our part about the American system or American Catholicism or from any false sense of an American independence in an interdependent world. The choice was not meant to blind us to the important issues of third-world poverty, the arms race, bitter suffering by third-world refugees whose displacement is often caused by first-world governments or corporations. Rather, we wanted to move beyond mere principle to a new and concrete view of the teaching for our own time and country. We wanted to urge the participants at the conference to come up with agenda items for bringing this treasured tradition forward to our own time and place. Rather than have a mere token representation from other continents and places, we decided to keep the focus American, without allowing it to be closed in on itself or parochial.

The volume is divided into four major sections. In the first section we treat what in the planning sessions we called "metasubjects" (what a barbaric term!). These referred to issues which cross-cut the three substantive areas of the tradition we wanted to celebrate, reevaluate, and bring forward for our time: the family, work, and peace. Basically, we wanted several essays to treat the historical background of the tradition, to place its origins and development in historical and sociological context. The chapters by O'Brien, Coleman, and Zahn do this. Zahn reminds us how much social Catholicism has been a social movement and not just a theoretical enunciation of moral principles.

We knew that the double foundation of Catholic social thought in scripture and human experience (sometimes caught in the older term *the natural law*) remained problematic and would likely be raised in each of the three substantive areas. We asked Charles Curran to address this theme. How are these two sources of the teaching interrelated, mutually codependent? This remains an important, still-unresolved theoretical issue in the tradition.

Moreover, fundamental ecclesiological issues get raised when debates rage over the competence, scope, style, and validity of the church taking stands in the social order. We asked Bryan Hehir and Bishop Raymond Lucker to address the ecclesial dimensions of the tradition. Hehir charts shifts from Leo XIII's time to our own in the understanding of the right and competence of the church to address social issues. Lucker reminds us that the church which preaches social justice must first be just itself, an exemplary witness of its own social doctrine.

THE FAMILY

The second main section in this volume treats the family in Catholic social thought. The family is a unique nexus that unites the private and public, the church (the family as a unit of the church) and economy and politics. Moreover, no other single theme has so exercised Catholic social thought from its beginnings. This has been expressed in diverse ways such as concern about a limited state which recognized parental rights to determine the education of their children, to espousals of a family wage, to recent Vatican efforts to enunciate a charter of family rights in debates about rights at the United Nations.

Catholic thought on the family as a social unit is grounded in a more fundamental theology about the sacrament of marriage. Lisa Cahill takes up this theme and James and Kathleen McGinnis probe the ecclesial dimension of the family as domestic church. Major demographic, cultural, and technological shifts have taken place which represent, simultaneously, assaults on or aids to the family in the modern economy, polity, and church.

8   *John A. Coleman, S.J.*

Sheila Ryan Johansson depicts the effect of some of these demographic changes on family morality. Johansson states it sharply when she says: "Catholic family morality in the form of modern papal encyclicals is not really a form of social thought. It is a set of dogmas which are being a-socially conceptualized in some context-free manner." If demography does not have the last word, it reminds us, nonetheless, that Catholic family norms of morality (for example, on birth control) have important social and economic consequences which do not, on the surface, always seem to promote justice and integral human development. Ernie Cortes addresses cultural shifts that diminish a theory of family rights and the needed institutional changes to make the family again a true social unit and mediating institution.

Sidney Callahan speaks to technology (especially the new reproductive technologies) and its impact on the family. She tries to discern what is of permanent value and what may need reevaluation in Catholic teaching on reproductive technologies. Finally, Richard McCormick asks whether Catholic social thought on the family is coherent and consonant, in its ethical method, with Catholic thought in the economy and politics. Is Catholic social thought, he asks, of a piece?

WORK

A third section turns to the topic of work in Catholic social thought. In line with our decision to reevaluate and bring forward Catholic social thought in the American context we turn, first, to the bishops' pastoral on the economy. Archbishop Weakland asks what was missing in that pastoral, what can be learned from its critics, and what needs to be addressed in new ways today. Two economists, Charles Wilber and Robert Kuttner, look to an area imperfectly explored in Catholic social thought: the organization of work. What would workers rights and responsibilities look like in a changed competitive context? Only by answering this question will we be able to find the equivalent of what championing labor unions in 1891 might mean for our very changed American conditions of work and its organization. What new forms of social contract between labor and capital, what new forms of worker ownership and co-determination are possible and desirable in our setting?

If Catholic social thought is pro-union, it is not anti-business. We have asked a business executive, Thomas Johnson, to address what kind of market economy will be needed and how we can humanize the conditions of work in large corporations.

Surely one major area of new appropriation by Catholic social thought will be a serious address to the criticism by feminists and attention to the conditions of women in work. Blindness to women's issues and insights not only impedes the effectiveness of Catholic thought on the family but also Catholic construals of work. Carol Coston asks what the Catholic social tradition could learn from women's experience of work and its organization. Where should Catholic social thought today stand on issues of day care, equal pay for equal work, a family wage for single mothers?

PEACE

The final section of this volume addresses peace in Catholic social thought. The American bishops have taken a lead in the world church in confronting the arms race and nuclear proliferation. In this section, Joseph Cardinal Bernardin takes a new look at the bishops' pastoral *The Challenge of Peace.* Mary Evelyn Jegen helps us see how this social thought is carried by real movements for peace. Bishop Gumbleton talks to the issue of peacemaking as a way of life that would allow for an entirely new attitude to questions of war and peace. William O'Brien reminds us of the realist's demand that we not forget the need to continue some policy of effective defense, perhaps even nuclear deterrence, in a world of nuclear weapons. Kenneth Himes asks whether the American bishops are really ethically consistent in their unique (and largely unsubstantiated) claim in *The Challenge of Peace* that pacifism and just-war thinking are complementary and mutually supportive ways of thinking. Eric Hanson addresses the organizational revolution in world order necessary to create the conditions of peace.

BRINGING THE TRADITION FORWARD

Not all of the authors in this volume stand in agreement. There is a lively argument. This is as it should be since no tradition of the social good worth its salt is not worth arguing about. Few of the authors simply want to stand on the laurels of a hundred-year tradition, however venerable and honorable. They see some lacunae and weak spots, some very important unaddressed questions. Our hope is that, on the occasion of this centenary of *Rerum Novarum*, we will take the tradition it inaugurated so seriously that we will want to know passionately how to apply it in new ways and with fresh insights to the unfinished agenda of our nation and our world. With all its fine principles about the family and family rights, new questions of working mothers and the need for child care, of cultural erosion of the family as a mediating institution, and new demographic conditions demand a fresh look at the Catholic understanding of the family as a locus of social responsibility, a repository of rights, a source and school for virtue and solidarity. New economic conditions force us to rethink what the dignity of labor will mean in the twenty-first century and in the large organizational structures of our society. New challenges to peace have moved us, as Cardinal Bernardin notes, to see the bishops' pastoral on peace as already, in part, dated.

The next ten years could well seal the fate of the American economy and its ability to compete in the world economy as innovative, humanizing, and productive. New threats to human dignity and the solidarity of workers force us to address freshly the meaning and institutionalization of human work. Similarly, the end of the Cold War presents us with unique opportunities for building a new set of institutions for a peaceful world. Our ultimate hope is that these essays can serve as a background to help us write our new, updated *Rerum Novarum* for the twenty-first century. A tradition worth celebrating is worth fighting over, worth revising and reevaluating and worth updating to face the new signs of the times.

I conclude with the words of the United States bishops in their 1991 pastoral message *A Century of Social Teaching:*

> It is the challenge of our Lord Jesus Christ who laid out our continuing challenge in the Sermon on the Mount. In 1991, let us explore together what it means to be "poor in spirit" in a consumer society; to comfort those who suffer in our midst; to show mercy in an often unforgiving world; to hunger and thirst for justice in a nation still challenged by hunger and the homeless, poverty and prejudice; to be "peacemakers" in an often violent and fearful world; and to be the "salt of the earth and the light of the world" in our own time and place.

There is no lack of challenge as we start the second hundred years of Catholic social teaching!

NOTES

1. The citation from Ambrose is found in Charles Avila, *Ownership: Early Christian Writings* (Maryknoll, N.Y.: Orbis Books, 1983), p. 66.

2. For the Thomas citation, cf. Paul Sigmond, ed., *Saint Thomas Aquinas on Politics and Ethics* (New York: W. W. Norton Company, 1988), p. 45.

3. Michael J. Schuck, "The Context and Coherence of Roman Catholic Encyclical Social Teaching: 1740-1987," doctoral diss., the Divinity School, University of Chicago, 1987. A version of this dissertation will be published in 1991 by Georgetown University Press.

4. Ibid., p. 5.

5. Ibid., p. 408. The citation from Monica Hellwig comes from *Understanding Catholicism* (New York: Paulist Press, 1981), p. 185.

PART I

THE TRADITION: HISTORY AND NEW DIRECTIONS

1

A CENTURY OF CATHOLIC
SOCIAL TEACHING

Contexts and Comments

DAVID J. O'BRIEN

On the fiftieth anniversary of *Quadragesimo Anno,* John Coleman, S.J., demonstrated how difficult it is to refer to the papal social encyclicals as providing a "tradition." Internal inconsistencies, discontinuities, and sharply differing positions on key questions make it very difficult to generalize about Catholic social teaching, much less to present a century of papal commentary as a single coherent tradition, itself a word loaded with meanings in Catholic theology. I do not want to repeat here Coleman's critical examination of the major documents. Instead, I would like to reflect on the broader contexts from which those documents emerged and within which they were received. What was going on when the documents were written? How did the settings of church and society, and perceptions of those settings, influence the general direction of the encyclicals? I will discuss *Rerum Novarum* (1891) and *Quadragesimo Anno* (1931) at some length, *Mater et Magistra* and *Pacem in Terris* (1961, 1963) more briefly.

RERUM NOVARUM

Leo XIII confronted a Eurocentric world at the height of the Victorian era. England and its navy spanned the globe, the new German empire outstripped even England in industrial skill and stood poised to challenge her for political dominance as well, while France nursed the twenty-year-old wounds left by its defeat at Prussian hands. A unified Kingdom of Italy, with its capital in Rome, seemed securely established, though unrecognized by the pope, who never tired of seeking foreign support for the restoration of his temporal possessions. In the English-speaking world, where Catholics were a minority, the church was prospering, but in the European heartland, at the height of Europe's world dominance, Catholicism appeared to most sophisticated people as an anachronism—bothersome, sometimes disruptive, but clearly doomed by its adherence to ideas, symbols, and structures which no longer fit.

It was a progressive age, sure that its achievements constituted the pinnacle of human possibility, toward which previous ages had striven and which non-Europeans would naturally seek to emulate. Political centralization around modernizing bureaucracies, mass education, accelerating technological innovation, new and highly secular philosophies grounded in the cult of science, all contributed to a sense of optimism among the now dominant middle classes and those older elites who had joined them.

The most important thing about the world facing Leo XIII was that it was working, at least in the opinion of the dominant classes. The idea of progress, inevitable, automatic progress arising from laws of nature and history, was at its peak, in part because individuals, important social groups, and nations had experienced real improvements. Liberalism in politics, economics, philosophy, and religion was the operative ideology even of regimes whose authority was still grounded in tradition, as in Austria or Russia, or had been established by force, as in Germany. Instability there surely was, arising from exclusion: the working classes, whose anger found expression in socialism, and suppressed nationalities, seeking political forms for new-found cultural self-consciousness. Both socialist and nationalist movements blended romantic, sometimes quite conservative, yearnings for community and tradition with more modern aspirations for improved living standards, political participation, and self-determination. Among socialists, the older, almost religious movements of utopian socialism were giving way to more militant, professedly scientific and obviously modernizing forms under the influence of Marxism. But in 1891 the threat of socialism was not yet critical and the most important national aspirations in Germany and Italy had been fulfilled.

Leo's church stood apart from the dominant mood of liberal optimism. For one thing liberals throughout the century had regarded the church as a major enemy; when in power, they almost always sought to eliminate its privileges and marginalize its role in public life. Catholics who sought dialogue with secular liberalism had been badly defeated. At the First Vatican Council, only two decades before *Rerum Novarum*, the ultramontane movement captured the church for its own brand of militantly anti-liberal theology and politics. In its most important decree the Council declared the infallibility of the pope and, equally important, defined the papacy's all but complete jurisdiction over the universal church.

Vatican I marked a remarkable organizational revolution, removing altogether the barriers of national hierarchies and crown authority that had stood between the vicar of Christ and the ordinary Catholic. The purpose of the whole ultramontane movement was to strengthen the church for resistance to anti-Christian forces and render it independent, able to act on its own. It was to be a fortress, marked by its distance from emerging modern culture, but by no means a passive one. Resistance was one stage, counterattack another. Leo's task was to institutionalize this Vatican I centralization and to provide that new construct with a less obscurantist ideology. If there was any doubt that he did so, that he was a man of the post–Vatican I church, it was quickly settled by a series of learned encyclicals which rejected religious freedom and pluralism, warned of subversive forces in society, praised the repression of firebrands and agitators, and presented the church, if taken into partnership, as a bulwark of order and authority.

The prospects for Catholic restoration were not promising. Not only was the pope himself a "prisoner in the Vatican," but in Germany the church had just emerged from the assaults of the *Kulturkampf.* In France it faced an anti-clerical republic and Leo's efforts to persuade Catholics to participate in its politics failed. But Catholics were increasingly well organized. Informal devotions gave way to sacramental practice and formal religious instruction. The church could carry out a strategy of building parish-based church practice because it was gaining control over its own officials. Freed now from governmental patronage, it developed priests and bishops devoted to the church, hopefully to their people but always to the institution. National churches all but on their own a century earlier now acknowledged Vatican authority even in the details of ecclesiastical administration. This apparently reactionary church enjoyed a certain popularity. If the confident bourgeoisie remained hostile and portions of the new working class were being lost, the church drew strength from social groups alienated by modernization: aristocrats, peasant proprietors, artisans and shopkeepers. In some areas like Ireland, Poland, and Quebec, the church was a vehicle for national cultural resurgence. In Germany the Catholic Center Party, strong in Bavaria and other traditionally Catholic regions, had fought Bismarck to a draw. With the Germans pointing the way, Catholics were exploring new forms of organization, including trade unions, which would consolidate their subculture while allowing them to act rather than simply react to persecution. In short, the pastoral strategy of promoting sacramental practice in organized parishes and bringing popular devotions under clerical control, thus providing a religious basis for group identity, showed promise of flowering in other, more militant organizations and movements through which the church could contend for cultural authority and social strength, if not political power.

Finally, and most directly relevant to the encyclical, there was in 1891 a Catholic social movement aimed at directing the energies of the church to the social question. Some Catholic leaders had argued for years that the church's future strength depended less on the struggles of church and state than on forging new bonds with those hurt by industrialization: the increasingly insecure peasantry and lower middle class and, most important, the new proletarian working classes. The latter, they thought, held the key to renewing the church's influence, and by 1891 they had built a variety of movements aimed at achieving that objective. But this new social Catholicism was itself deeply divided.

One strategy was to join the working class in protest against bourgeois civilization, show how the church, too, rejected the inhumanity and brutality of industrial capitalism and an individualism that had destroyed guilds and churches alike and left the powerful free to exert their will. Paternalistic employers of an aristocratic bent, perhaps even a benevolent monarchy, would speak on the workers' behalf and fight for the restoration of Christian civilization. In parts of eastern and central Europe, where guilds still existed, Catholic social leaders stood in all-out opposition to capitalism, seen as an alien import associated with the Jews, and clung to a romantic vision of a bygone Christian social order. The church alone had answers to the social question; return to the church would have to accompany effective action for justice, and until then, there was no choice but to stand against liberalism, democracy, economic progress, and personal freedom as it had come to be understood since the Enlightenment. The alternative to this reactionary corporatism was posed in Germany, where the church organized workers and other social groups as part of its pastoral response to social change and then, challenged by Bismarck's modernizing reforms, formed the Center Party to present its defense against anticlerical legislation in the Reichstag. By organizing Catholics as workers, as economic actors, and by supporting a political party which had to compete with others for popular support, the German church necessarily had to accommodate its ideological radicalism to the practical requirements of such organization. At least temporarily, Catholics would have to accept the legitimacy of parliamentary government and capitalist economic organization. In doing so they could appear to be compromising their commitment to a Christian social order. So conflict arose between reformers, strong in Germany, and the radicals dominant in Austria and, to a lesser degree, in France.

Three things could be said about *Rerum Novarum* in this context. First it was reformist, not a radical document. Faced with a confident liberalism, and worried about the growth of socialism, Leo came down on the side of the Center Party, not on the side of the more extreme corporatists. Earlier he had attempted to lay the basis for Catholic participation in France's anticlerical republic, judging that they would be better able to forward their cause from inside than from outside the system. Similarly he had decreed the use of Thomistic philosophy in seminary education and encouraged biblical and historical studies because he wished to free the church from an inflexible, doctrinaire dogmatism that isolated it from modern claims of truthfulness. Just as he had tried to free the church from inflexible identification with royalty and with outmoded anti-intellectualism, he tried in *Rerum Novarum* to free it from paralyzing resistance to bourgeois civilization by shifting attention from the intractible problems of church and state to the social question, where a more flexible pastoral and evangelical approach might be possible.

Leo rejected the counterrevolutionary stance of the corporatists, while offering some reflections on the sources of modern problems that could confirm their alienation. But he chose the reformist option, evenhandedly condemning both socialism and laissez-faire liberalism. He endorsed workers associations, affirmed the positive responsibility of the state to intervene on behalf of the poor, and upheld the claim in justice to decent wages, hours, and working conditions. The church would engage in a mission effort to workers, defend their rights, and help them organize. Disentangled from medieval restorationism, the church would be free to adjust pragmatically to the social conditions of different nations, while continuing its critical stance toward capitalism.

Participation was acceptable (at least outside Italy); Catholicism need not be simply a counterculture. The dream of a restored and unified Catholic culture was postponed, not discarded. The encyclical made clear that the source of modern problems was the Reformation and the ensuing decline of Catholic influence, but the heart of the document, its elaboration of human rights and responsibilities, the positive role of the state, and the importance of organization all provided a foundation for active participation in modern society which the more stringent ultramontanes, and in some sense the reigning theology of the day, would not allow. It is no wonder that United States Catholics, when they thought about their role in public life, lifted Leo's Thomistic discussion of human rights out of their corporatist and ultramontane settings to construct a rationale for their participation in politics and nondenominational associations.

But, and this is the second point, this was a document of the ultramontane church. Priests, not laity, were urged to take up the cause of the workers. Leo intended Catholics to participate through Catholic organizations, and he expected such organizations to be under clerical control. Indeed the entire text reads as an analysis of and prescription for society from the point of view of the institutional church. Winning workers to the church is as important as defending their rights. The extremes of individualism and socialism not only hurt people and disrupt society, they also demonstrate the danger of organizing society without a clear commitment to the faith and the church. In the aftermath of the encyclical, Leo regularly warned against independent lay action, demanded hierarchical supervision of social action, and urged Catholics, as he told the Americans, to associate as much as possible with other Catholics and practice a docile submission to the church's authority. One might work with others for short-term reform, but as a tactic in the larger strategy of "recovering the world for Christ," the explicit goal of his successor forty years later.

Finally, *Rerum Novarum* was one expression of Leo's search for an independent middle ground between the perceived extremes of the age. In negative terms Leo issued a plague on both houses of capitalism and social- ism; more positively he claimed that the church could reconcile the classes and bring both social order and distributive justice. Thomism, with its bal- anced rationalism, was the intellectual foundation of this Catholic middle way; the *ralliement* was its political expression; the reformism of the encyc- lical its social agenda. Eventually, to be sure, it would be necessary to carry out corporatist reconstruction in a renewed Christian (read Catholic) civ- ilization, but for now that hard edge was muted by the strategic needs of the church in a period of triumphant capitalism.

QUADRAGESIMO ANNO

The atmosphere of 1931 was quite different. While it is too simple to say that liberal Europe died in the trenches of World War I, or at Versailles, or with the Bolshevik revolution, these events did dramatically change the European political, social, and cultural landscape. Liberalism remained— and remains—an important element of Western culture, but its adherents were chastened by the tragic events of the new century and by the dramatic challenges to Enlightenment rationalism which accompanied those events. By 1931 nationalism had destroyed the central European empires, while socialism, especially the communist wing now backed by the Soviet Union, had taken on authentic revolutionary potential. Frightened by the Reds, out of patience with the compromises and indecision of parliamentary gov- ernment, and no longer sure that the combination of technology and free markets meant progress, people responded to promises of authority, order, and harmony made by fascist movements.

Then came the worldwide depression, the immediate setting of Pius XI's encyclical. Here was an economic situation altogether different from that Leo faced. Now nothing seemed to work. Collapse of the banking system, spreading unemployment, inflation out of control in some countries, all suggested that liberal capitalism had failed. Liberal governments seemed unable to cope, fascists and communists fought in the streets, the world was on the brink of dramatic change.

Liberalism's crisis could seem Catholicism's opportunity. The church had clearly distanced itself from parliamentary regimes, multi-party systems, and free markets. It had no stake in the institutions created by nineteenth- century liberalism; its isolation of forty years ago now seemed an asset. At the same time its credentials as an opponent of the left, of socialism and communism, were unassailable. Untainted by association with liberalism and socialism, might the church not appear well-positioned to help restore traditional values, order, and stability? At the very least it might be easier for the church to reach accommodations with single-party states resting on such foundations, a judgment seemingly affirmed by the 1929 Lateran Treaty and Concordat with Mussolini.

The church of 1931 was even more unified under papal direction than forty years earlier. The condemnation of modernism had set back Leo's efforts at awakening scholarship, but it had also made the church a more formidable organization, especially when the insistence on uniform doctrine and discipline found expression in lay movements and organizations under clerical and episcopal direction. Catholic Action, the officially organized bodies of lay Catholics, constituted a means to exert influence and thus occasioned conflict with the state. Lay militants, in response, attempted to emulate their fascist and communist counterparts in dedication and discipline.

The Catholic strategy had moved from defense to counterattack. From the family to the League of Nations modern culture was in trouble and the church had the answer, indeed the only answer. Efforts to solve such problems without the church would prove futile, if not suicidal. Pius XI (and his successor) issued a steady stream of encyclicals on a tremendous variety of subjects, presenting those Catholic answers. To back up those answers, there were the organizations of Catholic Action and a tremendous number of committed priests, religious, and laity.

So, unlike *Rerum Novarum, Quadragesimo Anno* was radical, even revolutionary; it was about reconstruction, not reform. Its proposed Christian social order was both an expression of the demands of faith, mediated through the church, and a practical response to the problems facing society. Those were problems of authority, order, and stability, to which the right was responding, and problems of basic human needs, equitable distribution, and balanced power, which the left addressed. Both perspectives exposed the systemic failures of liberal capitalism, evident in the collapsing economies of 1931. With passion the pope denounced the system of organized greed; with equal passion, and no more attention to the claims of religious liberty and religious pluralism than his predecessors had exhibited at Vatican I, he proclaimed the need to rebuild the social order on Christian foundations. The corporatist vocational (or occupational) group system, organized around common, not class, interests, free from both state control and the contentious anarchy of classes and parties, would bring about a society marked by both order and justice.

The keynote of *Rerum Novarum* was the living wage, a prescription based upon human rights, the right to life, and to the means necessary to sustain life. It thus provided grounds for dialogue and participation in liberal societies. The keynote of *Quadragesimo Anno* was *social justice*, a term introduced in this document and specifying the directive principle of social institutions, not competition but the common good. This emphasis on the common good reflected the systemic character of the encyclical's critique and prescription. The marginalized church of 1891 could not speak with authority about sharing responsibility for the common good, because it was outside the circle of power; emphasis on human rights drew on a commonly accepted, increasingly consensual language to create common ground with other outsiders, in particular the workers. Now, in 1931, the center was open, and emphasis on social responsibility, on duty, order, and discipline, could create common ground with the right and legitimate Catholic move back to the center of national life. At the same time reaffirmation of Tho- mistic categories of rights retained a foundation for resistance to totalitar- ianism and appeals to liberal allies if that became necessary.

In democratic contexts, social justice could be read as calling Catholics to share with others responsibility for the common life and to persuade interest groups to act with attention to the general welfare: a voluntaristic exhortation to be unselfish and public spirited. John A. Ryan and his fol- lowers in the United States constructed on such foundations detailed pro- posals for a unique form of industrial democracy. They took for granted that unions and trade associations, adding co-partnership and other schemes of shared responsibility to the agenda of collective bargaining, could provide vehicles both for protecting individual and group rights and for participating in defining the common good at the level of the shop and the industry as well as the larger community. But where there was no interest in the give and take and negotiations of pluralism, the term had to do with constructing organizations based on common values and common interests, with institutional change, not education or moral conversion. Sub- sidarity, another new idea, supposedly guaranteed decentralization, but it left unclear how the content of the concept would be defined.

The problem of *Quadragesimo Anno*, then, was that its proposed Chris- tian social order would be difficult, perhaps impossible, to implement in a pluralistic society. How could differing interest groups be persuaded to subordinate group interests to the general welfare? More important, who would define the specific requirements of the common good? The church had always regarded the democratic answer of negotiation and compromise as incompatible with natural law. Fascism and communism would utilize the state, but the church could not allow such a powerful state, especially in non-Catholic hands. So in the end the new system could only work if whole nations returned to the church, accepted its teachings and its sanc- tions, and automatically and freely accepted the demands of right reason. The Christian social order was the economic and social expression of the post–Vatican I ultramontane church. In the absence of a Catholic majority, it would be necessary to acquiesce in a single party, which would coordinate the various elements of the economy and integrate them into the political system. It was an ideology of counterattack and Catholic restoration, grounded in the romantic corporatism of central European Catholics. It could and did inspire selfless devotion to a revolutionary cause; it could and it did attract deeply compassionate and committed churchmen all over the world, but it was a utopia, and a dangerous one.

Both Leo and Pius had spoken to Catholics and to the wider public from the standpoint of the post–Vatican I church. They were churchmen in the modern sense, loyal to the faith but also (might one say even more?) to the organization which claimed to be the living embodiment of that faith, indeed to be Christ's very presence in the world. Such men took for granted that what was good for the church was good for everybody. From this confident position, they and many others like them could discern in authentically prophetic fashion the foundational weaknesses of modern industrial capitalism, of liberalism, and of socialism. While few would risk the status and safety of the institution on behalf of those hurt by social change, many did see those hurts, denounced them publicly, and to some degree at least ministered to them. In some places, the church succeeded in winning the hearts and minds of men and women damaged by modern social change. What it failed to do was to see, and to identify with, the hopes and aspirations awakened by those same social changes. The popes saw and denounced the cruel treatment of workers, but did not affirm the workers' claims to a better life. They saw and denounced the rampant inequalities of modern life, but never made their own the idea that ordinary people have the right to share responsibility for the life of their communities. Refusing to acknowledge the legitimacy of pluralism, they could hardly understand the necessarily messy, ambiguous ways of democratic politics. In the end the church understood the damage caused by modernization, but it lacked insight into its liberating role; it could advocate and at times defend those in need, but it could not yet affirm a future in which all might participate. It played a critical, and not a constructive role, and in the end had to share responsibility for the outcome.

MATER ET MAGISTRA AND PACEM IN TERRIS

The world of 1961, the date of John XXIII's *Mater et Magistra,* differed from the world of Pius XI thirty years earlier even more than his world had differed from that of Leo XIII. Another world war, even more devastating than the first, left behind awesome weapons, disintegrating empires, and a divided and heavily armed Europe. To the East, the Soviet Union now ruled over heavily Catholic states and threatened to exterminate the church, while the Chinese communist regime seemed to have succeeded in doing exactly that. Western Europe was rebuilding, with United States help and often under the leadership of heavily Catholic political parties. The Cold War was the dominant fact of the day; the threat of communism gave the church and Western democracies a common enemy. What mattered was not the church's association with the political right before and sometimes during the war, but its long-standing opposition to communism.

There was another dominant fact, inseparable from the Cold War, the fact of nuclear weapons. These weapons rendered war between the major states unthinkable and made one or another form of coexistence inevitable. Two world wars had provided one common experience; fear of another rendered that experience immediate. Yet there was violence and the threat of violence everywhere. The strategy for keeping the peace was deterrence, the credible assurance of mutual destruction. Repression of anti-colonial rebellions, movements of national liberation, ethnic, racial and religious conflicts all made war a continuing reality of twentieth-century life.

The postwar world was increasingly tied together by new technologies of transportation and communication, and by an increasingly global and interdependent economy. Economic issues of the kind dealt with by the popes could no longer be adequately understood within the framework of the nation-state alone.

The situation of the church in the postwar world was paradoxical. At first glance the church was well-positioned. The papacy, seemingly rendered ridiculous by its intransigent resistance to modernity, now was a major factor in Western society and culture. Thirty years earlier the popes had responded to anti-liberal yearnings for authority, order, unity. Now, with even greater skill, the papacy set aside its disdain for pluralism, religious freedom, parliamentary government, and international organization. The new teaching of Christian democracy coincided with the emergence of Christian Democratic political parties as dominant elements in the politics of Western Europe. At the same time the church in captivity to the East gained prestige by martyrdom, while its presence outside the West gave it a global perspective that was almost unique.

Yet the church was less triumphant than it seemed. For one thing, serious Catholics had been deeply shaken by the war, the holocaust, and the decline of the colonial empires. The former events occasioned soul-searching among theologians and pastoral leaders. In France the latter forced a long search for the appropriate form for native churches in non-Western settings. If liberalism had been weakened by the First World War, royalism and reaction were destroyed by the Second. The church had no choice but to move to the left, but the pastoral, as opposed to the political, foundations for that move were weak. Low religious practice and limited acceptance of church discipline marked its European middle- and working-class members. In France, at least, the image which emerged was one of a minority church in a de-Christianized milieu; this image had great influence on pastoral and theological reflection during the period.

John XXIII, in his two encyclicals, responded to this new situation. First, *Mater et Magistra* and *Pacem in Terris* were far more democratic than the statements of his predecessors. The change had begun under Pius XII, but Pope John carried the affirmation of human rights, support for welfare state social reforms, and insistence on popular participation much further. For one thing, his list of human rights included both the social and economic rights developed in the social encyclicals and the political and civil rights, including the right to religious liberty, about which the popes had long seemed more doubtful. Because they drew heavily on neo-scholastic philosophical categories, John's encyclicals recalled those of Leo XIII, but now these affirmations of human dignity and human rights were placed in a democratic context: individuals and states had the obligation to share responsibility for constructing institutions in which these rights could be protected.

Second, John's writings were genuinely internationalist, appealing to the entire human community on the basis of a presumed concern for peace, freedom, justice, and human rights, without the insistence of earlier popes that only acceptance of Christianity and the church could enable the human community to find its proper political and cultural form. This reflected the sense of urgency created by nuclear weapons and the Cold War, to be sure, and the need for the church to reach out beyond the West, but it also reflected the quality most notable in John's writings: their standpoint within the human community rather than within the Catholic subculture. On the surface John XXIII was a churchman like others since Vatican I. But in the setting of the postwar world, he saw that the church must take its place in the middle of the historical experience, as brother and friend rather than simply teacher or judge.

At about the time *Mater et Magistra* appeared, theologian Karl Rahner wrote that the church, as church, could, in the name of faith, identify and name social evils and demand, in the name of faith, action to address them. But it could not, as church, prescribe how those evils were to be eliminated. The Christian must be a peacemaker, but the way to peace is complicated and involves human judgments. John XXIII wrote in that spirit, pointing to dangers, insisting on the Christian requirement to act, and expressing confidence that people of good will could in fact find ways to overcome the problems that confronted them.

In contrast to earlier (and some later) social teaching, John's was a message of hope and confidence. Leo and Pius, like the social movements which gave rise to their writings, played a critical, but not a constructive role; they could name with great force the evils of the day, but they stumbled when trying to present a credible alternative. John XXIII abandoned the very idea of a Christian social order as a specifically Catholic prescription for societal ills; the alternative was one which the human community would have to construct for itself in truth, justice, charity, and freedom. The church wished to be a companion in that project.

CONCLUSION

Leo XIII had written for an insecure church to what appeared to be a confident and secure world. Pius XI spoke for a more triumphal church to a world on the point of despair. John XXIII addressed a weary and worried world from the standpoint of a more humble and chastened church. In doing so, Pope John reopened the door to participation in liberal and pluralistic societies on the basis of natural law principles which had been ever so tentatively opened by Leo XIII. His opening was crippled by its location within the post–Vatican I Catholic subculture. With the changes of the Second Vatican Council, especially the *Declaration on Religious Lib-*

erty, Catholics could explore the requirements of citizenship (as done, for example, by John Courtney Murray and, more recently, by the United States Bishops) without the inhibitions the older church even at its best had imposed. In *The Pastoral Constitution on the Church in the Modern World* the Council claimed that the church had no political agenda of its own but participated in political life to defend human rights, promote human dignity, and build up the unity of the human family. On this basis the church speaks to issues from a standpoint deeply within the society, winning support by persuasion and seeking common ground with others, including non-Christians.

After Pope John this liberal position stood in tension with various survivals of older, more church-centered theologies and political strategies. On some issues, like sex, and in some settings, like those of persecution, the church adopted sect-like separatist strategies, speaking from its own distinctive standpoint, sometimes demanding resistance and renewing its subculture precisely by separation from the wider community. Similar impulses exist wherever Catholic identity is unclear and the unity and discipline of Catholic organization seems threatened. At the same time, freed from the intellectual and cultural barriers of the older subculture, Catholics around the world opened themselves to gospel-based, enthusiastic movements which produced more independent and evangelical styles of social and cultural action. These too had sectarian tendencies, judging events from an explicitly Christian perspective. Subcultural and evangelical Catholics, like the earlier popes, have a firm basis for discerning evils and denouncing them. But, also like the earlier popes, they find it difficult to define and build alternatives or to win attention and support from others who are not Catholics or Christians. As in the older conflicts of liberal Catholics with ultramontanes and corporatists, the more sectarian and separatist groups appear to speak with more integrity as Catholics, while liberals seem soft and accommodating. But if the task is to construct a world more genuinely human, that is, to persuade all persons to realize their full humanity, the liberal project of living as Christians in the midst of an ambiguous history, and to share responsibility for that history, seems indispensable.

At the least this analysis suggests that it is important for the church and its members to be ever conscious of their own location in particular cultures and in particular expressions of church. It is necessary to discern the assumptions about the relationship of church and world often buried in social pronouncements. Knowing that language itself is a cultural product, that the church is always in this world, while the world is never outside the church and is always in some sense religious, perhaps we can develop Catholic social teaching in ways appropriate to the needs of the church and the human community at our moment of responsibility.

2

NEITHER LIBERAL NOR SOCIALIST

The Originality of Catholic Social Teaching

JOHN A. COLEMAN, S.J.

Despite many shifts and changes in Catholic social teaching during the past one hundred years, Catholic social teaching remains a distinct and original social ideology, with a sort of unity based on its Janus-faced opposition both to liberalism and socialism. Others have pointed to the unity and originality of this corpus of teaching by appealing to the notion of a preferential option for the poor or the developing sense of human rights.[1] Both approaches are legitimate. I want to highlight the way in which Catholic social teaching in the nineteenth and early twentieth century was rooted in a distinct social location, which put it at odds with both liberalism and socialism. Responding to real social movements for social change both within and without the church, Catholic social teaching came up with a distinctive and original social ideology. Despite real and important shifts in the conceptual focus of this teaching (for example, toward a balance of scriptural vision against a more pure natural-law approach; to a change in the theory of private property as first espoused by Leo XIII; toward a more dynamic and historical understanding of natural law), it remains today a distinctive alternative conceptual scheme and direction-giving philosophy (a social ideology) to the regnant variations of classical socialism and liberalism. As these last two have changed, over time, so has social Catholicism. Selectively, it has incorporated elements from these other two competing modern ideologies, yet generally based them on uniquely Catholic philosophical and theological grounds.

25

HISTORICAL PERSPECTIVES ON THE PAPAL SOCIAL
IDEOLOGY

Several excellent historical studies exist which treat Catholic social movements in nineteenth- and twentieth-century Italy, Germany, France, Austria, the Lowlands, Brazil, Argentina, and the United States.[2] My purposes here are much more modest than any attempt at an adequate retelling of the history of social Catholicism as seen from the vantage point of the groups which embodied its social ideology. I want merely to give some flavor of the diversity of such groups, their social location and competing political positions. Second, I want to show that despite a spectrum of unresolved positions there are some common motifs and direction-giving orientations in the tradition stemming from its opposition to both liberalism and socialism.

The church's deep involvement in politics dates from the early Middle Ages. Christian theology, for its part, has developed from the time of Origen and Augustine through Aquinas a sophisticated theory of the appropriate relation of Christianity and the state—the purposes, autonomy, and limits of state authority, and the obligations and limits of Christian citizens to obey political authority. At the time of the rise of the modern state this tradition was extended by the scholastic theorists such as Suarez, Vittoria, and Molina. This larger theological tradition forms a background to the modern papal ideology.

The idea that humans could actually transform society by creating new political, economic, and social institutions dates only from the eighteenth and nineteenth centuries, most particularly since the French Revolution. Recognition of a distinctively "social question" only came about with the uprooting of a landed peasantry and their migration into industrial cities. These two important nineteenth-century revolutions—the French and the Industrial Revolution—evoked Christian assessments and response, as they evoked modern liberalism and socialism also as responses. They gave rise, in the late nineteenth century, to that distinctive amalgam of currents of thought, concepts, and principles which became social Catholicism. In a strict sense, I would argue, the Catholic social ideology is a product of a precise history.

In general, France was the chief testing ground for Catholic reactions to the political and industrial revolutions. The church broke with the French Revolution and the principles of 1789 over the issues of the civil constitution for the clergy, the oath of allegiance to the state, and an *église salarie*. As one historian has put it, "the revolution wanted not orderly cooperation but the subordination and incorporation of the church."[3]

If the Catholic social ideology, in Alfred Diamant's phrase, represented "a two-front war against Adam Smith and Karl Marx, against laissez-faire and socialism," Catholic social theory was less forged in grand philosophic isolation than in the crucible of actual political struggle.[4] Liberal governments and movements in nineteenth-century France and Italy were decidedly laicist and anti-Catholic. They sought to place severe restrictions on the freedom of the church. The church lost the workingman in France and Belgium as the peasants migrated to the cities and later turned socialist. The social location of the distinctive Catholic constituency—active, practicing, and self-consciously Catholic—in France, Austria, and Italy in the nineteenth century was in the aristocracy, the peasantry, and the small artisan and petit bourgeois class.[5]

The upper middle and professional classes—the constituency for classic nineteenth-century liberalism—and the proletariat—the constituency for socialism—were either outside the church or unfavorable to it. Hence, the social location of the typical constituency for Catholic politics in nineteenth-century Europe almost guaranteed a social stance different from both liberal and socialist social programs.

After 1789 one of the key issues being raised was whether the republican form of government was compatible with Catholic social teaching. A related issue was the appropriate measure of state activity to guarantee the common good. The Catholic view of the state favored neither the Girondist caretaker state nor the Jacobin omnicompetent state. In general, Catholic thinkers completely rejected Rousseau's way of construing political obligation and individual rights, the notion that society is created by a social contract. Instead, they stressed the organic nature of society, the importance of intermediate groups and natural hierarchies. As Leo XIII would put it in his encyclical *Libertas Praestantissimum*, the liberties of 1789 were unacceptable because they denied the divine origin of civil authority and individual liberties.[6]

Connected to these issues of the liberal parliamentary state and liberal ways of construing natural rights and civil liberties, questions arose about a liberal economic philosophy based on the myth of the free market. A leading historian of Catholic social movements, Joseph Moody, states the issues involved in the challenge of nineteenth-century liberal economic and political philosophies to the Christian faith of the church:

> The dominant economic philosophy was basically hostile to Christianity and irreconcilable with it. Economic liberalism was, in a sense, a rival faith founded on the worship of technique as its central mystique, on science viewed as religion, and on a boundless faith in human reason, narrowly understood. Its utilitarian ethics ignored all values that did not immediately contribute to man's economic needs. Religion was banished from the market place and in its niche was enshrined the goddess of unrestrained freedom in the pursuit of economic satisfaction. Equally in politics, the claim of religion to be heard in public affairs was denied. . . . More fundamentally, the unlimited optimism of the age led to the rejection of the basic Christian doctrines of original sin and redemption.[7]

THE SPECTRUM OF CATHOLIC SOCIAL MOVEMENTS

Moody reminds us of the great diversity of Catholic groups and movements responding to the social question in nineteenth-century France.[8] We need a thumb-nail sketch of this variety.

The Reactionary, Traditionalist Authoritarians

In the immediate aftermath of the French Revolution, the French emigre community produced two major Catholic social theorists who combined criticisms of the revolution with a call for the reestablishment of the old monarchical order. Joseph de Maistre in *Considerations sur la France* and *Du Pape* and A. de Bonald in *Theorie du Pouvoir Politique* stressed the values of concrete experience over abstract reason, of society over the individual, order over progress. De Maistre contended that national sovereignty needs a counterweight in order to prevent its deterioration into limitless despotism. He suggested that the temporal power of the papacy and the papacy's indirect adjudication of other temporal sovereignties serve as the needed counterweight to the rise of the sovereign nation-state. None of the popes accepted whole cloth de Maistre and de Bonald's reactionary, traditionalist authoritarianism. This was partly because these reactionaries' theory of religion reduced religion to a social utilitarian support for traditional societal authority. It denied a genuinely independent role to religion above and beyond its social function. Still, the hankering for a renewal of an idealized medieval polity typifies and informs much of Catholic social thought until the eve of the Second World War. Especially noticeable in this regard are the proposed schemes for a corporatist vocational order which — even when divorced of de Maistre's explicitly authoritarian and nostalgic motifs as in Pius XI's *Quadragesimo Anno* — implicitly looks back to medieval social harmonies (to a world before either liberalism or socialism) as normative.

The Paternalistic, Reformist Aristocrats

A second group of Catholic social thinkers included men such as Villeneuve-Bargemont, who argued, in his 1834 book *Economie, Politique Chretienne* that workers had a right to their own organizations and that state intervention was necessary to combat wage slavery. Other paternalistic monarchists in France such as Count Albert de Mun, the Marquis Rene de la Tour du Pin, and Frederick LePlay showed genuine, if paternalistic, interest in ameliorating the position of the lower classes and reasserting an authentic Christian aristocratic elite. Like the red Tories in England, these social Catholics took up, in a paternalistic way, the cause of the working class, basing their cause on a nostalgic retrieval of the medieval romantic view of aristocrats, organic social solidarity, and a guild society of peasants and skilled artisans. The paternalistic reformers looked upon the emerging proletariat as a species of new "barbarians" who might provide fresh energy for a renewed Christendom in a tired and spent Europe. The church sought a way to baptize these proletarian barbarians and bring them under its tutelage as it had the barbarians of old. While basically intransigent on the political question of a republican form of government—de Mun and la Tour du Pin helped organize a counter-centenary celebration for France in 1889—the reformist aristocrats were relatively progressive in advocating reform measures in the economy (child labor laws, reduced working hours, state regulation of a legal standard for a minimum just wage). They also adhered much more to statist and interventionist premises than nineteenth-century laissez-faire liberalism would have allowed.

Liberal Catholicism

A third group of social Catholics, which formed the group around the journal, *L'Avenir*, included Lammenais, Lacordaire, and Montalembert. These liberals desired an accommodation with the principles of the republic. Their ideas generally coincided with those of Alexis de Tocqueville. Republican democracy was seen as an inevitable fact in the design of providence. It had stood the test of time and should be tolerated.

The *L'Avenir* group accepted the liberal civil liberties and representative parliamentary government. On the other hand, they resisted French laicist notions that restricted the cultural and political voice of the church. They also fought against the Rousseauian bias against intermediate groups. They denied to the state any basis for a claim to exercise an educational monopoly. In their view, intermediate groups would serve as a buffer and zone of creativity for individuals vis-à-vis the state.

Hans Maier has argued that the liberalism of these "liberal" French Catholics rests on radically different premises—among them, the divine origin of all human authority—than the regnant political liberalism of "secular" Rousseauian France. The *L'Avenir* group consisted of accommodationists rather than strict liberals. Unfortunately, however, the members seemed, to some extent, to have made a *theologoumenon* of democracy, thereby sacralizing a historically relative form of polity.[9] This led to their condemnation by the church.

Gregory XVI condemned most of the propositions of the *L'Avenir* group in his encyclicals *Singulari Nos* and *Mirari Vos*. Unfortunately for their cause, the group's famous slogan, "A free church in a free state," had been taken up by Cavour in Italy as a cudgel against the papacy. The condemnation of the liberal Catholicism of Lammenais, however, did not end the Catholic movement for accommodation with the major political tenets of liberalism such as separation of church and state, a charter for civil and political rights of individuals against the state, and so on. In Belgium, especially, the revolt against the hegemony of the Netherlands in 1830 brought Catholics and liberals together in a coalition of a nationalist agenda of founding the freedom of the nation. Although checked in France, the ideas of Lammenais flourished among Catholics in the Lowlands, the United States, and Ireland.

When later in the century the political tenets of liberalism were again condemned in Pius IX's encyclical *Quanta Cura*, Bishop Dupanloup of Orleans countered the papal condemnation with his famous distinction between a thesis and a hypothesis: "A wrong theory which must be repudiated as a general principle and rejected in all cases as a true thesis, can however contain so many truths that it can lead to a materially practicable solution, if it is applied to adequate circumstances (as a hypothesis) in a prudent and cautious way."[10] Dupanloup's casuistry fought for space to keep alive some dialogue between social Catholicism and liberalism. The bishop sought to juxtapose history to ahistorical essentialist thinking.

Variations of this Dupanloup distinction would be used through the nineteenth and early twentieth centuries by progressive Catholics to allow some accommodation and Catholic appropriation of given elements of liberalism and socialism. A variation of Dupanloup's casuistry was evoked by John XXIII in his encyclical *Pacem in Terris* to justify a new partial accommodation with socialism. Nevertheless, the excessive individualism, voluntarism, and positivism of liberalism would remain areas of Catholic contention with liberalism, just as the three issues of a right to private property, a materialist interpretation of history, and the doctrine of class warfare would set off social Catholicism from Marxist socialism. Even when appropriating elements from either of these nineteenth-century economistic theories, social Catholicism would base them on radically different premises.

The Christian Democrats and Meliorists

Frederic Ozanam is the major French source for a meliorist, nonromantic view of social reconstruction. He endeavored to discover, behind the unresolvable French political question concerning the legitimacy of a republican form of government, the deeper issue of a social question. "Avoid politics and concentrate on the social question" was his resounding battle cry to fellow Catholics. The Christian democrats, following the lead of Ozanam, nurtured no desires to restore the past, nor did they feel that the masses needed to be guided by the ruling classes. Ozanam's position—similar in many ways to the meliorist position of Bishop Emmanual von Ketteler in Mainz—had four major planks:

(a) Economic liberalism is a materialist system that degrades the dignity of the human person. Persons become mere utilitarian means—even machines—in this economic philosophy rather than the ends of all action. The hierarchy of human values is distorted and reversed by liberalism. In

Leo XIII's famous phrase from *Rerum Novarum* "man precedes the state" and, presumably, also the economy.

(b) The system of capitalist production is basically unjust, and the economy leaves the determination of wages to an impersonal law of supply and demand instead of adjusting them to foster decent, minimal conditions for human life. Workers must not be treated as commodities whose price (or right to work) rises and falls with the market.

(c) Charity may bind the wounds of the poor, but it is not an adequate remedy. Only justice can establish a true human relationship between employer and laborer.

(d) The labor market must be regulated by the free organization of the workers into unions and by some state control of wages and conditions of labor.

Hans Maier has summarized what he sees as the most important characteristics of this Christian-Democratic school in nineteenth-century France: "the primacy of the social over the political, Ozanam's contribution; the complimentarity of human rights and civic duties; the limitation of state sovereignty in favor of individual and corporate rights; the demand for a subsidiary structure of society through political decentralization and a corporate economic system."[11]

The Christian Socialists

A final group, the Christian socialists, is best typified in the representative figure Philippe J.B. Buchez, who wrote a monumental forty-volume Christian interpretation of the French Revolution. Buchez, a follower of Saint Simon, founded a journal and movement for workers, *Atelier*, in the 1840s. He was vice-mayor of Paris and the first president of the National Assembly in the revolution of 1848. Buchez' program sought to neutralize the conflict between capital and labor by uniting both groups in an all-embracing corporatist *organization du travail*. Buchez also severely criticized the liberal principles of human rights by insisting on a list of civil duties and social rights (as an extension of the principles of 1789). He added a "socialist" set to the "individualistic" principles of 1789. From the beginning, social Catholicism has always included its minority movement of "red abbés."

Social Catholicism would continue — into the twentieth century — a horror of class conflict and perpetuate "the naive assumption, common to all corporatists, that social conflict could be alleviated and perhaps eliminated by the simple expedient of bringing the social classes together into the same organization."[12] Until World War II social Catholics would remain enamored of a corporative ideal for society. In this view capital and labor would constitute a joint economic parliament, separate from the state, as such. Catholic social thought never really probed the anarchic potentialities in this theory. In more recent years this ancient theme of the unification of capital and labor has been taken up by social Catholics in an espousal of industry councils and co-determination and profit-sharing schemes, endorsed strongly in the social encyclicals of John XXIII.

Some such varied spectrum of social ideologies among Catholics ranging from authoritarian reactionaries, paternalistic romantics, liberals, democratic meliorists, and Christian socialists, was no less typical of nineteenth-century Austria and Germany, where the main juxtaposition pitted the romantic medievalists who rejected capitalism as immoral (Joseph Goerres and Karl von Vogelsang) against the meliorists (such as the solidarist school of economics and Bishop von Ketteler).[13] Within this spectrum the position of the meliorists won out in determining Catholic economic and social policy. Some such variety and spectrum of social positions, moreover, continued in European Catholicism through the Second World War and beyond. Over time, the reactionary and romantic positions have waned. By the end of World War II they had dropped out as effective voices within the Catholic social spectrum, at least in Europe and North America, although residues of these traditions lived on in Latin America. The liberal and Christian democratic stream became dominant in the post-World War II period. Between the two wars and in the aftermath of World War II, a species of Catholic socialism—personalist socialism—emerged in various movements. Its ideology is best stated in the works of Emmanuel Mounier.[14] The older dream of a "corporative society" reconstructed on medieval organic principles was quietly dropped by the end of Pius XII's papacy, never to be heard from again.

COMMON ASSUMPTIONS ACROSS THE SPECTRUM

Despite the variety, there is a peculiar tilt and drift in this Catholic social spectrum. The social ideology is strongly rooted in the social location of nineteenth-century European Catholicism and the social questions of that continent and age. The social ideology forged in that period—creating formative ideas, principles, and metaphors that perdure into the late twentieth century—is a historically distinctive constellation of social thought. Several important biases in this ideology, generally subscribed to across the Catholic spectrum, can be briefly summarized:

An Anticapitalist Bias

The major economic debates which lie behind the texts of *Rerum Novarum* of Leo XIII and *Quadragesimo Anno* of Pius XI involve reactionary, medieval romantics who rejected capitalism hook, line, and sinker and incorporated a Catholic version of the labor theory of value, who were pitted in dispute with "reluctant capitalists," reformers who accepted capitalism as a system while rejecting its abuses. These latter reformers, following the lead of Bishop von Ketteler, Heinrich Pesch, and the German

Solidarists, were reforming capitalists. Nevertheless, an anticapitalist bias (or, minimally, suspicion) remains a perduring residue in the papal social ideology.

Socialism is also rejected by social Catholicism. This rejection is rooted in the antireligious animus of much of nineteenth-century continental socialism. With the organization of Catholic groups concerned with the working class — labor unions, benevolent associations, and such — and eventually the rise of multi-class Catholic denominational parties in Europe, socialist parties and labor unions competed for the Catholic working-class votes. Many of the historic Catholic pronouncements condemning socialism closely relate to the electoral fortunes of Catholic confessional parties in Italy, Belgium, Germany, and elsewhere. In that sense, their high doctrinal formulations often represent rationalizations of confessional self-interest. Nevertheless, the economic philosophy of the dominant German (and Jesuit) solidarist school of economics — so influential on social Catholicism through the end of World War II — derived from the armchair or "salon" socialism in German academic economics.[15] This source of social Catholicism diverged from classic liberal and neo-liberal positions and their corresponding social ideologies.

A Bias toward the Social rather than the Political Revolution

This second Catholic bias — strongly stated in the papal strategies of Leo XIII and Pius XI, but still alive today — led to a peculiar amalgam of a relatively progressive economic position coupled with a decisive distrust of political parties, civil libertarianism, and parliamentary democracy. The incorporation of a decidedly democratic predisposition into the papal social ideology did not occur until the papacy of Pius XII, although the Christian democratic strain formed an unbroken subtradition in social Catholicism since the time of Lammenais. In the post–World War II period this strand became dominant. Earlier authoritarian views based on paternalism (the masses are as children in need of leadership from above) or a Catholic animus against liberal civil liberties grounded in individualism, the social contract, and the denial of a divine origin of all societal authority have progressively ebbed away. The liberal liberties are currently accepted but on a philosophical ground other than their basis in liberalism.

The bias toward addressing the social rather than the political question, Ozanam's perduring legacy, continues unabated in papal social thought. It has been forcefully restated by John Paul II. This bias is the reason some Catholics have seen the papal social ideology as a crypto-justification for the liberal capitalist order. With Gregory Baum, they argue that

> The difficulty of Catholic social teaching was that it did not correspond to any actual historical movement. . . . Catholic social teaching was "idealistic" in the positive Catholic sense, inasmuch as it demanded faith, sacrifice and

selflessness, and "idealistic" in the pejorative Marxist sense, inasmuch as it was a pure creation of the mind, outlining what ought to happen according to an abstract ideal of justice, and not a social theory based on the actual historical experience of people struggling for emancipation. The "third way" beyond capitalism and socialism was not a concrete, historical political option in western society.[16]

Baum contends that an ideology unrelated to real social movements is bound to seem abstract and sterile. Yet, if Catholic social teaching did not correspond to any actual historical *movement,* as we have seen, it did correspond to the social location of Catholics in the late nineteenth and early twentieth century: peasants, aristocrats, petit bourgeois.

A Bias toward a Pluralist View of Authority

Social Catholicism stresses the "natural" organic nature of society and the necessity of protecting "natural," intermediate, voluntary groups such as neighborhoods, regions, guilds, labor unions, and social and familial groupings of all kinds from encroachment or suppression by the expanding state. Catholics share an instinct—embodied in Pius XI's principle of subsidiarity—that such intermediate groups are the real locus of creativity, social freedom, and spontaneity. They should be supported—the root meaning of the Latin word *subsidium*—rather than supplanted by the state. As Pius put it, the state can and should intervene to "encourage, stimulate, regulate, supplement and complement" these intermediate groups.[17] Pius' teaching on this issue was reiterated by both John XXIII and Paul VI.

In this regard the classic nineteenth-century Catholic criticism of liberalism—shared widely along the spectrum of social Catholicism from reactionaries to Christian democrats—accused the liberal state of being simultaneously omnicompetent and powerless. Liberal legal theory was condemned because it denied the existence of a higher law and thereby entrusted vast powers to the font of positive law—the state. Against this view Catholic legal theory rooted positive law in a divine "natural" law and recognized social authorities in intermediate groups such as the family, the church, and voluntary social groups that did not derive their authority from the state or exist at its good pleasure. Their intrinsic, underived authority flowed from the very sociality of human nature.

On a second front, Catholics criticized liberal political theory for defining the sphere of public law so narrowly that the state had become powerless to regulate social and economic affairs. Throughout the spectrum of social Catholicism, Catholic ideologies have never assumed that that state is best which governs least. Classic Catholic views maintain a strong statist expectation. Catholic social teaching, following the classical tradition, holds governments responsible for the well-being of society.

A Bias toward Social as well as Individual Rights

Catholic rights theory—following the lead of Buchez—invariably juxtaposes the civil liberties of 1789 with social rights to such things as a just wage, workers' rights to organization, just prices. This Catholic rights theory—ultimately rooted in Catholic notions of human dignity and social solidarity—led to a quite different Catholic justification for private property than that of theories resting on liberal premises. Catholic theories stress the social nature of private property, its historically relative character. Catholic social ideology can envision, in the words of John Paul II, a social mortgage on all property, or, in the view of Pius XI in *Quadragesimo Anno*, forms of property that only the state can control since "they carry with them an opportunity for domination too great to be left to private individuals."[18]

The work of the major theorists of social Catholicism in this century—Pesch, Sturzo, Maritain, Mounier, LeBret—as well as contemporary political and liberation thinkers, incorporate these four major Catholic social biases. Continuously the Catholic social ideology distances itself from both liberalism and socialism. This view is explicit in *Rerum Novarum, Quadragesimo Anno,* and *Sollicitudo Rei Socialis. Quadragesimo Anno* refers to Leo XII as seeking "help neither from liberalism nor socialism. The former had already shown its utter impotence to find a right solution of the social question, while the latter would have exposed human society to still graver dangers by offering a remedy much more disastrous than the evil it was designed to cure."[19] The same rejection of both liberalism and socialism is found more recently in the *Medellín* and *Puebla* documents of the Latin American episcopacy. A dramatic statement of this theme can be found in Paul VI's apostolic letter *Octogesima Adveniens*:

> The Christian who wishes to live his faith in a political activity which he thinks of as service cannot without contradicting himself adhere to ideological systems which radically or substantially go against his faith and his concept of man. He cannot adhere to the Marxist ideology, to its atheistic materialism, to its dialectic of violence and to the way it absorbs individual freedom in the collectivity, at the same time denying all transcendence to man and his personal and collective history; nor can he adhere to the liberal ideology which believes it exalts individual freedom by withdrawing it from every limitation, by stimulating it through exclusive seeking of interest and power, and by considering social solidarities as more or less automatic consequences of individual initiatives, not as an aim and a major criterion of the value of the social organization.[20]

PAPAL SOCIAL IDEOLOGY: AN IDEAL TYPE
AND THEMATIC SUMMARY

In his historical survey of the papal ideology up to Vatican Council II, Richard Camp assesses the achievement of this body of thought. It represents a serious and often distinguished tradition of investigation into the social significance of the modern nation-state. The popes' approval of state activity never became utter dependence upon it. Their ridicule of anti-statist individualism never degenerated into scorn for individual rights or dignity. Nor did their differences of interpretation conceal the fundamental unity of their basic hope — that the modern state would become a means of more abundant life, not an instrument of tyranny.[21]

My own view sees the papal ideology as a product of history, a unique constellation of ideas, norms, and principles derived, in part, from classical, pre-modern notions of authority in society based on organic solidarity in a hierarchical social structure. This pre-modern understanding underwent adaptation in the nineteenth century in response to the rise of liberalism and socialism and was carried by the unique class location of European Catholicism at that time. While social Catholicism endorsed neither liberalism or socialism, it gradually accepted elements or emphases in each, passing them through its own discernment model. In so doing it became a complex, separate modern ideology for social life. In the twentieth century, papal-social ideology has strongly embraced democratic participatory themes in state and economy and strongly stressed the interdependence of nations. Although it shares elements with other traditions, social Catholicism is not reducible to any of them. The consistency of the evolving papal social ideology can be summarized under five thematic rubrics. Its understanding of state authority and citizen participation is (1) religious; (2) communal; (3) personalist; (4) pluralist; and (5) social democratic.

Authority and Citizen Participation as Religious

In the Catholic view, all authority is ultimately derived from God. Consequently, every state authority involves a *limited* sovereignty. The limitation of the state's rightful power rests in the belief that the authority of the state is not *sui juris* but a delegation from God. State power can not be exercised merely for the benefit of the rulers or in a way that perverts justice and human dignity.

State authority is limited by what is set above it in ultimate judgment (divine transcendence and natural law). It is also limited by a sphere (the spiritual) within society itself, which contains its own autonomy. The government is simply incompetent to make judgments about religious liberty of conscience, truth, and revelation.

The political implications of Christianity are unique among the world religions because Christianity sets the kingdom of God over against the principalities and powers. Caesar is granted a realm — legitimate, even extensive, authority — provided that realm is seen as also limited in the scope of sovereignty, checked by another realm, the things of God, which is its superior. As sociologist David Martin comments, "Christianity creates counter-cultures above and below the unity of natural society." Martin also notes the totalitarian tendencies in a purely secular view of authority, its propensity to divinization. In this regard, "the only tradition which can inhibit the tradition of secular divinities, collective or individual, is the tradition which maintains secular and sacred in a complex balance. Unless you have sacred *and* secular, you cannot control the destructive potential of divinization."[22]

Although it roots all authority ultimately in the transcendent, Catholic social theory nevertheless respects the autonomy of the secular. What it cannot accept is any view of the secular which would destroy or totally isolate the sacred. In the Catholic view no human authority is self-grounding. It is subject to judgment in accord with the purpose of every civil authority, which consists in the furtherance of the common good.

Authority and Citizen Participation as Communal, Personalist, Pluralist

Catholic social theory is not anarchist. It does not denude the state of essential authority. Rather the state represents the highest, indispensable, and most responsible agency for determining the common good. Notoriously, against liberalism social Catholicism maintains a very strong social sense of human nature. Against liberalism Catholic social teaching holds governments responsible for the well-being of society. The Catholic concept of a "common good," which is something *structural* and more than the mere additive summation of individual goods, militates against the nightwatchman state of classical liberalism.

If the Catholic notion of a substantive common good is foreign to most prevailing liberal views of authority and participation, the Catholic insistence on the personalist ends of society contrasts with overly collectivist views. The personalist theme runs throughout the encyclical tradition, beginning with Leo XIII's insistence that "man is older than the state." Pius XI took up the same refrain. "Society is for man and not vice versa. This must not be understood in the sense of the liberalistic individualism which subordinates society to the selfish use of the individual but only in the sense that by means of an organic union with society and by mutual collaboration the attainment of earthly happiness is placed within the reach of all."[23] Closer to our own times, Paul VI in *Populorum Progressio* sees the goal of society as aiming at a complete humanism. On the basis of this personalism the modern papacy has engaged in a human rights strategy. In *Pacem in Terris,* John XXIII compiled an extensive list of civil, political, and economic rights necessary for human dignity.[24]

Perhaps no one theme has so consistently been remarked on by commentators on the papal encyclicals as their insistence on a pluralism of societal authority and the right — derivative from the very sociality of human nature — of individuals to form associations intermediate between the state and individuals. The most usually cited exemplification of this right to inter-mediate associations is the right to form labor unions, but the latest for-mulation of the grounding principle for this right, "justice as participation," really envisions a rich associative life in civil society. Catholic pluralism is rooted in a distinction between state and society. This distinction represents the founding source of the principle of subsidiarity; that is, wherever a task can be satisfactorily achieved by the initiative of the individual or that of small societal units, the fulfillment of that task must be left to the initiative of the individual or that of small social units. This is the basic Catholic principle of "small is beautiful" or at the least, in Andrew Greeley's felic-itous phrase, "no bigger than necessary." Catholic social thought favors, without absolutizing them, decentralized forms of authority. It insists on the zone of civil society and its inherent logic, which must not be usurped by the imperialistic logics of states and markets.

This principle of the autonomy of intermediate groups needs to be jux-taposed against a no-less-strong counter-principle of state authority; that is, wherever the welfare of a community requires concerted common action, the unity of that common action must be assured by the state. "No bigger than necessary" has as its corollary "as big as needed to achieve the com-mon good." Even when the state legitimately and necessarily intervenes, however, to "encourage, stimulate, regulate, supplement and complement" the action of intermediate groups, Catholic social thought assumes that, as much as possible, the state should act in ways that utilize and favor rather than simply supplant voluntary associations. In one of the most pithy state-ments of this Catholic distinction between state and society, Paul VI remarks in *Octogesima Adveniens* that "the domain of politics is wide and comprehensive, but it is not exclusive."[25]

Authority and Citizen Participation as Social Democratic

Despite the inherent ambiguity of papal encyclical language and the Vatican's desire in such documents to cast a wide net and conciliate many groups, most commentators see a decided tilt in the tradition, certainly since the time of John XXIII, toward economic or social democracy.[26] Like the Christian democratic parties in Europe, which had much influence on this tradition, contemporary social Catholicism has become a tradition of the welfare state. It assumes a priority to meeting basic needs in determin-ing the direction of the economy. It justifies some cases of nationalization of property and champions workers' co-determination schemes in industry. It is very difficult to see how a careful reading of this social tradition can yield an essential defense of capitalism as it is presently practiced. Neither socialist in a classic sense nor capitalist, the tradition is best described as social democratic in its thrust.

Philip Land, for many years on the Vatican Commission on Justice and Peace and a consultant in the writing of *Mater et Magistra*, has written an excellent essay that illustrates the social democratic nature of this tradition. In that essay Land distills nine middle axioms, which he draws from the Catholic social ideology, for judging any economy. They form an excellent summary of the social democratic strain in the papal teaching. Each of his summary principles can be found in recent social encyclicals:

> 1) The economy is for people; 2) The economy is for being, not having; 3) The economic system ought to be needs-based; 4) The economy is an act of stewardship; 5) The economy must be a participatory society; 6) There must be fair sharing; 7) The system must permit self-reliance; 8) The economy must be ecologically sustainable; 9) The economy must be productive.[27]

CONCLUSION

I have not dwelt in this essay on the weaknesses or *lacunae* in the papal social ideology. I see, basically, four such weaknesses. First, the economic thought, while rightly stressing the need for just distribution, pays too little attention to the necessity of increased productivity as a social good. No one can distribute a wealth that does not exist. This is a major flaw.

Second, Catholic social thought too easily assumes the possibility of social harmony. It acts as if all that is needed is to get the social classes together into one organization for conflict to cease. In this regard Alfred Diamant has suggested that the pluralism assumed by Catholic social thought is based on the implied premise that the various groups which make up the pluralistic system are fundamentally homogeneous and subscribe to a single consensus on values.[28] In fact, modern societies are only tenuously homogeneous. Catholic social thought has not really faced the full reality of pluralism, especially the political implications of living in societies with especially deeply diverging views on fundamental social values. This is its deepest challenge from the North Atlantic nations. Catholicism's sense for social harmonies is a residue of earlier medieval organic models for society and theological models for the church as a communion in harmony. Although the medieval organic models have long since been explicitly abandoned by the papal social ideology, they live on implicitly in the continuing assumptions about a harmonious social order. Nor am I convinced that this present pope in his encyclical *Laborem Exercens* totally overcomes the liability of the tradition on this point, as some commentators, such as Donal Dorr, suggest.[29]

A third flaw in Catholic social ideology is the failure of this tradition to propose workable alternative institutions and ideals to the regnant liberal and socialist institutions. Because of this failure, many critics have accused the papal social ideology of being unduly idealistic. In actual fact, in the absence of alternative models for institutional implementation, social Catholicism will embrace the status quo. As many have seen, to function as an effective guiding social ideology, social Catholicism will need to engage in alternative model-thinking. It will not do to distance itself from both liberalism and socialism philosophically, if it is unable to embrace forms of institutional life which avoid the flaws in both systems. Even more fundamental, most of the encyclical genre lacks even an institutional imagination.

Finally, the distinction between the social and the political implicit in the Ozanam epithet, "Avoid politics and concentrate on the social question," will not withstand closer scrutiny. If the social question calls for societal transformations—even structural changes which run deep, as Paul VI argued—politics is the appropriate arena for imagining alternative structures and calculating, among realistic alternatives, the chances of achieving one rather than another. Too great a dichotomy between politics and the social question entails either: (1) a narrow, purely technical view of politics, which neglects its deepest meaning as the arena for expanding freedom and human possibility, or (2) a trivialization of the complexity of the social question. Short of a flight from real history and societies, there is no way to completely avoid politics and simultaneously genuinely concentrate on the social question.

This has led some critics to suspect that the epithet should really read "Avoid the *appearance* of politics (in order to protect the institutional interests of the church) and concentrate, moralistically, on the social question." To most political scientists or sociologists, at any rate, the church's claims to stand above politics and above every socially conditioned ideology will seem either illusion, ideology in the pejorative sense, or a shell game to cover the church's covert political interests and goals.

I do not doubt the legitimacy and fruitfulness of a more theological reading of Catholic social teaching than I have given here (I have done this in other contexts). I have tried, within a more phenomenologically social science perspective, to look at the attempt of Catholic social teaching to be neither socialist nor liberal as a creative source of its originality and uniqueness. I have argued that, historically, this neither/nor stance made sense because of the social location of nineteenth-century Catholicism. Indubitably the neither/nor stance runs as a leit-motif from Leo XIII to John Paul II. It might be appropriate to end with some remarks of David Martin about the relation of Christianity to liberalism and socialism. Martin does not avert explicitly to social Catholicism. His remarks, however, capture what I see as the deepest intention behind social Catholicism's critique of both liberalism and socialism and a source of its originality as a direction-giving set of principles in the modern world:

> It may be that as the contradictions of liberalism and socialism reveal themselves as inherent and as Christianity can be seen distinct from either, that a celebration of a community yet to be fully realized, a recognition of tragedy written in the nature of life and of a hope not exhausted by the necessary imperfection of social arrangements, will seem once again relevant. Religion

has to find a way of detaching itself from liberalism without contributing to
the defeat of freedom and tolerance, and of distinguishing itself from socialism without being thrown directly into the arms of socialism's enemies or
denigrating the impulse to the equalization of human opportunities.[30]

If my reading of the originality and consistency of Catholic social ideology
is correct, social Catholicism in its best moments and breakthrough points
in the last hundred years has done just what Martin hopes Christianity
would do when faced with liberalism and socialism.

NOTES

1. For an argument that the unity of the social teaching rests in a preferential
option for the poor see Donal Dorr, *Option for the Poor* (Maryknoll, New York:
Orbis Books, 1983); for a view of this tradition through the lens of human-rights
theory see David Hollenbach, *Claims in Conflict* (New York: Paulist Press, 1979).

2. See, among other sources, Joseph Moody, ed., *Church and Society* (New York:
Arts, Inc., 1953); Robert Kothen, *La Pensee et L'Action Sociale des Catholiques 1789-
1944* (Louvain: Em. Warny, 1945); Hans Maier, *Revolution and Church: The Early
History of Christian Democracy 1791-1901* (Notre Dame, Indiana: University of
Notre Dame Press, 1969); J.B. Duracelle, *Les Debuts du Catholicisme Sociale en
France* (Paris: Presse Universitaires de France, 1951); Alec Vidler, *A Century of
Social Catholicism* (London: SPCK, 1964); for Germany, besides Alfred Diamant,
Austrian Catholics and the First Republic (Princeton, New Jersey: Princeton University Press, 1960) see the book length contribution of Edgar Alexander, "Church
and Society in Germany," in Moody, pp. 325-583, and Franz Mueller, "The Church
and the Social Question," in Joseph Moody and Justice Lawler, eds., *The Challenge
of Mater et Magistra* (New York: Herder and Herder, 1963), pp. 13-154.

3. Moody, p. 123.

4. Diamant, p. 15.

5. For Catholic class structure in nineteenth-century France, see Duracelle, pp.
73ff; for Austria, Diamant, pp. 96ff; and for Germany, Alexander, p. 479.

6. English title, "Human Liberty," in *The Great Encyclicals of Leo XIII*, ed.
John Wynne (New York: Benziger Brothers, 1903), p. 142.

7. Moody, p. 14.

8. Ibid., pp. 128ff.

9. Maier, p. 191.

10. Cited ibid., p. 200.

11. Ibid., p. 284.

12. Richard Camp, *The Papal Ideology of Social Reform* (Leiden: E. J. Brill, 1969),
p. 128.

13. For these groups see Diamant, pp. 33-60.

14. Mounier rejected Christian democracy and called for a direct collaboration
with the left. He was the "personalist" editor of the influential lay Catholic French
journal *L'Esprit*. See his *Oevres*, vol. 1-4 (Paris: Editions Seuil, 1963).

15. For Solidarism see Diamant, chapter 5. The founder of Solidarism, Heinrich
Pesch, had been a student of Adolf Wagner and Gustav Schnoller, both *katheder-
socialisten*. For Pesch, see Richard Mulcahy, *The Economics of Heinrich Pesch* (New

York: Henry Holt and Company, 1952), and Franz Mueller, *Heinrich Pesch and the Theory of Christian Solidarism* (Saint Paul: College of Saint Thomas, 1941). This economic theory of Solidarism lies behind *Quadragesimo Anno*.

16. Gregory Baum, *Catholics and Canadian Socialism* (Toronto: James Lorimer and Company, Publishers, 1980), p. 80.

17. *Quadragesimo Anno*, in Oswald von Nell-Breuning, *Reorganization of the Social Economy* (Milwaukee: Bruce, 1936), p. 422. The principle of subsidiarity is restated by *Mater et Magistra* (see David O'Brien and Thomas Shannon, eds., *Renewing the Earth* [Garden City, New York: Doubleday, 1977], p. 62) and also in *Populorum Progressio* (O' Brien and Shannon, p. 324.)

18. *Quadragesimo Anno*, in Nell-Breuning, p. 431.

19. *Quadragesimo Anno*, in Nell-Breuning, p. 403.

20. *Octogesima Adveniens*, in O'Brien and Shannon, p. 366. The Medellín document "Justice" also makes an appeal to social Catholicism as neither liberal nor socialist: "Both systems [liberal capitalism and Marxism] militate against the dignity of the human person" (O' Brien and Shannon, p. 553).

21. Camp, p. 157.

22. David Martin, *The Dilemmas of Contemporary Religion* (Oxford: Basil Blackwell, 1978), p. 37.

23. *Divini Redemptoris*, in Nell-Breuning, p. 456.

24. *Pacem in Terris*, in O' Brien and Shannon, p. 328.

25. *Octogesima Adveniens*, in O'Brien and Shannon, p. 378.

26. See Samuel Hux, "An Outsider's Look at Catholic Social Thought," *Commonweal* 108, no. 7 (April 10, 1981), pp. 200-205.

27. Philip Land, "The Earth Is the Lord's: Thoughts on the Economic Order," in *Above Every Name: The Lordship of Christ and Social Systems*, ed. Thomas E. Clarke (New York: Paulist Press, 1980), pp. 237-38.

28. Diamant, p. 287.

29. See the chapter on *Laborem Exercens* in Dorr. I agree with Dorr that some movement (at least in verbal acknowledgment) has taken place in Catholic social thought to give room to conflict models of society. I do not think, however, that Catholic social thought has really budged all that much from its historic bias toward harmony models.

30. Martin, p. 104.

3

SOCIAL MOVEMENTS AND CATHOLIC SOCIAL THOUGHT

GORDON C. ZAHN

More than a quarter century has passed since I last taught a course in papal social encyclicals, an assignment I always enjoyed even though I knew the subject matter caused many raised eyebrows on the part of my more empirical colleagues in the sociological fraternity. Such a course — especially when offered at a Catholic university — seemed to them to reek of moralistic preachment, if not outright theological contamination of our purportedly value-free social science.

Their fears, if I may say so without naming names, were probably justified more often than not, certainly often enough to cause me many moments of acute academic discomfort. Not often enough or severe enough, however, to convince me that the study of the "Five Great Encyclicals"[1] then in vogue could not be approached empirically in a thoroughly legitimate sociological exploration of the social thought of a major religious community as expressed in official proclamations by its authoritative spokespersons. I still maintain this is the case and sincerely regret that today's graduates of Catholic higher education generally are not familiar with the encyclicals, their contents, and most important of all, their implications for Catholic attitudes and behavior. Indeed, I would argue that this educational gap has contributed significantly to the failure of Catholic education to produce what another of those "great" social encyclicals defined as its ultimate purpose: nothing less than the "true and perfect" Christian.

Too much time has passed; too many changes have taken place in Catholic social practices and attitudes for me to use my old class notes, were I able to find them. Then, too, new "great" encyclicals collections have since been issued and several of those original five demoted to lesser rank and deleted from current compilations. The one we honor here, however, retains undiminished both its prominence and its importance. As the *New Catholic Encyclopedia* states: *Rerum Novarum* deserves the honor we pay to it as "the first of the great social encyclicals" because it "marked the bestowal of significant papal approval on the then emergent Catholic social movement."[2]

That it did, and more. That bestowal of approval opened the way to the further emergence and development of a wide range of other new Catholic social movements on a scale almost certainly beyond its eminent author's expectations, a proliferation that shows little sign of slowing or coming to an end.

Many, perhaps most, of these newer movements can claim — or would seek to claim — substantive, if not always direct, linkage to that first great encyclical. Not only was this result unanticipated; it was almost certainly unintended. One might go so far as to say that today's more activist Catholic social movements would be regarded by Leo XIII as too radical, even dangerous, departures from his principal themes and intentions, and the policies and programs they promote would be for him a source of serious concern meriting disapproval or even condemnation.

CONTEMPORARY MOVEMENTS AND LEO XIII

Consider, if you will, a few contemporary examples: ecumenism; feminism; the familiar clutch of movements for social justice as defined by demands for racial, social, and economic equality. To trace these back to Leo and his encyclical would require a generous exercise of imaginative extrapolation. Then there are the more exotic examples of spirituality-centered movements involving participants in "personal fulfillment" adventures featuring what might best be described as free-style — sometimes *extremely* free-style — religious attitudes and practices. These are worlds apart from the rather archaic psychology upon which the encyclical's conclusions are based and the religious formulation given those conclusions by Leo.

Most offensive of all to him, there is little room for doubt, would be contemporary Catholic movements of the "democratic Left" and the extent to which they borrow from, and sometimes openly adopt, the socialist ideals and propositions *Rerum Novarum* was so clearly intended to counteract. This is not to say, one must hasten to add, that the encyclical's teachings provide full endorsement or support for the contrary commitment to individualistic capitalism so devoutly fostered by today's competing Catholic movements of "the ultra- or neo-conservative Right."

Nor can one deny that by contemporary standards the style and much of the encyclical's content could be characterized as triumphalist, elitist, and sexist to a degree thoroughly out of keeping with what we would regard as an appropriate, or even acceptable, vehicle for Catholic social thought and behavior. Thus, when Leo affirms "without hesitation that all the striving of men will be in vain if they leave out the Church" (par. 13) and later declares that "all men must be persuaded that the primary thing needful is to return to real Christianity" (par. 45) the Christianity of which he speaks is not today's ecumenically sensitive Christianity but, rather, the exclusivist "one true Church" jealously defending its claim to the only authentic set of keys to the kingdom.

That church would have little in common with the "community of the faithful" model of Vatican II. Leo's image of the "church" was the rigidly hierarchical structure that prevailed in his ultramontanist day—a model, many find reason to fear, which could prevail again in the near future if certain recent and troubling trends in the exercise of ecclesiastical authority and direction persist. The difference finds expression even in its literary form and style. The encyclical holds to the traditional pattern of address that was to obtain until John XXIII broke the cast. Where John and his successors have made a point of including "the clergy and faithful of the whole world" and "all men of good will" in the salutation, *Rerum Novarum* and its message were addressed to his "venerable brethren," the patriarchs, primates, archbishops, and bishops of "the Catholic World"—all in their proper order.

Its sexism finds clearest evidence in, but is not limited to, the characteristic papal use of noninclusive language. Whatever offense one may take from that stylistic fault, all too often elevated by our more contentious feminists into crusades for posthumous censorship and correction, pales into insignificance when, as in this document, one encounters "the real thing."

Women, to Leo, are "not suited to certain trades" but instead are "by nature fitted for homework," the calling most conducive to preserving their modesty and promoting "the good bringing up of children and the well-being of the family" (par. 33). This naturally leads by implication to an even more shocking display of patriarchal familism in the pope's warning against what he regarded as dangerously intrusive action on the part of state authority into family affairs. Such intrusion, as he saw it, represented a threat to a natural order in which "the child belongs to the father" as "the continuation of the father's personality" and "takes its place in civil society not in its own right, but in its quality as a member of the family in which it is begotten" (par. 11).

Even when he deals with what is intended to be the central focus and purpose of the encyclical—the elaboration of the rights of labor—one encounters concepts and formulations few of today's workers or their leaders would find acceptable. Catholic social movements striving to create a society marked by greater economic and social equality will find little direct support here for specific programs designed to achieve this goal. This does not, of course, negate or undermine the value of the contribution which this "magna carta" of labor did represent in its open endorsement of the rights of workers to form "Workmen's Associations" for their mutual benefit and protection. Without the opening it provided, such movements may never have come into being.

It is sometimes overlooked that the encyclical may have found its point of origin in the religious controversy in the American church arising from ecclesiastical efforts to condemn the Knights of Labor. The struggle within the hierarchy provided the occasion—and quite possibly the inspiration—leading to the issuance of this "first great social encyclical." The Knights, probably the first successful forerunner of modern unionism (it already claimed a membership of a half-million!) had been formally condemned by a Canadian bishop as a forbidden secret society, and some of the more prominent prelates of Canada and the United States took the issue to Rome in an attempt to have the condemnation validated and extended by the Holy See. Their efforts failed thanks to the equally determined efforts on the part of Cardinal Gibbons and Bishop Ireland on the Knights' behalf.

In response to their urgent appeals[3] (personally carried to Rome by Ireland), the Knights were formally "cleared" by Leo in 1887. In effect, then, the encyclical, coming along as it did four years later, elevated what was a juridical decision on a "local" problem to a definitive statement of "the mind of the church." The central issue, as Gibbons would remember it more than thirty years later, resolved itself into a simple—perhaps too simply stated—moral choice: "If the Knights of Labor were not condemned by the Church, then the Church ran the risk of combining against herself every element of wealth and power. . . . But if the Church did not protect the working man she would have been false to her whole history; and this the Church can never be."[4]

Without seeking to diminish the importance of that struggle and victory, Gibbons may have been premature and overly enthusiastic in asserting that the "whole history" of the church to that point had been a record of protection of the working man and his rights. Had that been the case, *Rerum Novarum* would have been an exercise in redundancy. Nor has the intervening century validated his optimism. If anything, it provides illustration enough that not only the previous but the subsequent record of the church in promoting and defending the rights of labor—*including Leo's encyclical and its reception and impact*—still falls far short of that ideal.

The controversy over the Knights may have provided a convenient occasion for issuing an encyclical proclaiming the rights of labor at that particular point in time, but a far more urgent stimulus must have been the Marx/Engels vision of a "spectre" haunting Europe. It certainly was haunting Rome. Deserving though it is of recognition as labor's "magna carta," it was even more a papal defensive reaction and counterattack provoked by the appeal of ideological socialism and the rapid advances socialist-oriented movements were making in the turbulent closing half of the nineteenth century.

Taken in the context of this challenge to the church and its teachings, *Rerum Novarum* becomes as much an effort to restrain as to free the workers. As already noted, much emphasis was placed on protecting the religious dimension of the "Workmen's Associations." "It is clear that they must pay special and principal attention to piety and morality, and that their internal discipline must be directed precisely by these considerations" (par. 42). But even this concern is overshadowed by the encyclical's energetic defense of private ownership and protection of property rights, its absolute rejection of the class struggle, and a far more restrictive definition of the role of the State and its economic rights and responsibilities than that envisioned in the socialist solution.

Recognition of these priorities of concern need not diminish or deny the encyclical's other, more positive, contributions. The explicit statements setting forth the responsibilities of capital and employers toward the laborers they employ—with special emphasis given to the protection of women and children against exploitation—would be justification enough for the praise it has received. If they seem overly cautious to us today, we must remember they were strong enough to account for the suspicion and opposition Pius XI would later admit it aroused "even among Catholics." *Especially* among Catholics perhaps?

But the encyclical issued no stirring call for the workers of the world to unite, no reminder that they had nothing to lose but their chains. It is not that the encyclical fails to recognize class differences. It not only recognizes them; it goes beyond recognition to statements which affirm the division as legitimate, even *natural*. In doing so, it introduces a dangerous overlap of concepts which, in effect, equates labor with poverty in the process of denying the need or justification for class struggle.

It is a "great mistake," Leo warns us, "to possess oneself of the idea that class is naturally hostile to class; that rich and poor are intended by nature to live at war with one another." Dismissing this as an irrational and false view, he declares that "it is ordained by nature that *these two classes* should exist in harmony and agreement, and should, as it were, fit into one another, so as to maintain the equilibrium of the body politic. Each requires the other; capital cannot do without labor nor labor without capital" (par. 15, emphasis added). Even making allowance for possible distortion in translation, the easy juxtaposition of terms—labor with poverty and capital with wealth—is significant. Not only does it reflect acceptance of the social realities of the time, but it leaves disturbing echoes in other more specific principles and applications of critical importance to Catholic social movements, not least the question of whether what he refers to, and apparently accepts, as the "equilibrium of the body politic" deserved to be maintained.

It is well to stress these considerations if only to demonstrate that what most interpreters (including *this* interpreter) celebrate as a watershed document opening the way to a completely new emphasis and direction for social and economic change was, in fact, conservative and traditionalist in its teachings and almost certainly in intent. However much stimulus and support *Rerum Novarum* has provided to social movements of a liberal and even radical character, Catholics on the other side have found and still can find similarly persuasive stimulus and support for their reactionary social movements as well.

If, as the encyclical has it, "humanity must remain as it is"; if "unequal fortune is a necessary result of inequality in condition"; if "to suffer and endure" is "the lot of humanity" and "no strength and no artifice will ever succeed in banishing from human life the ills and troubles which beset it" (par. 14)—if all these things are true, what point would there be in joining in organized efforts to reform society and its institutions? It is no accident that statements like these coupled with the encyclical's nostalgic appeal to the model of medieval guilds (an appeal elaborated further forty years later in Pius XI's commemorative and its embrace of a corporative social order) have provided, whether so intended or not, a mantle of religious justification for Catholic support for and active participation in the fascist and neo-fascist movements in Europe and Latin America and here at home.

Nevertheless, I have come to praise the encyclical, not bury it. *Rerum Novarum*'s claim to recognition as the first of the "great social encyclicals" is beyond challenge, and it is fully deserving of the honors paid it. If intellectual honesty requires that we also recognize it was the product of its time as, of course, was its author, this should not detract from the honor due it. To say it did not do all it could have done (and, perhaps, *should* have done) may seem to some to be praising it with faint condemnation, but that is certainly not my intention.

WHAT *RERUM NOVARUM* WROUGHT

What did it do? To revert again to the words of the *New Catholic Encyclopedia*, "it marked the bestowal of significant papal approval on the then emergent Catholic social movement." Or, more accurately, on the "then emergent" Catholic social *movements* and, indirectly by extension upon the multitude of such movements that have emerged since and are still emerging.

The importance of that "bestowal" should not be minimized. Whatever else the encyclical achieved or did not achieve, it represents a distinct though not yet dramatic breakthrough that opened the way to that proliferation of social activity *by predominantly lay-staffed and directed organizations* that characterizes so much of Catholic social action today.

At the risk of breaking continuity, this seems an appropriate time to introduce a sociological definition of *social movement*. Most such definitions, of course, can claim neither conclusive nor universal acceptance. With this reservation as a warning, then, I define a *social movement* as a more or less *organized* effort on the part of a *significant segment* of a population to *change* an existing social order in a manner its participants believe *ben-*

eficial to the whole. Please note, each of the emphasized terms is essential to an understanding of the concept as I use it.

A *Catholic* social movement would be either (a) one in which Catholics constitute the significant segment of the larger population that is to be affected or influenced by the movement, or (b) one in which the movement's participants represent a significant segment of the total *Catholic* population and are seeking to change the church in ways they deem beneficial to it and its mission.

Without going into overly precious or confusing detail, let it be said that the significance of the segment in either instance may lie simply in the number of participants or, if the number is small, in recognized status or valued characteristics of those participants (wealth, rank, intellect, virtue, and so on) as determined by the society or social unit targeted for change at a given time. The success of political revolutions, we might assume, will most often depend upon mass support and participation; on the other hand, organized efforts seeking less extensive or more gradual changes could involve at most a relatively small number of respected individuals or influential elites.

From the beginning of church history significant individuals and groups (some holding positions of ecclesiastical power, some emerging from obscurity) have won and inspired followings to oppose situations they saw as socially evil and proposed solutions or practices they considered to be more in accord with God's will. Occasionally such movements originated as religious orders. Sometimes, in the process of achieving their goals, they decided to perpetuate their activity in the religious state.

The historical context in which Leo XIII issued his challenge to the threatening dynamism of socialism already found Catholics, clerical and lay, at work "in the world" founding *secular* organizations promoting policies and programs they viewed as religious in spirit and objectives. Then, as now, such movements could be found working both sides of the ideological street. Opposing an ultramontane and hypernationalistic *Action Française*, for example, was a *Le Sillon* and other more liberal (though rarely radical by today's standards) movements dedicated to social reform and universalistic visions of peace and an end to human suffering.

A number of these latter movements drew inspiration from Bishop von Ketteler's address to the Frankfurt Assembly in 1848. Many of the points this eminent German nobleman and politician made would later find echoes in the major themes developed in *Rerum Novarum.* Leo XIII, in fact, is reported to have acknowledged him as his "great predecessor." In a more practical application, Ketteler's speech was pivotal to the development of the social welfare program instituted by Bismarck in Germany.

The ideal of achieving social justice through social reform spread and resulted in a proliferation of Catholic organizations in Austria, France, Belgium and, somewhat later, Italy and Great Britain. Some were limited in their focus and program; others were more comprehensive in their approach to necessary social change. Some, like the Kolping Society founded in 1849, still survive. Allowing for adjustments of priorities imposed by a changing social situation, the Society continues to perform its original mission of providing hostels and adult education opportunities for journeymen artisans, more recently expanding this to include facilities for boarding families as well. With many such developments and activities well under way in 1891 — and, in Germany at least, already adopted as public policy — the papacy could scarcely avoid becoming involved. Even without the challenge presented by socialism. The Knights of Labor controversy, though certainly not the definitive cause, provided a helpful final nudge.

To repeat, the encyclical's "bestowal of papal approval" may not have been intended to be as broadly interpreted and applied as soon proved to be the case. Though its immediate objective seems to have been to establish the right of workers to organize into benevolent and protective societies, given the nature of papal style it was perhaps inevitable that this affirmation of right would be elaborated into a pattern of moral and religious principles opening the way to broader application centering upon other issues of social reform and justice. This unanticipated extension of papal social thought turned out to be the major and most lasting contribution of *Rerum Novarum*. Whether so intended or not, it legitimized and even *invited* open criticism of the established social order and, without spelling out specific guidelines, encouraged activity designed to translate that criticism into corrective reform and social betterment.

This represented a significant shift in the church's temporal relationships in two important respects. Cardinal Gibbons, as cited earlier, saw that by refusing to condemn the Knights "the Church ran the risk of combining against herself every element of wealth and power." For centuries church officialdom had maintained close, indeed often familial, ties of affinity with those "elements." By almost every measure of prestige, power, wealth — not excluding lifestyle — high ranking ecclesiastics matched the nobility and rulers of the secular order. Indeed, in many instances those ecclesiastics and rulers were one and the same person.

Leo's family background, described as noble, but by no means wealthy, may not have fit that pattern fully, but it came close. True, some popes (like his sainted successor, Pius X) were born to families of modest circumstances, but even in such instances it can be taken for granted that no one, no matter how modest his origins, would have reached the papacy without establishing himself as at least a familiar, and more likely an intimate associate of wealth and power. For this pope, then, to align himself with the cause of the worker was to risk being charged with going over to the socialists and revolutionaries and abandoning — if not betraying! — his "kind" and their interests. As Pius XI noted, this was the reaction of many to *Rerum Novarum*, its cautious warnings and reservations notwithstanding.

The other departure from nineteenth-century church practice was, in retrospect, more fundamental in nature. The church had always recognized the divinely imposed obligation to comfort, protect, and serve the needs of the poor and helpless. To fulfill this obligation religious orders devoted to charity and human services were founded, a great network of institutions created, and massive emergency collections of funds and valuables gathered whenever necessary to aid victims of catastrophe. If the true identification of the Christian lies in demonstrating to others how they love one another, this has found repeated and impressive illustration in such acts and outpourings of charity over the centuries.

Rerum Novarum goes beyond charity, however, in demonstrating its concern for labor (which, remember, to Leo was virtually interchangeable with "poor") and speaks instead of *rights*. Its argument, while it certainly does not ignore charitable appeals to consider the worker and his spiritual and physical welfare, is based on a carefully elaborated development of the demands of justice and recognition of the essential equality of all in God under which "there is no difference between rich or poor, master and service, ruler and ruled." It is from this concentration upon unity and equality that, even after proclaiming ownership of private property as a right grounded in nature, Leo derives his striking distinction between possession and use of property and wealth under which "man should not consider his outward possessions as his own, but as common to all, so as to share them without difficulty when others are in need" (par. 19).

Although this is not yet the preferential option for the poor now offered as the measure of a truly Christian public policy, the seed is there. So, too, with the careful distinction between the two dimensions of human labor — personal and necessary — which serves as the theoretical basis for defining the just wage and leads by direct inference to what must have been a truly shocking conclusion to the nineteenth-century employer: "If through necessity or fear of a worse evil, the workman accepts harder conditions because an employer or contractor will give him no better, *he is the victim of force and injustice*" (par. 34). Indeed, we may safely assume there are employers or contractors in our day and in our country who still consider such talk incomprehensible, if not openly subversive. Some Catholic employers and contractors might even sense implications of heresy.

Apart from its recommendation that "Christian Associations" be formed for the specific purpose of serving the spiritual needs and protecting the rights of the laboring population, *Rerum Novarum* did not anticipate or endorse the formation of Christian movements addressing a broader range of social reforms or proposing the comprehensive restructuring of society itself. Nevertheless, it did provide the pattern of moral justifications which has been expanded and modified as needed to validate organized efforts of Christians concerned with other social problems and their correction. To illustrate the linkage one need but refer to movements active in our own country and in our own time: the Catholic Worker promoting the personalist "revolution" keyed to communitarian ideals and vision in voluntary poverty while serving the needs of the homeless and rejected of the nation's slums; Friendship House and its successors living out their goals for interracial justice; Pax Christi with its pacifist commitment to a world freed from violence and war; and all the other groups of Catholics who have similarly dedicated their lives to demonstrating the link between belief and behavior.

This is not to say that such organizations or their efforts have always been welcomed or even approved by the institutional church and its leadership — or, for that matter, that they are today. There was a time when participation in religious conferences with other Christians and Jews made one vulnerable to suspicions of disloyalty, if not outright apostasy; when working for interracial justice was deemed too radical and possibly even a sign of communistic leanings; when promoting pacifism and conscientious objection was not only un-American but unorthodox if not heretical.

THE *MAGNA CARTA* OF LABOR

Though it often involved stretching the point to claim *Rerum Novarum* and the other "great" social encyclicals and papal statements as official ecclesiastical endorsement for these positions, the opening was there to be exploited. In this sense, though this *"magna carta* of labor" fell short of assuring or even recognizing the full rights of the worker of its time, its bestowal of papal approval at least implied acceptance of the general principle behind organized efforts to achieve and protect those rights. This would have lasting significance in many unanticipated applications. Not only did it furnish legitimacy for what, especially under Pius XI, was to become a vast network of *official* Catholic Action organizations — with capital letters and operating under ecclesiastical direction — it also inspired a host of unofficial (lower case) Catholic action groups and organizations, like those mentioned above, dedicated to translating the Christian message and mission into tangible works of mercy and justice.

Rerum Novarum, then, was the first in a series of impressive papal documents addressing the needs of contemporary society. It may well be that the time of the "great" encyclicals is now past. The last in the series may have been John XXIII's world-shaking *Pacem in Terris.* This is not to ignore those issued by his successors, Paul VI and John Paul II, but merely to observe that these efforts have not had anything like the impact such commentaries on the moral state of the world once enjoyed. This may be due in great part to the increased frequency and variety of papal statements and a more sophisticated exploitation of the media. Certainly a major factor is the break with tradition represented by a peripatetic papacy in which personal visits and ceremonial tours command more attention as an exercise of the teaching authority of the church than formal (and lengthy) proclamations issued from Rome.

Collegiality and the proliferation of more local pastoral statements from episcopal conferences are a factor too. Finally, there is what might prove to be the most basic explanation of all: a serious decline in the extent to which religion and the utterances of religious leaders are considered relevant to social practices and policy. Or authoritative. Today it is clear, even among loyal and committed Catholics, when a pope speaks on matters of public or even private behavior, fewer are ready to listen and not all of those who do are ready to accept what they hear.

CATHOLIC SOCIAL THOUGHT FROM BELOW

This does not mean the game is lost. Catholic social thought is alive and well, perhaps in better shape than ever. The locus and source has changed. No longer centered solely in the statements and actions of those in charge of "the home office," that social thought now finds more vital development and expression in discussions and debates involving segments of the believing community that were previously all but excluded from policy deliberations and decisions. In tone and content, today's Catholic social thought more accurately reflects the encounter between the faithful and the world, the world it is their mission to redeem.

This may beg for empirical validation, but I am convinced—both as believing Catholic and professional sociologist—these free exchanges of openly contested statements of moral principles and proposals for their application will do a much better job of fulfilling that mission. The record of the past few decades adds weight to my conviction. The more significant contributions made by or in the name of the church—in supporting programs for economic justice; in opposing the evils of racism and anti-Semitism; in denouncing the weapons and strategies of modern war and defending the priority of conscience—all of these originated from "below," from individuals and movements which at first were denied official recognition and support and obliged to overcome official suspicion and outright opposition. Later, often much later, these would become formally proclaimed policies of the church.

It is well to keep this in mind as we celebrate the one-hundredth anniversary of *Rerum Novarum*, a papal document that really did make a difference as "the first great social encyclical." Leo, too, benefited from the beginnings made by others, beginnings not always recognized or approved. It does not lessen the spirit of celebration to speculate how different the history of the world would be if Rome, not Marx, had been the first to recognize and protest the evils of the capitalist industrial order. After all, the basic philosophical principles and religious teachings upon which Leo XIII based his exposition of the rights of labor had been professed centuries before.

Perhaps that should be the lesson for the church today—for popes, for bishops, for everyone who claims the privileges and shares the responsibilities of being Christian: we must resolve to be more sensitive to what those responsibilities may be and, no less important, more willing to take the risks they may involve. Too little and late though it might have been, *Rerum Novarum* did give witness to the primacy of justice in social and economic affairs. To this extent it has provided and can still provide inspiration and support, indirect at times though it may be, for individuals and movements serving the twin causes of peace and justice.

NOTES

1. References and citations to *Rerum Novarum* are taken from the collection *Seven Great Encyclicals* (Glen Rock: Paulist Press, 1963).
2. *New Catholic Encyclopedia* (Publishers Guild, 1967), vol. 12, p. 387c.
3. See *New Catholic Encyclopedia,* vol. 6, p. 467b; vol. 7, p. 610d.
4. Cited in "My Memories," *Dublin Review* (April 1917).

4

THE RIGHT AND COMPETENCE
OF THE CHURCH
IN THE AMERICAN CASE

J. BRYAN HEHIR

The assigned topic of this essay concisely combines two dimensions of the life and ministry of the Catholic church. The "right and competence" of the church to address political, legal, social, and economic issues is rooted in the nature of the church. More precisely, it is rooted in the prophetic ministry of teaching and service that has been articulated in the Catholic social tradition. To address the right and competence question is to speak at the level of principle—ecclesiological and ethical principles valid for the universal life of the church. The right and competence of the church to speak and act in the public arena has been asserted in widely disparate settings: by Ambrose and Augustine in the Roman Empire; by Innocent III and Boniface VIII in the medieval commonwealth; by Bellarmine and Vittoria in Italy and Spain; and by Leo XIII, Pius XII, and John Paul II in the century of Catholic social teaching.

The "American case" illustrates how the universal principles take shape in the particular setting of a local church. At this level the analysis shifts to an assessment of variable political, social, and cultural conditions. The emphasis in this analysis is on how the right and competence of the church is exercised through particular policies and choices.

The argument of this paper will address these two questions in three steps. First, a synthetic statement of how the right and competence of the church has been formulated since Leo XIII. Second, an examination of the setting and substantive debate occurring in the United States about the exercise of right and competence. Third, a concluding comment made about future directions.

THE RIGHT AND COMPETENCE OF THE CHURCH:
THE TRADITION, THE COUNCIL, AND THE POPE

The need to assert and defend the right and competence of the church to speak and act arose early in the life of the Christian community. The exercise and defense of the right forms a major chapter in the history of Roman Catholicism.[1] I will identify three moments from the last century when the right and competence question took shape and also changed in its formulation. The altered statement of right and competence has changed the public and social role of the church. The development in the position on right and competence also illustrates a growth in the church's understanding of itself and of the world.

Leo XIII and Societas Perfecta

Leo XIII (1878-1903) spanned two distinct periods of the church's relationship with the world. One dimension of his teaching was addressed to recasting the church-state question, the dominant social issue for the popes of the nineteenth century. The second dimension of the Leonine corpus inaugurated "the social teaching" by shifting papal attention from the politics of church and state to the socio-economic questions of church and society. In both areas, church-state and church-society, Leo XIII inaugurated a process of development in Catholic teaching which went far beyond the ideas he used.[2]

While these two themes are distinct and have different histories, the right and competence question is a common thread uniting them. In his conflicts with continental liberalism and in his response to the Industrial Revolution, Leo XIII was determined to defend the right and duty of the church to enter and engage the public order of society. In his inaugural address to the social question in *Rerum Novarum*, he stated the theme:

> We approach the subject with confidence and in the exercise of the rights which belong to us. For no practical solution of this question will ever be found without the assistance of religion and the church.[3]

The formula Leo XIII used to assert "the rights which belong to us" was the concept of the church as a *societas perfecta*. The lineage of the concept ran from Pope Gelasius' (+496) "two swords" theory through the "two powers" theory of medieval Christendom to Leo XIII's attempt to salvage the substance of Gelasius in the face of the modern nation-state. The phrase *societas perfecta* was not coextensive with this history, but it was the dominant concept in use after the medieval union of church, state, and society had dissolved.

The meaning of the phrase *societas perfecta* was that *the church possessed all the power and capacities needed for it to achieve its specific objectives as a religious community.* Perfect in this sense meant "complete," not morally impeccable. An imperfect society was in some way dependent upon other communities or authorities for an essential dimension of its existence; *imperfect* meant "lacking self-sufficiency." The church was a *societas perfecta*, because it could identify the source of its existence, specify the objectives it existed to fulfill, and define the powers (or resources) which allowed it to accomplish its mission.

The primary function which the formula *societas perfecta* fulfilled was to distinguish the church definitively from the civil power or the state, and to assert the church's independence — in the order of being and action — from the state. To use John Noonan's phrase, the *societas perfecta* language invoked the metaphor of "line-drawing,"[4] establishing a clear sphere of unfettered action for church and state. By implication the formula also acknowledged the independence of the state and affirmed an equally clear sphere of competence for the temporal or civil authorities. But the principal goal of the formula was to support the independence — hence the right and competence — of the church, then secondarily to seek an area of collaborative activity for church and civil authority, both of which were obligated to serve the person.

While the *societas perfecta* formula can be understood as a clear statement of ecclesial principle, it also was, in part, shaped by the conditions of nineteenth-century church-state relations. Leo XIII desired to move away from the conflict between the church and "the modern world," which had marked the pontificates of Gregory XVI (1831-46) and Pius IX (1846-78). He faced, however, an objectively hostile environment toward the public life of the church on the part of the major European powers. Both Bismarck's *Kulturkampf* and the French Republic's policy sought to limit or eliminate the public influence of the Catholic church. Leo XIII was pushed and pulled into a posture of "line-drawing" with the civil society of his time. He sought to establish constructive relationships with temporal powers (*concordia* was his often-stated goal), but the objective margin for positive action was very limited.

Leo XIII's line-drawing metaphor began with a conception of "the church *and* the world"; it defined this relationship cautiously and defensively, conscious of the philosophical, political, and religious differences which set Catholicism apart from dominant nineteenth-century ideas.[5] From this carefully defined starting-point Leo XIII sought to rebuild a right order of relationships of politics, culture, and economics. More precisely, he sought to restore the right order which existed before the double revolt of the Reformation and the Enlightenment had created chaos. Leo XIII's restoration was not cast in the hostile terms of *Mirari Vos* or in the defiant rejectionist character of the *Syllabus of Errors*, but it assumed a church-world relationship that contemporary Catholic teaching finds both defensive in tone and minimalist in its expectations for church-world relationships.

Vatican II and "The Sacrament of Unity"

The difference is best exemplified by contrasting the *societas perfecta* world-view with that of Vatican II. The Council's principal contribution to Catholic social teaching is found in two documents, *Gaudium et Spes* and *Dignitatis Humanae*. While both texts address a range of moral issues which have been at the core of Catholic social teaching (church and state, religious liberty, socio-economic issues), the primary contribution of Vatican II has been the ecclesiological foundation it provides for social ministry. Together these texts define both the church-state and the church-society relations. In that sense they provide the conciliar response to the right and competence question.

In a wider view of the Council's work, however, it is useful to look at the link between *Gaudium et Spes* and the central doctrinal affirmation of Vatican II, *Lumen Gentium*. While this text is primarily concerned with the "inner life" of the church, it stands as the foundation for *Gaudium et Spes*. A specific link between the two texts is *Lumen Gentium*'s description of the church as "like a sacrament or sign and instrument of a closely knit union with God and of the whole human race."[6]

The sacrament of unity formulation does not directly address the right and competence question, nor does it provide specific guidance for the church's activity in the world. But the premises sustaining the conception of the church as a sacrament of unity are rooted in a different view of the world and the church's relationship to it than those sustaining the *societas perfecta* world-view.

Yves Congar called attention to the shift in perspective and principle achieved by Vatican II:

> In full agreement with the Dogmatic Constitution *Lumen Gentium, Gaudium et Spes* has a profoundly different outlook on the relations between the spiritual and the temporal to the one which the Middle Ages bequeathed and which prevailed in classical doctrine down to Chapter IX of the schema *De Ecclesia* of the Preparatory Theological Commission. It is clear that what was involved was not so much a contradiction as a development; the problem itself had altered, by moving from the juridical and political plane to the anthropological plane of personal belief.[7]

One way to illustrate the development of which Congar speaks is to focus on a linguistic shift. The medieval conception spoke of the "church *and* the world"; the Council's conception—in both the sacrament of unity and in the title of the pastoral constitution—is "the church *in* the world." The church does not address the world across a boundary; the conception is rather that the world is the context for the church's eschatologically oriented ministry. The concept of sacrament of unity calls the church to be both a sign and a source of unity in human affairs.

The *societas perfecta* model stressed the equality of the church with civil society; it secured independent ground from which the church could confront and limit temporal power. The sacrament of unity model stresses the solidarity of the church with the world. Its emphasis is on providing a place within civil society from which the church can offer its unique form of service.

The development in the view of the world and the church which the Congar quote identifies is evident in *Gaudium et Spes*. There is a much more positive conception of the world than seemed possible in the nineteenth century. Pius IX saw the church in a desperate struggle, philosophically and politically, with the dominant ideas of his time. Leo XIII sought to build bridges, intellectually and politically, with the world, but his starting-point was a conviction that a profound rupture existed between the Christian and contemporary vision of God, the person and society. The Pian pontificates of the twentieth century did not fundamentally change this conflicted view of church and world, even though Pius XII pressed Leo XIII's conception of dialogue on a much broader range of themes and issues.

The foundation and legitimation of Vatican II's conception of church-world relations was provided by theological developments in the 1940s and 1950s, and by papal texts of John XXIII (*Pacem in Terris* and the Opening Address to Vatican II) and Paul VI (*Ecclesiam Suam*). There is a clear connection in substance and style between *Ecclesiam Suam* and *Gaudium et Spes*. Both in turn sustain the conception of the church as a sacrament of unity.

Ecclesiam Suam places the church in a series of dialogues with an ever-expanding constituency. *Gaudium et Spes* defines its posture and purpose in this way: "This Council can provide no more eloquent proof of its solidarity with the entire human family with which it is bound up, as well as its respect and love for that family, than by engaging with it in conversation about these various problems."[8]

The emphasis in the conciliar texts is not on the issues of right and competence but on the nature of the relationships which can be shaped between church and world, church and state, and church and society. The right and competence themes, that is, how to protect the necessary independence of the church, are addressed in two ways.

First, there is a clear, strong affirmation in both *Gaudium et Spes* and *Dignitatis Humanae* on the transcendence of the church in the face of any and all political systems. The church must protect this spiritual transcendence by preserving its temporal independence. Second, the defining principle of church-state relationships is the freedom of the church. The church asks not a favored position in society (this can erode independence) but the freedom to function.[9]

Transcendence and freedom protect the right and competence of the church to speak and act. The concept of the sacrament of unity locates the church in a position to shape those relations with the world, society, and state which make service possible. The final contribution of *Gaudium et Spes* is its description of how these relationships should be structured. Essentially the bond between the church and the world (society and state) is the person; paragraph 76 defines the work of the church as safeguarding the dignity of the person. Then paragraphs 40-42 tie together an affirmation of the church's transcendence with an equally strong assertion that the eschatalogical ministry of the church includes its work in history to protect human dignity, promote human rights, foster the unity of society, and provide a sense of meaning to all areas of societal life.

At Vatican II the ideas of right and competence are subsidiary to the pursuit of these four objectives. Transcendence and freedom are the preconditions for a ministry of service mandated by the church's vocation to be a sacrament of unity.

John Paul II: Solidarity and Service

John Paul II has been shaped by and is reshaping the social legacy of Vatican II. In his encyclicals, addresses, and actions the decisive impact of the Council, and specifically of *Gaudium et Spes*, is evident in his conception of society, the state, and the role of the church. The social legacy of the Council had two dimensions: it simultaneously "depoliticized" the role of the church and "resocialized" its ministry. *Dignitatis Humanae* disengaged the church from specific ties to civil authorities by establishing freedom as the key principle of church-state relations. In perception and in policy this freed the church from ties that bound it to certain states. In turn, the freedom to function achieved by *Dignitatis Humanae* was put to effective use by the impetus given to the social ministry by *Gaudium et Spes*. The ecclesiological foundation for social ministry provided by the Council generated a qualitatively new kind of social engagement by the church in situations as disparate as São Paulo and Seoul, Manila and Managua, Warsaw and Washington.

John Paul II has intensified both dimensions of the legacy of Vatican II.[10] His distinctive contribution to the right and competence debate should be interpreted in this conciliar context. A fundamental characteristic of his pontificate has been his determination to lead a nonpolitical but socially engaged church.

This determination is particularly evident during papal trips (often to the most volatile social situations in the world). The trips are governed by two criteria. He has ruled out any specific identification of the church with political parties or institutions (particularly by forbidding priests and religious to hold public office). Simultaneously, he has advocated a broad range of deep social reforms, cutting across local, national, and international lines.

John Paul II's specific contribution to the right and competence question has a distinctively post-conciliar character to it. He defends "the right" of the church to a public role in a way which contrasts sharply with Leo XIII's style. He does not need to defend the public rights of the church in the kind of apologetic style which the political character of the last century forced Leo XIII to adopt. The public role of the church is articulated and defended in terms of both the transcendence of the church (not dependent upon political authority) and the right of religious freedom (understood to mean not only the rights of personal conscience, but the right of religious communities to speak, act, and influence society).

The post-conciliar style also means that defense of "the right" to speak and act is a secondary theme to "the exercise of the competence" of the church in the social arena. In brief, the right is defended by exercising it broadly and vigorously as a socially engaged church. An example of the primacy of exercise was John Paul II's address to the United Nations in 1979, a benchmark of his pontificate. While the pope made it clear at the opening of his address why the church had the right to participate in the United Nations, he moved quickly from this theme to enter the substantive issues of human rights and world order as seen in Catholic teaching. The dominant impression of the address was a church much more concerned with the issues of the day than with the defense of its rights and specific role in the world forum.

The U.N. address was a benchmark in the sense that it set a pattern for his ministry. John Paul II has enhanced the right of the church in the public arena by the way he has exercised the competence of the church in the social ministry. In terms of the *Gaudium et Spes* agenda of church-world issues, John Paul II has engaged papal diplomacy and advocacy on a scale unprecedented in this century.[11]

Leo XIII, Pius XII, and Paul VI all gave high priority to the diplomatic arena, but John Paul II combines traditional diplomatic contacts with direct local advocacy of issues through his trips. Together, the diplomacy and advocacy are de facto assertions of the church's "right and competence" to engage the public arena at the local, national, and international level.

In a style reminiscent of Leo XIII, however, John Paul II has joined papal diplomacy with extensive papal teaching. The right and competence of the church is legitimated by the scope and substance of papal teaching addressing an extraordinary range of issues in the last twelve years. As he made clear in the opening section of *Sollicitudo Rei Socialis*, this pope sees his teaching in direct continuity with the social teaching of his predecessors. While this lineal descent is evident, equally clear is the distinctive character of John Paul II's social teaching.

Yves Congar and John Courtney Murray both observed that the effect of Vatican II was to move the church-world question from primarily a juridical-institutional format to a more theological interpretation of the role of religion and the church in addressing the contemporary world.[12] John Paul II's social teaching is regularly cast in terms of how the vision of Catholic faith should address both the public and personal dimensions of existence. The teaching uses biblical and theological categories much more extensively than any social document since *Gaudium et Spes*.

From *Redemptor Hominis* through *Sollicitudo* John Paul II has pressed a vision which is both addressed to the world at large *and* is substantially cast in theological terms. In *Sollicitudo* the pope described social teaching as one way in which "the Church fulfills her mission to evangelize for she offers her first contribution to the solution of the urgent problem of development when she proclaims the truth about Christ, about herself and about man, applying this truth to a concrete situation."[13]

In the same vein John Paul argued that failure to probe empirical issues down to their theological roots in the nature of the person will result in an inadequate understanding of the problems the modern world faces. John Paul uses this theological address to the world on questions as different as medical ethics, work and the economy, the arms trade, and human rights.

The theological character of his social teaching is complemented by its moral and political specificity. While affirming the church's nonpolitical role, John Paul has not hesitated to draw specific conclusions about social and economic conditions, the arms race, and regional conflicts. Moral specificity is also combined with a willingness to comment on the geo-political character of the superpower relationship and its consequences for others. The combined affect of the theological basis of John Paul's teaching, his moral specificity, and his political evaluations set his exercise of the competence of the church off from his predecessors.

Right and competence remain as necessary ideas in Catholic social teaching, but they are asserted indirectly today, often less as a claim to be vindicated than a protection needed so the church can enter the dialogue with the world in a spirit of solidarity and service. These terms characterize John Paul II's teaching, but they are also the product of the evolution in Catholicism's dialogue with the world over the last century.

In the last decade of the twentieth century the right and competence of the church to speak and act is less contested than a century ago. The moral principles the church invokes and the conclusions drawn from them often are contested. But this debate has less to do with right and competence than with how the Catholic moral vision engages the major social issues of the day. The response of the church at this level must be about the quality and character of its ministry, not right and competence.

THE AMERICAN CASE

The right and competence question in "the American Case" will be assessed here in light of the constitutional and social setting within which the church functions, and of the ecclesiological debate about how the church in the United States should fulfill its ministry.

The status and role of *the local church*, understood analogously to apply to the diocese and the church within a nation, have taken on new significance in the social ministry since Vatican II. The establishment of episcopal conferences by *Christus Dominus* and the invitation of Pope Paul VI in *Octogesima Adveniens* to the local churches to become articulators of the social vision have focused attention on how the universal teaching is received and how it can be implemented in diverse social and cultural settings.

The Significance of the Social Setting

The American Case means that the Catholic church pursues its ministry in a religiously pluralist culture; the culture is part of a post-industrial society, and it is governed by a secular, democratic state. These three characteristics were all part of the American Case before they were themes addressed in Catholic social teaching. In 1991 they continue to be major elements of the setting in which the church works and they have been explicitly evaluated in Catholic teaching. Each needs to be assessed to capture some sense of the American Case.

Religious pluralism has been the native condition of American society from its beginning; the constitutional guarantee of religious freedom is a cornerstone of the political and legal system. In contrast to this pervasive, central role in the American experience, religious pluralism has received systematic address in Catholic theology only in the past century. During this time the evaluation of religious pluralism has moved from a condition to be surpressed or overcome to a recognition that pluralism is the presumed context for the ministry of the church.[14]

In this process of development in Catholic thought, the American Case played a significant role. In the nineteenth-century church-state controversies (Gregory XVI to Leo XIII), religious pluralism was an exception to be tolerated when it could not be overcome. The Vatican I formulation of "Thesis/Hypothesis" was the normative method for evaluating pluralism. The American Case was the hypothesis—that which could be tolerated but should be changed. The work of John Courtney Murray, using the American Case as a laboratory and an example, led to *Dignitatis Humanae* at Vatican II, the text which displaced the "Thesis/Hypothesis" formulation. In the teaching of Vatican II religious pluralism was not "Thesis," but it was the accepted setting in which the church pursued its ministry in freedom, dependent only on its own resources and the quality of its witness.

The acceptance of religious pluralism did not change the practical situation of the church in the United States. It simply legitimated the American Case in principle within the church. At the practical level the pluralist setting has become more complex since Vatican II. First, partly due to the ecumenical collaboration of the post-conciliar period, and partly due to the nature of the issues involved (war, race, poverty) the Catholic and mainline Protestant churches found much common ground in spite of pluralism. Second, at the same time an agenda of issues arose—principally in the biomedical issues of genetics, abortion, and euthanasia—which has already created (abortion) or threatens to create (euthanasia, fetal tissue transplants) deep public divisions in the ecumenical relations of the Christian churches.

The basic dynamic of religious pluralism remains similar to the analysis offered by Murray in the 1950s and 1960s.[15] But the content of the issues and the emergence of new actors (for example, evangelicals) mean that Murray's analysis by itself is insufficient to chart the course of ministry in the 1990s. Murray never had to address the abortion issue; it was a "settled" public policy question in the 1950s and 1960s.

In the past decade abortion has been the most intractable issue in the public arena, explicitly argued along religious-moral lines. But the lines of division are not clearly Catholic *vs.* Protestant. Conservative Protestants tend to join Catholics in opposing abortion even though there is little theological agreement with the Catholic style of argument; mainline Protestants share much theological and social ground with Catholic social teaching but often divide over the abortion question. In neither case—"left" or "right"—can the consistent ethic be used as the basis of Catholic-Protestant dialogue.

Pluralism is the societal context of the American Case; a democratic state, defined in terms of specific secular purposes, is one of the central facts confronting the church. Once again, in the practical order American Catholicism had achieved a *modus vivendi* with the secular state (the constitutional state) long before Catholic teaching came to terms in principle with the reality.

The acceptance of a secular democratic state was foreshadowed in *Pacem in Terris*, then confirmed at Vatican II. Coming to terms with the constitutional state involved a complex journey, addressing aspects of Catholic thought which are held in tension. Unlike liberal political philosophy, Catholic teaching holds that society and the state are organic developments rooted in the nature of the person. This premise inclines Catholic teaching to accord a broad role to the state, particularly in pursuit of moral and religious values. It was this conception of the state's *cura religionis* which made acceptance of religious liberty so difficult for Catholicism.

At the same time the principle of subsidiarity—found in Catholic social teaching—sought to preserve a pluralist structure of power in society. This, in turn, provided grounds for setting limits on the range of state power and influence. A complementary notion that made the move to limit state power possible in Catholic teaching was the traditional principle investing the right to educate children with their parents, a right held prior to the state.

The acceptance of religious pluralism, the affirmation of the right of religious liberty, and the recognition of the role of the constitutional state all occurred at Vatican II. Taken together these developments both reflected the influence of the American Case in the wider church, and in turn legitimated this particular church-state-society configuration in Catholic theology.

A third characteristic of American society now also reflected in papal teaching is the post-industrial organization of society. The term *post-industrial* is a product of American social science and does not carry the theological overtones which religious pluralism and the role of the state conveyed. The new classic reference for the concept of post-industrial is Daniel Bell's *The Coming of Post-Industrial Society.*[16] The elements of Bell's analysis, if not his terminology, are woven through *Octogesima Adveniens*, and since then have helped to frame the "Social Question" in Catholic teaching. Bell's 1976 description of post-industrial society (for example, the centrality of theoretical knowledge, economies of information, a change in the character of work, the changed role of women) is remarkably similar to Paul VI's description of the "new social questions" in 1971.

These new questions pose a double challenge for the social ministry of the church in the United States. First, on the domestic front the coming of post-industrial society has produced a conjunction of the "old" with the "new" social questions. The old issues of poverty, race relations, employment, housing, and hunger are still with us. At the same time the new questions, which Senator Daniel P. Moynihan has called the social issues of the Post-Industrial Age, include AIDS, drugs, and the threat that a percentage of the population will be locked into poverty because they do not have the skills to function in a post-industrial economy.[17] In addition, post-industrial advances in medical technology generate choices about the beginning and end of life that are social and moral as well as medical questions.

Second, the new social question, as it is found in Catholic teaching from *Octogesima Adveniens* through *Laborem Exercens* and *Sollicitudo*, involves examination of how post-industrial societies are to relate—in their policies and practices, for example—to developing societies, often still in the first stage of the Industrial Age.

These two broad challenges—the domestic and international dimensions of the Post-Industrial Age—symbolize the social agenda facing American Catholicism. They grow out of the American Case, and they are central to themes of Catholic social teaching.

An Ecclesial Response to the American Case

The American constitutional system guarantees "the freedom of the church," which Vatican II established as the basic principle to protect the right and competence of the church. The church is assured "space" to pursue its ministry. The space must be used by a style of ecclesial engagement; hence the ecclesiological debate about social ministry. The issue is not confined to "whether" the church should be socially engaged, but "how" it should exercise the right and competence of the church.

Because Vatican II tied the social ministry securely to an ecclesiological foundation, the post-conciliar period has witnessed an extensive debate on ecclesiology and social witness.

Professor David O'Brien distinguishes three different styles of social witness, cutting across the two hundred years of American Catholicism: the immigrant model, the republican model, and the evangelical model.[18] Father Avery Dulles has sorted through the Catholic social debate in terms of traditionalist, neo-conservative, liberal, and radical postures.[19] These classifications are based on different historical horizons and use differing criteria, but they point to the attention given today to the "how" of social engagement. To some degree this attention reflects the shift from defending the church's right to determining how to exercise its competence.

In this essay, I will focus on the ecclesial debate catalyzed by two examples from the American Case: the two NCCB pastoral letters on peace and the economy. In response to them and in light of the longer and larger ecclesial argument summarized above, three distinct proposals for a style of social ministry have been advocated in the United States in the past decade. They are an educational-cultural model, a legislative-policy model, and a prophetic-witness model. While each has an internal logic and distinct consequences, I propose them here as a spectrum of ecclesial views, sharing some common ground.

The *educational-cultural* model holds that the most appropriate (theologically) and effective (socially) role for the church's social teaching is to concentrate on broad themes of public philosophy, personal character, and family values. This view, represented — in different ways — in the writings of J. Brian Benestad of Scranton University and George Weigel of the Center for Ethics and Public Policy, reflects Paul Tillich's argument that culture is the framework for politics and religion is the soul of culture. The fundamental public task for the church — part of its evangelizing ministry — is to shape the religion-cultural conception of society. These ideas will then find their way into the policy process. In a critique of an address by Cardinal Joseph Bernardin, Benestad synthesizes the educational-cultural position:

> Looking at the church's relation to the political and social orders primarily as an advocate of just policy, however, diminishes the scope of the church's impact on society. . . . When expounding Catholic social teaching, the church needs to find a way to talk in the public forum about virtue and the common good. Hardly any opinion-molders talk about these things in a profound way anymore. In my judgment, Catholic bishops are particularly suited to perform this service.[20]

Benestad's position does not rule out making specific policy choices, but he believes too much emphasis has been given to this task, to the detriment of Catholic teaching authority. Moreover, he argues that the broader themes of Catholic moral vision, for example, an ethic of virtue, a conception of the common good and a critique of the modern conception of human rights, are precisely what the American public debate needs today.

The educational-cultural model understands the social ministry as a subcategory of the teaching mission of the church, and it conceives of social teaching in a style reflective of classical political philosophy, focusing on the character of the good regime, the duties of citizenship, and the relationship of personal and public virtue. In this model of social ministry, the Catholic contribution is strong on perennial principles, but restrained about policy choices. The church is clearly a teacher of wisdom, less clearly an advocate in the public life of society. The effect of this model is to keep the church "in the debate" but "above the fray," because the Catholic position is stated in such general terms.

This model has a long history, but it rests on two assumptions which highlight its limits as a strategy of social ministry. First, the model places great faith in the ability to move from important but broad social principles held by a citizenry to the specifics of policy choice. The model seems to hold that if the citizenry thinks correctly in general terms, the society will act wisely and effectively on specific choices. Second, the basic conception of virtue, rights, and common good, which animates this model, amounts to a fundamental challenge to existing patterns of policy discourse in American society. This fact is a very good reason for pursuing the fundamental themes, but also a good reason to question whether the educational-cultural model is an adequate style of social ministry.

The method of this model (from the conscience of the citizenry to the choice for policy) and the objectives of the model (reshaping the moral vision of society) make it an indispensable element of ministry, but its *only* time frame is very long-term. In the short to middle range, this model may leave the Catholic voice out of public life.

It is this fear which is one of the driving forces behind the *legislative-policy* model of Catholic social ministry. This style has been represented by the history of the National Catholic Welfare Conference and the United States Catholic Conference's engagement in the Washington policy arena. The post-conciliar emphasis on episcopal conferences enhanced the stature (including budget, staff, and visibility) of this model. The pastoral letters of the 1980s exemplified its style.

The legislative-policy model shares with the prior position the conviction that the institutional church enters the public arena in fulfillment of its teaching ministry. This model, however, has a different conception of how the teaching function should be related to social ministry, and how it should be exercised. To use the NCCB pastoral letters as an example, the teaching style found there is a mix of the exposition of principles espoused in the educational-cultural model, and an application of those principles in the concrete details of the policy debate. The legislative-policy model is based on the conviction that the strength of the Catholic moral tradition resides in *two* factors: a systematic body of principles *and* an ability to illustrate the meaning of the principles through casuistry. In short, the legislative-policy model believes that Catholic social teaching should be *both* systematic and specific.

The differences of the two models extend to the place of social ministry in the church. The legislative-policy perspective is not satisfied with the restricted role for advocacy implied by the educational-cultural position. The legislative-policy view is that social ministry is *rooted* in teaching ministry but should not be simply *subsumed* by it. There is a distinct dimension of ministry which involves engagement in the public life of society, using both teaching and advocacy, espousing both principles and policy positions. To hold this position, however, the second model must address two questions.

First, what authority should be attributed to teaching which is a mix of principles and policy choices? The first model fears that this mix will mortgage the moral authority of the church. If the same authority is attached to both principles and choices, the apprehension would be well-founded. The appropriate response is to distinguish levels of teaching and to espouse a procedural principle for teaching, that is, increasing empirical specificity means declining moral authority. Such an approach, found in the pastorals, seeks to protect principles and allow for advocacy.

Second, if the institutional church advocates specific policy recommendations, how will unity in the church be preserved on worship and doctrine? The specific policy choices must be understood to be not only limited in their authoritative weight, but also open to debate and differing positions within the ecclesial community. Such specific choices as "no first-use," increasing the federal housing program, and advocating a constitutional amendment to oppose abortion, all have reasons to commend them; none has the intrinsic power to command universal assent in church or society.

In spite of their differences, both the first and second models share a view of a "transformationist" role for the church in society. The third model, the *prophetic-witness* position challenges the transformationist consensus. The questions raised are fundamental ones, touching on the sources for social teaching, its mode of discourse, the premises of church-world relations, and the goals of social ministry. One finds these questions in several Catholic movements, but they are most systematically raised by Stanley Hauerwas of Duke University, a Protestant with an abiding interest in the Catholic social role.[21]

The prophetic-witness model has always been a compelling view of ecclesial presence in the world. It offers a definite vision, held with integrity by a community whose boundaries are fixed, firm, and clear vis-à-vis civil society. The witness model seeks to create within the church a clear counterpoint ("a choice not an echo") to existing societal vision and policies. It disputes the transformationist strategy because the latter concedes too much to the world (society or state) and usually entails concessions on the part of the church.

In contrast to compromises and concessions the prophetic-witness model draws a distinct line between the ecclesial and civil communities, and it then offers individuals and institutions a difficult but clear choice: forsake the wisdom of the world with its balances of power, calculation of consequences, and continued compromises and embrace the wisdom of the kingdom, including its understanding of the cross. The prophetic-witness model seeks transformation as the product of a prior conversion; without conversion, it believes the transformationist strategies will always fall short of what the kingdom requires.

The questions which the witness model inevitably faces are as old as its history. They are questions about the church, the world, and how the two relate. Regarding the church, is a witness model possible for all members, expected of all? Or, conversely, what conception of the church is needed to sustain the witness model? Regarding the world, is conversion an appropriate *social* strategy? Short of conversion is any common ground possible between the civil and ecclesial communities?

There are examples of ecclesial communities in the Protestant tradition which have answered these questions decisively: the witness model is for all members, and the world will never be the church, hence, radical divergence is expected daily; common ground is a strategic illusion probably based on a theological mistake. Now that the prophetic-witness model is so well represented in Catholicism, with its conception of the complementarity of nature and grace, church and world, the prophetic-witness logic faces new tests and likely will produce a modified posture from its Protestant ancestors.

A CONCLUDING NOTE

Right and competence are permanent categories in a Catholic theology of church-world relations. But permanence must be distinguished from significance. At both the universal and local level, in the church-world relationship the right and competence question has been subordinate to issues of apostolic witness, social advocacy, and a ministry of solidarity with and service in the world. Particular events, that is, a frontal challenge to the church's public existence, would bring right and competence back to center stage—hence the need to keep the categories clearly defined and readily available. But they are not the primary ideas needed to address the challenge of social ministry in the 1990s.

Those ideas surface more readily in the analysis which cuts through the three models of ministry just outlined. Here the questions are what constitutes faithfulness to the gospel vision, how the vision is articulated convincingly, and how it can be shared socially. The different answers produced by the three models should not be superficially reconciled or collapsed into a soft consensus position. The differences do make a difference in how the Catholic church seeks to be present in the world. The tension in the ecclesial debate sharpens strategic thinking and deepens theological reflection. The first and second models need each other; the temptation for either is to seek to banish the alternative conception. Together these frame a Catholic social witness which is less stringent in its inner discipline than the witness model, but more viable as a social alternative in the intricacy of a post-industrial society; it is a Catholic witness less clear in its challenge to society, but more complex in its understanding of the "new social question." Both the social strength and capacity for complex assessment are needed in the American Case.

The third model presents a perennial and irreducible challenge to the first two. The challenge of the prophetic-witness model has often been relativized in Catholicism, but never rejected. It has returned in the post-conciliar period with renewed vigor. It is less easily joined with the other two than they are with each other. The inquiry about how the three models relate and remain part of a single Catholic witness is the question which has overtaken right and competence today.

NOTES

1. For a sampling of the literature see Y. Congar, "Eglise et Etat," in *Catholicism: Hier, Aujourd'hui Demain*, vol. 3, col. 1430-1442; B. Tierney, *The Crisis of Church and State 1050-1300* (New Jersey: Prentice-Hall, 1964); J. C. Murray, "The Problem of Religious Freedom," *Theological Studies* 25 (1964) pp. 503-75 (hereafter *T.S.*); E. Troeltsch, *The Social Teaching of the Christian Churches*, vol. 1 and 2 (New York: Harper and Row, 1960); A. Rhodes, *The Vatican in the Age of the Dictators (1922-1945)* (New York: Holt, Rinehart and Winston, 1973).

2. The best analysis of Leo XIII on church-state relations is still John Courtney Murray's work. See "Leo XIII on Church and State: The General Structure of the Controversy," *T.S.* 14 (1953), pp. 1-30; "Leo XIII: Separation of Church and State," *T.S.* 14 (1953), pp. 145-214. For an assessment of Leo XIII on church-society relations, see F.H. Mueller, *The Church and the Social Question* (Washington: American Enterprise Institute, 1984), pp. 66-83. For a comparison of Leo XIII on political and economic themes, see Murray, "Leo XIII: Two Concepts of Government," *T.S.* 14 (1953), pp. 551-67.

3. Leo XIII, *Rerum Novarum* (1891), no. 13.

4. John Noonan, "Responding to Persons: Methods of Moral Argument in the Debate over Abortion," *Theology Digest* 21 (1973), pp. 297-300.

5. Murray, "Leo XIII on Church and State," pp. 10-18.

6. Vatican II, *Lumen Gentium* (1965), no. 1.

7. Yves Congar, "The Role of the Church in the Modern World," in *Commentary on the Documents of Vatican II*, vol. 5, ed. H. Vorgrimler (Freiburg: Herder, 1968), p. 208.

8. Vatican II, *Gaudium et Spes* (1965), no. 3.

9. See J. C. Murray, "The Issue of Church and State at Vatican II," *T.S.* 27 (1966), pp. 604-6.

10. For an analysis of John Paul II on church, state, and society, see G. H. Williams, *The Contours of Church and State in the Thought of John Paul II* (Waco, Texas: Baylor University Press, 1983).

11. For an assessment of John Paul II's diplomatic role, see J. Bryan Hehir, "Papal Foreign Policy," *Foreign Policy* 78 (Spring 1990), pp. 26-48.

12. Congar, p. 208; Murray, "Church and State at Vatican II," pp. 581-85.

13. John Paul II, *Sollicitudo Rei Socialis* (1987), nos. 1-4.

14. Murray, "Church and State at Vatican II," pp. 585-86.

15. J. C. Murray, *We Hold These Truths: Catholic Reflections on the American Proposition* (New York: Sheed and Ward, 1960), pp. 27-78.

16. Daniel Bell, *The Coming of Post-Industrial Society: A Venture in Social Forecasting* (New York: Basic Books, 1976), pp. xvi-xvii.

17. Daniel P. Moynihan, "Toward a Post-Industrial Social Policy," *The Public Interest* 96 (Summer 1989), pp. 16-27.

18. David O'Brien, *Public Catholicism* (New York: Macmillan, 1989), pp. 230-52.

19. Avery Dulles, "Catholicism and American Culture: The Uneasy Dialogue," *America* (January 27, 1990), pp. 54-59.

20. J. Brian Benestad, "Cardinal Bernardin and the Need for Catholic Social Teaching," *Center Journal* (Winter 1984), p. 18.

21. Hauerwas has developed his systematic position over several years; examples of a prophetic-witness position can be found in parts of *Vision and Virtue: Essays in Christian Reflection* (Notre Dame, Indiana: Fides Publishers, 1974); *A Community of Character: Toward a Constructive Christian Ethic* (Notre Dame, Indiana: University of Notre Dame Press, 1981); and *Against the Nations: War and Survival in a Liberal Society* (Minneapolis, Minnesota: Winston Press, 1985).

5

CATHOLIC SOCIAL TEACHING AND HUMAN MORALITY

CHARLES E. CURRAN

The methodology of contemporary Catholic social teaching sometimes uses Christian warrants and sometimes employs more inclusive human appeals which do not presuppose any distinctive religious beliefs. These two approaches to Christian social ethics are not new, but there are new and different aspects involved in the discussion about these approaches today.

A traditional debate has taken place in Christian ethics between the advocates of a scriptural approach and those of a natural-law methodology. In general, Roman Catholic moral theology strongly endorsed and exemplified the natural-law approach. Catholic moral theology for the most part did not base its teaching on exclusively Christian approaches. However, the natural law has a strong and important theological foundation, which has been developed by Thomas Aquinas among others. God's plan for the world and for the life of humankind is the eternal law, but law for Aquinas is primarily an ordering of practical reason. Through creation, God has given human beings their reason. Human reason reflecting on human nature can discover God's plan. Creation and mediation thus constitute the foundations for the traditional Catholic acceptance of natural law. The plan or law of God is discovered through human reason's ability to reflect on human nature and discover how human beings should act in accord with the plan and work of the creator. The natural law is the participation of the eternal law in the rational creature. Some Protestant ethicists, especially Barthians, strongly criticized a natural-law approach, but other Protestants recognized at least some place for human reason in their ethics.[1]

The thought currents associated with the Second Vatican Council brought about some profound changes in Catholic life in general and in moral theology. The council called for moral theology to be more thoroughly nourished by the scriptures. The older manuals of moral theology were criticized for being legalistic, minimalistic, individualistic, and not truly theological. The Second Vatican Council also deplored the split between faith and daily life in the attitudes of so many Catholics. The natural-supernatural distinction or even dichotomy in the manuals of moral theology and theology in general was severely criticized at this time. Faith, scripture, and theology must be relevant to the daily life concerns of members of the church and to the theological reflection on social and political life.[2]

Official Catholic social teaching and its methodology illustrated this change in approach. *Pacem in Terris,* the 1963 encyclical of Pope John XXIII, was the last document to employ an exclusive natural-law approach, the same methodology which had been used by Leo XIII in *Rerum Novarum* and in subsequent documents.[3] *Pacem in Terris* clearly sets out its methodological presuppositions in its introduction (par. 1-7). The laws governing the relationships between human beings and states are written by the Creator in human nature and human beings made in the image and likeness of God with intelligence and freedom can discover and act in accord with this plan of God. Note that in the discussions of peace in this document no appeal is made to Christian warrants such as grace, Christian reconciliation, or the gift of Jesus and the Spirit to the disciples. However, the *Pastoral Constitution on the Church in the Modern World* of the Second Vatican Council in its consideration of the human person, human community, and human activity in the world appeals to the Christian warrants of creation, sin, redemption, and, to some extent, eschatology (par. 12-39). Subsequent documents have appealed to Christian warrants and sources as well as to inclusive human appeals.

Two types of questions arise in this new context. The first never-ending discussion concerns how each of the two different approaches should be used. What is the meaning of natural law or human reason? Should reason be used inductively or deductively? How does one move from the time, culture, and place of the scripture to the contemporary time, culture, and place? Should one employ an ascending or a descending Christology? These important continually recurring questions lie beyond the scope of this essay. The second type of question concerns the relationship between these two different approaches and the reasons for choosing one approach rather than another. These documents are dealing with the question of a good and just social order. In discussing this area, one issue is fundamental and basic. Does official Catholic social teaching recognize one social moral order that is the same for all, or are Christians and Catholics called to do something different from what is required of others in trying to bring about a more just society?

The question is framed in such a way as to avoid certain presuppositions which might go along with it. For example, the question under discussion does not necessarily presuppose a deductive or an inductive methodology. These documents of official Catholic social teaching deal with what perhaps can best be called the social moral order or social justice in the broadest sense of the term. These are matters that admittedly affect all human beings and belong to the public forum. The challenge for all humankind is to bring about a more free, just, participative, and sustainable society. Are Christians called to do something different from others in trying to bring about the social moral order? In my judgment, the answer to the question is there is only one social moral order and all humankind, including Christians, are called to work for the same social justice.

ONE SOCIAL MORAL ORDER

This chapter will defend the thesis that contemporary official Catholic social teaching recognizes there is only one social moral order for all. Christians and Catholic Christians are not called to do something other than what is required for all others. Two preliminary reasons give credence to this thesis. First, a negative argument which by itself cannot be totally convincing. Nowhere in these documents can one find an explicit statement that there is a different moral content in the social order for Catholics or for Christians. Such an argument is not totally convincing because it could well be that the documents presuppose and imply what they do not say explicitly. However, if such a position were taken, one would expect some references to it since the documents want to teach the members of the church about their social responsibilities.

Second, the documents are often addressed not only to church audiences but to all men and women of good will. Pope John XXIII started this practice with his encyclical *Pacem in Terris* of 1963. Before that time the documents were generally addressed to the Catholic church, its members, and its leaders in keeping with the very concept of the encyclical, which is a letter sent around to the churches. The natural-law method of the earlier encyclicals made them in principle open to all other human beings, but as a matter of fact they were not specifically addressed to all humankind. Now, even though appeals are often made to scripture and Christian warrants, the letters where applicable are addressed to all humankind. Thus, Pope John Paul II's *Laborem Exercens* (1981) and *Sollicitudo Rei Socialis* (1987) are addressed to all men and women of good will. Such an address does not necessarily prove there is only one social moral order for all, but it points in the direction of such an understanding.

An examination of the most significant documents of contemporary official Catholic social teaching indicates that they explicitly and implicitly admit there is only one social moral order. Christians and Catholics are not called to do something different from others in working for the common good. *Gaudium et Spes, The Pastoral Constitution on the Church in the Modern World,* recognizes that "the social order and its development must

unceasingly work to the benefit of the human person. . . . This social order
. . . must be founded on truth, built on justice, and animated by love; in
freedom, it should grow every day toward a more humane balance" (par.
26). "The subject and the goal of all social institutions is and must be the
human person, which for its part and by its very nature stands completely
in need of social life" (par. 25). "Christian revelation . . . leads to a deeper
understanding of the laws of social life which the creator has written into
the spiritual and moral nature of human beings" (par. 23). *Gaudium et Spes*
explicitly recognizes "the rightful independence" and "autonomy" of
human affairs. Yes, the autonomy and rightful independence of earthly
affairs can be misunderstood to mean that these created realities do not
depend on their creator and have no relationship to God. The constitution
explicitly employs the concept of mediation to explain both the autonomy
of created things and their dependence on God. "The autonomy of earthly
affairs . . . mean(s) that created things and societies themselves enjoy their
own laws and values which must be gradually deciphered, put to use, and
regulated by human beings" (par. 36). From the faith perspective, this is
the will of the creator. "For though the same God is saviour and creator,
Lord of human history as well as of salvation history, in the divine arrangement itself the rightful autonomy of the creature, and particularly of the
human being, is not withdrawn. Rather, it is reestablished in its own dignity
and strengthened in it" (par. 41).

The *Pastoral Constitution on the Church in the Modern World* thus clearly
comes down on the side of one social moral order based on human nature
and human dignity, which is the same for all. One might maintain that this
document as the first one to bring in distinctively Christian warrants is a
transitional document that still holds on to the basic presuppositions of the
earlier documents with their natural-law basis. However, later documents
do not justify such an interpretation. A brief analysis of the more significant
later documents indicates that the same fundamental acceptance of one
social moral order for all remains.

In Pope Paul VI's *Populorum Progressio* (1967) the basic criterion of a
just social order is the complete development of the human being, which
is expounded throughout the whole of part one of the encyclical (par. 6-
42). True to the Catholic insistence on the social aspect of human existence,
the second and final part of the document deals with "the development of
the human race in the spirit of solidarity" (par. 43-80). In this section the
pope refers on occasion to his visit to Bombay where he called for mutual
understanding and friendship so we can all work together to build the
common future of the human race (par. 43). *Populorum Progressio* ends
with a final appeal to the sons and daughters of the church, to Christian
brothers and sisters, to non-Christian brothers and sisters, and to all people
of good will "to achieve a responsible development of humankind in which
all human beings will have an opportunity to find their fulfillment" (par.
84).

Octogesima Adveniens, the apostolic letter of Pope Paul VI on the eightieth anniversary of *Rerum Novarum,* cites *Populorum Progressio* to point out "the church's duty to put herself at the service of all, to help them grasp their serious problem in all its dimensions, and to convince them that solidarity in action at this turning point in human history is a matter of urgency" (par. 5). This letter discusses at length the new social problems confronting human society and calls for all to work together to solve these problems and to work for a destiny that is shared by all (for example, par. 12, 21). The basic criterion of what should be done remains the human person and the human family (for example, par. 11, 13, 14, 15, 16, 17, 19, 20, and 21). The second part of the letter calls to mind two human aspirations which are making themselves felt in these new contexts — equality and participation, two forms of human dignity and freedom (par. 22). Political activity which is to be based on the common good for the human person is social by nature (par. 23, 24, 46). The common good has been a central theme in Catholic social teaching. Thus, Catholics are called to recognize the problems confronting the contemporary world and to work with all others to bring about a just transformation of society based on the criteria of the nature of the human person, the human family, and the common good.

Justitia in Mundo, the document issued by the 1971 synod of bishops, recognizes that the forces working for bringing about justice in the world are "rooted in the awareness of the full basic equality as well as of the human dignity of all. Since human beings are members of the same human family, they are indissolubly linked with one another in the one destiny of the whole world, in the responsibility for which they all share."[4] The very title *Justice in the World* indicates the one social moral order which is common to all. "The right to development must be seen as a dynamic interpenetration of all those fundamental human rights upon which the aspirations of individuals and nations are based" (O'Brien, p. 393). The church is not alone responsible for justice in the world but her responsibility is a part of her mission. "Her mission involves defending and promoting the dignity and fundamental rights of the human person." "Christians . . . testify to the power of the Holy Spirit through their action in the service of human beings in those things which are decisive for the existence and the future of humanity" (O'Brien, p. 399). This synodal document ends with a call for collaboration with other Christians, other believers in God, and also with those who do not recognize the author of the world in fostering social justice, peace, and freedom (O'Brien, p. 404). Again the implications are clear. There is one social moral order and one social justice that all must work together in trying to attain.

Evangelii Nuntiandi, Pope Paul VI's 1975 document on evangelization, is most revealing on the question under discussion. The document deals primarily with evangelization but sees the social mission of the church as part of the evangelizing function. The pope sees human development and liberation as part of the evangelizing mission of the church, but the gospel involves much more than this dimension. "Evangelization involves an explicit message . . . about the rights and duties of every human being, about family life without which personal growth and development is hardly possible, about life in society, about international life, peace, justice, and development — a message especially energetic today about liberation" (par. 29). Between evangelization and human development there are profound links of an anthropological order because the human being to be evangelized is not an abstract being but is subject to social and economic questions. There are also links of a theological order since one cannot disassociate the plan of creation from the plan of redemption. There are links of the evangelical order because one cannot proclaim the new commandment without promoting in justice and in peace the true, authentic advancement of human beings (par. 31). Thus redemption and the gospel do not exclude but include true human advancement, which appears to be the same for all human beings. Talking about the specific contributions of the church, *Evangelii Nuntiandi* does not propose that Christians should do something different from what others are called to do in the service of justice and true human advancement. The church provides Christian liberation with the inspiration of faith, the motivation of fraternal love, and a social teaching. No specific mention is made of a special content for Christians which is different from the justice, human advancement, and social good for which all human beings are called to work (par. 38).

Laborem Exercens, the 1981 encyclical of Pope John Paul II, very clearly affirms the reality of one social moral order for all. "The church considers it her duty to speak out on work from the viewpoint of its human value and of the moral order to which it belongs" (par. 24). A strong point in the encyclical concerns the priority of the person and of the subjective aspect of work. "Thus the principle of the priority of labor over capital is a postulate of the order of social morality" (par. 15). The truth that constitutes the fundamental and perennial heart of Christian teaching on human work is that human work has an ethical value of its own which clearly and directly remains linked to the fact that the one who carries it out is a person, a conscious and free subject, that is to say, a subject that decides about oneself (par. 6). The ethical nature of work emphasizing the primacy of the subjective "should also find a central place in the whole sphere of social and economic policy, both within individual countries and in the wider field of international and intercontinental relationships" (par. 7).

One section of *Laborem Exercens* (IV, par. 16-23) is devoted to the rights of workers. These rights are for all workers. Such rights must be seen within the broad range of human rights which are connatural with human beings and which constitute the fundamental conditions for peace in the modern world: peace both within individual countries and societies and in international relations (par. 16). Note again the emphasis on universal human rights which belong to all human beings and must be recognized by all human societies. *Laborem Exercens* closes with a long section (V) on the spirituality of work. Here a specifically Christian approach is developed in contrast to the moral teaching part of the document which proposes what is required of all.

Sollicitudo Rei Socialis issued by Pope John Paul II in 1987 to commemorate the anniversary of *Populorum Progressio* incorporates many of the themes already seen which point to the fact that there is one social moral order to which all, Christians, other believers in God, and nonbelievers, are called to strive and work for. The human person is the basis for a just social order. All people are called in solidarity to work for the true and authentic development of human persons. The conclusion of *Sollicitudo* makes this point. "At stake is the dignity of the human person whose defense and promotion have been entrusted to us by the creator. . . . Every individual is called upon to play his or her part in this peaceful campaign, a campaign to be conducted by peaceful means in order to secure development in peace in order to safeguard nature itself and the world about us. The church too feels profoundly involved in this enterprise and she hopes for its ultimate success" (par. 47).

Thus documents of contemporary official Catholic social teaching acknowledge there is one social moral order or social justice to which all, including Catholic Christians, are called to work. There are references to the moral order and the order of social morality. The basis for this one order is the nature and dignity of the human person and of authentic human development both as individuals and in solidarity with others. Universal human rights furnish an important criterion of social morality. These documents also insist on the need for all to work together in order to achieve this justice, be they Catholics, other Christians, other believers in God, or even nonbelievers who are people of good will.

Another way to prove the thesis of this paper is to examine the content of official Catholic social teaching. Is the teaching that is proposed something which is proposed just for Christians or for all human beings? Part of the problem here is to produce an accurate and succinct statement of the content of official Catholic teaching. The danger is that in summarizing this teaching one will propose it in such a way as to support one's own thesis.

"A Pastoral Message," proposed by the United States bishops in conjunction with their pastoral letter on the economy, succinctly summarizes the content of Catholic social teaching on the economy. The following summary of the principal themes of Catholic social teaching will depend heavily on this pastoral message.[5] The bishops develop briefly six moral principles which "give an overview of the moral vision that we are trying to share" (par. 19). Note the universalist intention of the document. The pastoral message uses the terms *principles* and *themes* synonymously. I prefer to use the word *themes* rather than principles. The word *themes* is broad enough to embrace the attitudes or dispositions of persons as well as the values, principles, and norms that should direct life in society.

The basis of official Catholic social teaching is the dignity of the human person. For the Christian such human dignity or sacredness is rooted in creation, but all humankind can and should recognize this fundamental dignity.

The human person is social and one develops and grows only in community with others. Thus society is not something foreign or opposed to the individual person, but human persons are called to live together in society with other human beings. The dignity and social aspect of the human person constitute the cornerstone of the vision of society in official Catholic social teaching.

Human rights have emerged in the last three decades as the criterion often proposed in official Catholic social teaching for determining the justice of a particular society. However, this teaching insists not only on political and civil rights (for example, freedom of religion, speech, assembly, and so on) but also on social and economic rights such as rights to food, clothing, shelter, and health care.

The justice that should flourish in society in the vision of Catholic social teaching recognizes both the personal and the social dimensions of the person. Commutative justice regulates the relationships between individuals. Distributive justice directs the relationship of society and the state to the individuals, whereas social or legal justice governs the relationships of individuals to society and the state. Commutative justice is blind, no respecter of persons, and involves arithmetic justice. If I borrow five dollars from you and five dollars from the wealthiest person in the world, I owe each of you the same. Distributive and social justice do respect persons and involve proportional and not arithmetic justice. Thus, for example, the wealthy should not only pay more tax but pay a greater percentage of their income in tax. One of the fundamental demands of social justice today is the need for all to participate in the life and direction of society and the state.

The proper role of government is directed by the principle of subsidiarity, which avoids the two opposing dangers of individualism and totalitarianism thus illustrating the basic anthropology at work. Society exists for the common good. Government should intervene to help individuals, voluntary associations, and local governmental authorities to do what they can, and the federal government should only do those things that the smaller and lesser bodies cannot do effectively. Property too has an individual and a social aspect because from the Christian perspective the goods of creation exist to serve the needs of all. But again, nonbelievers can and should recognize this social dimension of property to serve the needs of all.

In recent years Catholic social teaching has emphasized the preferential option for the poor which originated especially in Latin American liberation theology. Although this option has strong roots in the Judeo-Christian tradition, nonbelievers can and should have this same preferential option as a value and as a hermeneutic principle or norm for what is just in society.

This synthetic summary of the major themes of Catholic social teaching indicates that such an approach is available to and required of all people living in a particular society. Christian motivation and intentionality definitely shape one's approach but all are called to accept and to put into practice this vision.

CORROBORATION

Other reasons can corroborate without conclusively proving the thesis that Catholic social teaching recognizes one social moral order or social justice which all, Catholics, Christians, believers in God, and nonbelievers are called to work for in solidarity. First, an older Catholic social teaching in the pre–Vatican II period and extending back to Thomas Aquinas insisted that the social moral teaching was based on the natural law, which is common to all humankind. Many people including myself have criticized the manuals of moral theology for their classicist, one-sidedly deductive, and physicalist view of natural law. The older Catholic understanding of one social moral order could definitely be wrong and in need of change. However, one can criticize severely the natural-law theory of the manuals and still come to the conclusion that there is only one social moral order for all. In fact, in the debate in Germany in the last two decades the defenders of the natural law or autonomous ethic, which sees all Christian morality as open to human reason, have generally belonged to the revisionist school of moral theologians.[6] These revisionists have disagreed with many of the conclusions of the manuals of moral theology and of official Catholic teaching especially in sexual areas. They disagree in many of the philosophical areas of what is meant by human reason and human nature, but they agree with the basic theological perspective that human reason reflecting on human nature can arrive at the moral order. Thus the thesis defended in this essay is in accord with the older Catholic tradition on this subject and has been affirmed even by many contemporaries who have somewhat severely criticized the philosophical presuppositions of neo-scholastic philosophy and of Thomism. This argument does not pretend to be totally convincing, but it adds some corroborative force to the argument made on the basis of Catholic social teaching itself.

A second corroborative argument again has its basis in Catholic universalism. The traditional Catholic teaching on the natural law and on the universal salvific will by which God calls all people to salvation illustrates catholicity or universality. In its relationship with the world and society, Roman Catholicism has not been a sect. In the famous typology of Ernst Troeltsch and Max Weber, the sect sees itself in opposition to the world and withdraws from the world rather than be corrupted by compromise with the world. The church as a type is a universal community open to all whose members live in the world and work together with all others for a better human society. Troeltsch saw Roman Catholicism as the best illustration of the church type.[7] Typologies are never exact, for reality does not always neatly fit into these typologies. However, all recognize that Roman Catholicism has not been sectarian. Roman Catholicism has always seen itself as living in the world and working to bring about a more just and human society.

One might object that for most of its history Roman Catholicism accepted a Constantinianism which called for the union of church and state. In such a unitary vision the independence and autonomy of the temporal order were not recognized. However, even in a Constantinian vision the temporal order retained what was thought to be its own finality and purposes. By its very nature, according to the reasoning often proposed, the temporal order is subordinate to the spiritual and hence should be subject to the spiritual. The control of the spiritual order was more often acknowledged to be indirect and not direct. Even in the theoretical acceptance of Constantinianism a relative autonomy of the temporal order was acknowledged.

All must recognize that Roman Catholicism has had great difficulty in coming to grips with some aspects of modernity, especially religious freedom and religious pluralism. Only in 1965 with the Vatican Council's *Declaration on Religious Freedom* did official Catholic teaching accept religious freedom and pluralism. However, in recent times Catholic social teaching has strongly recognized the need for all people in society to work together for a just temporal order.[8] As noted earlier, *The Pastoral Constitution on the Church in the Modern World* does not hesitate to speak about the autonomy of the temporal.

A third reason tending to confirm the thesis of this essay comes from an interpretation given by the United States Catholic bishops in their pastoral letters on peace and the economy. In the letter on peace the bishops explicitly recognize that Catholic social teaching on peace and war is directed to two different audiences. When addressing the Catholic faithful, the emphasis is on Christian aspects. When addressing the wider pluralistic audience, the document employs a more inclusive human approach. The pastoral letter on peace points out how these two different styles and approaches have been used in past Catholic social teaching. In this context the document clearly affirms the existence of one social moral order or social justice for which all must work in solidarity. "The wider civil community, although it does not share the same vision of faith, is equally bound by certain key moral principles. For all men and women find in the depth of their consciences a law written on the human heart by God. From this law, reason draws moral norms. These norms do not exhaust the gospel vision, but they speak to critical questions affecting the welfare of the human community, the role of states in international relations, and the limits of acceptable actions of individuals and nations on issues of war and peace."[9]

Bishop James Malone, then the president of the National Conference of Catholic Bishops (1984), explicitly treated the same issue in a significant address. The American bishops not only want to speak to Catholic believers but they also want to make a religiously informed contribution to the public policy debate in our pluralistic society. "When we oppose abortion in that forum, we do so because a fundamental human right is at stake – the right to life of the unborn child. When we oppose any such deterrence policies as would directly target civilian centers or inflict catastrophic damage, we do so because human values would be violated in such an attack. When we support civil rights at home and measure foreign policy by human rights criteria, we seek to do so in terms all people can grasp and support."[10] Thus the American bishops recognize that on public policy questions they are not proposing values and norms only for Catholics but for all humankind.

FURTHER CONSIDERATIONS

This section will develop in greater length two significant aspects of the thesis defended in this paper: a more precise understanding of the social moral order and the relationship of this thesis to the ongoing discussion in contemporary Catholic moral theology.

What does the social moral order mean and include? I have employed this term on the basis of its use in various official documents in Catholic social teaching. *Order* and *ordering* are important and traditional concepts in Catholic ethics. Law in the Thomistic understanding was looked upon as the objective norm of morality. In the Thomistic tradition law is seen primarily as a work of practical reason whose function is the proper ordering of things. Such a generic understanding of law applies to the different types of law – the eternal law, the natural law, and human law. These different types of laws are related through mediation. The natural law is the participation of the eternal law in the rational creature. Human law either makes known the requirements of natural law or makes specific what is left indeterminate in the natural law. Thus, for example, the natural law requires that one drive automobiles carefully and safely, but human law decides which side of the street drivers should use.[11] The moral order thus refers to the way that all things should be ordered. The social moral order refers to the ordering that brings about a just society.

The manuals of Catholic moral theology in the pre–Vatican II period truncated the Thomistic understanding of morality and reduced it almost totally to the role of ordering and of law. In my judgment morality, and also the moral order, involves more than just norms. Social morality by its very nature is always going to give more importance to ordering and to structures and institutions for these are the very reality of the social order. The social order does not directly deal with the private, the internal, and the invisible. However, the social moral order does depend heavily upon the attitudes, dispositions, or character of the people who comprise the society. Social morality demands two realities—a change of heart and a change of structures. In addition to the attitudes and virtues that should characterize the person living in the society, a proper understanding of the social moral order also includes the values, the norms, and the principles that should direct the life of society. Finally there is the level of concrete structuring of social realities and of the particular judgments that must be made. The social moral order must embrace all these three different levels.

The more objective levels of values, principles, and norms on the one hand and particular structures, institutions, and judgments on the other hand are in my judgment the same for Christians and non-Christians and for all human beings. All human beings are called to live together in a particular political society and as part of the total human family. The social moral order thus understood is open in principle to every human being. By no means do all human beings accept the values, norms, and institutions that are proposed, but all by reason of being human are called to accept these and there is no insurmountable reason (for example, the lack of explicit Christian revelation) which prevents their acceptance of this social moral order. From a purely pragmatic perspective in order to have a society there has to be some fundamental and basic agreement about what the society is and how it should function, but the position taken here is not just a pragmatic one.

Attitudes, virtues, dispositions, and character refer to the more subjective aspects of human morality where one can and should expect a greater degree of differences depending upon the differences of the individual. All people living in the same society must ultimately come to some agreement about the type of society they want to live in and the values that should be present in such a society, but individual human beings will retain their own dispositions, preferences, character traits, and so on. However, the fundamental attitudes and dispositions governing life in society are the same for all. For example, concern for the poor is frequently proposed as an important attitude in Catholic social teaching and often grounded in the Hebrew and Christian scripture. However, concern for the poor should characterize all people in the society and not just those who accept the Christian faith or some other religious faith. Concern for the poor does not necessarily require any religious basis. The basic dignity of all human beings can serve as the foundation for a special concern for those human beings who are most in need. Intentionality and motivation will definitely differ, but concern for the poor is an attitude required of all human beings.

How does the thesis of this essay fit into some of the ongoing discussions about similar issues? One question concerns the best way for Catholic social teaching to address its subject matter. All must admit that Catholic social teaching is addressed not only to Catholics but to all others. With such an audience the documents at times will use Christian warrants but at other times will use more inclusive human warrants. The tactical question will continue to be present. What the present thesis adds to this question is that the tactical question is really the only question that has to be addressed. One does not appeal to Christian sources and themes because there is content which is meant only for Christians. However, I would strongly disagree with the contention that the documents should appeal only to inclusively human sources and warrants. In addressing the Catholic community the documents should appeal to those realities shared by this particular community. In fact, I do not think the documents in the past have appealed enough to the relationship between liturgy and social practice. The Catholic community is primarily a eucharistic community, and this sacramental reality should have an important relationship to life in human society.

The broader context of the subject matter under consideration here is the question about whether there is a unique moral content to Christian morality. The question has been discussed from different contexts and in different countries. As in any ongoing debate there have been clarifications and developments as the discussions ensued. Norbert Rigali has recently helped the discussion by focusing on what is the precise question involved and what are extraneous questions. The debate is not about the distinctiveness of Christian morality, for all admit many things such as love of God and neighbor are distinctive about Christian morality. The issue does not concern moral theology or Christian ethics, which is the thematic and systematic reflection on Christian morality. The precise question is: Does Christian faith add any unique material content to morality, the moral order, or the moral life?[12]

In the present issue the focus is even narrower. We are talking about the social moral order. Such an order is obviously more limited than the moral order. As noted above, the social moral order deals only with one part of morality and does not touch the private, the purely personal, and that which does not have an effect on society. Also within the confines of any given society we are dealing only with the social moral order for all people who belong to this one society. The presupposition is that these people have to live with one another in peace, justice, and harmony despite their many differences, which often involve religious differences. One could logically maintain that faith does not add any material content to the social moral order but still hold for different material content in the broader moral order.

I have maintained that there is only one moral order for Christians and for all others. In trying to explain this I have found helpful another suggestion made by Norbert Rigali, which he later abandoned. Rigali distinguished four different spheres: essential, existential, Christian essential, and Christian existential. Essential morality is that required of all persons because they are human persons or, in the narrower context of the present discussion, is that which is required of all people in order to live in a just human society. Existential morality refers to the particular calls, gifts, and dispositions of individuals, such as one's profession, state in life, place of living. Christian essential morality refers to responsibilities incumbent on one as a member of a Christian faith community and which belong to all such members. Christian existential morality refers to the particular vocation or call of a person within the faith community; for example, to dedicate oneself to the service of peace. Rigali has rejected this earlier distinction because it is based on a classicism which sees a uniform moral order based on a universal human nature. In the name of historical consciousness Rigali argues for a multiform moral order based on concrete persons in history.[13]

There is no doubt that my position is universalist. I do not think it necessarily has to be classicist. Part of the problem is in knowing the precise way in which historical consciousness is to be understood. I believe that historical consciousness is compatible with human universality. Universality and classicism are not necessarily opposed; in fact, they exist on two different levels. Rigali and I agree that the difference between morality and ethics is very important and significant in this discussion. Morality refers to a normative ordering which involves what should be or be done. Ethics is a second-order discourse that reflects on morality in a thematic, systematic, and reflexive way. Rigali rightly points out that the issue under discussion is on the level of morality (whether or not there is a unique moral content to Christian morality) and not on the level of ethics. I am asserting a universality on the level of morality. The discussion about classicism and historical consciousness is not on the level of morality but on the level of ethics. One could hold to a general and an "in principled" universality on the level of morality without necessarily embracing classicism on the level of ethics.

Rigali can be pushed from the other extreme to reply to the charge that his position tends toward sectarianism. On the narrower question of the social moral order, Rigali needs to address the question of how people in a pluralistic society can work for justice for all its citizens. Will he admit any universal values or principles such as those proposed by Catholic social teaching? Can one have justice in human societies if people are radically incapable of agreeing on what justice is? Rigali could continue to help the discussion along by responding to questions about universality. Does he admit any universality? And, if so, where? On the level of the social moral order, of human rights, of the dignity of the human person?

In the current discussion about the uniqueness of Christian morality questions have arisen about what scripture contributes to morality. Some with whom I share the position of affirming there is one moral order for all claim that scripture gives only paranesis or moral exhortation but no normative morality.[14] I disagree, and I think Catholic social teaching also uses scripture to provide some normative content. However, the level of the normative as found in scripture is on the whole rather general because the scriptures themselves are historically and culturally limited. Thus, for example, the preferential option for the poor as found in scripture is normative. The common destiny of the goods of creation to serve the needs of all is often based on Christian warrants. Yet the normative aspects that are found in scripture are not unique to the faith community but can be accepted by all others. This essay has defended the thesis that official Catholic social teaching today recognizes one social moral order. Catholics, Christians, believers, and nonbelievers are called to work together for the common good of society. In accord with this thesis Catholic social teaching will continue to address the two audiences of the church and of all human beings and will appeal both to Christian warrants and to more inclusive human appeals. However, all are called to work together in solidarity for authentic human development and liberation.

NOTES

1. For an overview of the discussion about natural law, see Charles E. Curran and Richard A. McCormick, *Readings in Moral Theology No. 7: Natural Law and Theology* (New York: Paulist Press, 1990).

2. For a description of this work of renewal and for an analysis and criticism of the relationship between faith and ethics especially as it was discussed in the last two decades in Germany, see Vincent MacNamara, *Faith and Ethics: Recent Roman Catholicism* (Washington: Georgetown University Press, 1985).

3. The pertinent paragraph numbers of official documents will be given in the text. These documents can be found in a number of different sources.

4. There are no official paragraph numbers for *Justitia in Mundo*. My references will be to David J. O'Brien and Thomas A. Shannon, eds., *Renewing the Earth: Catholic Documents on Peace, Justice, and Liberation* (Garden City, New York: Doubleday Image Books, 1977), p. 391.

5. National Conference of Catholic Bishops, "A Pastoral Message," in *Economic Justice for All: Pastoral Letter on Catholic Social Teaching and the U.S. Economy* (Washington, D.C.: United States Catholic Conference, 1986), par. 12-18, pp. ix-xi.

6. For this discussion in Germany, see MacNamara, *Faith and Ethics: Recent Roman Catholicism*. The theologians associated with this approach include Alfons Auer, Franz Böckle, Josef Fuchs, and Bruno Schüller.

7. Ernst Troeltsch, *The Social Teaching of the Christian Churches,* 2 vols. (New York: Harper Torchbooks, 1960).

8. One of the early and perduring concerns of John Courtney Murray, whose scholarship prepared the way for the Catholic acceptance of religious liberty, was the need for cooperation between Catholics and all others in the social sphere. In the 1940s Murray justified such intercredal cooperation on the basis of natural law, which is shared by all. See John Courtney Murray, "Intercredal Co-operation: Its Theory and Its Organization," *Theological Studies* 4 (1943), pp. 257-86.

9. National Conference of Catholic Bishops, *The Challenge of Peace: God's Promise and Our Response* (Washington, D.C.: United States Catholic Conference, 1983), par. 17.

10. *Washington Post,* August 19, 1984.

11. John Mahoney, *The Making of Moral Theology: A Study of the Roman Catholic Tradition* (Oxford: Clarendon Press, 1987), pp. 224-58.

12. Norbert Rigali, "The Uniqueness and Distinctivenes of Christian Morality and Ethics," in *Moral Theology: Challenges for the Future: Essays in Honor of Richard A. McCormick,* ed. Charles E. Curran (New York: Paulist Press, 1990).

13. Norbert Rigali, "On Christian Ethics," *Chicago Studies* 10 (1971), pp. 227-47; Rigali, "Morality and Historical Consciousness," *Chicago Studies* 18 (1979), pp. 162-68; Rigali, "The Unity of Moral and Pastoral Truth," *Chicago Studies* 25 (1986), pp. 225-29.

14. Bruno Schüller, "Zur Diskussion über das Proprium einer christlichen Ethik," *Theologie und Philosophie* 51 (1976), pp. 321-43.

6

JUSTICE IN THE CHURCH

The Church as Example

BISHOP RAYMOND A. LUCKER

"Anyone who ventures to speak to people about justice must first be just in their eyes." These words of the Synod of Bishops held in Rome in the fall of 1971 provide the context for my remarks concerning justice in the church. I speak from almost forty years of pastoral experience as religious educator, seminary professor, education administrator, parish pastor, and bishop of a small, rural diocese in Minnesota.

I attended minor and major seminaries in the 1940s when the social justice teaching of the church had an important place in the curriculum. We studied the "great encyclicals," especially those of Pope Leo XIII, Pope Pius XI, and Pope Pius XII. We learned of the dignity of the human person, and especially the dignity of workers and their right to organize and to bargain collectively. We were taught the concept of the common good and the call of the church to work for the transformation of society.

As a seminarian I eagerly read the *Catholic Worker* and studied the teachings of Canon Joseph Cardijn on the Young Christian Worker movement. I was excited about the priest worker movement in France. I read books by Cardinals Suhard and Saliege and Abbe Godin. Together with other seminarians I visited apostolic centers such as Friendship House, the Peter Maurin House, Catholic Worker Houses in Chicago, St. Paul, and Milwaukee. I was inspired by Dorothy Day, Catherine de Hueck, and Father Virgil Michel. I participated in special summer courses on Catholic action and on the social justice teachings of the church. I was a member of a small study group of seminarians who met each week to learn about and to apply the gospel message to social issues and to our own lives. Often, the great cry was for the active participation of priests as chaplains or spiritual directors in lay apostolic movements.

I was influenced by "labor priests" like Monsignor Francis Gilligan, who actively supported the labor union movement and who taught leadership and organizational skills in labor schools. (Later on, I was especially touched by Monsignor George Higgins, a colleague and friend, who epitomized clerical leadership in this field.)

At the same time, I grew up during a period when we thought of the church as the "perfect society," meaning that the church has within itself all of the means to reach its end. Nevertheless, we thought of it as a society which had all the answers and knew all the questions and, in general, could do no wrong. We never thought that the social justice teaching of the church had to be applied to the church itself. Such teaching was directed to society, to the world, and to conditions of injustice "out there."

Church leaders blessed the troops and the fleet as they went off to World War II to protect the world for democracy and freedom. In so many parts of the world the church was clearly allied with the political powers of the state. Only a few voices reminded us that the bombing of cities and the indiscriminate destruction of population centers was evil.

Pope John XXIII and Pope Paul VI advanced the church's social teaching and the documents of the Second Vatican Council laid the groundwork for calling every member of the church, especially the laity, to work for the transformation of society. The poor of the world were to be given special concern. We were becoming truly a world church, and we were beginning to see that all people and all of creation were related throughout this small planet.

There was only a gradual awareness on my part, and I suspect many in the church, that work for justice was a duty of everyone in the church, including me. As a young priest I looked at social justice concerns as something that merited the interest of church people, but such interest was a free choice. Some people could address social concerns and others could just as well be interested in some other aspect of the work of the church. My special work in the church was to promote religious education. Others, I felt, were called to social action.

Since the Vatican Council we have come to see more clearly that action on behalf of justice is indeed constitutive of preaching the gospel and essential to the ministry of the church in the redemption of humanity. The task of evangelization is intimately connected with working for justice. The Second Vatican Council called us to look at the joys and hopes, the griefs and anxieties of the whole world as the joys and anxieties of the whole church.

THE POOR OF CENTRAL AMERICA

A strong influence on my growing awareness of the call to justice has been the relationship of the Diocese of New Ulm to the church in Central

America. The Bishops of Latin America, meeting in Medellín, Colombia, in 1968 and in Puebla, Mexico, in 1979, gave a new meaning and vision to the concept of a preferential option for the poor.

In the early 1960s Pope John XXIII urged all of the dioceses in North America to send missionaries to Central and South America. It was a call for a more just distribution of the personnel and resources of the church. The Diocese of New Ulm accepted an invitation to staff and support the parish of San Lucas Toliman in Guatemala.

The blessings that have returned to the Diocese of New Ulm through this over twenty-five-year commitment have been enormous. One of the most important is that the people of the Diocese of New Ulm have learned so much about poverty, injustice, hunger, oppression, torture, and killing. We have learned about the value of the widespread distribution of the land and the human rights of every individual. We have come to know of a church, which had aligned itself with the rich and the powerful, now having turned to the poor and oppressed, becoming a church of martyrs.

The church in Guatemala became for us a "church as example," calling us to look at our lifestyle, to work for justice and peace, to commit ourselves to nonviolence, to value human life and human rights.

In all of this we see the social justice teaching of the church as calling Christians to work for the transformation of the world. Only in recent years have we begun to look at the church itself as in need of reform. I was in Rome as a graduate student in theology during the Second Vatican Council. I remember how surprised I was when I learned that the church could, indeed had to, reform itself.

We came to realize more clearly that the church which speaks for the sacredness of all human life, for justice, for the poor, for peace must indeed be concerned about justice within its own life and institutions. We were being led by the Holy Spirit to reform and renewal within the church itself. The church must be an example of how members of society ought to live.

How are we as a church community to apply the message of the social encyclicals and the church's social teaching to our own institutions and practice? I write these pages as a few pastoral reflections drawing from my life and experience. I hope to shed a little light on this question by reviewing what is said in some recent church documents about justice in the church and by outlining the rights of church members as contained in council documents and in the Code of Canon Law. Further, I will offer some reflections on the nature of the church and consider a few examples of issues of justice within the church.

1971 SYNOD

The church must itself strive to be a just institution if it desires its social teaching to be taken seriously by others. I refer to the synodal document, *Justice in the World* (particularly the third section, "The Practice of Justice:

The Church's Witness"), where the bishops call for an "examination of the modes of acting and of the possessions and lifestyle found within the church itself." The words with which I began this essay ring out: "Anyone who ventures to speak to people about justice must first be just in their eyes," say the synodal delegates from all over the world. Strong words indeed!

The document's words continue to prod us and perhaps make us uneasy. We are urged to promote and to secure the rights of persons within the church. We are reminded of our responsibility to give to those who work within the church a "sufficient livelihood." Lay employees are to be given "fair wages and a system for promotion." Lay people are to "exercise more important functions with regard to Church property" and "share in its administration."

Women are to "have their own share of responsibility and participation" in the life of the church. The church is to recognize "everyone's right to suitable freedom of expression and thought," including "the right of everyone to be heard in a spirit of dialogue." Church members have a right to proper and speedy judicial procedures. All church members have a right to "share in the drawing up of decisions," and such participation is to be fostered through "the setting up of councils at all levels."

With regard to "temporal possessions" and "positions of privilege," "it must never happen that the evangelical witness which the Church is required to give becomes ambiguous." "Our faith demands of us a certain sparingness in use, and the Church is obliged to live and administer its own goods in such a way that the gospel is proclaimed to the poor."

Finally, the lifestyle of all church members is to exemplify "that sparingness with regard to consumption which we preach to others as necessary in order that so many millions of hungry people throughout the world may be fed." While strides have been taken in some of these areas, we must admit that we have a long way to go.

ECONOMIC PASTORAL

Fifteen years after the 1971 Synod, the United States bishops issued a pastoral letter on Catholic social teaching and the United States economy, *Economic Justice for All.* In paragraphs 347-58 of the pastoral, the bishops speak of "the Church as economic actor," and they reiterate the Synod's teaching that the church's own life and action must reflect the justice it preaches. The bishops recognize that "on the parish and diocesan level, through its agencies and institutions, the Church employs many people . . . has investments . . . extensive properties for worship and mission."

The bishops stress that "all the moral principles that govern the just operation of any economic endeavor apply to the Church and its agencies and institutions; indeed the Church should be exemplary." The notion of the church as example runs through this part of the pastoral letter. The church in all its institutions from the Holy See to small rural parishes, from dioceses to families, from schools and universities to hospitals and nursing homes must teach justice, practice justice, and exemplify justice.

The institutional church is challenged to give just salaries and benefits to its employees, and church members are reminded of their responsibility to donate a just share of their time, talent, and treasure toward the church's support. Obviously the institutional church cannot meet its obligations in justice if its members do not meet theirs. Church institutions are urged to "fully recognize the rights of employees to organize and bargain collectively," and "to adopt new fruitful modes of cooperation."

Attention is called to the "continuing discrimination against women throughout the Church and society, especially reflected in both the inequities of salaries between women and men and in the concentration of women in jobs at the lower end of the wage scale." The church is also reminded of its responsibility to be a just steward of its properties and investments, of its "special call to be a servant of the poor, the sick, and the marginalized," and of its obligation "through all its members individually and through its agencies . . . to alleviate injustices that prevent some from participating fully in economic life" (the Campaign for Human Development is an example of the church's action in this area).

So, the church is called "to become a model of collaboration and participation," a model of justice. Church teaching regarding justice should reflect that the church is aware of its vocation to practice the justice it preaches. Sometimes, this is not the case.

The Congregation for Catholic Education, for example, issued a set of guidelines in 1988 for the study and teaching of the church's social doctrine in the formation of priests. It is an excellent summary of Catholic church teaching on social justice and social action. But, the ninety-one-page document does not mention the issue of justice in the church.

RIGHTS IN THE CHURCH

A centerpiece of the social justice teaching of the church is its concern for the rights of all persons. The revised Code of Canon Law issued in 1983 has a section that outlines the obligations and rights of all of the faithful, clergy and lay, and the obligations and rights of the lay Christian faithful.

This list of the rights of the Christian faithful flows from the Second Vatican Council's understanding of the church as the people of God. Every member of the church is called to participate actively in the life and mission of the church, and this call stems from baptism and confirmation. This foundational teaching of the Council is found in several places in the Council documents (*Lumen Gentium,* 33; *Apostolicam Actuositatem,* 3, 1522, 24; *Presbyterorum Ordinis,* 9).

The basis of all rights in the church is baptism. "As members, they share a common dignity from their rebirth in Christ." They are given the same grace and are called to the same life of holiness. "They possess in common one salvation, one hope and one undivided charity. Hence, there is in Christ and in the Church no inequality on the basis of race or nationality, social condition or sex" (*Lumen Gentium,* 32).

All Christians are equal, as the Second Vatican Council stated. The Second Vatican Council document on the church stated that "every type of discrimination, whether social or cultural, whether based on sex, race, color, social condition, language or religion, is to be overcome and eradicated as contrary to God's interest" (*Gaudium et Spes,* 29).

Throughout the Council documents there are other references to rights in the church and this led, after the Council, to the development of lists of rights in the church. In the project of revising and bringing up to date the Code of Canon Law, there was a proposal to add to the code a "fundamental law" of the church, which would list among other things the rights of members of the church.

CODE OF CANON LAW

There is a list of rights contained in the Code of Canon Law in the section on the people of God. The Christian faithful are all called to holiness (c. 210) to proclaim the message of God and to spread the gospel (c. 211). Every member of the church has a right to receive the word of God and the sacraments and has a right to worship (c. 213, 214). Members have a right to establish and to participate in associations (c. 215).

All the Christian faithful "in accord with the knowledge, competence and preeminence which they possess ... have the right and even at times a duty to manifest to the sacred pastors their opinion on matters which pertain to the good of the Church, and they have a right to make their opinion known to the other Christian faithful, with due regard for the integrity of faith and morals and reverence toward their pastors, and with consideration for the common good and dignity of persons" (c. 212). Every member has a right to participate in the mission of the church (c. 216).

All of the Christian faithful have a right to their good name and to protect their own privacy and to vindicate and defend their rights in the church before a competent ecclesiastical court (c. 220, 221).

In addition to these rights, which all Christians enjoy, lay people in the church have additional rights. They have a special duty to perfect the order of temporal affairs with the spirit of the gospel, the right to educate their children, to be installed in certain ministries. If they are church employees, they have the right to decent remuneration by which they are able to provide for their own needs and for those of their family. They likewise have a right to a pension, social security, and health benefits (c. 231). Other rights are acknowledged for members of the church throughout the Code of Canon Law.

Thus, there has been a growing awareness in the life of the church during these last one hundred years of human rights and the gradual recognition and application of those rights in the life of the church itself.

THE CHURCH: A MYSTERY, HUMAN AND DIVINE

Before considering specific issues of justice within the church, I want to reflect on some aspects of the nature of the church.

The church is a sacrament, a mystery. Jesus is the head of the church; the Holy Spirit is the life of the church; and we are its members, with all of our weaknesses, sinfulness, ignorance, and mistakes. While the church is the body of Christ, it is poor, broken, human. Though called the Spotless Bride of Christ, the church can be unjust. Though marked by holiness, the church can be unholy. The members and leaders of the church are all human beings, born in original sin, prone to sin and mistakes, yet capable of growth and holiness.

It is hard for us to recognize our own sinfulness, sinfulness in the church. There can be a tendency to divinize the church. One effect of that is to minimize or even deny the way in which our doctrine, worship, and pastoral practice are historically conditioned and culturally limited. The principle of the incarnation has us take seriously the implications of human fallibility, vulnerability, change, growth, creativity, and flesh. All this within a community which Jesus promised to be with and to guide in all truth!

Karl Rahner often reminded us that the church needs to recognize its mistakes. It does grow; it always needs to reform. There have been many changes in noninfallible but authentic teachings in the church. This should not surprise us. We have changed in our teaching about women, about race, about human liberty, about Galileo, about the Mosaic authorship of the Pentateuch, about torture, about who is a member of the church, about abstaining from sexual relations before going to communion, about church and state.

According to *Mysterium Ecclesiae* (Congregation for the Doctrine of the Faith, 1973), we are to recognize the historical, time-conditioned character of church pronouncements. Though the church can teach infallibly, doctrinal definitions may be expressed at first incompletely, and may be limited by the language and by changeable conceptions of a given time. The gospel needs to be incarnated in every culture, in every time, in every social and economic system.

The social teaching of the church continues to grow as well. In celebrating one hundred years of *Rerum Novarum*, we recognize that today it is an inadequate document and superceded by the Second Vatican Council's *Constitution on the Church in the Modern World* and the two social encyclicals of Pope John Paul II, *Laborem Exercens* (1981) and *Sollicitudo Rei Socialis* (1987). Catholic social teaching must continually keep pace with changes and needs in society.

Once we say as official church teaching that authentic but noninfallible teaching can change (as we did in the Vatican II *Declaration on Religious Liberty*), once we say all people are equal, all people have rights, then we set ourselves on a course, a trajectory, that is not easily stopped or changed. We are then willing to say that we have made mistakes and we have grown in applying Catholic social teaching within the church. With that in mind, I now want to focus on a number of particular issues.

SALARIES AND BENEFITS OF LAY EMPLOYEES

In recent years increasing numbers of lay persons are exercising ministerial roles traditionally carried out by priests, sisters, and brothers. People give their talents, their gifts, their energies, their lives to promote the mission of the church. For this, they are supported by parishes, institutions, dioceses, and religious congregations.

In 1986 the National Association of Church Policy Administrators published a position paper, "Just Treatment for Those Who Work for the Church," calling on "Church-related institutions to model just treatment for all persons working for them." Among the personnel practices recommended were clearly written personnel policies, involvement of employees in decisions affecting them, just salaries and benefits, fair and honest performance evaluations, grievance and termination procedures, and the right to join employee associations.

The bishops' pastoral on economics identified salaries and benefits of lay employees as a matter of special concern. They committed themselves to the notion that all those who work for the church should receive sufficient livelihood and social benefits and called on all of the members of the church to recognize that this would call for increased contributions on their part.

In 1987 the National Conference of Diocesan Directors of Religious Education undertook a research project on just wages and benefits for lay and religious church employees. Fifteen other national Catholic organizations joined the project. The purpose of the study was to give guidance to church employers on decisions affecting salaries and benefits for those who work in the church. The study revealed that, depending upon what model of compensation was followed, church employees received anywhere from seventeen to forty percent below what was needed for a family to live in basic dignity or in comparison with people in similar positions.

Catholic schools throughout the country struggle to continue to provide quality education and at the same time bring pay scales to a more equitable level in relationship to professional scales in the public schools. Base starting salaries for teachers in Catholic schools are frequently sixty to seventy percent of what their counterparts in public schools make. After twenty or more years a Catholic school teacher is likely to be making fifty percent of a public school teacher's salary. The Catholic school teachers may be willing to work for less and be committed to this challenging and rewarding ministry. Still, justice demands that they receive "a sufficient livelihood," "fair wages," and "a system for promotion" (*Justice in the World*, 351).

STIPENDS AND RETIREMENT OF RELIGIOUS

Another issue of justice in the church concerns the retirement of members of religious congregations, especially women religious. In November of 1987 the bishops of the United States voted to have a national, annual collection to raise retirement funds for religious congregations.

I believe that all of us have a responsibility and should be given an opportunity to contribute to the support of retired religious men and women, who have given so much toward building up the church in our country.

We have been told by the Tri-Conference Retirement Project that religious communities were 2.9 billion dollars short in their retirement funds. In the past we simply did not provide for the retirement costs of religious women. Religious communities had set little aside for retirement. The stipend given to an active sister was hardly enough to provide even basic necessities much less put aside something for future retirement.

For ten or twelve years some dioceses, including the Diocese of New Ulm, had been regularly consulting with representatives of religious communities and stipends were instituted for sisters that took into account their needs, including the need to support elderly members of their communities. This has not been the practice throughout the country. The average stipend given to religious women in this country last year was something like $8,000. Religious women tell us that the minimum stipend needed is in the neighborhood of $15,000, not including housing, transportation, continuing education, and retirement needs. If the approximately fifty thousand active sisters received an average of $5,000 more per year, that would add 250 million dollars annually to the support of retired religious women. In ten years we would be closer to meeting the 2.9 billion dollar past service liability.

The Catholic people of the United States have been generous in supporting the national collection for the retirement needs of religious, and that effort needs continued support. We need to recognize, however, that the ten-year collection, even if it continues at a generous level, will never meet the needs or solve the longterm problem. It can only hope to generate ten percent of the support that is really needed.

A more just solution to the problem, in my opinion, calls for larger basic stipends or larger compensation packages based on some other system from parishes and institutions in which the sisters are employed throughout the country.

The sisters that I talk to are not asking for charity. They are asking for basic justice. The pastoral of the bishops of the United States on economics said, "It would be a breach of our obligations to these dedicated women and men who taught in our schools, worked in our hospitals, with very little remuneration, to let them, or their communities, face retirement without adequate funds."

RACISM IN THE CHURCH

While church teaching has developed with regard to racial justice, the church needs more effectively to practice such justice. When I attended the seminary in the 1940s and 1950s, it was almost impossible for a young black man or woman to attend a seminary or join a religious community. I was proud, I remember, that the St. Paul Seminary admitted black students, but this was an exception. They could join a few religious communities; some of them were set up especially for black candidates.

The official church at every level has condemned racism and the actions of racists. For example, the Pontifical Peace and Justice Commission declared, "Racism and racist acts must be condemned. The Church wants first and foremost to change racist attitudes including those within her own communities" (November 3, 1988, *Origins*, February 23, 1989). Pope John Paul II has led the way in clear, unambiguous teaching on racism and discrimination.

Yet we have been told over and over again by African Americans, Hispanics, Native Peoples, and others that racism is found within the Catholic church in the United States. The same racism that exists in society can be found in the church. Some efforts have been made in recent years to overcome racism and to change the attitudes of Catholic people.

In their pastoral letter, "What We Have Seen and Heard," the African-American bishops forcefully remind us, "Blacks and other minorities still remain absent from many aspects of Catholic life and are only meagerly represented on the decision-making level. ... This racism, at once subtle and masked, still festers within our Church as within our society. This stain of racism on the American Church continues to be a source of pain and disappointment to all, both Black and White, who love her and desire her to be the Bride of Christ" (p. 20).

SEXISM IN THE CHURCH

In 1981 I joined Bishop Victor Balke in issuing a pastoral letter to raise awareness among our people of Christian feminism and the sin of sexism. We also hoped that our pastoral letter would lead to a greater and fully just participation on the part of women in the life of the church.

We defined sexism as "the erroneous belief or conviction or attitude that one sex, male or female, is superior to the other in the very order of creation or by the very nature of things." We identified sexism as immoral and a social evil contrary to gospel teaching. "Sexism is a lie," we said. "It is a grievous sin diminished in its gravity only by indeliberate ignorance or by pathological fear." We were led to issue this pastoral letter by the growing awareness of a pervasive attitude of sexism in society and in the church.

In 1975 Pope Paul VI, speaking of the United Nations International Women's Year, noted that one of the aims of the year was "winning equal rights for women," and declared that "there are still millions of women who do not enjoy basic rights." He called for an examination of conscience. He said, "The examination has to do with the manner in which rights and duties of both men and women are respected and fostered and also with the participation of women in the life of society on one hand and in the life and mission of the Church on the other."

The very cornerstone of Catholic social teaching is that every human being is created equal and every person has human rights. Jesus demonstrated this to us by his life and teaching. Women accompanied him in his ministry. Jesus taught Mary, the sister of Martha, as a rabbi instructed a disciple. Jesus revealed himself as Messiah to the Samaritan woman, and she became one of the first evangelizers. He touched women, healed them, forgave them. Women were among the first to whom Jesus revealed his resurrection. Women took an active part in the early life of the church. "For all of you who were baptized into Christ have clothed yourselves with Christ," Paul wrote to the Galatians. "There is neither Jew nor Greek, there is neither slave nor free person, there is not male and female; for you are all one in Christ Jesus" (Gal 3: 27-28).

Through a whole series of historical and cultural circumstances society continued to regard women as unequal, as property, as unclean, as tempters of men. Such sinful attitudes entered into the very fabric of church life. Only in recent years has our awareness of sexism been raised, mostly through the development of the feminist movement and the many Christian feminists and women theologians who have examined their experience in the light of the gospel message. We, as a church, need to listen to their voices, examine our conscience as Pope Paul VI asked us, and apply the social justice teaching of the church in this very important area to our lives, to our institutions and through our daily practice.

In the consultation leading to the development of the Bishops' Pastoral Response to Women's Concerns, women from around the country told us that sexism is found at every level of the church. The church is a patriarchy; that is, an institution under the rule of men. It is a male-led and male-dominated church, rather than a discipleship of equals.

The second draft of the pastoral response concludes by saying, "Equality is not a privilege to be earned by women, but a right which belongs to them by virtue of their creation in the image of God." Equality leads to acceptance, respect, sharing, mutuality, appreciation, friendship and partnership; inequality to domination, superiority, disrespect, lack of appreciation, devaluing and stereotyping—in a word, to sexism. The bishops pledge themselves to work for the elimination of every trace of sexism or unequal treatment. They promise to "oppose the destructive power of sexism" by working to change structures, attitudes, and misconceptions that perpetuate this evil.

Some efforts have been made to mitigate this injustice, especially now that awareness has been raised on the issue. Still, women are not allowed certain positions of power and leadership in the church, and sexist language continues to pervade church hymns, documents, and pronouncements. The denial of women to serve at the liturgy continues to convey second-class status, even though they can participate as song leaders, cantors, lectors, and extraordinary ministers of the Holy Eucharist. Pressure will continue to be made on church leadership and on church members in general to work toward the full equality of men and women in church and society.

DUE PROCESS

It is one thing to have church statements and canon law speaking about rights of people in the church. It is another to set up procedures that will protect individuals who have been treated unjustly by either another member of the church or by one of its institutions.

Due process in the church provides the means to guarantee fundamental rights and freedom. It is a method of resolving disputes by setting forth and protecting the rights of persons involved in a conflict with church personnel, institutions, or those who have been wronged by administrative decisions. It is a protection against arbitrary exercise of power.

Certain rights are protected by due process: the right to fair employment practices, the right to be informed of proposed actions which affect individuals, the right of a person to be heard in defense of their rights, the right in the face of accusation to confront one's accusers, and the right not to be judged by one's accusers.

Due process procedures have been set up in over half of the dioceses in the United States. It is an in-house and in-family process. Where a due process system has been established in a diocese, usually two services are available: conciliation and arbitration. Most disputes can be resolved through conciliation. The two parties of the dispute come together with a third party, a conciliator, to resolve a problem. The process for arbitration is more formal and difficult and adds an important dimension that the two parties are willing to abide by the decision of the arbitrator.

Experience has shown that most of the conflicts presented to the diocesan due process boards have been conflicts around the hiring and firing of teachers and other church personnel and accusations about the arbitrary exercise of authority by pastors. Actually, where due process procedures are in place, few cases have been initiated. The availability of due process in the church is not yet widely known, and the very existence of due process procedures makes people more aware of the importance of treating others fairly. A committee on arbitration has been established by the National

Conference of Catholic Bishops to resolve conflicts where a bishop or one of the conference agencies is involved.

There are still many widespread complaints that such procedures are needed in the offices in Rome as well, especially in regard to the treatment of theologians and priests who are seeking laicization.

ORDINATION OF WOMEN

One of the most divisive and controversial issues facing the church as we enter the third millennium is the ordination of women. The declaration issued by the Congregation for the Doctrine of the Faith in 1976, "On the Question of the Admission of Women to the Ministerial Priesthood," said that the church "in fidelity to the example of the Lord, does not consider herself authorized to admit women to priestly ordination" (5). The actions of Jesus and the practice of the apostles are seen as normative.

Karl Rahner believed that the practice of the church can be understood as a human tradition and not as divine revelation and, therefore, can be changed.

The Pontifical Biblical Commission in 1976 declared that the New Testament by itself does not permit us to settle whether women can be ordained priests. A report from the American Biblical Association came to a similar conclusion.

It is necessary that this issue be open to discussion. The very fact that we are not able to teach openly about it or even discuss it is a sign of injustice in the church. This is such a critical issue in the church that it deserves full and open study by the best minds in the church.

As we celebrate the one hundredth anniversary of modern Catholic social teaching, we can be proud of a rich heritage. Justice and human rights have been promoted—this we celebrate. We continue to be challenged by our own teaching. The words of Jesus still echo, "This is the time of fulfillment. The reign of God is at hand! Reform your lives and believe in the gospel!" (Mk 1: 15).

PART II

THE FAMILY IN
CATHOLIC SOCIAL THOUGHT

7

MARRIAGE

Institution, Relationship, Sacrament

LISA SOWLE CAHILL

The Roman Catholic understanding of marriage has been shaped by four factors: 1) a *Western* historical and social context for understanding sexuality, kinship, and individuality, essentially within a social and patri archal model, but with a modern emphasis on personal freedom; 2) a *sacramentalizing* tendency, accepting human institutions but also transforming them in distinctive ways (for example, by seeing marriage as permanent); 3) *canon law*, the medium by which Western Christianity has controlled sexuality and protected marriage as an institution via juridical definitions; and 4) a struggle to balance *the physical and the interpersonal* aspects of marriage. Of special current importance is the "personalism" of the recent magisterium. The latter ambiguously assimilates modern understandings of the person, of freedom, and of interpersonal relationships to a pre-modern emphasis on the physical "nature" of sex and reproduction, and on the social functions of sexuality and family within a hierarchical and patriarchal order.

THE WESTERN THEOLOGICAL PERSPECTIVE ON MARRIAGE

Historically, Christianity has understood marriage to be the only appropriate channel for human sexuality; it is a relationship of social and domestic partnership typically characterized by sexual intercourse and shared parenthood. Christian interpretations of marriage have built upon its cultural patterns. Until modern times, the relationship of the couple to one another has been secondary to blood kin relations, especially that of parent and child. Until the mid-twentieth century, companionship, friendship, and love have been subsidiary and nonessential aims of sex and marriage. Lineage and inheritance along male descent lines have been in Western and in most other cultures the major structures of social organization, and marriage has functioned both to provide a controlled mechanism of descent and to link distinct lineage-based kinship groups. Men have seen women as primarily childbearers, essential to the male's contribution to the intergenerational kinship network. And women have seen marriage primarily as a way to ongoing economic and social affiliation with a descent group, and as a way of securing their own status within it by means of their children, especially sons. Extramarital sexuality is unruly sexuality, which threatens social organization. Perhaps worse, it results in offspring who suffer the burden of their parents' irresponsibility to these social roles. Because it has seemed to pose a threat to the ordering of passion by reason, and because it can disrupt fundamental social patterns, sexuality has appeared as a necessary but intractable aspect of human life, in need both of explanation and of domestication.

Augustine's understanding of the meaning of marriage for Christians has been perhaps most formative for our religious tradition. Its dangers are redeemed by three purposes or attendant "goods": sexual faithfulness, a restricted and ordered expression of genital sex with one's spouse only (*fides*); the raising of children (*proles*); and the indissoluble bond, which in Christian marriage stands for the union of Christ and church (*sacramentum*).[1] Augustine resisted contemporary philosophical and religious dualisms (particularly Manicheeism), which rejected all sex. Augustine justified sex and marriage as the necessary means of procreation.

Despite its possible adequacy to the realities of his time and that of several later generations, the Augustinian defense of matrimony looks appallingly insufficient today. Familiar critiques focus on Augustine's negativity toward sexual passion in general, his limited view of sex as good only when deliberately procreative, and his and his culture's suppression of the interpersonal value of sexual intimacy as well as their complacent assumption of gender inequality. Thomas Aquinas appropriated Augustine's three goods from the *Sentences* of Peter Lombard, so perpetuating their influence.[2] More innovatively, Aquinas saw marriage as a "friendship" of the most intense kind[3] and saw sexual passion as good as long as it is rightly ordered (to procreation). Nonetheless, women were subordinate, and procreation, not love or sexual pleasure, remained the only legitimate reason for sexual relations and the primary purpose of marriage until the twentieth century. As a framework for sexual roles and corresponding duties, Christian marriage has functioned, in line with Augustine's categories, as an appropriate sexual outlet; as a nurturant source of the next generation; as a secure institution that undergirds the interdependence both of the sexes and of the generations; and as a symbol of humanity's equally secure dependence on divine salvation.

Three ongoing problems must be faced in any discussion of Catholic marriage teaching. The first is the dialectic of the social and the personal in marriage, which is both a relationship and an institution. This dialectic includes the relation of the physical realities of marriage, especially sex and reproduction, to both poles. Second is the problem of gender, or of the roles of the sexes in marriage and in other functions onto which marriage opens. While older teaching was based on the assumption of women's inferiority to men, recent incomplete efforts have been made by the magisterium to speak of women and men as equals, while still retaining many of the moral outcomes of the framework in which procreation was explicitly primary. Third is the formation of the marital commitment or union, whether by mutual consent or sexual consummation, and as provisional or indissoluble.[4] Theological views of sacramentality and indissolubility have been heavily molded by juridical interests in defining clear criteria of the existence or nonexistence of the marriage bond and in locating a particular moment at which it begins to exist irreversibly.

MARRIAGE AS SACRAMENTAL REALITY

A sacrament is a human interaction or event that provides the setting and becomes the substance of a relationship between God and humans.[5] The sacraments of the Christian churches (from a minimum of baptism and eucharist to Roman Catholicism's maximum of seven) ritualize basic experiences which give definition to the life cycle (birth, growth, marriage, social vocation, death) and to daily existence (food, forgiveness). These events become gateways to divine friendship, forgiveness, and reconciliation.

Marriage in early Christianity was not immediately taken over from a secular reality into a specifically "sacramental" one. Nonetheless, it was one among many spheres of life which Christians transformed by discipleship.

> The first Christian community had no precise notion of sacrament. They simply tried to experience and relate their whole life to the Risen Christ, into whom they were baptized . . . and in whom they were a "new creation" (Gal 6:15).[6]

In addition to the fact that they held up marriage as a permanent relationship instead of a dissoluble contract, Pheme Perkins describes a couple of other ways in which early Christians set themselves off from the culture by sacralizing marriage.[7] Authors like Paul (1 Cor 7:3-5) rejected the extreme asceticism which commended celibacy even in marriage, but adopted a moderated asceticism by preferring celibacy (1 Cor 7:7,8). Christians also subsumed marriage into a religious world-view by linking it with religious symbols as a graced or transformed relationship (Eph 5:25; 1 Cor 7:13-14).

Historically, the sacramentalization of marriage became detached from its biblical base in the eschatological idealism of communal life and was tied instead to its canonical regulation. When Peter Lombard formulated the list of seven sacraments in the twelfth century, he included marriage. At the Council of Trent (1563) marriage was formally declared a sacrament in response to the Reformers' view that it is a human and dissoluble institution. In subsequent developments the sacramentality of marriage has been reduced virtually to its attribute of permanency as contract — an attribute more susceptible of juridical scrutiny and enforcement than the presence of divine love through a relationship. Permanent fidelity is often linked to God's salvific love as a practical norm by means of Ephesians 5:25, "Husbands love your wives, as Christ loved the Church"; and 5:32, "This mystery [the "one flesh" unity] is a profound one, and I am saying that it refers to Christ and the Church."

But the analogy of husband and wife to Christ and church is obviously meant by its author as an exhortation to Christians regarding specific and practical marital behavior. It can hardly be taken as an abstract principle, to be turned around as a statement of fact about all actual marriages. There is also no indication by Paul that all Christian marriages will in fact reach the level of Christ's love for the church. As Theodore Mackin so rightly observes, "An analogy consisting of Christ's metaphoric marriage with a metaphor of the Church cannot produce an ontological effect in an actual marriage."[8] So one can conclude at most that "the ideal model of Christian marriage has been assumed into the love relationship of Christ and the Church."[9] Abstract predications about marriage, based on biblical texts taken out of context and interpreted to substantiate ecclesiastical law, must be replaced by a more experiential approach which recognizes both the provisional and the progressive nature of marriage as a human relationship and the paradoxical bearing of gospel ideals on all human enterprises.

Although the New Testament gives the formative evidence that marriage is a graced reality, that evidence is insubstantial as a base to support all the accumulated sacramental and canonical traditions about marriage. Indeed, the influence of scripture on the Catholic view of marriage has been minimal, though scripture is cited frequently (for instance, Matthew 5 on divorce; Ephesians 5 on marriage as sacrament of the church; and 1 Corinthians 7 on sexuality in marriage). Quotations are largely supportive or ornamental in relation to the sacramental, canonical, and moral Catholic marriage traditions. An important question to which we shall return is what message of renewal the Bible might offer to Catholic thought about marriage today. My basic answer will be that, while the gospel affirms for all cultures and human relationships the eradication of the standard criteria of exclusion (race, class, and gender), the Bible also demonstrates that the particular forms and institutionalizations of moral relationships like marriage, transformed in discipleship, have to be worked out concretely within particular cultures.

MARRIAGE IN CANON LAW

Mixed agendas and practical lack of clarity plague the course of marriage in canon law. Since the Middle Ages the church has assumed that marriage is created by consent to a contract; the contract constitutes both the substance of the marriage and the sacrament. At the same time the church has attempted to maintain that marriage is an effective sign of Christ's presence to the church, a presence defined as saving love, not as a stipulation of rights and duties.[10]

Historically, discussion about the nature and establishment of marriage reflected three different perspectives on what is most essential to the reality and experience of marriage: sexual intercourse, spiritual communion, and living together (consistent with the marriage of Mary and Joseph), or a social institution for the raising of children.[11] In medieval scholasticism the theologians tended to defend consent to a mutual personal and social relationship, with canonists siding with the more practical criterion of sexual intercourse. Already in the early Middle Ages, when the church had complete jurisdiction over marriage, influential families had brought to it cases for adjudication. This made it necessary to determine precisely what constituted the bond, and indissolubility became linked to consummation. In the twelfth century Gratian's decretals and Pope Alexander III established what continues to be Roman Catholic practice: marriage is valid and sacramental by virtue of the partners' consent (and hence ostensibly indissoluble). Yet a valid unconsummated marriage can be dissolved on the condition of a legal declaration within the church that it is "null and void." What is indissoluble in principle differs from what is indissoluble in fact.[12] Perhaps this inconsistency handles in an inept juridical manner the insight that Bernard Cooke expresses more directly and biblically as an eschatological ideal for marriage: "A Christian marriage is indissoluble, but short of the eschaton it is incompletely indissoluble."[13]

The church's stipulation that any marriage of two baptized persons is by definition sacramental (and thus indissoluble) is a result historically of a struggle for jurisdictional control over marriage between the ecclesiastical and civil authorities in eighteenth- and nineteenth-century Europe. Since contracts fell under the jurisdiction of the state, the church insisted that for Christians the contract is the sacrament and that marriage thus comes within the concerns of canon law.[14] A theological conundrum and practical problem which today results is the situation of so-called baptized nonbelievers, whom the church must regard either as administering to one another a sacrament which they do not accept, or as having no right at all to marriage, otherwise regarded as a natural human prerogative.[15]

PERSONALIST INTERPRETATIONS OF MARRIAGE

In the last fifty years "personalist" philosophy has made broad inroads into the Catholic understanding of sexual relationships. Stimulated, for instance, by the work of Herbert Doms and Dietrich von Hildebrand,[16] authors of the middle decades of this century found the meaning of both sex and marriage in the love relationship of the couple, specifically, of heterosexual spouses. According to von Hildebrand, for instance, it is love that gives marriage its primary meaning, and love consists not primarily in socio-economic cooperation or parenthood, but in a complete and exclusive self-offering or self-surrender of each spouse to the other.[17] The Holy Office decreed in 1944 that "certain modern writers" who "either deny that the primary end of marriage is the generation and education of children, or teach that the secondary ends are not essentially subordinate to the primary end" are condemned.[18]

Nonetheless, church teaching itself was to become gradually but heavily influenced by the modern emphases on the dignity of the person and the importance of interpersonal relationships to human society and welfare, and by the emerging awareness of the dignity (if not full equality) of women. Hence increasing recognition has been accorded by the magisterium to the potential of sex to express and enhance psychological intimacy and bonding, and to marriage as an interpersonal union of spouses in which love as well as procreative and social partnership is a definitive element. Since the 1960s the magisterium has treated love and procreation equally as ends of marriage. But many practical expressions of this changed understanding have been ambivalent if not schizophrenic. According to *Humanae Vitae* a specific physical openness to procreation (identified with the "natural" integrity of the physical act of sexual intercourse) can never be set aside out of consideration for the love relationship of a couple or even in light of a marriage which over time includes both contraception and parenthood. The norm of procreation continues to govern love's sexual expression; women's procreative contribution continues to define their primary gender role as domestic and maternal.

Rerum Novarum (1891), the first of the modern social encyclicals, addresses marriage only in defending private property as a right contingent upon "man's social and domestic obligations," including God's command to be fruitful and multiply. The encyclical exhibits the assumptions about the place of the individual in society that undergirded the pre-modern understanding of marriage. As John Pawlikowski notes,

> The responsible fulfillment of role-designated duties by each member of society guaranteed social tranquility. In the medieval vision the discussion of social policy was largely limited to the discussion of the *a priori duties* and responsibilities assigned to every social office and function in the community.[19]

In particular, the father as head of the family has an obligation to provide his children "with all that is needful to enable them honorably to keep themselves from want and misery in the uncertainties of this mortal life" (9). Women, correlatively, are "not suited" to "trades" outside the home, but are "by nature fitted for home-work," and should "promote the good bringing up of children and the well-being of the family" (33). We note that marriage is relevant to the church's *social* teaching as defining an important set of social roles within an organic order; the roles of married persons are defined "outward" rather than in terms of the interpersonal spousal community itself. Forty years later *Quadragesimo Anno* adopts essentially the same approach (71).

But *Casti Connubii* (1930), written like *Quadragesimo Anno* by Pius XI, expands upon the meaning of marriage. Pius attends to the relationship of the spouses as well as to their familial and social roles. "By matrimony . . . the souls of the contracting parties are joined and knit together . . . by a deliberate and firm act of the will; and from this union of souls by God's decree, a sacred and inviolable bond arises" (7). Reiterating Augustine's three goods, Pius goes on to give the child first place among the blessings and ends of marriage (11, 17), whose education indissolubility serves (18). But at the same time, Pius continues, marriage is not merely an institution for the education of children. It is a "blending of life as a whole and the mutual interchange and sharing thereof." Moreover, the "mutual inward molding of husband and wife . . . can in a very real sense . . . be said to be the chief reason and purpose of matrimony" (24). This shift toward personal mutuality as the basis of marriage is as significant as it is poorly integrated with the primacy still given to procreation and with the commendation to women of "ready subjection" in the order of domestic love (27).

As in earlier documents, the brief treatment of marriage in *Gaudium et Spes* places it in the context of family. But the Council document moves the idea that marriage is a "community of love" unequivocally to center stage. The language of "intimate partnership," "conjugal covenant of irrevocable personal consent," "marriage covenant of conjugal love," "intimate union," "mutual gift of two persons," and "mutual self-bestowal" (48) replaces both the contractual approach of canon law and the theological-moral approach, which subordinated spousal love to parenthood and family. Sexual expression is depicted primarily as the outcome of marital love, and children as its fulfillment rather than as the primary reason for the marriage relationship itself. Following on these personalist affirmations, *Humanae Vitae* (1968) — although like *Casti Connubii* condemning artificial birth control — elevates love to a level with procreation and supports the "mutual self-gift" language so pervasive in the writings of John Paul II.

Is the emphasis on conjugal love as the foundation and basic meaning of marriage inconsistent with a continuing norm against interference in sex's procreative outcome, at least when the good of spouses or of their love would be so served? This possibility was specifically introduced by the papal birth control commission, which preceded *Humanae Vitae*.[20] According to the advisory report procreation is "a specific task of marriage," but cannot be interpreted outside the context of the "totality" of the relationship, in which sexuality has a unifying as well as a procreative function. In light of the unitive meaning of sex, the papal advisors thought that it is morally legitimate to regulate births (even artificially) in light of conjugal and familial needs, as long as the relationship is over-all receptive to procreation. However, this recommendation was rejected by *Humanae Vitae.*

In that encyclical Paul VI specifically recognized changes in the status of women and in the evaluation of love in marriage and in sexual acts (2). Among these are the parity of the unitive and the procreative meanings of the conjugal act, stated to be inseparably connected (12); and the duty of a "responsible parenthood" (10). The love of wife and husband is a "reciprocal personal gift of self," a "communion of their beings in view of mutual personal perfection," "free," "total," and "a very special form of personal friendship" (8-9). For the baptized it "represents the union of Christ and Church" (8, cf. 25). Citing *Gaudium et Spes,* Paul grounds children in marital love, which "is not exhausted by the communion between husband and wife, but is destined to continue, raising up new lives" (9). Although couples not only may but sometimes should deliberately intend nonprocreative sexual intercourse, this responsibility must be implemented only through "natural" means.

John Paul II reinforces the advances and ambiguities of *Humanae Vitae. Familiaris Consortio* idealizes marriage as a "covenant of conjugal love freely and consciously chosen, whereby man and woman accept the intimate community of life and love willed by God himself" (11). This love, indissoluble and sacramental, "aims at a deeply personal unity" that "leads to forming one heart and soul" (13). "Fecundity is the fruit and sign of conjugal love, the living testimony of the full reciprocal self-giving of the spouses" (28). The pope is adamant about the position on birth control[21] — perhaps already sabotaged by personalist emphases on the marital "communion." The limitation of means of birth control to those which not only subordinate to biological processes the spontaneous and "natural" sexual deepening of love and intimacy, but are also less reliable for many couples, seems to rest upon two assumptions. First, in the area of sexuality the interpersonal aspects of moral agency ought to be governed by (not just respectful of) its physical preconditions; and, second, women should be perpetually prepared to subordinate their public roles to the domestic ones which may at any time be occasioned by a new birth. Although the pope recognizes the emergence of women as social actors outside the family, he reserves the true fulfillment of women to motherhood (*Familiaris Consortio,* 23). Many married couples will wonder whether their experiences of the relational value of sexuality have not been co-opted in the service of an impossible (and hence judgmental and discouraging) ideal, which, far from supporting true mutuality, continues to subordinate women and to narrow stereotypically the roles of both sexes.

PERSONALISM AND CANON LAW

The 1983 Code assimilates Vatican II personalist themes while leaving essentially intact the juridical mechanisms and criteria by which marriage is controlled. Marriage is defined as both a "covenant" and a "contract" (can. 1055).[22] This language replaces the earlier definition of marriage as a contract by which spouses consent to reciprocal rights to one another's bodies with regard to those acts naturally leading to procreation (can. 1081 in the 1917 Code). Marriage is the establishment by consent of "a partnership [*consortium*] of the whole of life" and is ordered both to the spouses' good and to the procreation and education of children. The term *consortium* steers a middle course between a purely external or socio-economic association and the highest form of interpersonal union (*communio*), which marriage does not in all cultures typically represent.[23] The essential properties of marriage are unity and indissolubility, even if neither partnership nor the good of spouses, nor parenthood, are ever actually attained; or, if they are attained, irreversibly cease to be possible (can. 1056).

It is readily observed that personalist understandings of marriage fit awkwardly into canon law because personal relationships do not easily yield to objective and universalizable criteria, and because personalist characterizations of the marriage relationship are normative rather than descriptive. Peter Huizing invokes an "evangelical principle" that "marriage is a mandate to accomplish," "a call and a mandate to lifelong fidelity," and as such "is exposed to irreversible failure."[24] The contractual aspects of marriage are in canon law wed too closely to its sacramental meaning, so that the sign value of the relationship is detached from what ought to be its basis in human reality.

SEXUAL MORALITY AND PERSONALISM

Roman Catholic teaching since *Humanae Vitae* has held that both sex and marriage have two purposes: union or love, and procreation. Another way to put this (when considering, for instance, reproductive technologies which can make procreation rather than sex the starting point) is that the Catholic view of sexuality holds a triad of values to be inseparable: sex, love, and procreation. The specific prohibitions typically derived from this inseparability are familiar. The inflammatory rhetoric surrounding related questions too often seduces us into thinking that prohibitions and permissions in themselves are the most important things in Catholic sexual teaching. But they are not. Behind or beyond any specific rules about sexual conduct, Catholicism gives a more basic, more fundamental message about sexual morality. It affirms marriage as an ongoing nexus of social and personal relationships in which sexuality's positive potential is best protected and realized. The message is: sexual pleasure is good, but it is not the whole meaning of sexuality; sex is an unparalleled avenue of intimacy and bonding; and, in addition to enhancing the relationship of the sexual couple, sex has in parenthood and family a distinctive creative power by which it extends and enlivens the couple's own relationship and reinforces the dialectic of their social identity and contribution. In other words, there is a radical and enriching unity to sex's several dimensions: physical pleasure, interpersonal intimacy, and shared parenthood. It is through all of these that a couple's relationship takes on its moral and its sacramental character.

SCRIPTURAL RENEWAL OF THE THEOLOGY AND ETHICS OF MARRIAGE

In the past the Bible, especially the Christian scriptures, has been used to substantiate specific norms and practices for Christians, primarily by adducing texts which seem to speak directly to the issue at hand. Salient instances regarding marriage are the divorce texts, Paul's instructions on mutual sexual rights, and the household codes of the pastoral epistles. But the rise of historical criticism has carried with it increased caution about assuming either that the Bible actually addresses our own concerns, or that, when it does, its "message" can be transposed in any direct and clear manner to our situation.

Contemporary interpreters recognize the limitations of focusing on isolated texts and turn to more pervasive biblical themes or general models to define moral ideals and norms, or views of specific relationships like marriage. At this level, complementary or even competing themes within the canon can be brought into contact with one another. Texts, books, or strands that may not speak directly to a particular moral concern can still yield some perspective on it. For instance, a critique of the patriarchy of the Hebrew scriptures might draw support from what some exegetes see as the more egalitarian connotations of the Genesis creation stories or the sexual mutuality of the Song of Songs. In the Christian scriptures, sayings about submission of women are understood as historical responses to social difficulties the early Christian communities faced[25] and are qualified by the connotations of the Pauline baptismal formula (Gal 3:28). Moreover, early Christianity contrasts to ancient Judaism in that for the former, marriage and family are no longer definitive of one's status within the religious community. Nor are kinship and descent the means by which the religious community survives and expands. This change is especially significant for the status and roles of women, as demonstrated in their discipleship (for instance, the attestation of all four gospels that Mary Magdalene was the first to see the risen Lord).

Contemporary exegetes also demonstrate that biblical texts and themes themselves arise as responses to historical situations, which may provide a fresh perspective on how biblical materials can function normatively. Scripture not only addresses the obvious and not-so-obvious issues, it also reveals how the originating communities responded on the basis of a new identity in Christ to the social institutions of the surrounding culture. The Christian community today may not face precisely the same situations, but its identity should be *analogous*; it should sponsor *analogous* kinds of response to the social challenges it does face. The test of normative proposals about Christian discipleship lies in social practice; this is a central conclusion to be drawn from the biblical literature itself.

The Bible can and ought to enable a resocialization process[26] whereby the meaning of human relationships is changed, even as Christians may continue to live in other, overlapping communities of identification with their own values. Christian identity may sometimes incorporate and sometimes challenge these other values. Although today's church may not want to replicate all the behavior patterns of the early Christians, the social embodiment of faith and discipleship should be analogous to the social relationships discernible through the biblical accounts. Christian narrative, parable, and symbol help to create a framing world-view out of which moral action and moral analysis can emerge.[27] The religiously sponsored worldview provides the background against which the present-day community discerns what is or is not analogous embodiment, tested again in practice shaped by that same set of religious beliefs, commitments, and expectations.

If we are to discover a shape for marriage which is "analogous" to the faith and life of the earliest Christian communities, we must first know what the "new" life of the first Christians was like. Several authors describing the subversive effects of early Christianity on the social order speak of a radical equality and solidarity within the religious community, which served as a critique of inegalitarian institutions, especially economic ones.[28] It is plausible to argue that the essential thrust of the gospel for human relationships is *equality*, also translatable as love and mercy toward whomever stands in need."[29] Equality as a Christian value must be paired with *solidarity*, the recognition that our interdependence with our fellow ("equal") human beings creates an obligation of mutual support.

Can such values be elaborated more concretely in relation to marriage? The themes of equality and solidarity in gender relationships are proclaimed most clearly in Galatians: "There is neither Jew nor Greek, there is neither slave nor free, there is neither male nor female; for you are all one in Christ Jesus" (3:28). But in marriage, even in the process of its sacralization, and despite the inclusion of women in discipleship roles both in Jesus' ministry (e.g., Mary Magdalene in Mk 16:9-11; Lk 24:1-11; Mt 28:1-10; John 20:14-18) and in Paul's churches (1 Cor 16:19; Roms 16:1-6, 15), the subordination of women gradually regained a hold. The *haustafeln* (household codes) enjoined the submissiveness of wives to husbands (as of slaves to masters and children to fathers) within the household as the basic unit of Roman society (1 Cor 11:2; Eph 5:24; Col 3:18; and 1 Tm 8). It has been argued, preeminently by Elisabeth Schüssler Fiorenza, that such texts betray the original "discipleship of equals" in favor of accommodation to the larger society by which second generation Christianity sought acceptance. Because they are inconsistent with the gospel's egalitarian thrust, they are, according to Schüssler Fiorenza, non-normative.[30]

However, at another level, these texts may still represent a model for "analogous" Christian community today. Despite their patriarchal substance, they reflect the transformation of secular marriage by Christian values, for example, some reciprocity in the household hierarchy (Eph 5:25; Col 3:19 and 21, 4:1). As Schüssler Fiorenza herself has said, the biblical materials and their communities are not archetypes whose every element must be reproduced in revised form by Christians today. They are historical prototypes, first attempts which can be improved upon by recognizably similar yet significantly different later embodiments.[31] The message of the *haustafeln* is that discipleship ought to transform the human realities of marriage and family. But basic gospel themes of equality and solidarity, as well as extrabiblical, experiential critiques of women's oppression, instruct Christians today to find better, more culturally subversive ways in which to do that than the accommodationist New Testament patterns represent.

Perhaps a better New Testament model of marriage is suggested by the divorce texts (Mt 5:31-32, 19:3-9; Lk 16:18; Mk 10:2-12; 1 Cor 7:10-11). These texts should be read as an eschatological ideal (see Mt 5:19-20, 48), rather than as the absolute rules or juridical presuppositions into which canon law later converted them. Jesus teaches his disciples to restore broken relations to the order intended by God at the creation (Mt 19:4-8). Marriage implies a solidarity and unity of two in "one flesh." Jesus is also portrayed as addressing the responsibilities of marriage equally to woman and man (Mk 10:10-11), whereas the Jewish custom was to place the prerogative of divorce in the hands of the husband. If a man does take advantage of this prerogative, he is responsible for its corrupting effects on the woman as well as himself (Lk 16:18). In the divorce texts, cultural practices regarding marriage are challenged as divisive and inegalitarian, and, where provisionally accepted (Mt 5:32, 19:9; 1 Cor 7:15), are narrowed in closer conformity to the Edenic and kingdom ideal of unity. The mandate for later communities is to challenge the culture analogously, while still allowing some flexibility at the level of application.

In summary, discipleship requires that Christian communities embody the gospel values of equality and solidarity in all human relationships, including those with an essentially secular or "human" meaning and function, such as marriage. Christian marriage can be a sacrament or avenue of God's graceful approach to humanity. It can convert sex, marriage, and family into relations through which the worth and dignity of each person is realized, and in which a mutually supportive solidarity leavens cultural situations of marriage and kinship.

This means that the specifics of a Christian view of marriage must be elaborated in response to particular cultural contexts. Two contrasting examples of cultural institutions which are challenged in different ways by Christianity are the North American (United States) and the African practices of marriage. The former is the context in which we are presently addressing this topic; it also has much in common with the Northern European cultures which continue to generate official church teaching. The latter is a useful counterpoint because it incorporates almost opposite values, and because the difficulty of meshing the African and the Western approaches has been noted repeatedly by African bishops.[32] In North American culture sexuality is seen primarily in relation to the personality of the individual. A high value is placed on sexual pleasure, for which the key moral criterion is mutual consent (an ironic return to the contractual model). Although lasting affective relationships and even marriage are regarded as ideals by most people, there also exists a high level of cynicism about fidelity and permanency in sexual relationships. Parenthood, still a goal of most married couples, receives cultural support, not primarily as a natural or necessary outcome of sexual intimacy and commitment, but as an option for those who choose it. The availability and potential effectiveness of contraception make it possible to think of procreation as a detachable feature of sexual relationships rather than as their natural accompaniment or as part of their moral character. The assets of this Western view of sex and marriage are its insight into the importance of the dignity and freedom of persons in defining moral relationships, of the quality of relation of the sexual couple (rather than their social role), and of the equality of women. But the deficits are the reduction of the moral criterion of sexual activity to consent (not commitment and parenthood), and a somewhat paradoxical idealization of marriage and family as existing to fulfill (and capable of fulfilling) all the emotional needs of individuals.

Once marriage becomes focused exclusively on personal fulfillment and dependent on romantic love, it is also cut off from social and kinship supports and purposes which augment the resources of the couple to sustain their relationship through times of difficulty. Hence an alarming incidence of divorce and the perilous situation in which the inner-directed and isolated nuclear family currently finds itself. Couples who choose to live together rather than to marry may intend to reduce the risks of commitment to an untested and possibly unstable marriage, yet their reluctance to make a public commitment further deprives their relationship of social support. It also avoids the social responsibilities implied by the establishment of an economic, domestic, and potentially procreative partnership. The Western marriage ideal recognizes equality, especially as the freedom to choose a sexual, marital, or parental relation, but it is inadequately attentive to the solidarity Christian values imply both for the couple and family and for the connection of the narrower relation to the wider social and religious communities.

On the other side, African marriages are still very much family affairs, and are heavily dependent on kinship support for their consolidation. At the 1980 Synod on the Family the bishops from Zaire reported: "The importance which is attached to the marital bond by the family is evident from the care with which the family group prepares for and progressively works out its institution."[33] Marriage joins two families, who engage in a prolonged process of exchanging visits and gifts before bride and groom come together sexually. The marriage does not begin to exist at any one definable instant, as in the Western contract or ritual. The couple may have sexual relations and even children before the marriage is completed. Should they encounter difficulty, families of lineage, who have an investment in the couple's commitment, become actively involved in helping them to negotiate a settlement of differences. In the event that a marriage does break apart, either before or after its completion, there are clear expectations about the economic obligations of members of the union and especially about support of children, who will subsequently be cared for, not by a "single parent," but within the kinship network. At the same time, the failure of a woman to achieve pregnancy can be a reason to break off the marital process. Polygamy is also common and is a means for men to augment their work force and enhance their economic and social status.

The assets of African customary marriage are its recognition of the social and familial nature of the marital bond; of its integral relation to parenthood; and of the progressive nature of human commitments, not easily captured by the contractual stipulations of Western ecclesiastical law. On the downside, there is a devaluation of interpersonal intimacy between spouses in favor of marriage's communitarian and procreative contributions. Women's role is seen almost entirely in economic and procreative terms, and is subordinated to the interests and needs of husbands and fathers. In Uganda, for instance, adolescent girls are married off for a dowry of cattle; women are responsible for much more physical labor than men, including agriculture and hauling water; women bear and care for many children; and women are frequently beaten by their husbands, who infect them with AIDS at an epidemic rate. To add symbolic denigration to material injury, women must kneel upon meeting any man, including their own sons.[34] While solidarity is high in the African cultural forms of marriage, recognition of the dignity and equality of spouses and of other family members is, from a Christian standpoint, unacceptably low.

While the Christian view of marriage will not be able to supply clear and culturally transcendent answers to all questions of sexual and marital ethics, it can be grounded in essential gospel values (equality and solidarity) which lend a critical perspective on particular cultural realizations. Moreover, the embodiments of Christian marriage achieved by different Christian communities can prophetically enlarge one another. Since equality and solidarity are rather too comprehensive to provide much detailed guidance for marriage, the Catholic Christian tradition has, learning from embodiments in many cultures, marked out some more substantive guides to marriage as a specifically sexual, unitive, and parental relationship. Catholicism in its interpretation of marriage affirms as normative the goodness of sexual desire and pleasure, but notes their insufficiency as guides to sexual behavior; "love" as affective intimacy, companionship, or mutual cooperation and support; shared parenthood; serious commitment to monogamous fidelity and permanency (represented as indissolubility); and confidence that God's forgiveness and reconciliation are available in marriage as an interpersonal partnership opening onto social roles (represented as marriage's sacramental quality). Although an initiating ritual of marriage is important as an effective sign of serious intent and social accountability, the marriage relationship is formed gradually, by both consent and consummation. I see this normative vision as a positive contribution Catholicism makes to a Christian appreciation of marriage.

Yet I mentioned at the outset that Catholic marriage teaching must deal with three problems: 1) the dialectic of the social and the personal, and the function of sex in relation to each pole; 2) gender roles; and 3) the formation and possible dissolution of the marriage bond. A few concluding reflections on each of these are in order here. Perhaps the major challenge for a modern Western perspective on marriage is to set our assumptions about personal relations in marriage against a historical and cross-cultural horizon. Looked at more universally, both the importance of parenthood as a meaning of sexuality and socio-economic linkage as a meaning of marriage and family have a prominence we Westerners are less inclined to notice than the importance of personal commitments and fulfillments. As Margaret Farley has observed, the marital commitment is a commitment to a whole framework of life, which sustains the love of the partners, but which also must be construed in terms of family, community, church, and wider society.[35] Catholic teaching needs to find a way to affirm the dignity, freedom, and happiness of persons in marriage and family while simultaneously linking parenthood, kinship, and social roles *to the integrity of* sex and marriage as intersubjective experiences that are also always embodied and social experiences. In other words, it is not enough to refer in sexual morality or marriage merely to the integrity of physical reproduction as such, or to tie the physical to the intersubjective in a forced or artificial way that does not ring true to the experience of married persons and parents. Spousehood and parenthood must be linked together as ongoing personal and embodied *relationships* that have a definitive sexual/procreative dimension, not through an analysis of *acts* of sexual intercourse.

On the problem of gender roles, I would deny that true mutuality in marriage can be sustained on the basis of stereotypic divisions, however idealized in a rhetoric of nobility. The aforementioned tendency to focus the meaning of parenthood on physiological processes feeds into a biologistic view of women's maternity, asymmetrically emphasized over the fatherhood of men. Equality and solidarity in marriage demand parallel participation by men and women in both the social and the domestic aspects of marriage.

On the issue of the sort of graced relation a Christian marriage is, indissolubility and sacramentality are ideals having normative force but not inviolability. Sacramentality is never something which exists in a marriage wholly and completely. Like commitment, fidelity, sexual consummation, and parenthood, it is cumulative and progressive, taking root slowly, requiring nurturance to bear fruit. Although the presence of God to humans within the creaturely relationship is God's own gift, and, from the divine side, irrevocable, God accepts a certain vulnerability in choosing a human vehicle for self-disclosure. The marriage as a human relationship is a living, organic, and creaturely reality, never immune to death through neglect, destruction, or catastrophe. Marital disintegration must be recognized institutionally and redeemed practically through forgiveness, reconciliation, and reparation—in the termination of the first spousal relation; in fidelity to its continuing claims, especially those of children; and in building new relationships, for which more successful Christian transformation can be hoped.

NOTES

1. Augustine, *On the Good of Marriage.*
2. *Summa Theologiae*, Suppl. 49.
3. See *Summa Contra Gentiles* 3/II.123.6 and *ST* II-II.26.11.
4. An extensive resource on these issues is Theodore Mackin, S.J., *Marriage in the Catholic Church* (a trilogy) (Mahwah, New Jersey: Paulist Press): *What Is Marriage?* (1982); *Divorce and Remarriage* (1984); and *The Marital Sacrament* (1989).
5. See Mackin, *The Marital Sacrament*, pp. 7-9.
6. Stephen Babos, "Marriage as a Sacrament," *Thought* 58 (1983), p. 6.
7. Pheme Perkins, "Marriage in the New Testament and Its World," in *Commitment to Partnership: Explorations of the Theology of Marriage*, ed. William P. Roberts (Mahwah, New Jersey: Paulist Press, 1987), pp. 26-27.
8. Mackin, *The Marital Sacrament*, p. 673.
9. Ibid, p. 634.
10. See ibid., p. 524.
11. E. Schillebeeckx, O.P., *Marriage: Human Reality and Saving Mystery* (New York: Sheed and Ward, 1965), pp. 291-92.
12. Schillebeeckx, pp. 168-69, 291-97. On the history of marriage in canon law, see also Ladislas Orsy, *Marriage in Canon Law* (Wilmington, Delaware: Michael Glazier, 1986), pp. 13-37.
13. Bernard Cooke, "Indissolubility: Guiding Ideal or Existential Reality?" in Roberts, p. 71.
14. Theodore Mackin, S.J., "How to Understand the Sacrament of Marriage," in Roberts, p. 37. See also Mackin, *The Marital Sacrament*, pp. 450-515; and Orsy, pp. 34-35. The relevant encyclical is Leo XIII's *Arcanum Divinae Sapientiae* (1880).
15. See, for instance, Peter J. Huizing, S.J., "Canonical Implications of the Conception of Marriage in the Conciliar Constitution *Gaudium et Spes*," in Roberts, p. 118.
16. Herbert Doms, *The Meaning of Marriage* (New York: Sheed and Ward, 1939), originally *Vom Sinn und Zweck der Ehe* (Breslau: Ostdeutsche Verlagsanstalt, 1935); and Dietrich von Hildebrand, *Marriage* (New York: Longmans, 1932), originally *Die Ehe* (Munich: Kösel-Pustet, 1929).
17. Von Hildebrand, pp. 5, 9, 16, 49.
18. The decree is cited in full by John C. Ford, S.J. and Gerald Kelly, S.J., *Marriage Questions* (Westminster, Maryland: Newman, 1964), pp. 27-28.
19. John T. Pawlikowski, O.S.M., "Modern Catholic Teaching on the Economy: An Analysis and Evaluation," in *Christianity and Capitalism: Perspectives on Religion,*

Liberalism and the Economy, ed. Bruce Grelle and David A. Krueger (Chicago: Center for the Scientific Study of Religion, 1986), p. 4.

20. The Pontifical Commission for the Study of Population, Family, and Birth was established by John XXIII and submitted its findings to Paul VI. There was only one formal report of the commission, the so-called majority report, though a dissenting minority authored an opinion under the leadership of John C. Ford.

21. See *Familiaris Consortio*, 34 and *Reflections on Humanae Vitae: Conjugal Morality and Spirituality* (Boston: Daughters of St. Paul, 1984).

22. Citations of canon law will be made in the text; unless otherwise noted, they refer to the 1983 revision of the 1917 code and are taken from the translation by the Canon Law Society of America, *Code of Canon Law: Latin-English Edition* (Washington, D.C.: Canon Law Society of America, 1983).

23. Orsy, p. 51.

24. Huizing, in Roberts, p. 126.

25. Elisabeth Schüssler Fiorenza, *In Memory of Her: A Feminist Theological Reconstruction of Christian Origins* (New York: Crossroad, 1983).

26. Wayne Meeks, *The Moral World of the First Christians* (Philadelphia: Westminster, 1986), p. 126. See also Meeks, "A Hermeneutics of Social Embodiment," *Harvard Theological Review* 79 (1986), especially p. 184.

27. William C. Spohn, S.J., "Parable and Narrative in Christian Ethics," *Theological Studies* 51 (1990), pp. 100-114.

28. See, for instance, Halvor Moxnes, *The Economy of the Kingdom: Social Conflict and Economic Relations in Luke's Gospel* (Philadelphia: Fortress Press, 1988), pp. 28-30; or Ched Myers, *Binding the Strong Man: A Political Reading of Mark's Story of Jesus* (Maryknoll, New York: Orbis Books, 1988), pp. 47-53. These and others draw centrally on Moses I. Finley, *The Ancient Economy* (Berkeley and Los Angeles: University of California Press, 1973).

29. This argument is made by Joseph G. Donders, "Inculturation and Catholicity in Relation to the World-wide Church," an address given at the Forty-fifth Annual Convention of the Catholic Theological Society of America, on June 8, 1990. Also in the *CTSA Proceedings*, 1990.

30. Schüssler Fiorenza.

31. Ibid., pp. 33-34.

32. See summaries of episcopal position papers from Black Africa, Southeast Asia, Latin America, and North America in Jan Grootaers and Joseph A. Selling, *The 1980 Synod of Bishops "On the Role of the Family": An Exposition of the Event and an Analysis of Its Texts* (Leuven: Leuven University Press, 1983), pp. 29-65.

33. As quoted in Grootaers and Selling, p. 31.

34. Jane Perlez, "For the Oppressed Sex, Brave Words to Live By," *New York Times*, June 6, 1990, A4.

35. Margaret A. Farley, "Divorce, Remarriage and Pastoral Practice," in *Moral Theology: Challenges for the Future*, ed. Charles E. Curran, (Mahwah, New Jersey: Paulist Press, 1990).

8

FAMILY AS DOMESTIC CHURCH

JAMES and KATHLEEN McGINNIS

INTRODUCTION

Since the overall theme for this book is a direction for Catholic social thought at the beginning of its second century with regard to family, peace, and work, this essay will address this question with regard to the family, exploring explicitly the links between families and the church's social mission and teaching. For too long, there has been a divorce, or at least a separation, between family and social action. People labelled conservatives in our church and society as a whole have tended to focus on family, while those labelled liberals have concentrated on social action. In fact, family has been used as an excuse for not being involved in social action. Christians who took, and still take, such a dichotomized view of the world tend to be better off economically and generally have not felt the sting of economic and/or racial injustice in their own life and family. But with the increase of violence in our society affecting all neighborhoods and households, perhaps there is a little more understanding that all families are victims to some extent in an economic system that perpetuates inequities. Maybe there is a little more openness to hear and see Catholic social teaching as pro-family. Perhaps, too, there is a little more openness for pro-family Catholics to consider involving themselves in social action, if only in defense of the family.

To bring these possibilities to fruition, the church in general and Catholic social teaching in particular need to do at least several things. First, Catholic social teaching must make these links between family and social action explicit, a task of analysis. Second, the church must continue to work for the services families need in order to survive and move beyond survival to engage in the church's social mission. This second task is one of direct service and advocacy. Third, the church must empower families to engage in the church's social mission. Two of the most important aspects of this task of empowerment are providing vision and support systems. It is in this task of providing vision that Catholic social teaching needs to help families see themselves as "domestic church" and all that such a vision implies. This essay will examine each of these three tasks, especially the first and third, analysis and empowerment.

ANALYSIS – MAKING CLEAR THE LINKS BETWEEN FAMILY AND SOCIAL ACTION

A first step for Catholic social teaching at this point is to help families see the relevance and urgency of the social agenda for their own well-being. Families of all races, classes, and localities are being victimized by powerful social forces in our society. It is in the self-interest of rich as well as poor families to embrace the church's call to peace and justice; otherwise, families will be victimized even further. While there are many social forces pounding away at families, this chapter will examine five: materialism, individualism, racism, sexism, and violence or militarism. Here we will consider the impact these forces have on families. In section three, we will consider how families can address and influence these forces. Families need not remain passive victims.

Materialism

While modern economies have provided a more decent life in material terms for hundreds of millions of people, they have also created a very real problem for Christian families, especially in capitalist societies. Papal social teaching has addressed this reality for a hundred years, with the message getting stronger with each succeeding pope. Pope Paul VI's warning that superfluous goods may be enslaving modern men and women[1] points to a tendency in affluent societies: objects are becoming more important than persons. Objects are personified and persons are made commodities.[2] Even a cursory study of modern-day advertising reveals that objects are presented as providing us with identity, companionship, joy, intimacy – all values traditionally associated with persons. Persons, on the other hand, are often treated as objects – sex objects, sales targets, units of labor. The effects of materialism and the "commodification" of the person devastate families in three distinct ways.

First, materialism sends the message that "more is better; happiness is having." This drive takes a terrible toll on both adults and children as recognition and affirmation come to center on what we have rather than on who we are. The more we seek security in money, goods, and huge insurance policies, the less we find our security in the Lord and in one another. Fearing economic consequences, we become afraid to take risks for the gospel. Material novelties, constantly dangled before us, threaten fidelity to our spouse, our children, and our work. This constant message to possess more and to enjoy the "good life" tantalizes children as well as adults, poor as well as rich, and threatens to shortchange the spiritual dimension of life, if not to jeopardize it altogether.[3]

A second effect of materialism, flowing directly from the first, is the tendency to look down upon the "have-nots." These people — the economically poor, the elderly, those with disabilities, the not-so-beautiful people of our society — are disregarded, disdained, and in some cases even killed.

A third effect centers on the exploitation of the earth. The prevailing "more is better" attitude threatens the earth itself, since the needs of future generations can easily be ignored in the face of pressing contemporary wants and desires.

Individualism

Not surprisingly, materialism fosters individualism. Generated by a mentality that exalts possessions,[4] individualism separates personal freedom from its social context and manifests itself in such forms as a private property ethic which entitles one to use private resources at whim. Such a use of private property is very different from Catholic social teaching, which reminds us that God intended the earth and all that it contains for the use of every human being. The right to private property, therefore, must never be exercised to the detriment of the common good.[5]

This individualism weighs heavily on families in a particular fashion. The highly competitive nature of our economic system and society, combined with the image of rugged individuals raising themselves up by their own bootstraps, high levels of mobility, and the ascendancy of nuclear families over extended families, have isolated many families. This isolation has increased the need for material security and fosters competition for grades, jobs, affection, positions, prestige, power. Supportive, noncompetitive relationships, even within families, become much more difficult in such an atmosphere.

Governments and economic systems also place great burdens on the family when they do not guarantee the basic necessities of life for each person. Often both parents are forced to work long hours. Frequently unemployed fathers are forced to leave their homes in order to secure minimal assistance for other family members. Unemployment, whether caused by automation, multinational corporations closing factories for cheaper labor elsewhere, government budget cuts, or the failure to plan and direct more capital to job-creating industries, affects workers and their families in many ways — spiritually, psychologically, physically, and economically, as noted in the United States Catholic bishops' pastoral letter on the economy, *Economic Justice for All*.[6]

Racism

The connection between economic problems families face in our society and the problem of racism is clearly pointed out in the United States Catholic bishops' pastoral letter on racism, *Brothers and Sisters to Us*:

> Racism and economic oppression are distinct but interrelated forces which dehumanize our society. Movement toward authentic justice demands a simultaneous attack on both evils. Our economic structures are undergoing fundamental changes which threaten to intensify social inequalities in our nation. . . . The poor and racial minorities are being asked to bear the heaviest burden of the new economic pressures.[7]

The letter also discusses the hard facts of racism and its effect on families — disproportionate unemployment, the stereotyping of people of color in the media and even in school textbooks, the low self-image of people of color, and the growing housing crisis that plagues families of color. It remains clear that racial discrimination "has only exacerbated the harmful relationship between poverty and family instability."[8] And the situation continues to worsen since that pastoral. According to the Campaign for Human Development in 1989, a typical African-American family earned slightly more than half (56 percent) the income of a white family. That was the poorest percentage in twenty years. In 1978 twenty-one percent of Hispanics lived in poverty. By 1987 that number had jumped to twenty-eight percent.

Sexism

Sexism is similar to racism in its intensity and consequences. The economic effects, for instance, are becoming clearly evident as more women, due to financial need, join the workforce. Problems such as unequal pay and unequal opportunity often create serious crises for a family, especially if the family depends solely on the woman's income for support. In 1989, according to the Bureau of Labor Statistics, women earned sixty-nine cents for every dollar men earned. By 1986 women represented sixty-three percent of all persons 16 years old and over with poverty level incomes. For women of color, a double burden of discrimination exists.

The cultural consequences of sexism are perhaps less blatant but no less serious for families, and thus for society as a whole. Stereotypes regarding what it means to be a "man" and a "woman" limit emotional, physical, and spiritual development of men and women, boys and girls. To view nurturing and service solely as the woman's role is to imprison woman and inhibit men in the development of the nurturing/service dimension of their person. As with racial stereotypes, sex-role stereotypes infect the books children and adults read, the toys with which children play, advertising, television, and films.

Similarly, to present women and men as mere sex objects threatens both friendships between men and women and marital fidelity. This presentation finds blatant expression in pornography and more subtle but equally pervasive expression in advertising, television, and film.

Violence and Militarism

Violence as a means of resolving conflict—from the interpersonal to the international level—constitutes a fifth problem for families in particular and for society in general. Child abuse and spouse abuse are increasing dramatically, and it is no coincidence that so are murders, foreign military interventions, prisons and executions of criminals, war toys and violence on the media, and the size of the military budget. A society that resorts to violence, for dealing with frustration or conflict, even glories in violence, will see its families suffer from violence.

This is in addition to the obvious suffering that results from decreases in federal spending for housing, food, education, health care, and so on, because of an expanding military budget. Catholic social teaching in this regard has been explicit and dramatic in its expression. For one, the Vatican stated in its 1976 letter to the United Nations: "The arms race is an act of aggression that amounts to a crime, for even when they are not used, by their cost alone, armaments kill the poor by causing them to starve."[9]

SERVICES—THE WORKS OF MERCY AND THE WORKS OF JUSTICE

The second major task on behalf of families that the church's social teaching should address is the provision of those services that families need to survive in today's world. This involves three basic approaches—providing services, promoting community organizations, and advocating for public policy change. The church has a long history in providing direct services on behalf of families, especially through all the agencies and programs connected with Catholic Charities departments. Parish social ministry offices and St. Vincent de Paul programs have often expanded such services at the parish level.

The church has also involved itself on behalf of families by helping them organize themselves to work for those rights and services they need. Such involvement has ranged from local credit unions, food co-ops, cooperative child-care efforts, block or parish-wide pooling of goods and talents, and buying groups, to such things as support of farm worker and other unions. The work of the Campaign for Human Development is especially notable in this regard.

Advocacy for public policies that would provide help at all levels of government is the third aspect of this task. Catholic social teaching has been more and more explicit in this regard, culminating in the United States with the pastoral letter on *Economic Justice for All.* Since this whole area of family and the economy is being addressed in other parts of this program and publication, let us move to the third and most important task for Catholic social teaching on behalf of families — empowering families as agents of change through vision and support systems.

EMPOWERING FAMILIES TO BE AGENTS OF CHANGE

Providing a Vision of Family as Domestic Church

Families need not remain passive victims in the face of the massive social forces enumerated above. Families can become the agents of their own development and in the process involve themselves in the transformation of the world. Reorienting family thinking about themselves is part of this process. Helping families see themselves as domestic church has wonderful possibilities along this line. But the understanding of *church* is critical in this. Church must not be seen primarily as a safe harbor where we protect ourselves from the winds of the world, as many of us experienced growing up in Catholic ghettos. As the gospel parables indicate, the church of God is to be a leaven in society, deeply involved in transforming the world, God's instrument in the completion of God's kingdom or reign. If this is how we understand church, then to invite families to see themselves as domestic church will help families move more fully into the world rather than retreat from it. There are three major aspects of thinking of families as domestic church that we want to explore here. We "go to church" for at least three things — spiritual growth and nurture, community and worship, and mission.

"Nurture the full human and spiritual growth of your children"
These words of the United States bishops to families in the 1983 pastoral letter on peace, *The Challenge of Peace,*[10] offer adults quite a challenge. Just as the parish church is a site or source of grace, so too is the domestic church. Family is the key place where individuals live their faith to a significant extent and are "graced" in the process. It is the primary place where individuals are affirmed and develop their gifts. In the words of the Second Vatican Council, "The family is the first school of those social virtues which every society needs. ... It is through the family that they [children] are gradually introduced into civic partnership with their fellow human beings, and into the People of God."[11]
The affirmation that can be experienced within the family is absolutely essential for the realization of the church's social mission. Neither children nor adults can be concerned about others unless they feel good about themselves first. They cannot deal well with difference — whether racial, economic, or religious difference — unless they feel comfortable about their own identity. They cannot take risks on behalf of others and participate in social change unless they have a good self-concept and some self-confi-

dence. They are unable to be different from the crowd and stand up for what they believe unless they feel good about themselves. For all these reasons, affirmation is essential for nurturing compassion and courage in people of all ages.

The possibilities for such affirmation within families are numerous. To cite just a couple of examples here, adults can verbally praise children not only for their successes but also for their efforts. Smiles, hugs, and other forms of physical affection are sorely needed in our society. Attending children's performances helps them feel appreciated and special. Listening is crucial; so is taking the ideas and needs of the young seriously. We can celebrate them in a variety of ways and times—birthdays, days and rites of passage, times when they tried hard, and on "just for being you" days.

Nurturing the emotional development of children, especially the tender and caring dimension of our humanity, has immediate as well as long-term consequences for peacemaking. An over-emphasis on what are generally labelled masculine values—toughness, power, control, winning—produces violent persons and a society that seeks to solve problems through force, as noted earlier in this chapter.

Our children's intellectual growth is equally important, since peacemaking requires creativity and critical thinking skills. The materialism and violence associated with the media, as noted earlier, can be addressed within families even as adults and children watch television with a more critical eye.

In that same paragraph addressed to families in *Challenge of Peace,* the United States Catholic bishops ask parents to "consciously discuss issues of justice." Instead of shielding their children from reality, which is often "bad news," adults can help children deal with all that they are hearing and seeing. This does not mean stripping children of beauty, play, goodness, and trust, and exposing them to realities they are too young to handle. But it does mean working through some often painful experiences and discussing issues of injustices in their own lives as well as in the larger world. News broadcasts, the morning paper, movies like "Gandhi" or "Romero" are all occasions for such discussion. As children mature, adults can share more of their concerns and actions with their children—asking their advice over a dinner discussion, inviting them to participate in an upcoming action or event, or to co-sign a letter to their political representatives. What children desperately need in the face of massive social forces and evil is to see significant adults in their life concerned and doing something about those evils. This is the single most important factor researchers and counselors have identified for nurturing hope and counteracting the despair and sense of helplessness so prevalent in our society and children especially.

Nurturing children's spiritual growth relates to social action in another way. Social action entails risk and suffering. Whether it is finding the courage to reconcile oneself with another person or to challenge a government policy, peacemakers are likely to pay a price. But so did Jesus. When adults share their faith with children, when they encourage a personal relationship with Jesus, when they help children understand the cross, they enable children to respond more generously to the call of Jesus to be a peacemaker. Long-term peacemakers are deeply spiritual persons. Praying within the family brings us to the second sense of family as domestic church that we want to explore.

Worship and community

Just as people go to the parish church for worship and community, so too should these be experienced within the family as domestic church. Some wonderful resources for family ritual and worship have appeared in the last decade, including such things as *The Blessing Cup,* Ed Hayes's *Prayers for the Domestic Church.* Mitch and Kathy Finley's book, *Christian Families in the Real World: Reflections on a Spirituality for the Domestic Church,* is an excellent overview of this whole theme and vision.

A variety of family reconciliation services have been published and many families are creating their own. These are important sources of community-building in the home as well as worship experiences. Family reconciliation events reinforce a forgiving, accepting environment in which family members readily apologize and forgive one another. These healing events can be as simple as a five-minute addition to a family meeting in which family members acknowledge and ask forgiveness for one way they have been unhelpful in promoting peace in the home. More elaborate reconciliation events can include bible reading, prayer, and symbolic actions such as writing down the negative behaviors on pieces of paper and burning them in the fireplace as a way of letting go of those behaviors and asking forgiveness.

One mechanism that has proven effective for many families for promoting a sense of community within the family is the family meeting. This shared approach to making family decisions and plans and resolving family conflicts is based on a mutual model of family life, where everyone contributes and is taken seriously; "Children are to be seen *and* heard." Obedience is not the primary virtue of family living. This does not mean that everything is negotiable, that there are no bottom lines. Adults must get in touch with their "nonnegotiables" and "bottom lines," distinguish those that should be truly nonnegotiable, and be able to articulate reasons for their positions. It is important to distinguish between basic values and particular ways in which these values can be lived out. To say that family worship, helping others as a family, less consumer-oriented living, helping out with chores, and so on are nonnegotiable family values is fine. Exactly how a family lives them out day-to-day and year-by-year can be and should be very negotiable. The more input that children have into family decisions, the more likely they are to internalize our values and the less resistance we are likely to encounter in trying to live the gospel. For example, deciding together what the family should do to help others (family service) avoids the situation of dragging reluctant children along to an event the parent or parents alone choose.

Furthermore, family meetings are an excellent opportunity to learn a variety of communication and conflict resolution skills, essential for community-building within the family as well as for more effective living and working in the larger world. In family meetings listening skills, expressing rather than repressing feelings, learning non-hurtful ways to express anger, expressing needs and wants in clear terms, weighing a variety of possible solutions to any given conflict, and negotiating skills are all called upon.

Because of how helpful such a mechanism has proven to be for so many families, it is important to identify some of the guidelines for conducting effective family meetings. They include the following:

—Schedule family meetings regularly, so there is some predictability. Otherwise the children will not trust the process.

—Schedule them at the most convenient time for *all* members of the family.

—Make the agenda available to everyone. It helps to have a piece of paper posted prominently on which to write agenda items. Otherwise children often forget what they want to discuss.

—Include agenda items that involve family plans, family fun events, family service opportunities. Do not limit the agenda to problems and conflicts only. Otherwise, it is likely to be too negative or heavy.

—Combine the family meeting with things that "taste good" such as a special dessert, a family game or fun night, a trip to the ice-cream store, individual affirmations, candlelight and/or other touches of beauty where the meeting is held.

—Rotate leadership so children get a chance to develop their leadership skills.

—Be sure that decisions are clear, tasks are assigned, consequences identified, and that a "check-in" time has been identified (that is, a time to evaluate how well a particular solution is working).

—Decide by consensus, not by voting. Otherwise, there may be losers. One helpful definition of consensus is that everyone is at least willing to try the proposed action for one week, even if one or more persons have some doubts about it.

—Give everyone a chance to speak. Help less verbal members of the family get their points across.

—When possible, consider the children's agenda items early in the meeting, so that they feel the process is working for them.

—When first starting family meetings, concentrate the agenda on "low stake" items, that is, items less likely to trigger defensiveness. Don't ask reluctant family members for a ten-year commitment to the process. See if everyone is willing to try it for a few times and then evaluate the experience and continue with any necessary modifications if the over-all process seems to be helpful.

Because of the increased sense of communication, affirmation, and cooperation that is generally experienced through family meetings, combined with a greater sense of community and joy that family celebrations and ritual generate, the family is likely to feel more together and have a greater sense of identity and purpose. These are indispensable when it comes to nurturing a sense of the church's social mission in families. The more "together" a family feels, the more willing it generally is to go out into the world as a family. And reciprocally, the more that the family as a whole involves itself in the community and the larger world, generally the more together it becomes. This brings us to the third aspect of family as domestic church — mission.

Nurture a sense of mission in families

Just as the parish church or community hopefully experiences a sense of being sent forth into the world from its celebration of the eucharist, so too the family as domestic church needs to feel sent forth. Parish community and family community are not solely or perhaps even primarily for their own sake, but are called to extend the love they experience in these communities to the world outside. Each is called to be leaven in the transformation of the world — a light for the world, salt for the earth. To embrace this mission, families need to have their imaginations expanded, their inspiration deepened, and their sense of isolation countered with ever-widening structures of support. Catholic social teaching and ministry can help with all three.

Imagination. To the frequently asked question, "But what can we do?," the church needs to be as specific as possible. The social forces identified earlier in this essay — materialism, individualism, racism, sexism, violence, and militarism — seem overwhelming, even insurmountable. "What's the use; what can one family do?" is too often the plaintive reply of persons who choose to do nothing because they can't do everything. Families need to have their imaginations stretched. To assist in this process, here are some possible first steps for families with regard to each of these social forces.

To challenge materialism and individualism, families can focus on their care for the earth. Recycling is an obvious place to start. Some families share economically by exchanging tools, toys, books, or outgrown clothes. A deepening sense of reverence for the earth is fostered by camping trips, contemplative walks in parks, even a family or community garden. To experience that it is not necessary to own in order to enjoy, many families turn to libraries, parks, and other public facilities. Teaching children to use and care for library books and records, because others want to enjoy them too, is a simple yet profound way to practice stewardship. Alternative gift-giving presents another opportunity to simplify the family lifestyle. Replacing costly and generally less personal gifts with homemade presents, providing the gift of one's time and talent, or purchasing the handicrafts of the economically poor, all promote a sense of stewardship.

Engaging in works of mercy provides a second channel to offset the problems of materialism and individualism. Hospitality is an excellent place for families to start practicing stewardship. To open the family home to a person in need of temporary or long-term housing—a teenager who cannot make it at home, an overnight traveler, an elderly relative, a foster child— is to welcome the Lord. Less demanding options, like inviting others for meals, are generally possible for all families. Sharing goods and time with the economically poor is possible for most families. Part of the savings from any sacrifices or cutting back on family spending should probably be shared with those who have less.

The works of justice—participating in social change—are readily available for families. Families can challenge corporations that pursue the maximization of profit at the expense of people and the environment. Participation in consumer boycotts is more and more common, especially with helpful resources for shoppers like the book *Shopping for a Better World*.[12] Families can also challenge the media—networks and advertisers— for some of the blatant materialism that they often promote.

With regard to the issue of racism, families can start with their own home and lifestyle and work to make it more multi-cultural; even simple steps like attention to the visuals in the home—the art work, magazines, toys, books—make a difference, especially for children. Whom we invite into our homes; where we shop, recreate, and worship; whom we seek out for professional services all have an impact on our attitudes and ultimately our actions. Where we live is probably the most important factor in this whole process, for it affects our access to all the above.

In addition to a lifestyle which fosters an appreciation of the rich diversity of racial and ethnic groups in our society, families can also challenge institutions and policies that encourage racism. Children as well as adults can write to publishers and networks to protest books and shows which portray racial stereotypes. Store managers can be encouraged to provide toys, greeting cards, and other items that reflect the diversity of our society. School systems, amusement parks, and other entertainment centers are just some of the other social institutions to which families relate that should be held accountable for their portrayal of diverse racial and cultural groups.

All these institutions can be held equally accountable for their treatment and portrayal of women and men, as a way of families challenging the sexism in our society. So too can the lifestyle diversification mentioned above be applied to sex-roles, for example, seeking out women professionals for some of the services families use. Nurturing the full human development of both boys and girls has already been noted as a daily and practical way for families to confront sex-role stereotyping.

In terms of challenging the violence and militarism of our society, much has already been said, especially in teaching nonviolent conflict resolution skills and promoting cooperation at home. There are many opportunities in our schools, community sports programs, and other areas where competition can be fierce for families to promote more cooperative alternatives. Families can challenge the violence that saturates the media. They can also participate in public policy advocacy around the local, state, and federal budgets—encouraging nonviolent alternatives to bigger prison systems, drug treatment programs *vs.* incarceration, diplomatic *vs.* military means for addressing international conflict, economic *vs.* military aid to third-world countries, disarmament *vs.* ever-more-costly and destructive weapon systems. Letter-writing, public demonstrations, and prayer gatherings, and a variety of forms of tax protest or resistance are open to whole family involvement. The family as well as individuals and corporate bodies all have a prophetic role to play in the transformation of the world. We all need our imaginations stretched as to how to be creatively and effectively faithful to this role. But we may need inspiration even more than imagination, because this prophetic role involves a lot of risk, as some of the action possibilities above clearly imply.

Inspiration. To embrace the risks involved in living out its social mission as domestic church, the family needs lots of inspiration. The four primary sources of such inspiration are deepening relationships with God/Jesus, with people who are hurting, with advocates for change, and with a community of faith. A word about each.

Christians are more likely to respond to the call to social involvement if they understand that call as part of the mission of Jesus which Christians now carry out in the world. Fostering a personal relationship with Jesus, especially through prayer and reflection on the scriptures, is essential to hearing the voice of God. The liturgical year, embodying the life of Jesus, also highlights his social mission. Advent/Christmas reminds us that God takes the world so seriously as to come among us as a human being, in simplicity, to serve rather than to be served. Lent marks the call to repentance for social sin as well as personal sin. Lent also calls us to respond to Jesus as he suffers today—in the hungry, the elderly, those victimized by racism or repression, and many others in our society and world. Easter and Pentecost are liturgical sources of hope and action, since the power of the Spirit who raised Jesus from the dead is continuously at work in the world.[13] The eucharist itself calls us to build the unity of the body of Christ, which we symbolize and celebrate in that sacrament. This deep, inexhaustible richness of the church's liturgical life must be made even more available to families for deepening their commitment to be sent as the domestic church into the world.

Inspiration also comes from being touched by both the victims of violence and injustice and by others who are taking great risks to respond with compassion and courage. We are moved to action by the lives and witness of others, not by statistics. The more we allow the stories of others to penetrate our hearts, the more "they" become our friends, the more likely we are to accompany them in their struggles. The parish and diocesan church can facilitate such encounters and relationships for families. And the importance of mutuality in these relationships must be stressed. "Doing with" rather than "doing for" should characterize social ministry, especially in working with the economically poor.

Lastly, inspiration, compassion, and courage are enkindled to the extent that families are touched and supported in small communities of faith. Reflecting, praying, celebrating, playing, and working with other families not only increase the effectiveness of social action, but also provides the accountability, challenge, support, and enjoyment without which families will not sustain their involvement over the long haul. This has been the experience and the gift of the base Christian communities of Latin America to the universal church. These small intentional communities combine faith-sharing, fellowship, and community action in a way that has unleashed a powerful force in the ongoing transformation of our world. The RENEW process in our own country has moved more and more in this direction, promoting clusters within parishes. It is here that the necessary structures of support in the empowerment process must begin.

Empowering through promoting support systems
    Family support groups. Three movements that have focused the need for support systems specifically on families are the Christian Family Movement, Family Clusters, and the Parenting for Peace and Justice Network.[14] From their experience have come the following guidelines for promoting family support groups, perhaps the most important component for Catholic social ministry in its efforts to empower families to participate in the church's social mission as domestic church.

    — Quality is more important than quantity. Even if only two families are initially interested, begin. Most family support groups have expanded over time.

    — Personal invitations are always more effective than mailings. Share an article, tape, or chapter in a book with others as a way of introducing them to the possibility of a family support group with a social action orientation.

    — Generally it is better to ask families to commit themselves to a shorter time span (such as three, six or twelve months), after which the group can evaluate itself and decide if and how it wants to continue. Long-term commitments from the outset tend to discourage many people.

    — It is preferable to let the topics emerge from the group itself rather than tying the group to someone else's outline. At the same time, however, it is helpful, especially at first, to have an outside resource to discuss.[15]

    — Family support groups that include the children, at least for occasional whole family events (e.g., picnics, holiday caroling, a family camp, a public action or service project and meal) seem to be more satisfying and enduring than adult-only discussion groups. Children need peer support for such values and lifestyles, perhaps even more than adults.

    — Sometimes family support groups can best emerge from existing adult or parent support groups, e.g., a Marriage Encounter follow-up group, a PET or STEP group, a church study or prayer group, a women's group, a parish RENEW group.

Models for such groups include Dr. Margaret Sawin's *Hope for Families*, in which she gives people who have experienced the family cluster model in a variety of settings the opportunity to tell their stories and reflect on their successes and failures. Her original book, *Family Enrichment with Family Clusters*, describes her process for a group of four or five whole family units to contract to meet together periodically over an extended period of time for shared educational experiences related to their living in relationship with the family. Both books are available from Family Clusters. The Parenting for Peace and Justice Network has an excellent workbook for families and leaders working with families, entitled *Helping Families Care*, in which the stories of five family support groups are presented.

Larger support structures. Family support groups are often more energized and effective if they see themselves plugged into, as it were, larger support systems. The parish is perhaps the first level in this process of networking. The parish can bring together a number of family and other support groups. The parish can model the kind of pooling and sharing that need to occur within and between families. A parish library, skills bank, recycling effort, clothes or toys exchange can all promote greater stewardship of resources. Parishes can also link or pair with one another, in the same community as well as in another country. In these pairings, individual families or groups within each group can be linked more personally.

Larger networks of families and family support groups exist as well. Both the Christian Family Movement and the Parenting for Peace and Justice Network link families across the United States and with families in other parts of the world. Membership in either of these networks, especially through their newsletters, gives families a greater sense of connectedness, that their actions are part of a much larger effort realizing God's Kingdom of Shalom little by little. Specific pairing possibilities between U.S. families and families in other countries are promoted in both networks. The more that families do connect locally and globally, the broader their vision becomes, the more joy and sense of purpose they experience, the deeper their commitment grows. Families need not remain passive victims of massive social forces. Families are called to be nothing less than God's instruments for the transformation of the world.

NOTES

1. Pope Paul VI, *A Call to Action: Apostolic Letter on the Eightieth Anniversary of Rerum Novarum* (Washington, D.C.: United States Catholic Conference, 1971), no. 9.

2. John Kavanaugh, S.J., *Following Christ in a Consumer Society* (Maryknoll, New York: Orbis Books, 1984). Kavanaugh develops this whole theme with wonderful insight.

3. For an elaboration of this point, see the Catholic Bishops of Appalachia, *This Land Is Home to Me,* in *Renewing the Earth: Catholic Documents on Peace, Justice, and Liberation,* ed. David J. O'Brien and Thomas A. Shannon (New York: Image Books, 1977), pp. 472-515.

4. Synod of Catholic Bishops, *Justice in the World* (Washington, D.C.: United States Catholic Conference, 1972), part 3.

5. Pope Paul VI, *On the Development of Peoples* (Washington, D.C.: United States Catholic Conference, 1967), nos. 22-23.

6. National Conference of Catholic Bishops, *Economic Justice for All: Pastoral Letter on Catholic Social Teaching and the U.S. Economy* (Washington, D.C.: United States Catholic Conference, 1986).

7. National Conference of Catholic Bishops, *Brothers and Sisters to Us* (Washington, D.C.: United States Catholic Conference, 1979), pp. 1-2.

8. Ibid., p. 4.

9. *The Holy See on Disarmament,* 1976.

10. National Conference of Catholic Bishops, *The Challenge of Peace* (Washington, D.C.: United States Catholic Conference, 1983), no. 306.

11. *Declaration on Christian Education,* no. 3, in *The Documents of Vatican II,* ed. Walter Abbott, S.J. (New York: Guild Press, 1966).

12. *Shopping for a Better World* (New York: Council on Economic Priorities, 1988). Also helpful is the *National Boycott Newsletter* (6506 28th Ave., NE, Seattle, WA 98115).

13. *Justice in the World,* no. 47.

14. Contact the Parenting for Peace and Justice Network at the Institute for Peace and Justice, 4144 Lindell Blvd, #122, St. Louis, MO 63108, 314-533-4445.

15. Some book possibilities include James and Kathleen McGinnis, *Parenting for Peace and Justice: Ten Years Later* (Maryknoll, N.Y.: Orbis Books, 1990); Kathleen McGinnis and Barbara Oehlberg, *Starting Out Right* (for families with younger children); Jacqueline Haessly, *Peacemaking: Family Activities for Peace and Justice.* The "Inquiry Books" from the Christian Family Movement are also quite helpful for adult discussion and family action.

9

THE MORAL IMPERATIVES
OF CHRISTIAN MARRIAGE

Their Biological, Economic, and Demographic
Implications in Changing Historical Contexts

S. RYAN JOHANSSON

When the serious scholarly study of European demographic history began in the 1960s, it soon became apparent that marriage patterns in premodern Europe were unique. Nothing was more demographically distinctive than the Western European marriage pattern when compared with marriage patterns in the rest of the world.[1]

In Asia, Africa, and elsewhere young girls were normally married by their middle teens to men who were eight or more years older. Marriage was virtually universal, and usually (in theory) polygamous. Almost everywhere marriage was a private contract, which could be cancelled through divorce. Husbands found it particularly easy to end an unsatisfactory marriage without social interference. Adultery within marriage was a serious violation of the marriage contract, but only for women. In many places a woman's infidelity was a crime against society which carried the death penalty, despite the otherwise private nature of marriage. In general the sexuality of women was highly regulated through law and custom; most men had considerable sexual freedom both before and after marriage.[2] Managing reproduction within marriage was a private or family matter; sometimes contraception and abortion were the discretionary prerogative of a woman, but infanticide was largely a father's right. Thus it is not surprising that relatively unconcealed infanticide was widespread in the non-European world;[3] in some countries it was clearly the principal means through which reproduction in marriage was regulated.[4]

In contrast, in early modern Western Europe (circa 1500-1750) marriage took place at a relatively late age. The average age at first marriage for ordinary Western European women was exceptionally high by world standards: 24-27 years rather than 12-16 years.[5] Western European men were only about two to three years older than wives, instead of a decade or more. But despite the fact that marriage was officially monogamous in Western Europe, which should have equalized the potential supply of spouses, not everyone married. Anywhere from ten to fifteen percent of all ordinary women and men remained single throughout their adult lives, whether or not the country was Catholic or (after circa 1500) Protestant. In the Christian tradition marriage was both sacred and secular. The sacramental character of marriage, which was not emphasized by Christian theologians until the twelfth century, made it increasingly incompatible with easy cancellation.[6] Spouses who could no longer tolerate one another could separate, but remarriage was difficult while a first spouse still lived.[7] Nevertheless, given that ordinary people married at a comparatively late age, many marriages were disrupted by death, and remarriage was surprisingly frequent.

The fact that so many adults remained unmarried could have led to high illegitimacy rates, but until the eighteenth century they remained surprisingly low. No more than two to seven percent of all recorded births took place outside marriage in sixteenth- and seventeenth-century Western Europe.[8] Low rates of illegitimacy were related to the fact that the sexual lives of both ordinary single women and men (who lived for the most part in small villages) were closely monitored by the local representatives of state and church, as well as by their own neighbors. The unmarried had no general right to privacy or any form of sexual expression with another person. When moral deviance was detected by the authorities, it was swiftly and harshly punished. But since both sexes were supposed to obey the same set of sexual norms, men were officially taught to accept abstinence before marriage and fidelity during it. In practice, punishment for breaking the rules came more often and more swiftly for deviant women.

In theory Christian women were not supposed to exercise much personal control over reproduction; to underline the fact that their fertility had been officially socialized, contraception, abortion, and infanticide were made both mortal sins and serious crimes.[9] Birth control and abortion were hard to detect, but the suspicious deaths of newborns were investigated with thoroughness by religious and secular authorities. Those women found guilty were punished with death.[10]

Ideally the good Christian couple was supposed to accept all the births God chose to send them, at least as long as they remained sexually active. But sexual fulfillment was not the purpose of marriage. Apart from its role in reproduction, few Christian theologians accorded sexuality any intrinsic value. Until the rise of Protestantism, the pursuit of sexual pleasure with one's own spouse was deemed incompatible with the pursuit of spiritual perfection. No other major religion ever made sexuality and spirituality so strongly and so consistently opposed to one another over the entire life-course of the ordinary married individual.

Although it is still debated how long it took Christianity to create the unique marriage pattern observable in sixteenth- and seventeenth-century Western European parish register data, very few demographers would actively reject the idea that its measureable demographic characteristics were the result of the slow diffusion and final triumph of a Christian mentality, with its distinctive sexual, marital, and reproductive moral imperatives.[11]

The fact that Christian rules for demographic behavior were eventually widely accepted in Western Europe, as the concrete basis upon which ordinary people appeared to have made day-to-day ethical decisions about their conduct, was a function of the creation and diffusion of an efficient and comprehensive institutional infrastructure designed to teach and enforce them. It took Christianity more than a thousand years to build a church in almost every village in Western Europe and to teach most European children the fundamental principles of Christian family morality. But by the sixteenth century the task had been accomplished, and almost every village, or set of villages, had some means for informally and formally enforcing Christian moral imperatives. From the sixteenth century, as religious controversies divided Christian Europe into two warring camps, the state offered further institutional support to Christian family morality as a way of preserving or imposing social order in rebellious times.

Thus it was in the sixteenth century that the state (in England and France) first instructed local churches to set up parish registers, so that all marriages would be officially recorded, every child baptized (as a specific type of Christian), and every one of the dead buried according to the rites of whichever version of Christianity was being supported by the dominant political authorities. Thus religious ferment and the institutional reforms which accompanied it may have been critical to the final drive toward the standardization of marital and reproductive behavior among early modern Christians, whether Catholic or Protestant. But not even an efficient set of institutions can make large numbers of people behave in ways they find biologically repugnant or economically impossible to put into practice.

Ultimately, in order to become the basis for standardized decision-making, the moral imperatives of any religion have to be institutionally and personally interpreted by individuals in some manner minimally compatible with their physical and social survival, as well as the material welfare of their families and communities. Since the demographic and economic bases for survival and welfare are not constant over time, timeless moral truths must be continually open to reinterpretation by people who have no choice but to try and reconcile their sacred beliefs with their biological drives and material resources, as these exist in any particular context.[12]

As biological beings, most humans have strong sexual drives which exist independently of their desires to have and nurture children. As economic beings, adults cannot ignore the fact that having children means finding extra resources to support them during the period of their dependency. Having invested in the welfare of the young, adults must consider the implications of their investment for their own old-age security. As social beings with spiritual aspirations, most people want to do the right thing for themselves and their children, but they have to decide what is right in a material context. Both Marxist and non-Marxist historians and anthropologists have long understood that sexuality, reproduction, production, and human welfare must be integrated with one another if a complex social system is to succeed in perpetuating itself over time.[13]

So when demographic historians note that Christian morality was probably the "deep" foundation for the unique marriage pattern that persisted in Western Europe for over four centuries, they also want to know what made these moral imperatives consistent with the biological, demographic, and economic imperatives of material survival in the preindustrial agrarian regimes of early modern Western Europe.

THE PRE-MODERN BIOLOGICAL CONTEXT IN WHICH INDIVIDUALS INTERPRETED CHRISTIAN MORALITY

We are accustomed to thinking of all human populations as having the same biological drives and the same reproductive physiology. But even the most innate (genetically programmed) drives do not come with inherited instructions for how drives should be expressed in a specific time and place. Timeless biological drives like those which govern the need for food and water are no different from timeless moral imperatives; both have to be interpreted in a time- and place-specific context. Inevitably that means that generalized biological drives (like hunger and thirst) must be translated into specific actions via culturally constructed programs about what and when to eat, whom to eat with, when and where to drink, and in what alternate forms water can be imbibed (tea, coffee, fruit juice, alcohol), and so on. Similarly, strong but vague sexual and reproductive drives/potentials must be culturally translated into a systematic basis for making concrete choices about when, where, and with whom to begin sexual activity and reproduction. Thus to a certain extent human reproductive biology is always socially constructed, usually under strong religious influences.[14]

As demographers have begun to understand that the measurable demographic differences between groups represent (to some extent) the culturally modified expression of a set of biological drives and potentials general to the human species, they have begun to take more seriously the potential influence of norms and values on human demography.[15]

Thus, to understand the sixteenth- and seventeenth-century context in which Western Europeans made sexual, marital, and reproductive decisions influenced by Christian moral imperatives it turns out to be important to understand that in former times the average body, particularly the female body, reached physical maturity later than at present, and probably ceased to be fecund slightly earlier. Data on the average age at menstruation from nineteenth-century Europe suggests that ordinarily females rarely reached maturity before the age of 15, and that 17 was not exceptionally late to begin having regular periods. Similarly, the average female apparently began to lose her normal biological capacity to bear children after 35 years of age. In other words the onset of menopause, which is much more difficult to date than menstruation, may have been closer to 40-45 years, rather than 47-52 years, as it is today. This means that the average early modern European woman had a potential childbearing span which lasted about fifteen to twenty years instead of twenty to twenty-five years. (Her modern counterpart begins to menstruate at 12, is fully fertile at 15, and is probably fecund until the early 40s—barring some kind of disease-related infecundity—for a total reproductive span of twenty-five years.)

The reduced reproductive capacity of women in early modern Europe was undoubtedly related to widespread poverty and very high levels of infectious disease, which also made Europeans, both male and female, much shorter than they are today, as well as much less healthy and long-lived.[16]

In this context, having a woman's body was not a demographic advantage as it is today, when women outlive men in the developed countries by six to eight years. In former times the life expectancy at birth of women was rarely more than two years greater than that of men, and this small advantage masked the fact that females often died at higher rates than males from childhood through mid-life.[17]

Women suffered from all the infectious diseases that commonly reduced life expectancy at birth in pre-modern Europe to 30 or 35 years; in addition, women were subject to the additional physiological stresses associated with experiencing five or six completed pregnancies and perhaps two or three spontaneous abortions or miscarriages. Historian Edward Shorter makes a persuasive case that, although most women were physiologically robust enough to survive repeated pregnancies (no more than one to three percent of women died while giving birth), few escaped some form of physiological damage to their vaginas, urinary tracts, and wombs.

Not all married women had children; about eight to ten percent seem to have been childless. Their anomalous condition was probably related to the prevalence of venereal or other diseases. Smallpox (the leading killer of children in early modern Europe) often rendered surviving girls sterile or sub-fecund, and syphilis (the great pox) led to sterility, miscarriages, and stillbirths, not to mention babies born blind or too frail to survive for long. The great pox along with other venereal diseases was widespread in early modern Europe, particularly in the towns. At best venereal disease inflicted pain and discomfort, at worst a slow and painful death. Everyone knew that sexually transmitted diseases were rampant, and so ordinary people had to take their existence into account when they made decisions about sexuality, just as they had to consider the biological hazards of repeated childbearing.

Some women at some time in their reproductive lives would have reason to fear further pregnancies. No doubt that is why the historical record contains references to contraception or abortion. But the resort to either was probably a last resort rather than a preference. Artificiai contraception was unpleasant and very inefficient; chemically or mechanically induced abortion, in addition to being a crime (at least after quickening), was probably more physiologically hazardous than childbirth.

It is in this biological context that the moral imperatives of Christian sexuality were heard, interpreted, and applied to the ethics of sexual decision-making in daily life. For women in particular it wasn't possible to separate sexual pleasure (and its dangers) from reproduction (and its dangers). The pursuit of sexual pleasure, in or out of marriage, could not have been contemplated apart from the contingent awareness that there was no good, safe, pleasurable way to separate the biology of sexuality from the biology of venereal disease and/or reproduction, even assuming that the institutionally enforced penalties for illegitimacy and adultery could be avoided.

Under these circumstances the practice of permanent abstinence outside marriage and periodic abstinence within it was likely to seem either the lesser of two evils or interpreted as an attractive alternative to disease, physiological injury, and premature death. In psychological terms the psychic costs of suppressing a strong sexual drive were likely to seem low compared to the probable biological costs of expressing them. This fearful, cautious mentality would have been more common among women than men, but a married man had to think about his wife's health, and a single man about his own.

Women or men whose unconscious sexual desires were directed toward members of their own sex would have found Christianity's emphasis on the virtues of heterosexual abstinence (in or outside marriage) fairly easy to internalize. In any case, if homosexual men and women had to suppress consciously and painfully their own sexual desires, they were not alone. They lived in a world where most forms of heterosexuality were just as sinful and stigmatized as homosexuality.

THE PRE-MODERN ECONOMIC CONTEXT FOR INTERPRETING CHRISTIAN FAMILY MORALITY

Despite the unfavorable biological context in which sexuality and reproduction had to be managed, most people nevertheless married and had children. This was not necessarily the result of their innate biological drive to reproduce themselves or a romantic search for love and fulfillment.

More likely it was the expression of the hard economic fact that most people in sixteenth- and seventeenth-century Europe were peasants, landless laborers, or rural and urban craftsmen. Their survival was dependent on maintaining a household economy, based on the family, which divided essential labor according to sex, and turned young children into laborers as soon as possible. In old age this family economy was likely to be the only means of support available outside of some minimal forms of religious or secular charity. In other words, in the framework of the household economy, as children grew older they became short-term economic assets to their parents and a potential source of welfare in old age, just as children still are in those parts of Africa where development is still in its early stages.[18]

Economically this meant that the real costs of raising children in pre-modern Europe may have been negative rather than positive, at least for ordinary families, if not for the rich. Then as now aristocrats and upper-middle-class families regarded having children as a costly form of consumption, which decreased rather than increased their own personal standard of living and did nothing to enhance their old-age security. In fact, after the birth of a son and heir, each new child was a threat to the status of upper-class families, unless they could be well-placed in the church or the army (sons), or sent to convents (daughters).[19] But this placement required some form of financial outlay. (Privileged Protestant families made the placement of unmarried daughters even more problematic by abolishing convents. Some historians trace the seventeenth-century origins of modern feminism to the production of roleless, single women in upper- and middle-class Protestant families.)

But peasant families could always find work for their children on the family farm, and artisans in the family business. Even landless families could usually put children to work in the fields or send them into domestic service. Ordinary parents could only be grateful for the fact that Christianity supported the family economy by exalting filial piety, stressing the rightness of submission to parental authority, and the responsibility of children to care for the elderly.

But like upper-class families, peasant families who owned their own land had to think in terms of limiting heirship to protect the family's economic and social status. Most propertied families in Western Christian Europe solved this problem by creating two classes of children within the same family—heirs and spares. One son (usually the elder) was designated heir apparent, and the other(s) as his stand-in. One daughter was selected for marriage and a proper dowry, and the other(s) for some other fate. In propertied Catholic families this usually meant a convent; in ordinary families, Catholic and Protestant, surplus daughters were expected to migrate in search of domestic or other employment; so were surplus sons who did not go into the army. The church often sponsored the education of some talented boys from ordinary families, but not on a large scale.

THE PRE-MODERN DEMOGRAPHIC CONTEXT FOR CHRISTIAN FAMILY PLANNING

But all families, rich and poor, shared a demographic regime which made it difficult to calculate how many children had to be born in order to ensure that at least one son or one child would survive to become an adult heir or source of assistance in old age. The extent of uncertainty they had to face was considerable.

Life expectancy at birth in sixteenth- and seventeenth-century Europe was in the range of 20 to 40 years, with 30 years being a particularly common value. In contrast, modern populations in the developed countries all have a life expectancy at birth higher than 70 years. In the latter case, all but a few unfortunate children reach age 20, and eighty-five to ninety percent reach the age of 45, where they might conceivably be of use to their elderly parents.[20]

But survival was much less certain in pre-modern Europe. Under the most ordinary demographic circumstances (a life expectancy at birth of 30 years), a little more than half of all children ever born survived to the age of 10 years, when they first began to be economically productive (if they lived in ordinary families); only half survived to age 20, when they could begin to think about marriage. If an average propertied couple wanted to be reasonably sure of having one surviving, married son, that meant producing at least two sons and two daughters (to have at least one to exchange in marriage with another family). Four children was an absolute minimum, and five or six children would add an extra measure of security. Again, raising extra children was not that expensive in the long run, since children (particularly sons) who survived to the average age of marriage (25-27) would have paid back all or some part of the cost of their upbringing, without expecting their parents to make any additional investment in them.

In this economic and demographic context Christian morality, which encouraged married couples to accept all the children God might send them, was an ethical imperative which made good biological, demographic and economic sense to most people. For one thing, if a man and woman married in their mid-twenties, practiced no form of artificial birth limitation, and survived jointly to age 40 (after which age the average woman rarely gave birth), the wife was unlikely to have more than five to seven completed pregnancies (for a total of three or four survivors). Demographers explain that the potential number of pregnancies was no greater than this because ordinary Western European women breast-fed for at least a year and often much longer. Given her poor nutritional status and high-frequency suckling, the return of ovulation was normally postponed for at least twelve months after birth. It took another five to ten months for a woman to start another pregnancy (assuming an intercourse frequency no greater than six or seven times a month) and an occasional spontaneous abortion. Thus the average married woman, who used no contraception whatsoever and did not even practice extended abstinence within marriage (or even a greatly reduced coital frequency rate), was unlikely to have a child more frequently than every twenty-four or thirty-six months. Those women who survived from the age of 25 to 40 in continuous marriages had between five and eight births, depending on their own individual relative fecundity.

In other words, for very sound economic reasons most married couples probably wanted to have at least four children, and for biological reasons they were (as non-contracepting couples) unlikely to have more than seven. Since seven births meant (on average) only three to four surviving adult children, this level of fertility may have been ideal in the ordinary pre-modern agrarian regime.

All the above estimates have made the assumption that a typical couple married in their mid-20s and survived jointly to their 50s. But when life expectancy at birth was only 30 years, almost half of all marriages were likely to be broken prematurely by the death of one spouse before they had completed fertility. In most places the typical first marriage only lasted fifteen to twenty years before death parted the spouses. In this context death covertly substituted for divorce or potential divorce. Unhappily married people could always imagine that they or their husband or wife would be carried away in the next epidemic or die from one of many competing non-epidemic diseases. At any rate few couples had to face the prospect of living together and remaining faithful to each other for more than twenty-five years. Today the average married couple can expect to live together at least fifty years before death ends their marriage.

In the pre-modern world those who lost a spouse remarried frequently and with surprising haste, unless they were old or poor or both.[21] Because marriage was an integral part of the household economy, being without a spouse was an economic and social handicap. All in all there were good economic reasons to get married, stay married, have a child every other year, and remarry (if widowed) for everyone who was not very poor (and virtually propertyless) or so rich as to be able to hire servants to do all forms of useful but arduous labor.

Thus far, exploring the biological, economic, and demographic context in which ordinary pre-modern Western Europeans interpreted and applied Christian moral imperatives to their own lives has made it seem as if there was very little tension between the ideals the church endorsed (as timeless guides to conduct) and the timely real world in which most people lived. But for a minority of the population, married and single, applying the moral imperatives of Christianity to their daily lives may have been much more biologically onerous than previously suggested. Not all the permanent spinsters and bachelors in early modern Europe wanted to lead celibate lives in order to escape the biological hazards of sexual activity and reproduction. Women in domestic service were frequently subjected to sexual harassment, or merely exposed to attractive sexual temptations in the houses in which they were employed. Many men forced to postpone or forego marriage purchased the services of prostitutes or kept mistresses. Homosexuality certainly existed and may have been rather common among the upper classes, where as many as thirty to fifty percent of all surviving children were not allowed to marry; respectable codes of conduct demanded that they lead virtually "homosocial" lives (that is, that they avoid unsupervised social intercourse with non-related members of the opposite sex).

UPPER- AND MIDDLE-CLASS FAMILIES AND TRADITIONAL CHRISTIAN MORALITY

Christian moral imperatives related to sexuality and reproduction were most problematic for middle- and upper-class families. Although only a small minority of pre-modern families belonged to these groups (they were no more than three to seven percent of the total population of families) the moral imperatives of Christianity made increasingly less sense to them. Like many middle-class families today (who comprise the majority of most modern populations) the pre-modern bourgeois family was already forced to raise very expensive children, children who would not necessarily be willing or able to support their elderly parents. Thus it is not surprising to find that the idea of systematically limiting the natural flow of births (through abstinence, withdrawal, artificial contraception, or even abortion) appealed first of all to families of this type.

The necessity of doing something to limit the number of children born to middle-class families was openly discussed as early as the seventeenth century.[22]

The small family idea was already clearly articulated in a French play performed in 1706:

All excesses are fatal to us bourgeoisie.
We must on occasion from pleasure abstain,
having only those children we well can maintain.
Tis better to nurture with care just one child,
than produce half a dozen and let 'em run wild.[23]

The quotation implies that fertility control within marriage can be achieved effectively through abstinence, but throughout the eighteenth century the French clergy denounced otherwise conventional, church-going, married Catholics for practicing withdrawal, artificial contraception, and even abortion within marriage.[24] In Protestant England clergymen (who still endorsed the traditional sinfulness of artificial contraception) were also noting and denouncing the practice of fertility control and abortion among privileged families.[25] But it was eighteenth- and nineteenth-century French Catholic families who pioneered *the normalization* of artificial contraception within marriage and the small family with no more than three children.

All during the eighteenth and early nineteenth centuries middle- and upper-class Protestant Northern Europeans frequently denounced the French for their immoral ways — until they too began to imitate them. The English middle and upper classes began to practice family limitation in the middle of the nineteenth century, closely followed by the urban working classes.[26] But the French were a century ahead of their Protestant counterparts, except in the United States, where a decline from exceptionally high levels of fertility has been detected among some middle-class groups in the late eighteenth century.[27] By 1900, in the context of rapidly urbanizing and industrializing societies, all European families, rich and poor alike, were practicing some form of family limitation.[28]

The problem was not the breakdown of Christian morality (in the sense that most ordinary Europeans openly rejected Christian sexual and reproductive norms), but a clash between two different ways of interpreting the Christian normative tradition. The reinterpretation of Christian sexual and family morality began with Protestantism. Most of the hundreds of sects which eventually emerged from the reformation agreed that marriage did not condemn a Christian to a state of spiritual inferiority. Moreover, despite the emphasis which was placed on the patriarchal nature of the family, a lot of Protestant rhetoric stressed the importance of affection between husbands and wives and the positive role that sexuality had in sustaining their relationship with one another.

But it was Enlightenment philosophers who were most responsible for directing social attention to the importance of fostering an affectionate relationship between parents and children, and what loving parenthood implied for the rights of children. Many secular humanists taught that parents who protected the social and economic status of their family by dividing their children into heirs and spares were violating their natural inclination (and duty) to love and protect all their children equally. They argued that all sons should be educated equally and made co-heirs. All daughters should also be treated equally as candidates for educations and/or marital dowries, and none should be stored in convents against their will.

This new morality was not yet interpreted to mean that sons and daughters should be treated equally. Such a radical claim took on moral force only in the twentieth century. Even so, by the eighteenth century, propertied families who had internalized the popular idea that marriage and parenthood should be based on love and affection were faced with agonizing material choices. To love your children equally meant looking out for their welfare equally. To love your spouse implied a continuing sexual relationship. But if a couple remained sexually bonded, without doing something to control their fertility, they could expect to subdivide the family's property and/or its liquid assets (in the form of dowries) between multiple heirs. In the context of most pre-modern economies, subdivision of a family's wealth or property was a certain path to downward mobility for their children.

In order to avoid choosing between their own intimate welfare and the future of their children the only material alternative seemed to be artificially limiting the production of equally expensive sons and daughters. It seemed morally superior to have one surviving child raised properly (educated, or endowed) than to give birth to a pack of children who would "run wild," that is, be deprived of an upper- or middle-class future. Those Christians who could not face a lifetime of virtual sexual abstinence within marriage (after the birth of one to three children over a period of two to eight years) felt forced to reject or reinterpret the church's moral imperatives about the absolutely sinful nature of withdrawal, artificial contraception, or even abortion. Rather than feeling guilty, they replaced the old moral imperatives with new ones—decent people, loving mothers, and prudent fathers practiced family limitation.

Interestingly, as the privileged, educated classes accepted the practical and moral necessity of artificially restricting the flow of births within marriage, their infant and child mortality rates also fell very dramatically.[29] Before the eighteenth century death rates among upper- and middle-class children were no lower (and sometimes higher) than those among relatively impoverished rural families. It was largely for this reason that life expectancy among the rich was just as low as it was among the poor in the sixteenth and seventeenth centuries.

One of the many reasons for this unexpected form of demographic equality was that so few upper-class women breast-fed their own children. Traditionally, most "privileged" Western European children were sent away to the household of a lower-class wetnurse, often for a year or more; thus they experienced the same harsh conditions to which ordinary children were subjected. Not all privileged children were sent away. Quite often the first-born son and/or daughter were nursed by their upper-class mother; and only the later-born children were consigned to a wetnurse. This form of selective maternal investment was only another reflection of the pervasive inequality which once existed among siblings.

Later-born children, who were much more likely to be unwanted than first and second children, died at much higher rates. In fact there is good evidence for believing that many pre-modern parents (not just upper- and middle-class couples) covertly practiced parity-influenced selective neglect as a form of "family planning."[30] Once they had two or three surviving children, privileged parents did not strive to preserve the lives of newborns to the same degree as they had earlier. But as fertility fell and fewer unwanted surplus births were produced, infant mortality rates fell even faster.

Catholic moralists were aware that pre-modern parents practiced differential investment in the preservation of their children, especially in the form of differential breast-feeding, but they were extremely conflicted about how to respond to it. As long as it was still widely believed that a lactating woman should not, or was not interested in, resuming intercourse with her husband, they thought that extended breast-feeding frequently led to extramarital sexual activity on a husband's part. Most Catholic theologians regarded this outcome as worse than depriving a child of the breast. A woman who denied the breast to her child for the sake of sexually satisfying her husband was thus encouraged to think of herself as doing the right thing. After all, the survival of an infant, breast-fed or not, was ultimately up to God. The virtue of a husband was (partly) dependent on his wife's compliance, and so selective breast-feeding was neither encouraged nor forbidden. It was a private decision, which was left up to the individual couple.

Catholic theologians were never in a strong institutional position to oppose forcefully the pervasive inequality between siblings, which characterized upper- and middle-class family life before the adoption of fertility control. The church drew most of its priests, monks, and nuns from the ranks of later-born upper- and middle-class children—the spares—who were not designated to inherit or marry. Without the maintenance of strict inequality between siblings, the normal system of clerical recruitment would have to be totally restructured. That is probably why the secular humanists were able to contemplate and advocate sibling equality with much more equanimity than most traditional Catholic moralists.

Whatever the case, over the course of several centuries, Protestants and secular humanists led the movement to reform family morality. The small family idealized today, with its highly educated children and couples who expect to maintain an active sexual life throughout their marriage (by separating sexuality from reproduction through artificial contraception), is their creation. The eventual triumph of this new family morality and its diffusion to the working classes was socially guaranteed by further reforms. Once the average couple could not legally employ their children, had to keep them in school for longer and longer periods, and did not need them for old-age security, they too adopted the small family ideal. But the nineteenth-century reform movements, which abolished child labor and made education compulsory, were only the logical, institutional extension of the new family morality developed to its fullest extent in eighteenth-century France.

THE DEMOGRAPHIC, BIOLOGICAL, AND SOCIAL CONTEXT
FOR MODERN SEXUAL AND FAMILY MORALITY

Today in the developed countries most married couples and most unmarried adults think about sexuality, marriage, and childbearing more like eighteenth-century upper- and middle-class French Catholics than their own agrarian ancestors. But they do their thinking in a biological context that is very different from anything that has previously existed.

Currently in the developed countries life expectancy at birth is more than twice what it used to be. Death rates are so low before old age that very few infants and children die before reaching adulthood (fewer than five to ten percent), and the average marriage can expect to last forty to fifty years before being broken by death. Since death is no longer a substitute for divorce, it is not surprising that as death rates declined, divorce rates rose, and the problem of remarriage returned to confront Catholic morality in a new guise. And not just remarriage, but sexuality in general, inside and outside of marriage.

In the modern world Catholics must now interpret Christian morality in a biological context characterized by very early maturity and much improved levels of health. For most girls menstruation now begins at 12 and meno-pause is delayed until 50 years or so. Properly educated middle-class chil-dren who delay marriage in order to complete their training (which increasingly lasts until the late 20s) must now cope with their biological drives for about five to seven years longer than they were once expected to do, and to do so in a society which provides them with a technology for separating sexual activity from pregnancy and disease. There is also an increasingly tolerant moral climate, which has removed the public stigma attached to sexual activity outside marriage and indeed has begun to glorify it. (AIDS, of course, is a new and frightening exception to ordinary modern conditions.)

Once adults marry they must consider reproduction in a biological con-text which has also greatly increased their potential fecundity. A modern, non-contracepting married woman can now expect to give birth every eight-een to twenty-four months until she reaches the age of 40 or even 45, even if she breast-feeds. Women are much better fed today, and very few are able to carry their babies around with them in order to nurse them on demand. Under these biological circumstances a lactating woman can resume ovulation while she is lactating and get pregnant fairly easily while still caring for a small infant. A non-contracepting woman of normal robust-ness, who married at age 24 could expect to have a total of at least eight and possibly twelve live births before her period of fecundity ended natu-rally. All of these children could reasonably be expected to survive to adult-hood.

There is of course the rhythm method for regulating reproduction. But people who practice the rhythm method usually manage to delay the next birth without efficiently preventing it. Instead of having eight to ten babies they might have five to eight births. These estimates assume breast-feeding on demand for at least six months after each birth; otherwise, the estimates would be even larger.

In the early 1980s economists estimated that it cost a married couple in a country like the United States about eighty thousand dollars to raise a child to the age of 18. To complete childrearing with a college education brought the total to over a hundred thousand.[31] If Catholic couples had large families, either they would have to earn much more money than the average couple or raise their children at a much lower standard than other couples.

The costs of feeding children adequately and keeping them alive in a very small house, wearing used clothing, and having them go to work after high school is much less than eighty thousand dollars. But as long as Cath-olics have the same aspirations for their children as non-Catholics, they will think of themselves as being unable to afford not to use contraception. To reject artificial birth control (supplemented by the occasional abortion) is perceived of as a way of doing harm to themselves, their children, or their marriages.

Marriages certainly need all the help they can get these days. The longer a marriage lasts, the more likely it is to go through emotionally stressful periods that suggest to one or both partners that the marriage has died, even though both spouses are living. Under the best of circumstances it is difficult to live in harmony and fidelity for half a century. Even the birth of one child threatens this ideal; a regular flow of new infants makes it virtually unobtainable.

But when Catholics reject traditional Christian sexual and family morality as a form of immorality designed to prevent happy marriages and properly expensive children, they frequently leave the faith. If they stay, they must individualistically adapt traditional moral imperatives to modern contexts in some way that makes living a Catholic life neither biologically impossible, economically threatening, nor socially irresponsible.

Moral individualism is truly antithetical to the Catholic tradition. But when traditional Catholic morality was widely accepted as the practical basis for making sexual and reproductive decisions, it made a lot of biological, economic, and demographic sense to ordinary people, even though they had no role in formulating its official expression. But those Catholic families who found traditional beliefs impossible to follow have chafed against the necessity of passively obeying moral imperatives over which they had no influence. No families were more quick to rebel than the upper and middle classes of Catholic France. In retrospect we can see that what French Catholics did was pioneer the modernization of family morality by rejecting the authority of traditional Catholic moralists. Of necessity they became moral individualists and established the dangerous or constructive precedent (depending on your point of view) that has led to what is currently called do-it-yourself Catholicism.

Until the sixteenth century adapting Christian moral truths to changing contexts was a complex process, largely under the control of the church itself, but not insensitive to the needs of ordinary people. In the Middle Ages local priests, some of whom still kept concubines, often mediated between the ideas of persuasive moral thinkers, the orders given by their bureaucratic superiors, and the over-all material situation of the people to whom they ministered. But as the church lost its once monopolistic control over Christian theology, philosophy, and the educational process, the hierarchy seems to have forgotten that its authority depended on listening, as well as making dogmatic pronouncements. From the time that some Protestant, some secular, and some Catholic voices began to articulate the moral interests of people who raised children in middle- or upper-class circumstances, the church refused to listen.

Once the Catholic hierarchy totally rejected the idea that some priests could marry, and it refused to tolerate concubinage, it became increasingly less well-positioned to conduct a meaningful moral dialogue with the voices who spoke openly for the interests of married people and those who whispered about the new aspirations and fears of the married women responsible for conceiving, giving birth, and raising successive generations of Catholics in the modern world. A church hierarchy run exclusively by unmarried men has no demographic, social, or political basis for entering into a moral dialogue with family men, married women, or even with single adults who are not single because they value celibacy. Moreover a church recruited from the ranks of surplus children probably had good reason to fear the spread of small-family ideals, since small families contain no surplus children whose only opportunity in life would come through the church.

Today many Catholic theologians, bishops, and priests are willing to listen to and work with ordinary people on the complex task of reinterpreting and adapting Christian-Catholic doctrine to modern times. But the most powerful and highly placed Catholic bureaucrats are opposing this trend. They are still unmarried men, convinced that priests should not marry, and that women, married or not, should continue to be excluded from the priesthood. Given this situation, it is not really surprising that Catholic family morality, expressed in the form of modern papal encyclicals, is not really a form of social thought. It is a set of dogmas, which are being asocially conceptualized in some context-free manner. Worse still, from the standpoint of most (virtually all) demographers, the papal encyclicals appear to expound an antisocial family and reproductive morality that works against the welfare of married couples and the children they must raise under modern demographic, biological, and economic circumstances.

Tragically, the fact that an all-male, celibate bureaucracy still retains its sterile control over official family morality may have already forfeited the church's opportunity to be a modern "moral clearinghouse" for both Catholics and non-Catholics concerned with maintaining some sexual and reproductive moral standards.[32] Today not much remains of the vital secular humanist tradition which once articulated the interests of married couples and voiceless children. It seems to have been reduced to, or replaced by, the idea that intense sexual pleasure should be valued above everything else, even maintaining stable, loving, adult relationships expressed in a context of continuing parental and/or community responsibility. Most morally sensitive people do not agree, but what *stable* means, what *loving* means, and what *continuing responsibility* means are matters which need to be collectively reconsidered in the demographic, economic, and social context of modern life.

In the meanwhile married Catholics, single Catholics, and gay and lesbian Catholics continue to go their own way, trying as best they can to modify individually their moral traditions so that they can lead lives which are Christian in spirit, without being biologically, economically, or socially impossible. In the course of so doing they have resurrected the traditional Western European marriage pattern in a new form. Delayed marriage has returned, and so have high (but not death-dependent) dissolution rates, extensive remarriage, and non-marriage for a substantial proportion of the adult population.

NOTES

1. J. Hajnal, "European Marriage Patterns in Perspective" in *Population in History*, D. V. Glass and D. E. C. Eversley eds. (Chicago: Aldine Publishing Co., 1965), pp. 101-46. Hajnal, a non-European, "discovered" the European marriage pattern in the sense that he was the first scholar to *quantitatively establish* its comparative uniqueness along three parameters: the average age at first marriage for women, the proportion of adults over 40 who had never married, and the small difference in age between spouses entering a first marriage. European demographers who had been working with parish registers and vital statistics dated from pre-modern Europe were initially unaware that the marriage patterns they observed were distinctive to Europe, particularly to Western Europe. For a summary of more recent quantitative research on the distinctive nature of pre-modern European demographic regimes see Michael Flinn, *The European Demographic System 1500-1800* (Baltimore: Johns Hopkins University Press, 1981).

2. Over the previous century an extremely large literature on European and non-European family patterns has been produced, which is demographic in the informal sense; that is, it makes generalizations about marriage and reproduction without the support of statistical data. Two classics in this genre are Stuart Queen and Robert Habenstein, *The Family in Various Cultures* (Philadelphia: J. B. Lippincott, 1967); and William J. Goode, *World Revolution and Family Patterns* (New York: The Free Press, 1970). Nevertheless, quantitative demographic history has generally supported rather than undermined the informal generalizations made about marriage and reproduction, although not necessarily about household structure. In all cross-sectional, quantitive data sets the nuclear household seems to be the most common form of domestic arrangement, irrespective of whether or not social norms affirm the superiority of nuclear or extended families. See the essays in *Household and Family in Past Time*, ed. Peter Laslett (Cambridge: Cambridge University Press, 1972). One of the reasons for the numerical dominance of nuclear households is demographic; when life expectancy at birth was 20 to 35 years it was relatively uncommon for a married couple with children to have surviving parents, particularly if the rules for domestic formation required a couple to live either patrilocally (with the husband's parents) or matrilocally (with the wife's parents).

3. Glenn Hausfater and Sarah Hrdy, *Infanticide: Comparative and Evolutionary Perspectives* (New York: Aldine Publishing Company, 1984). Infanticide is widespread among animal as well as human populations. It functions as a means to adjust the relatively steady flow of birth through time to short-term environmental constraints. In the higher primates it has an even more complex character. Experts do not agree on why it exists among humans, probably because it has so many context specific causes, and can take so many forms, both active and passive. Some of the data available on infanticide in human populations and the controversies over its causes are reviewed in the four essays in Section 4 of the book cited above,

including my own, "Deferred Infanticide: Excess Female Mortality During Childhood," pp. 487-502.

4. Japan is the most notable example. For a history of infanticide in Japan and its probable extent, see Irene Taeuber, *The Population of Japan* (Princeton, New Jersey: Princeton University Press, 1958).

5. Hajnal in Glass and Eversley, pp. 101-46. The type of detailed quantitative data required to characterize and contrast marriage patterns only existed in Europe from the sixteenth century onward and in some non-European countries since the early twentieth century. Thus Hajnal could not say for certain when the Western European marriage pattern actually emerged, but he could see that it began to lose its demographic distinctiveness from the late-nineteenth century through the mid-twentieth century.

6. Christopher N. Brooke, "Marriage and Society in the Central Middle Ages" in *Marriage and Society Studies in the Social History of Marriage,* ed. R. B. Outhwaite (London: Europa Publications, 1981), pp. 17-34. Annulments based on kinship were rather freely used as a substitute for divorce until the fifteenth century. Thus if two married persons "discovered" that they were third cousins once removed, this could be used as grounds for declaring the marriage null and void.

7. Roderick Phillips, *Putting Asunder: A History of Divorce in Western Europe* (Cambridge: Cambridge University Press, 1988).

8. For England, see Peter Laslett, "Long Term Trends in Bastardy in England" in *Family Life and Illicit Love in Earlier Generations,* ed. Peter Laslett (Cambridge: Cambridge University Press, 1977), pp. 102-59. For France, see Jean-Louis Flandrin, *Families in Former Times,* trans. Richard Southern (Cambridge: Cambridge University Press, 1979). For Renaissance Italy (Florence) the best detailed and quantitative study of traditional family and marriage patterns is David Herlihy and Christian Klapisch-Zuber, *Tuscans and Their Families: A Study of the Florentine Catasto of 1427* (New Haven: Yale University Press, 1978).

9. John T. Noonan, *Contraception. A History of Its Treatment by the Catholic Theologians and Canonists* (New York: A Mentor-Omega Book, 1967; first published by Harvard University Press in 1965). Readers of Noonan will recognize the above statement as a simplification of a long and complex doctrinal history, but it is not inappropriate given the generalized level at which contrasts are being drawn between Christian and non-Christian traditions.

10. M. Piers, *Infanticide* (New York: W. W. Norton Company, 1978). See also, P. C. Hoffer and N. E. H. Hull, *Murdering Mothers: Infanticide in England and New England 1558-1803* (New York: New York University Press, 1981). There was an "infanticide craze" in sixteenth- and seventeenth-century Western Europe, which may have resulted in the executions of more women than the witchcraft persecutions. Indeed, witches were themselves frequently accused of committing or abetting infanticide. Peter Stallybrass, "Patriarchal Territories" in *Rewriting the Renaissance,* ed. Margaret Ferguson, Maureen Quilligan and Nancy Vickers (Chicago: University of Chicago Press, 1986), p. 131.

11. There are several good histories of the centuries-long struggle between Christianity and paganism for control over the institutionalization of morality. For the first three centuries of its existence, see Robin Fox, *Pagans and Christians* (New York: Harper and Row, paperback edition, 1988). For the medieval period, see James A. Brundage, *Law, Sex and Christian Society in Medieval Europe* (Chicago: University of Chicago Press, 1987).

12. Noonan, pp. 565-631.

13. Jack Goody, *Production and Reproduction: A Comparative Study of the Domestic Domain* (Cambridge: Cambridge University Press, 1976). For Goody's study of the evolution of the European family under Christian influences, see idem., *The Development of the Family and Marriage in Europe* (Cambridge: Cambridge University Press, 1983). For a more detailed study of the integration of demographic imperatives and economic realities in late medieval Europe, see Richard Smith, ed., *Land, Kinship and Life-cycle* (Cambridge: Cambridge University Press, 1984).

14. It is useful to think about moral imperatives as part of the comprehensive set of instructions coded in the cultural programs universally used to standardize human behavior patterns for social purposes. Cultural programs, however, are printed out in the collective behavior of populations, whose members must have the biological and economic capacity to fulfill those imperatives. See S. Ryan Johansson, "The Computer Paradigm and the Role of Cultural Information in Social Systems," *Historical Methods* 21 (1988), pp. 172-88.

15. The effort to understand the role of cultural influences on human reproductive biology has gone furthest in the study of living human beings in African countries. See Hilary Page and Ron Lesthaeghe, eds., *Child-spacing in Tropical Africa. Traditions and Change* (London: Academic Press, 1981).

16. Edward Shorter, *A History of Women's Bodies* (New York: Basic Books, 1982).

17. Ibid., chap. 9. Also S. Ryan Johansson, "Mortality, Welfare and Gender: Male/Female Mortality Differences over Three Centuries," *Continuity and Change*, forthcoming.

18. John C. Caldwell, *Theory of Fertility Decline* (New York: Academic Press, 1982).

19. For a review of the literature on this point, see S. Ryan Johansson, "Status Anxiety and Demographic Contraction of Privileged Populations," *Population and Development Review* 13 (1987), pp. 439-70.

20. See Ansley J. Coale and Paul Demeny, *Regional Model Life Tables and Stable Populations*, 2d ed. (New York: Academic Press, 1983), pp. 42-54 and 55-79.

21. J. Dupaquier, E. Helin, P. Laslett, M. Livi-Bacci, and S. Sogner, eds., *Marriage and Remarriage in Populations of the Past* (London: Academic Press, 1981).

22. Artificial forms of contraception are found among some technically primitive peoples; techniques for separating sexuality from reproduction were already being practiced in the ancient Mediterranean world. Although consciousness of the existence of artificial contraception was never lost from Christian Europe, it is unlikely that it played a major role in the regulation of reproduction in medieval Europe. See Norman Himes, *Medical History of Contraception* (New York: Schocken Books, 1970; first published in 1936), p. 168.

23. Translated and quoted in Flinn, p. 45.

24. See Flandrin. Despite its title, *Families in Former Times*, the book is largely about French families in the seventeenth and eighteenth centuries among whom the struggle over the morality of contraception began.

25. Andrew McClaren, *Reproductive Rituals* (New York: Methuen, 1984). McClaren covers mostly English and American materials.

26. For the English middle classes, see J. A. Banks, *Victorian Values* (London: Routledge and Kegan Paul, 1981).

27. Robert Wells, *Revolutions in American Lives. A Demographic Perspective on the History of Americans, Their Families and Their Society* (Westport, Connecticut:

Greenwood Press, 1982). Around 1750 American women tended to marry by 20 and complete their first marriages by surviving to age 45. In between they normally gave birth every twenty-four to twenty-seven months and had between eight and ten children, well over half of whom survived to adulthood.

28. Ansley J. Coale and Susan Watkins, *The Decline of Fertility in Europe* (Princeton, New Jersey: Princeton University Press, 1986).

29. S. Ryan Johansson, "Centuries of Childhood/Centuries of Parenting: Philippe Aries and the Modernization of Privileged Infancy," *Journal of Family History* 12 (1987), pp. 343-65.

30. Flandrin, p. 153. For some quantitative estimates of the major role played by differential parental investment and selective neglect in the high infant mortality rates of privileged and ordinary families see S. Ryan Johansson, "Neglect, Abuse and Avoidable Death: Parental Investment and the Mortality of Infants and Children in the European Tradition," in *Child Abuse and Neglect: Biosocial Dimensions,* Richard Gelles and Jane Lancaster, eds. (New York: Aldine De Gruyter, 1986), pp. 57-93.

31. See Valerie Oppenheimer, *Work and the Family. A Study in Social Demography* (New York: Academic Press, 1982), Appendix C, "Dollar Estimates of Expenditures on Children," pp. 425-36.

32. Peter Steinfels, "State of the Church: Has Catholicism Lost a Chance to Be Our Moral Clearinghouse?" *New York Times,* Week in Review, (April 8, 1990), p. 1.

10

REFLECTIONS ON THE CATHOLIC TRADITION OF FAMILY RIGHTS

ERNIE CORTES

Given the turbulent nature of the times and the pressures impinging on the institutions of family and community, it is our view that new social institutions need to be created, old institutions recast, and the tradition and meaning of Catholic social thought reinterpreted. In the new millennium the worlds of work, of politics, and of intimate life will be much different for our children. To help them prepare for this new world and to fashion the institutions and relationships which will support them, it is important that the church be bold both in its interpretation of its tradition and in the praxis that flows from that tradition. Just as in a time of tremendous turbulence Paul and the early church Fathers guided the development of dramatically new institutions out of the fabric of the older institutions and traditions of the Greek, Jewish, and Roman worlds, the church in this epoch faces the opportunity of drawing on the best of its tradition to revitalize its mission.

Our subject in this chapter is the family and its well-being, and the ability of the church to protect and enable its members' lives as moral beings. We begin with the notion of "family rights" in the sense of legal entitlements of human beings to family life as a necessary but not sufficient protection of the integrity of families and human beings. But we argue that the church must focus at least equal concern on the texture of the society and community in which human beings live their daily lives. We argue that what matters is not just their entitlements, but their relationships to others and the role of social institutions in their lives.

The church in the American context, with which we are most familiar, has played a vibrant role in protecting and enabling its members' social relationships. The social institutions of the parish, neighborhood, extended family, parochial school, local public school, political machine, labor union, and fraternal and social associations mediated the relations between newly-arrived Catholics and the larger American society.

With the dramatic changes in society, the American Catholic Church has lost much of this role and is closing many of its former ethnic, inner-city parishes. As second-generation Catholics have moved their families to suburbia and a new wave of Catholics enters America's cities, little except television has replaced these institutions. The organizations of the Industrial Areas Foundation (I.A.F.) have been working to recapture the sense of this historic role of the church and other social institutions which mediated the relationships of individual human beings to larger society. The arguments here are part of that effort. We wish to explain to others what we are doing and how we have drawn on the traditions of Catholic social thought and practice. We also wish to suggest how the church can use Catholic social thought to recapture once again its tradition of building and supporting mediating institutions.

It is to this history and to the foundation of Catholic social thought that we appeal in arguing that the church should build the institutions to support a meaningful public and community life for families and their members. It should take care to shape the parish as an institution of public life. It should participate in building broad-based organizations from coalitions of parishes and congregations.

The following pages develop this argument in several steps:

1. We acquaint the reader with the Industrial Areas Foundation, which for fifty years has been struggling to build new democratic and pluralistic institutions to replace the lost mediating institutions of American society.

2. We then discuss briefly the role of the American Catholic Church in shaping institutions of immigrant civil society over the last century and a half.

3. We discuss our reading of Catholic social thought, in particular how it has laid the foundation for but not yet elaborated the full richness of the church's support of social relationships and institutions.

4. We then discuss the perspective of the I.A.F. in approaching the institutionalized relationships among people—within their families, churches, and other associations, including the I.A.F.'s broad-based organizations.

5. As an illustration of our argument, we draw on the experience of families in Allied Communities of Tarrant in Fort Worth.

6. We discuss the urgency of this task. It is not only desirable but imperative for the church to recapture its support of mediating institutions. We agree with Father Philip Murnion that the parish must concern itself with building a public life for its members and a sense of responsibility for its community.[1] In the vacuum of meaningful mediating institutions, families are left no countervailing institutions to limit the ways in which the state

and the market erode the values and relationships of the family in contemporary society.

7. In conclusion, we call on the church to continue to act as a leaven to society by exercising its prophetic role. It has a proud history of efforts to assert family rights and to make them substantive. It must persevere in this task. Beyond this, however, the church must also examine closely the nature of civil society and the need to build institutions which will mediate the relations between families and larger society. The church must be emboldened — not discouraged — by the vacuum that exists in social relations. It must come together with other congregational institutions to create a new, democratic public life for its families.

THE FAMILIES OF THE INDUSTRIAL AREAS FOUNDATION

The reflections of this essay are drawn from the experience of the organizations of the I.A.F. For fifty years the men and women of the I.A.F. have been creating new democratic institutions to empower families and congregations to defend their integrity and to participate meaningfully in public life. Some twenty-eight organizations in poor and minority communities across the United States now relate to the I.A.F. for leadership training.[2] They consist of over six hundred congregations and nearly one million families from a broad range of faiths and ethnic backgrounds. They include Catholic, Protestant, Muslim, and Jewish congregations, and Anglos, Hispanics, and African-Americans.

In the Southwest, one of the more powerful experiences has been that of San Antonio Communities Organized for Public Service (C.O.P.S.), organized sixteen years ago and the oldest organization currently associated with the I.A.F. C.O.P.S., an organization of twenty-six Catholic parishes on the Mexican west and south sides of San Antonio, was founded to empower low-income people in one of the poorest and most segregated cities in America. (Peter Jennings of ABC News once said that San Antonio reminded him most of Johannesburg because of its juxtaposition of extreme wealth and poverty.) Through the hard work of thousands of I.A.F.-trained leaders, C.O.P.S. won over 750 million dollars in new streets, drainage, parks, libraries, and other improvements, reversing a long history of disinvestment in the inner city.

Inspired by C.O.P.S., eleven other I.A.F. organizations have been formed in Texas and two more are in the process of forming in Arizona. Their purpose is not simply to deliver physical improvements to poor neighborhoods, but to change the very way in which a city or community conducts its public business. The C.O.P.S./I.A.F. strategy is to build an agenda which comes out of the experiences of families. The I.A.F. organizations establish issue platforms and hold public officials and corporate leaders accountable to commitments to those platforms. They do not participate in elections in traditional ways because, while they engage in voter education efforts, all

I.A.F. organizations are radically nonpartisan, endorsing neither candidates nor political parties. They are building a new democratic institution that organizes families and engages them in an ongoing dialogue with other power centers of the community. By doing so they are incorporating the political into the daily life of thousands of people. As Sheldon Wolin has written: "Democracy means participation, but participation is not primarily about 'taking part,' as in elections or officeholding. It means originating or initiating cooperative action with others."[3]

THE INSTITUTIONAL STRATEGY OF THE AMERICAN CATHOLIC CHURCH

The church in its American setting has a history of supporting the health of civil institutions. This role was essential to the success of Catholic immigrants and to its own success. This history forms an implicit theory, which has not become a fully articulated part of Catholic social thought. Although there is a scholarly history waiting to be written here, we are not attempting to write it. Our purpose is instead to urge a return to this tradition, much of whose vitality has been destroyed by the economic and social changes of the last fifty years.

The success of Catholic immigrants to America would have been impossible without the church. One American bishop, when his middle-class flock argues that they owe their success to themselves alone, reminds them that the American church educated them in Catholic schools and organized their fathers into the American labor movement. He could add that the church also sustained the cultural life of the ethnic neighborhoods in which they grew up. The social institutions of the parish, neighborhood, extended family, parochial school, local public school, political machine, labor union, and fraternal and social associations mediated the relations between individuals and the larger society. They provided protection against other, more powerful groups in the new society. They provided support networks for new immigrants, access to jobs, and access to political power. They acculturated immigrants to a new language and culture, and in turn gave them channels to influence that culture.

Now these institutions of immigrant Catholic society are gone, and the church is closing many of the parishes which were their site. Yet, as the children of the former immigrant families move to the middle-class suburbs, and the new immigrants from Latin America, Ireland, Southeast Asia, and the Caribbean move to the old cities, little except television has replaced them. The fabric of family rights wears thin without institutions which will vigorously defend them and empower persons to act on them.

The organizations of the I.A.F. are mediating institutions through which families create a space to learn about power and leadership and to act on what they learn. Like the institutions of immigrant Catholic society, they act to counter the pressures on families and to reshape other institutions in their relationships to families. In many ways they are a replacement for the mediating institutions the Amcrican church has lost over the last half-century.

THE STRATEGY OF CATHOLIC SOCIAL THOUGHT

This perspective on the history of the American Catholic church has not yet been captured in its full richness by Catholic social thought.[4] Important thinkers and leaders of the church havc laid the groundwork and elaborated the entitlements of families. As Donal Dorr has argued, Catholic social thought since *Rerum Novarum* has maintained a clear and continuing commitment to the vitality of all families and, in particular, the poorest families.[5] Catholic leaders and thinkers have defended the need of families for adequate food, shelter, clothing, and income, among other material needs. They have not only asserted the moral imperative of such needs but the legal entitlement to their satisfaction. They have had the courage to educate the church on social issues and to speak out to broader society. They have discussed the importance of a meaningful social life in the lives of persons.

Yet while they emphasize the importance of associations and institutions and the importance of "imbuing" them with religious meaning, they have not offered a theoretical framework of social relationships which enables people to operate competently within these associations and institutions. As we shall arguc in the next section, the nature of institutions is critical to their significance for persons. Our point in this discussion is not to write an exhaustive intellectual history, but to search Catholic social thought for its understanding of the social relationships in which human beings are immersed. We have found very important and useful intellectual foundations in them. But we have not yet found as complete a conceptualization of social relationships as needed — especially of the relationship between public and private spheres of social life.

The concern of Catholic social thought for the needs of families has deepened steadily since *Rerum Novarum* and has been increasingly conceptualized as the entitlements of their members. Pope Leo outlined the needs of families for shelter, clothing, nourishment, leisure, and protection of their property, and then called on the wealthy and the state to respect these on the basis of equity, moral obligation, and prudencc.[6] While asserting the justice of these claims, Pope Leo conceived of them as the obligations of the powerful rather than as the rights of the weak. He asserted that the poor had some rights, but more as the universal entitlement to private property than as welfare guarantees.

In the *Charter on the Rights of the Family*, the clearest and most recent papal statement on the topic of this essay, John Paul II unequivocally qualifies the preconditions of family life as the entitlements of all people.[7] The *Charter* outlines a comprehensive list of entitlements deserving protection, including voluntary marriage, control of childbearing, protection of children, family determination of education, support of family in public policy, practice of religion, voluntary association with other families, minimum welfare needs, minimum income, decent housing, and the ability of immigrants to keep their families intact.

Both of these documents, as well as intervening ones, have not been afraid to instruct the powerful institutions of broader society. Leo addressed much of his document to the wealthy, whom he hoped would restrain their advantage and perhaps go as far as to advise or even join with workers in creating harmonious "private societies."[8] John Paul explicitly directs his document to political institutions of national governments and international organizations.[9]

We think, however, that Catholic social thought needs to move beyond these foundational concepts of entitlements. It needs to develop a paradigm of the creative and interactive tension of the social relationships and institutions through which a person develops his or her capacities as a moral being and effective agent for change. Pope Leo's document asserted the right of workers to associate, but outlined the relationships within his "private societies" with only a vague appeal to "religious perfection."[10] He did not elaborate how individuals would relate to each other within these institutions, or how these institutions would relate to other institutions such as the family. Nor did he outline the different roles that institutions should play in persons' lives.

In *Quadragesimo Anno*, the most in-depth analysis of the place of voluntary institutions in social life with which we are familiar, Pope Pius XI articulated the "principle of subsidiarity."[11] He asserted the value of intermediary associations and insisted that the state not usurp any more power over them than necessary for the common good. Later leaders, in particular John XXIII in *Mater et Magistra* and *Pacem in Terris* and the authors of *Gaudium et Spes*, reaffirmed the principle for both national and international societies. However, in all four documents the authors used the principle more to argue for a limitation on the power of the state over individuals than for a specific role for voluntary institutions in the social life of families.

In our reading of Catholic social thought, we have found the most helpful discussion on the themes of social relationships in *Gaudium et Spes*.[12] The authors outline what we consider one of the great strengths of the Catholic tradition — its conception of the individual human as a social being. This tradition locates the development of a human being not within himself or herself, nor in others per se, but in relationships with others. Thus *Gaudium et Spes* taught us that "through [man's] dealings with others, through reciprocal duties, and through fraternal dialogue he develops all his gifts and is able to rise to his destiny."[13] This conception imagines human beings as "persons," not as "individuals." They are mothers, fathers, brothers, daughters, workers, employers, pastors, governors, and so on, not isolated, self-directed singularities.

Nonetheless, while *Gaudium et Spes* stresses and defends the importance of relationships to the human self—in contrast to the more individualistic conception of the self of the modern age's classical liberal conception—it gives little guidance on the nature of social relationships, the institutions within which they exist, and how the church should view them. It asserts the importance of relationships in the same way that *Rerum Novarum* did and adopts the strategy of the church to "imbue" institutions with religious meaning.[14] Such a strategy stresses the ability of the church to inform participants with moral sensibilities, but does not elaborate a theory or framework for developing the character and culture of these relationships. Nor does it elaborate how the parish as an institution might empower the laity to act appropriately within such a culture.

PERSON AND CHURCH, FAMILY AND COMMUNITY, PRIVATE AND PUBLIC

The I.A.F., its broad-based organizations, and their member congregations are intensely concerned with the nature of social relationships and institutions and their importance to the lives of people. While we agree with the documents of Catholic social thought that it is important to give religious meaning to institutions, we hope that the church will do more than proclaim its values to its people. It must have a strategy to create for them a culture which is a way of engaging others and themselves. It needs to create and inform what Richard John Neuhaus calls a "public square."[15] Human beings in society need institutions in society in which they can engage each other, reflect upon their values and experience, teach their lessons to each other, and act in concrete, specific ways. It is only in this way that they gain deeper insights into religious meanings.

In our vision, the ability to act effectively depends on our success in the two separate but interdependent spheres of public life and private life. We see the sphere of private life as based in the relationships of family and friendships, within which we discover our fundamental identity. This private life is where we experience love, in the sense of unconditional loyalty and an intimate union with others. It is a protected sphere, which we deserve to have privileged from the demands of strangers and the larger society. It is a region in which we seek relief from tension in relationships. We seek out people like ourselves; we look for acceptance, not challenge; we give without expectation and can depend on the same.

This sphere of private life, however, will not alone allow us to deal with all our needs as autonomous, self-directed moral agents. It will not allow us to build relationships with the people—strangers and otherwise—upon whom we depend in the modern division of labor. Nor will it allow us to build relationships in which we strive to grow beyond our intimate identities, to become something more than ourselves. In the sphere of public life we relate to each other not as intimates who share identities, but as dramatic personae who have responsibilities to each other. Those relationships may be warm, personal, and familiar, but they are not intimate. They have boundaries. Familiarity in this public sphere is not comparable to the intimacy of the private sphere; we seek others because they are different from us and have something to offer us. Public life is where we seek power — not power in the sense of control of others, but in the sense of collaborative enabling or what Bernard Loomer calls "relational power."[16] We exchange — rather than give — the things which we need. In our public relationships, the defining principle is accountability, not unconditional loyalty.

Such a public life is based in the institutions of community — among which we include politics, work, education, and to a large extent, church. The social relationships of these institutions empower us in the material sense of participation in the collective efforts which provide us the means of subsistence. They also empower us in the more social sense of recognition of the roles we play for others — as their leaders, teachers, pastors, followers, students, congregants, neighbors, citizens, owners, employees, partners, and so on. In public life, we see ourselves reflected in our relationships with others.

The family and church play critical roles for persons in succeeding in both the private and public spheres. The family, though the base for private life, is critical to public life. We see the family's significance to public life as the site in which people learn what de Tocqueville called the "habits of the heart," which will inform them in their lives as citizens, workers, and parents. He visited our early Republic and found a striking resilience and energy in its families, religious life, and townships. In his analysis the family had a paradoxical but sustaining role in a democratic society. On the one hand, it served as a protected sphere which insulated adults from the "turmoil" of public life. On the other hand, by virtue of its integrity and through the specific mores derived from religion and inculcated by a nurturing adult, the family sustained its members and gave them the moderate judgment and "love of order" important in public life.[17]

In this role, the family forms — or fails to form — persons able to relate to each other in public life. Families teach the first lessons of relationships among persons, some of which are central not only to private life but to public life as well. Within the family one learns to act upon others and to be acted upon. It is in the family that we learn to identify ourselves with others — or fail to learn to love. It is in the family that we learn to give and take with others — or fail to learn to be reciprocal. It is in the family that we learn to trust others as we depend on them — or learn to distrust them. We learn to form expectations of others and to hold them accountable. We also learn to hold ourself accountable. These lessons of reciprocity, trust, discipline, and self-restraint are important to the forming of relationships in public life, in which we must play our roles and hold others accountable to their roles.

The church plays a key role in the protection of private life and in the nurturing of families. It must protect the integrity of families from the penetration of modes of relationships which threaten private, intimate relationships. It both advocates for families and helps families protect themselves.

Yet despite the importance of church to private life, it is an institution not wholly of private life but also, to a large extent, of public life. It is not only family but also community. As community, it is the forum for one to seek power. The church can support persons in their efforts to build private relationships, but it also seeks growth for its members. It is to build a priestly, prophetic, and kingly people, who will proclaim their values to the world, not only to each other. Churches become sects when their members forget their public identities.

In its role as an institution of public life, the church serves as a base from which to act. These families brought together by the church support each other in caring for each others' needs and in serving as the collective repository of wisdom and faith for developing people as human beings. These congregations of families also create a space in which people recognize each other and act in the way that the ancient Greeks met in their *ecclesia* to exchange honor and to deliberate their collective actions.

In the simultaneous separation and interdependence of these two spheres, and the various roles of family and church in supporting persons in them, there is much opportunity for confusion and failure. Understanding these helps us to understand their appropriate roles and boundaries.

Pastors play a specific, accountable role with their parishioners and the society at large. We know the confusion that can arise when pastors seek relationships with their parishioners which are only appropriate to private life.

We see in American public life how politicians sometimes seek to appropriate the loyalty of private life to obscure their accountability in public life. Some who operate without a base in private life sometimes seek their intimacy in public relationships. Others manipulate people's needs for intimacy to increase their own influence.

On the other hand, we see that the understanding of the women's movement has been held back by narrow views of the family and the need for public life. The desire of women to acquire legitimate, empowered roles—which are found not in the family, but in the institutions of public life such as work, politics, education, church—is perceived as a rejection of family life. Instead, what is needed is a conception of the appropriate integration of private and public lives.

We also see problems when people fail to learn to build reciprocal relationships in the family. They then cannot act reciprocally in public. They tend to be rigid and uncompromising.

The I.A.F. organizations, as organizations which bring together congregations of different faiths and ethnic backgrounds, create a new institutional culture for families' lives. They offer opportunities for people to combine numbers to bargain effectively with other groups in society, as do other associations such as conventional trade unions, lobby groups, grass-roots pressure groups, and so on. However, they transcend simple utilitarian political association; much as the *ecclesia* existed for Classical Greece as a forum for speech and action and for the early Christians as a space within which they created the first congregations, the I.A.F. organizations offer a public space in which modern human beings experience the open-ended-ness of relationships and of themselves.[18] Members meet, discuss, argue, convince others, change their minds; they deliberate collective action and act together. These institutions not only allow families to defend themselves, but to discover and to develop their potential. They enable humans to participate in the kind of politics that comes closest in the contemporary world to the essence of the Athenian *polis*.

Catholic social thought, if it is to be useful, must elaborate a theory and a practice of competent social relationships. One of the church's strengths has always been to recognize the power of original sin; in Niebuhr's formulation, we have the capacity to do justice, but the inclination to be selfish. We become just and overcome our selfish inclinations as we become relational. Relationships with others give us growth in our capacities to make choices in the exercise of our free will as moral agents.

Institutions in this conception must embody a framework for making choices, a culture of developing political judgment. They must carry a tradition of priorities among competing values. This tradition must exist within a culture in which there is a cultivation of leadership qualities and a genuine mentoring of persons in developing their capacities to make choices.

This role of such an institutional culture is now more essential than ever. There is a dynamic quality in all our institutional relationships that requires that autonomous human beings have deep capacities to make choices and to participate competently in democratic politics. Such participation, when informed by an institutional culture which teaches people to be their own moral agents, has the potential to instill the needed growth and confidence in a person's power. Without such a culture, without its pastors being able to teach people about power, the church runs the danger that at some point people will recognize a chasm between a static view of the world and the dynamism of their own lives.

The I.A.F. seeks integrity and robustness in private life for the family—relationships which will allow them to build healthy relationships in both private and public life. For the church we seek an integrity and robustness in public life—relationships which will protect families, both by instructing them in their private lives and by preparing their members for a meaningful public life. Let us illustrate what we mean with a story of our work.

FAMILY, CHURCH, AND SCHOOL IN FORT WORTH

One of the twelve Texas organizations of the I.A.F. is Allied Communities of Tarrant (ACT) in Fort Worth, composed of fourteen thousand families from twenty-two congregations of diverse faiths and ethnic backgrounds. It is very broad-based, involving African-American, Anglo, and Hispanic leaders from both Protestant and Catholic congregations. Formed in 1982, ACT has organized its families in a number of efforts to direct public investment to the inner city. Among other accomplishments, it guaranteed the passage of a bond referendum to finance 57 million dollars of new streets, sewers, and other improvements in 1985.

In 1986 its leaders began to work closely with the principal of a primarily African-American middle school that had all but ceased to function as anything other than a holding place for children and adults. Its students ranked last on measures of performance among the district's twenty middle schools. Half of the children were failing at least one subject. Half failed the state's writing skills test. The police were called to the school two to three times a day. Its parent-teacher organization had one or two persons attending its meetings.

ACT leaders developed a plan with the principal to rebuild the relationships among the parents, teachers, and students of the school to revitalize the school. The principal took the lead to build a leadership team within the school's staff. ACT built leadership among the parents through a two-pronged strategy.

First, congregations belonging to ACT near the school organized periodic "Recognition Days" in which the congregation as a whole would applaud children for progress at school. Each congregation takes care to recognize *every* child for some form of progress, no matter how far it has to stretch, even if a child has only raised his or her grade from an F to a D or has started attending classes more regularly. These ceremonies generally form part of the worship service. Often the homilies are directed toward recognizing and supporting families in their efforts. These ceremonies represent both a theological change in the understanding of the church's role as connected with other important areas of family life and a concrete commitment to action. Currently, twenty or more local congregations hold Recognition Days for the children of the school.

Second, ACT leaders organized a process of individual meetings in which they met or attempted to meet with every child's parent(s), regardless of whether they belonged to an ACT congregation or to any congregation at all. The building of relationships in individual meetings is slow, hard work, but there is no shortcut or substitute. The one-on-one meeting is a process of give and take. It is the means by which people begin to recognize and understand their own interests. It is how they articulate their vision of themselves and their hopes for their families. It is how they build reciprocal relationships with others.

The leaders conducted over six hundred meetings in a period of a year and a half. While leaders learned about parents' concerns through a standardized survey, they, more important, began to build relationships with them to draw them into involvement with the school. Parents attended training sessions on how to support their children's study habits. They began to meet more often with their children's teachers individually.

ACT's work renewed the vitality of the churches' families in two ways. First, it created new public spaces within each congregation, within ACT as an association of congregations, and within the institution of the neighborhood school. Families met within each institution to recognize and celebrate the worth of their children. They met together to learn about themselves, their community, and education, and to teach these lessons to others.

Second, the web of relationships forming each institution took on new, more interesting and vital significance for the families. The congregations acquired a new significance in their ability to respond to the needs of families. Relationships with administrators and teachers, which once were at best benign and at worst hostile, became collaborative. Indeed, it is unlikely that efforts to improve the school could have succeeded without the institutional support of ACT's congregations.

The most visible sign of change was the school's transformation into a successful institution. The children's performance on standardized tests rose from twentieth of the district's twenty middle schools to third. The percentage of students passing the state writing skills test increased from fifty to eight-nine percent. The percentage of children failing at least one subject decreased from fifty to six percent. Police calls fell off to virtually none. Now it is not unusual for two hundred or more to attend parent assemblies at the school to learn about drug awareness, study habits, or other education-related themes. Parents also staff an afterschool enrichment program, which ACT and the principal of the school jointly conceived and implemented. Leaders in other churches and schools have begun to duplicate this effort in another middle school and three elementary schools that feed students to them.

Beyond making the school a more successful institution, parents became successful in ACT, a mediating institution, and now could negotiate with other institutions to pursue their interests and the interests of their children. In the second middle school, parents identified the need for substantial physical renovation of the building. They drew up a 1.8 million dollar plan and negotiated it with the school board. The board approved the plan and doubled the capital spending originally allocated to the school.

Such accomplishments are only the outward signs of the organization's real achievement—the development of churches into institutions of public life which shape and support their families in both their private and public lives. Whereas before the children had been failing, the new relationships built among parents strengthened their family lives and enabled them to succeed in school. One ACT leader has commented that the project calls parents to be parents, changing the culture within families. Through their experiences in ACT, a broad-based organization committed to public life, they learn how to organize and how to act. They become empowered. They do not merely celebrate their values and their hopes as fantasies in the privacy of home or pew, but acquire the power to make them a real part of the public life of Fort Worth.

FAMILY, CHURCH, STATE, AND MARKET

As traditional institutions have declined, fewer and weaker intermediate structures operate as buffers between the individual and the larger society. In fact, Margaret Thatcher once claimed that "there was no such thing as society" at all, only individuals and families.[19] The individual operates within the market and the state without the support of the relationships of social institutions.

In this conception of society, the family no longer plays the role of a mediating institution that de Tocqueville thought so important to the development of a public persona. Instead, it is an isolated refuge, a "haven in a heartless world."[20] The family is imagined as a closed, private sphere of comfort and leisure deliberately disconnected from the stress and tension of work and politics in public life. Often the church is seen in a similar vein as a retreat disconnected from the hurly-burly of life's vicissitudes.

The principal institutions of contemporary social life are the state and the market. Whereas for earlier society, political and material life were functions integrally imbedded in other institutions such as the household or the tribe or the city, the state and market are now separate and superior in influence to other social institutions. Whereas before material relations among persons were personal and dependent upon social roles and institutions, now individuals do not control these relationships directly, but find them subject to the movement of prices through an obscured mechanism, Adam Smith's famous "invisible hand." Relationships with others are abstract, no longer the free interchange of ideas but the exchange of goods and services mediated by a myriad other unseen exchanges determining the price level.

And as we know, these relationships can become punitive when market relations become mere transactions limited only by consent, however circumscribed by inequalities of power. When market players do not have equivalent bargaining power, Adam Smith's "invisible hand" becomes an invisible fist.

Similarly, political relations in the contemporary state become abstractions, a body of impersonal rules enforced on citizens. In the state's democratic form, citizens externalize rules and then enforce them on themselves. In its authoritarian form, an elite formulates the rules. In both, the state demands conformance of actions to external rules. Its chief purpose is to create laws and to enforce obedience, not to create a forum for public life. The state is not the means to development of a person through relationships with others in public life, but a mechanism for the satisfaction of needs originating in private life independently of others. Citizens experience political life as a simple expression of internal preferences and an abstract body of rules with no higher purpose than the utility of its constituents or its elite.

It is important to recognize that if the power of the state and the market are unconstrained by other institutions, the family will not be able to sustain its role as a protected refuge for meaningful private relationships – at least not for long. Nominally external economic and political institutions will penetrate the family and shape its relationships directly.

The most direct penetration by these now-autonomous institutions can be seen in advertising and television, which now play a major role in raising families (given that American children spend more time watching television than attending school). Until recently, advertisers could not market television programs based on toys; the assumption was that such programs were designed more to increase sales of particular products than to entertain or inform in their own right. Through recent changes in Federal Communications Commission regulations, children now receive concentrated and reinforcing messages to buy particular products. Ninja Turtles, for example, are not just a movie, but a cartoon series, videos, toy dolls, games, kids' pajamas, lunchboxes, coloring books, and more. These ads saturate children's television and are designed expressly to mediate children's decisions about what they want.

To note developments such as these is not to argue against the market or against advertising per se, but to argue for counterbalancing institutions in the development of private lives, the chief of which should be the family. Unless the family is strong enough to challenge such powerful messages and teach children a different way of making decisions, the advertiser and not the family will shape the family's wants. In the current conception of market morality, neither the family nor the state nor any other institution is presumed to instruct the individual in his or her choices nor limit the advantage of the more powerful. The only limit is an individual's enlightened self-interest.

We recognize the role of the market for the coordination of economic activity. The tools of a market mechanism – money and prices – are effective signals for what is to be produced, how much, and for whom. The market is also an effective mechanism for the creation of wealth.

Yet the market has fundamental limits. It accepts grossly unequal distributions of income and power, which distort the very workings of the market process. The market mechanism seems oblivious to the many examples of market failure that lead to the externalities of pollution, environmental degradation, and social imbalance – what John Kenneth Galbraith pointed out as private splendor in the midst of public squalor.

But more important, the healthy functioning of an enterprise-market system depends on balanced relationships among society's major institutions – family, community, and church – and the market mechanism. These institutions teach the values of social intercourse, reciprocity, trust, exchange, and accountability, which are requisite for the effective functioning of the market system.

In a similar fashion, the rules of the state may initially leave for the individual and family a larger or smaller area of private life, but if unchecked by other institutions, the state will ultimately reduce it to a hollow shell. Not only does it shape public life as empty obedience and coerced profession, as Vaclav Havel has noted, but it will shrink private life to a narrow circle of consumerist pleasure. Both will be experienced as passive and ultimately inauthentic.[21] I suspect that the Eastern Europeans will discover, as we have in the West, that the market alone will not serve to organize social life satisfactorily without countervailing institutions.

As we have argued throughout this essay, we see the family as the first of the institutions essential to creating an authentic private life for people. However, it alone will not be sufficient either to support a fully meaningful moral life or to protect its own integrity. The members of families need the mediating institutions of public life that serve as forums through which they can act politically. The first of these institutions is the church, which both creates that public space and organizes associations of congregations into larger institutions.

OUR TASK

We have a twofold task for thought and action. First, we need to ensure that the family is a strong institution in and of itself. The church must continue with renewed vigor its promotion of the family's material security. Catholic leaders have long defended the concept of a family wage, an income sufficient for one wage-earner to support a spouse, children, and home. The *Bishops' Program of Social Reconstruction* first mentioned the concept in 1919.[22] The *Program* was an explicit reform agenda for national public policy, including how to structure the minimum wage, employment of women, social insurance, and other labor issues to maintain the working-class living standards raised by the war economy. The pastoral letter of the same year was less pointed in its recommendations to the state, but clearly asserted as entitlements presumably deserving the state's protection the rights of labor to organize and to a living wage.[23]

The recent pastoral on the American economy, *Economic Justice for All*, stands in this tradition. It calls on society at large and the state to make a commitment to full employment, welfare guarantees, progressive fiscal policy, and equal opportunity.[24] Such a commitment is the underpinning of a family's security.

John Paul's *Charter on the Rights of the Family* was unequivocal in supporting a decent family income:

> Remuneration for work must be sufficient for establishing and maintaining a family with dignity, either through a suitable salary, called a "family wage,"

or through other social measures, such as family allowances or the remuneration of the work in the home of one of the parents.[25]

Given the deterioration of the family wage and general economic security, the church's renewed commitment to the family's security is more important than ever. In the 1950s and 1960s an average man could earn enough to support a family comfortably. Such is no longer the case. In 1949 an average young man between 25 and 34 years old earned twelve thousand dollars per year (in 1984 dollars) and the cost of an average house represented fourteen percent of his income. By 1973 a young man of the same age earned an average of $23,500 and the cost of an average house represented twenty-one percent of his income. By 1984, however, the income of an average man in that age group had fallen to $17,500 and the cost of an average house represented *forty-four percent* of his income.[26]

The church must persevere in its effort to establish a solid economic base beneath the family, especially since other institutions—particularly the political institutions—have failed to address the family's situation. From Nixon's failed Family Assistance Plan to Carter's 1980 Families Conference to the Reagan Administration's attacks on the welfare system to Bush's veto of the family leave bill, every recent American Administration has failed to enact substantive policies to protect the family.[27] Recently a cabinet-level advisory group in the current Administration reviewed innovative approaches to reducing poverty. It decided not to do anything substantive; in the words of one unnamed official, it decided to "keep playing with the same toys. Let's just paint them a little shinier."[28]

Second, as we have argued throughout this chapter, we need to conceptualize and pursue a vision of civil society appropriate to the new demands of this age. We believe that the two primary institutions in modern times, the market and the state, have their places in social life, but must be kept in their places.[29] Without strong countervailing institutions, we face Esau's choice of selling our birthright for a mess of pottage without knowing what we have done to ourselves.[30] The imperialism of the market will dominate and penetrate all relationships, in both public and private spheres.

We have already seen contemporary politics—both electioneering and governing—reduced to mere marketing strategies. In other words, politics no longer mediates the market but is part and parcel of the market. The ad men and the consultants now shape campaigns centered not around debates of public philosophy or the governance of what Daniel Bell called the "public household," but around slashing thirty-second television ads. We now suffer even worse as the ad men and consultants attempt to govern, fashioning the rationale of war and peace by opinion polls. The result is an incoherent, inarticulate, and trivial political leadership, and a growing, cancerous cynicism and alienation among the led. The failure to center public life around genuine discourse is poisoning the reservoirs of good will in social relationships. Trust is unraveling not just in the political sphere, but in other public spheres—between doctors and patients, pastors and parishioners, teachers and students.

The culture of the twenty-first century will be one of transformation. Just as parliamentary institutions of medieval English history had to be re-created to serve in the new society of the Industrial Revolution, our existing political and corporate structures must be re-created. The family must be imbedded in new democratic institutions, which are effective mediating institutions between persons and the larger institutions of the market and the state. The family is where human beings learn the values that will sustain them as citizens, workers, and parents. It is where they learn to trust and to build reciprocal relationships. The church, centered in public life, must support them as they build forums to engage in a meaningful public life. It is to serve as an institution which organizes them and their families to act as priests, prophets, and kings.

This could be the Catholic moment, but only to the extent that the church chooses correctly between tradition—the living ideas of the dead—and traditionalism—the dead ideas of the living. It must inculcate a new spirit of entrepreneurialism, mentor its clergy in an understanding of power, empower the laity, and agitate a vision which will reconstruct the mediating institutions of public life. We must empower these efforts with the tradition and spirit of family, church, and community. For this we shall need the best of the social teachings of the church.

NOTES

1. Philip Murnion, "The Complex Task of the Parish," *Origins,* vol. 8, no. 28 (December 28, 1978).

2. These organizations include Alliance for a Better Tomorrow in Knoxville, Tennessee; Allied Communities of Tarrant (A.C.T.) in Fort Worth, Texas; Austin Interfaith in Austin, Texas; Baltimoreans United in Leadership Development (B.U.I.L.D.) in Baltimore; the Border Organization in Eagle Pass/Del Rio, Texas; Communities Organized for Public Service (C.O.P.S.) in San Antonio, Texas; East Brooklyn Congregations in New York; East Valleys Organizations in Los Angeles; El Paso Interreligious Sponsoring Organization (E.P.I.S.O.) in El Paso, Texas; Fort Bend Interfaith Council near Houston, Texas; Gulf Coast Organizing Effort in Victoria, Texas; Interfaith Action Communities in Prince Georges County, Maryland; Interfaith Community Organization in Jersey City, New Jersey; the Metro Alliance in San Antonio, Texas; The Metropolitan Organization (T.M.O.) in Houston, Texas; Pima County Interfaith Council in Tucson, Arizona; Queens Community Organization in New York; Shelby County Interfaith in Memphis, Tennessee; South Bronx Churches in New York; Southern California Organizing Committee in Los Angeles; United Neighborhoods Organization (U.N.O.) in Los Angeles; Valley Interfaith in the Lower Rio Grande Valley in Texas; Valley Interfaith Project in Phoenix, Arizona; and Valley Organized in Community Efforts (V.O.I.C.E.) in Los Angeles.

3. Sheldon Wolin, *The Presence of the Past* (Baltimore: Johns Hopkins University Press, 1989), p. 150.

4. Our reading of the tradition of Catholic social thought is based on a review of the following documents (in addition to various secondary materials): *Rerum Novarum, Quadragesimo Anno, Populorum Progressio, Pacem in Terris, Mater et Magistra, Dignitatis Humanae, Gaudium et Spes, Octogesima Adveniens, Redemptor Hominis, Laborem Exercens, Sollicitudo Rei Socialis,* the Medellín documents, and *Charter on the Rights of the Family.* We have chosen these documents as important and representative works.

5. See Donal Dorr, *Option for the Poor: A Hundred Years of Vatican Social Teaching* (Maryknoll, New York: Orbis Books, 1983), chap. 12.

6. Pope Leo XIII's document asserted these needs couched in terms not of the rights of the weak, but of first a just exchange and second the duties of the strong. Nay, in this respect, [the workers'] energy and effectiveness are so important that it is incontestable that the wealth of nations originates from no other source than from the labor of workers. Equity therefore commands that public authority show proper concern for the worker so that from what he contributes to the common good he may receive what will enable him, housed, clothed, and secure, to live his life without hardship (*Rerum Novarum: On the Condition of Workers* [Boston: Daughters of St. Paul, 1942], par. 51).

Leo also argued to the powerful that it would be prudent to protect these rights in order to avert the disruption of strikes and riots (Ibid. par. 56).

7. *Charter on the Rights of the Family* (Vatican City: Vatican Polyglot Press, 1983), cited in *In All Things: Religious Faith and American Culture,* ed. Robert J. Daly, S.J. (Kansas City: Sheed & Ward, 1990), pp. 83-94.

8. See *Rerum Novarum,* par. 71ff.

9. *Charter on the Rights of the Family,* pp. 83-94.

10. See *Rerum Novarum,* par. 72, 77ff.

11. *Quadragesimo Anno,* in *The Papal Encyclicals, 1903-1939,* Claudia Carlen, ed. (Raleigh: McGrath, 1981), pp. 415ff.

12. *Gaudium et Spes: Pastoral Constitution of the Church in the Modern World, 1965,* in *Renewing the Earth: Catholic Documents on Peace, Justice and Liberation,* ed. David J. O'Brien and Thomas A. Shannon (New York: Image Books, 1977).

13. Ibid. p. 200.

14. Pursuing the saving purpose which is proper to her, the Church not only communicates divine life to men, but in some way casts the reflected light of that life over the entire earth. This she does most of all by her healing and elevating impact on the dignity of the person, but the way in which she strengthens the seams of human society and imbues the everyday activity of men with a deeper meaning and importance (ibid., p. 214).

15. See Richard John Neuhaus, *The Naked Public Square* (Grand Rapids, Michigan: William B. Eerdmans, 1984).

16. Bernard Loomer, "Two Conceptions of Power," *Criterion* (Winter, 1976), pp. 12-29.

17. But when the American retires from the turmoil of public life to the bosom of his family, he finds in it the image of order and of peace. There his pleasures are simple and natural, his joys are innocent and calm; and as he finds that an orderly life is the surest path to happiness, he accustoms himself easily to moderate his opinions as well as his tastes. While the European endeavors to forget his domestic troubles by agitating society, the American derives from his own home that love of order which he afterwards

carries with him into public affairs (Alexis de Tocqueville, *Democracy in America*, vol. 1 [New York: Alfred A. Knopf, 1945], p. 315).

See also the argument of Robert Bellah, et al., *Habits of the Heart: Individualism and Commitment in American Life* (New York: Harper and Row, 1986), p. 86.

18. See Richard J. Bernstein, "The Meaning of Public Life," in *Religion and American Public Life: Interpretations and Explorations*, ed. Robin W. Loven (New York: Paulist Press, 1986), pp. 29-52.

19. Margaret Thatcher, cited in Kenneth O. Morgan, *The People's Peace: British History, 1945-1989* (New York: Oxford University Press, 1990), p. 438.

20. For the development of this argument, see Christopher Lasch, *Haven in a Heartless World: The Family Besieged* (New York: Basic Books, 1977).

21. See Vaclav Havel, *Living in Truth* (London: Faber and Faber, 1989), pp. 3-35.

22. John Tracy Ellis, ed., *Documents of American Catholic History* (Milwaukee: Bruce Publishing Company, n.d.), pp. 611ff.

23. *The National Pastorals of the American Hierarchy (1792-1919)* (Westminster, Maryland: Newman, 1954), pp. 265ff.

24. See *Economic Justice for All: Catholic Social Teaching and the U.S. Economy*, in *The Catholic Challenge to the American Economy*, ed. Thomas M. Gannon, S.J. (New York, Macmillan, 1987), pp. 297ff.

25. *Charter*, p. 93.

26. Frank Levy, *Dollars and Dreams: The Changing American Income Distribution* (New York: Russell Sage Foundation, 1987), pp. 79, 68.

27. See Daniel P. Moynihan, *Family and Nation* (San Diego: Harcourt, Brace, Jovanovich, 1986).

28. *New York Times*, July 6, 1990, p. 1.

29. See Arthur Okun, *Equality and Efficiency* (Washington: Brookings Institution, 1977).

30. For a discussion of the Esau story, see Wolin, pp. 137-50.

11

THE FAMILY

The Challenge of Technological Change

SIDNEY CALLAHAN

The family and technology are uniquely characteristic of human beings. Only humans develop self-conscious kinship systems or create innovative complex operations for work. While other animals can be conscious, execute intelligent moves, and possess preferential bonds, only human beings create technology or family ties. These creations are inextricably linked in human history because they both depend upon large capacities for abstract thinking, upon human abilities to feel a wide range of intense emotions, and upon the possession of mobile and incredibly complex bodies.

To understand one's membership in a family requires high intelligence. However we define the structure or delimit the boundaries of the family, it is conceptually a lawful kinship system which consists of interrelated roles and identities — mother, father, husband, wife, sister, brother, grandparent, cousin, and so on. Only humans have the brain power to imagine and keep in mind the abstractions involved in a set of kin relationships; "my family" is a complex conceptual abstraction that has an existence for me beyond my experiences of concrete face-to-face interactions. Moreover, human kinship bonds require an ability to maintain intense, enduring emotional attachments beyond immediate gratifications and frustrations.

Family formation, family bonding, and family survival depend upon human capacities for foresight, memory, promises, commitments, and an ability to feel intense emotional attachments enduring across generations and over spatial separations.[1] More to the point, human kinship bonds are the crucible for developing responsible duties and the unique human sense of moral obligation to others.

Technology is also a distinctive human characteristic that requires high-

174

powered rational and emotional abilities. If we loosely define technology as purposely applying knowledge in order to effect a predictable outcome in the environment, then technology includes all rational methods, tools, and operational techniques devised for reliably accomplishing goal-oriented enterprises.[2] Today we recognize that technology is far more than the creation and operation of tools and machines for industry or transport. After all, a machine is essentially a material representation or crystallization of a set of efficient operating principles employed to solve problems by deploying laws of energy and force. Technology is materialized problem-solving or embodied rational thinking, today developed in tandem with modern science. Since the electronic revolution, many sophisticated subtle technologies have been employed in medicine, communication, information processing, and psychosocial forms of behavior control.[3]

Like the creation of kinship, the creation of technology also depends upon high capacities for human reasoning, human emotions, and human imagination. Humans can imagine and desire the perceived world and present conditions to be different than they are. To create technology human beings must first imagine that there can be better, as yet unknown ways to live and work, and then persevere in efforts to create new solutions to complex challenges. Chimpanzees and children may use simple tools for immediate short-term aims, but they cannot imaginatively reason well enough or sustain enough unwavering desire to work or to invent new complex operations.

Once a new technology is devised, however, creative human intelligence is built into the machine or technique; it takes less brains or emotional commitment to use the technology invented by others. This built-in intelligence inherent in technological inventions can present dangers. Children, adolescents, and mentally warped and retarded thugs can pull triggers or push buttons to produce consequences that they could never have created on their own. Technology amplifies human capacities so that even stupid people can do great harm.

Unfortunately it is also true in a fallen world that highly intelligent humans can choose to pursue destructive goals inventing and using technological means. We only have to think of the Nazi Holocaust or Hiroshima to understand the dangers of invention. Technology, like all other human cultural creations (even things as basically good as language, religion, or the family), can be used or abused. Ever since the invention of the hand axe, if not before, it has been obvious that many technological inventions can be used for either good or bad ends, depending upon the goals and intentions of the user. The tool can serve as a weapon—power, human agency, and increased efficiency can be two-edged in effect.[4]

More intriguing and worrisome still is the fact that some technologies over time may change their nature and effects; some rational operation once begun with good motivations for a good end may over time produce unanticipated harmful side effects. Or a technology may become a runaway process endangering human flourishing or destroying the physical environment. Even well-meaning intelligent people can reason incorrectly and initiate technological disasters. The annals of medicine and case studies in the new discipline of environmental ecology are replete with instances of promising technical innovations which later turned out to be harmful and destructive.

With increasing human capacities for freedom, reason, creativity, and technical control there are increasing choices to be made. With every increase of power individuals and groups must assume increasing moral and ethical responsibility to do good and avoid harm. The morality of creating, employing, and prudently managing an exponentially exploding technology is a complex task — and grows more difficult as technological progress moves closer to the biomedical sources of human life, death, reproduction, and the family.

Human societies and governments have been challenged to keep pace with the speeded-up developments of scientific and technological innovation. Technology builds upon itself and upon scientific discovery; once something is done new things never before imagined become possible and thereby may become the object of new desires. The force of what has been called the technical imperative drives a society to do what can be done.[5] Such forces stimulate continuing, undirected, and mindless technological innovation. The prudent human response is to initiate and exercise ever more vigorously reasoned human capacities for self-conscious moral evaluations followed by political control of technology.

New disciplines of technology assessment, risk assessment, and bioethics have emerged to try to assess social environmental costs and moral dangers *before* a technological innovation is discovered or widely deployed. We cannot always wait to see the data on whether some innovation is harmful, for a technology once introduced may bring irreversible and destructive consequences. Governments have slowly begun to act to assess, control, limit, ration, or ban technological progress as well as initiate and shape progress.[6] Professional groups and other institutions (like the church) have also recognized the importance of regulating technology. Medical technology and reproductive technology have been a particular focus of concern, since such technologies intimately affect life, death, and the health and well-being of individuals, families, and society.

THE FAMILY AND REPRODUCTIVE TECHNOLOGIES

Every technology has to be analyzed and assessed within its social context. The challenges of new reproductive technologies have to be understood within the existing social conditions of a particular society. In the industrialized twentieth century, technological innovations have transformed work, medicine, communications, housing, education, the landscape, leisure, and every other facet of life, including reproduction. The invention of antibiotics, infant formula, electricity, refrigeration, television, the automobile, the factory, computers, and so on, have had a profound impact on family life.

The family always mediates between the individual and the larger society; families affect society and in turn are affected by the society's technological and economic system. The family's reproductive, caretaking, and nurturing functions—producing, feeding, sheltering, and socializing the dependent young, as well as caring for the dependent old—are shaped by the technology available to the family. The family in a nomadic hunter-gathering social group operates differently from the family in a settled agrarian society, or the family in an industrialized or post-industrial world with access to modern medicine and modern reproductive technologies.

Reproductive technologies can be loosely defined as all those methods for initiating or limiting fertility that depart from traditional cultural and folk practices. Humans have always used sexual abstinence, delay of marriage, withdrawal, long lactation, abortifacient herbal potions, and infanticide to limit the number of children. On the other hand, efforts to induce fertility and increase reproduction—by folk medicine, magic, polygamy, and early marriage—can claim an equally long pedigree. The custom of procuring children through adoption is also an ancient practice. It is well to remember that families decreased the average number of their offspring in Europe before modern technological methods to control births were introduced.[7]

After worldwide industrialization new medical technologies developed and have radically changed the family by changing infant mortality rates, life expectancies, childbirth, health care, illness, dying, and reproductive technology. With modernity, mandatory schooling, and the passing of agrarian economies, family values and reproductive behavior change. Children in agrarian societies are cared for and educated at home and, in addition, can be immediate social and economic assets by providing labor and help in caring for siblings. But children in post-industrial societies require extensive education away from home and in general require longer and longer periods of vigilant protection, emotional nurturing, and economic support.

With the growth of ideologies that value individual children as unique potential persons—and when medical care ensures that children will have a good chance of surviving to adulthood—family reproductive strategies change. Parents tend to shift from producing high quantities of children to producing fewer children who are given a high quality of parental investment over longer periods of time.[8] Most families in complex technological societies cannot give large numbers of children the educational resources their children will need to participate in the economy as independent adults, capable of founding and supporting families of their own.[9]

As agrarian groups give way to societies with increased economic, educational, and psychological standards of childrearing, family size decreases. Ironically, the small families once characteristic of nomadic hunter-gatherers are again adaptive in modern industrialized societies. Mothers may not have to carry physically their nursing and toddler offspring during the tribe's long treks in search of food and water, but modern demands on parents to provide, protect, educate, and socialize children are equally arduous—and undoubtedly more psychologically stressful.

Changes in family conditions and the high values placed upon children have stimulated in modern technological societies the production of an increasing array of reproductive technologies. Contraception, sterilization, abortifacients and surgical medical abortions have been technological innovations used in the limiting of reproduction. Sophisticated uses of new medical and physiological information about fertility cycles, coupled with technological methods for information feedback, such as taking body temperature by thermometers, have also been used in limiting fertility.

At the same time, other extensive and increasingly sophisticated medical technological innovations have been devised and employed for treatments of infertility. As the steps in the cycles of fertility and processes of conception have been understood by medical research, new therapies have been devised to remedy infertility in married couples who do not conceive.[10] As all who watch television now know, some of these processes employ artificial extracorporal fertilization and the creation of embryos in the laboratory, often with the subsequent freezing of "spare" embryos before insertion in the mother. Other new techniques, more mindful of concerns for embryonic life, do not attempt fertilization outside the woman's body, but try to induce pregnancy by artificially procuring and conveying the parental couple's sperm and eggs to propitious locations at propitious moments in the fertility cycle.

The most drastic technological interventions have separated genetic, gestational, and social reproduction by using third parties, who supply what an infertile couple lack. There now exist an array of various new forms of collaborative reproduction in which third parties supply sperm, eggs, embryos, and wombs for gestation, in various combinations, in order to achieve the reproductive goal of taking home a child. Collaborative reproduction with sperm donations, egg donations, embryo donations, and surrogate mothering in two forms, challenge the traditional legal and social definitions of the family. Who is the mother? Who is the father? As the notorious Baby M case made clear, these new reproductive technologies produce new social, legal, and moral problems. Surrogate motherhood has been the subject of numerous state task forces charged to devise new laws and social policy.[11]

Another controversial array of reproductive technological innovations involves techniques of prenatal testing, genetic assessments, and prenatal treatments for the fetus. Extensive enterprises of genetic counseling and genetic screening aim at avoiding genetic disease or the presence of other birth defects in the family's offspring. The use of abortion as a means of controlling the genetic quality of offspring has been widespread—even to the point of genetic testing and abortion for sex selection. Moral questions about the use of all of these extensive new reproductive technologies have arisen and engendered a great deal of moral uncertainty as well as more legal and social conflict.[12]

The society now faces basic questions about the purpose of sexuality, the nature of parenthood, and the definition of the family. What are morally acceptable goals and morally acceptable means in the realm of human reproduction? Is there, for instance, an individual moral right to reproduce so that single persons or homosexual couples should not be denied access to reproductive technologies? Who should be allowed to use what medical reproductive technologies for what purposes? Are there destructive or immoral reproductive technological processes which should not be permitted? These are religious, moral, and political questions of great complexity and of great import. What guidance can be given by Catholic social thought to individuals, families, and societies facing the challenges of reproductive technology?

MORALLY EVALUATING THE CHALLENGE OF REPRODUCTIVE TECHNOLOGY

In the light of faith informed by reason Catholics approach the questions of reproductive technology and the family. I think there is an emerging Catholic consensus on these questions despite the number of disputes and disagreements which also exist. Beyond the differences over method and substance that divide the church, the general affirmations which follow have also become clearly envisioned and agreed upon.[13]

1) God has created humankind in God's own image and enjoined humans to be creative and procreative. Human creation of technology and the founding of families are both intrinsically good exercises of God-given stewardship over the creation.

2) The goal of human work and family living is human well-being and dignity as persons. This goal is in accord with God's revelation that love, equality, solidarity, and justice should reign on earth, in the church, and in the family as domestic church. Human technology and human cultural creations of family are to be judged by how closely they embody and further the love, truth, and justice revealed in the gospel news of redemption. All members of the human family and of particular families, no matter what their power, sex, and status, are morally equal.

3) Sin and evil exist. Reproductive technologies, like other human capacities and powers existing in a broken world, can be used to harm individuals, families, and society—whether through ill-will or ignorance. Human beings must individually and collectively morally evaluate specific reproductive technologies and attempt to further good consequences and deter harmful effects by social and legal means.

While all within the church might agree with the above general affirmations, there are disputes when the discussions become more specific. Science and technology, for instance, have not always been seen as compatible with religion. One thinks of recent fulminations against organ transplant technology, against secular humanism, or the not-so-distant persecution of Teilhard de Chardin. Yet today most Christians will celebrate the creative enterprise of science and technology as a human achievement which is God-given.

As God creates, works, and loves, so humans made in God's image are called to create, work, and love, and to exercise a grateful stewardship of their powers in developing the world. Christians who believe in an infinite, benevolent Creator of a dynamically evolving lawful universe naturally imagine that there are greater and greater understandings of reality waiting to be discovered and comprehended. The religious and scientific quests for Truth are alike in their imagining of the existence of intelligible realities and truths beyond what is visible to the eye. All creation awaits human discovery, development, and transformation, for the greater glory of God and the love of humankind.

This general affirmation of science and technological progress is tempered, however, by the Christian recognition of the existence of sin and evil. We know that technology can also be a means for humans who choose to reject the good and harm others and themselves to do so more efficiently. Severe critics of the human condition have often repudiated all use of power and technology. Other more radical critics affirm the ascetic path of complete detachment from the world, even declaring that the individual self and ego which desires, wills, and becomes attached to one's work, or one's family, must be overthrown in the final search for spiritual transcendence. Family ties, technology, and all organized social institutions are seen as obstacles for the purist. Catholic Christianity has for the most part clung to its incarnational beliefs and never gone the radical route of total asceticism and repudiation of embodied selves, love, sex, marriage, procreation, or work in the world.

God's mandate to Christians is not to leave the world but to transform it for the glory of God. When evil, sin, and scandals come, human minds and hearts must discern the deformations of the institutions and creations of culture, and work for reform. Using our God-given reasoning powers and our God-given faith, Christians embark upon the work of prudent appraisal of reproductive technology. But at this point, when it comes to how we are to go about making detailed moral prudential judgments of sex, marriage, family living, and reproductive technology, differences and disputes within the Catholic church appear.[14]

My own view is that Christian exercises of prudential moral judgments consist of holistic recursive reflexive processes in which many sources of knowledge are integrated. In the process of morally deciding challenging dilemmas we mull over the questions and engage in many circuitous, back-and-forth activities of consciousness. We weigh revealed truths (as they are currently expressed and understood); consider the church's tradition and its evolution over history; listen to religious mentors and the current magisterium; apply rational ethical principles (as they are currently understood); gather current scientific and social facts and paradigms (always fairly "soft" and constantly changing); search our minds, hearts, and imagination for insights, as well as hidden sources of personal irrationality and self-deceit; and consult our personal experiences of life through memories, dialogues, literature, art, worship, and prayer. Out of all of this practical reasoning and pondering, we decide. This is neither a deductive, inductive, nor single infallible authority-driven process, but rather an inward, outward, top-down, bottom-up, reflexive, recursive process engaging all of our personal resources.

After much reflection perhaps it can be seen that reproductive technologies, like other technologies, fall into three main groupings. There are technologies which are always destructive and harmful, and there are technologies that are almost always enhancing of the person's dignity and well-being. Then there are fairly neutral technologies that can be used either for good or bad ends, depending upon personal intention, context, and the conditions of their employment.

Destructive technologies are characterized with built-in harm-doing. Poison gas, napalm, germ warfare, nuclear bombs, and torture and brainwashing techniques can be seen as intrinsically evil in their assaults on human dignity and well-being. Certain technologies should never have been invented, but once invented should be banned and absolutely forbidden. Many of the disagreements within the church over reproductive technologies have to do with which interventions should be judged as being always immoral. (Similar arguments seem to take place in arguments over weapon technology and theories of just war.) Do technologies which directly assault, dismember, and destroy embryonic and pre-born human life fall into the immoral group? Should technologies which use third parties to separate genetic, gestational, and social parenting be seen as socially destructive and so forbidden? I think the answer to these questions is yes, but here can only sketch out my reasoning.[15]

Should, on the other hand, non-abortifacient contraceptives, sterilization, and in vitro fertilization which artificially aids a couple to have a child be seen as technological acts which are immoral? I think not. In my judgment these are instances of reproductive technologies that can be used either for good ends or for immoral purposes, depending upon an array of subjective and objective factors and existing conditions. These are technologies which do not inherently destroy embryonic life or destroy the rights or bonding or dignity of persons. With these technologies the moral challenge is to analyze and discriminate between acceptable and unacceptable intentions, conditions, contexts, goals, and outcomes. Of course in doing so one has to remember that harmful side effects or long-term destructive consequences of a technology can be physical, psychological, social, or moral.

By contrast we can see how certain technologies can almost always by their operation be life-giving, curative, and enhancing of the whole person's welfare. Many educational, rehabilitative, and medical technologies are wholly beneficial and can inspire only gratitude for their invention and development. Reproductive technologies which enhance maternal and fetal health are such good inventions. Other techniques of fertility regulation which are based upon fertility awareness, information feedback, and consensual marital cooperation can be seen as in this category. So too, certain sophisticated prepared childbirth techniques enhance personal freedom and dignity by employing the whole person and partners actively in the technique.

TECHNOLOGIES AND HUMAN DIGNITY

Many technologies endanger human dignity by their tendency to turn a human being into an object or thing. Evil depersonalizes, destroys, numbs, and negates integrity and personhood, and technology can sometimes contribute to depersonalization and numbing. Humans can be degraded by becoming enmeshed and subsumed in a technological process. A person becomes a mere cog in some assembly line, an interchangeable appendage to a machine or repetitive production technique. The whole person is no longer integrated, or willing and acting as an "I," but becomes an "it," a pair of hands or a back, or a machine's guiding system. In reproductive technologies a person can be reduced to the part or function of sperm donor, egg provider, or gestating womb. Feminist analyses of the new reproductive technologies have criticized the regressive and potentially exploitative effects of many of the new techniques.[16]

It is dehumanizing for a whole person to be reduced solely to an isolated part or function, even if it is a talent, a skill—or a reproductive function. It is also obvious that one can be more totally depersonalized by technology when one's body or mind is the passive object of a technique or the subject of research and experimentation. Medical technological treatments for infertility can end up treating a person as nothing more than an object or technical problem.[17] All sorts of "people work" in which persons become entities in ongoing technological operations have their psychological and social dangers for those who control the process and for those being controlled or worked upon.

The pervasive use of efficient technologies can subtly engender expectations that persons take on the characteristics of their machines or machine-like operations. "I am a camera," or "I am a programmed computer, with only input and output." While prevailing market forces may tend to turn persons into their external money value, pervasive impersonal technologies can tend to reduce persons into machine-like operating systems to be efficiently programmed by outside powers. We begin to think of ourselves as powerless before larger forces in the environment — and expect those around us to be equally helpless, or compliant cogs. Our worst nightmares are no longer of becoming a weak animal among jungle predators, but of becoming a numbered mindless slave robot in a grinding concentration camp factory. In new feminist dystopias, the nightmare goal is being reduced to existence as a reproductive slave.[18]

Humans can lose their sense of wholeness, their inner sense of subjective well-being as unique sources of agency, personal action, and creative work. As the self is deformed so is the other; other human beings are no longer seen as the source of their own personal will, desires, attachments, and social interactions. Sexual partners can become objects and offspring viewed as commodities to be made and unmade at will. In reproductive technologies there is a danger that the desire for a child can be deformed. Instead of accepting the gift of a child who will be an equal member of one's human community, the child becomes an object of parental desire who must meet certain criteria to be acceptable.

There can be many immoral completely selfish motivations for having children, just as there are for avoiding procreation. The technological imperative can lead persons to put personal self-will, control, and efficiency before other values. In this sense "a contraceptive mentality" can encourage a personal entitlement to absolute technological control of reproduction; when reproduction is seen as a personal right, to have or not have a child, then the culture can be on the slippery slope to social abortion and exploitative methods of collaborative reproduction.

There are major moral problems with collaborative third-party reproduction such as artificial insemination by donor (AID), egg and embryo donations and maternal surrogacy. First, donors or surrogates are reduced to a reproductive function so that their reproductive powers are separated from the rest of their person. These practices may also be economically exploitative when commercialized, since the rich will always hire the poor. Moreover, the moral tie between one's reproductive potential and morally responsible parental behavior is broken. Societies should not wish to encourage men and women to be able to donate sperm and eggs, or gestate offspring, disavowing future long-term commitments.

Moreover, the child who is the result of collaborative reproductive technology is deprived of the family ties that all other humans enjoy. One intentionally acts beforehand to cloud genetically the child's existence so that genetic father, mother, and other extended kinship relations are either unknown or unavailable. Bonds between generations and grandparents and their grandchildren have also been severed in collaborative third-party reproductive technologies. Sibling ties and bonds are also threatened, especially if surrogate mothers have children and then give their children's half-brother or half-sister away. When such things are countenanced, children are even less secure in their families. On the other hand, children who have been made to order under contract enter into the family less as an equal to all other entrants and more under the inordinate pressure of the exercise of parental will.

When third-party collaboration involves the genetic contribution of a male or female donor or surrogate, the exclusive bond between parents is broken. The symmetry of relationships within the family is disturbed; one parent is biologically related to the child, while the other is not. There are intrafamilial repercussions from asymmetry in biological kinship. In adoption, on the other hand, two parents can be equal in their contractual commitment to rescue a child or meet an accidental or unplanned social crisis. Using third-party reproductive technologies to give lesbian and homosexual couples their claimed right to a child is a completely unknown innovation and social experiment in which children are subject to risks and subjected to parental will and desire. The moral problems and drawbacks of collaborative reproduction are increased by such procedures.

Technological challenges to the nuclear family have made us reassess and reappreciate the family as an institution. The nuclear family existing within an extended kinship network is a socio-cultural invention that has stood the tests of time and cultural competition. Male and female pair-bonding within a supporting kinship network has worked to ensure that offspring are nurtured and socialized. Single parenting, communal parenting, and state parenting have all been seen as inadequate—particularly in a culture like our own in which a person has to operate at high levels of individual initiative and responsibility.

With new understanding of child development, family systems analysis, and the importance of psychological nurture and lifetime kinship connections, we realize how important healthy families are for the fate of a civilization. Not only is the family the humanizing means for moral socialization and acculturation, but the goal of most human effort and the source of most human happiness. The intense bonds of family serve as a humanizing bulwark against the depersonalizing forces of the marketplace, the world's worship of achievement and productivity, and technological bottom lines.

Equal well-being, equal rights, and moral dignity of all members within the family are not only components of a Christian moral ideal, but also furthers the flourishing of a family as a strong cohesive group. Good morality and good psychology and good social policy are in accord. Unitive bonding between sexual partners is valuable for its own sake, but also because it strengthens the stable nurturing available for dependents. In strong families persons learn to value and feel obligations to their own future progeny, both as their kin and as fellow human beings with morally equal status. Extended kinship relationships in the family should also be strengthened, since kin help young parents support the nurturing enterprise.

Sexual bonding, marriage, and procreative ties of kinship are such important goods that they sanction the use of reproductive technologies which are not destructive. In my judgment, remedial technological efforts to help a couple have their own child can strengthen the bond between parents and their child, when carried out properly. The effort to have a child — with all of the personal sacrifices of time, money, and cooperation involved — tests the parental commitment to each other and the child. These children, even when extracorporally conceived in IVF, are not collaboratively manufactured by third parties, but are the result of parental sacrifice and cooperation aided by the remedial power of medicine.

But as remedial technologies for married partners, such fertilization techniques should not be used except for parents who in normal conditions would be able to have their own children and be able to give them good enough parenting by cultural norms. The moral difficulties with technologies which aid parents to have their own children lie not in deforming a biological act or breaking a marital bond but in protecting the human conceptus from abuse.

Mammalian in vivo reproduction has the advantage of protecting the offspring within the mother's body and through long gestation predisposing further investment and protection. Human embryos or humans in the embryonic stage of development, which can be separated from parental protection and can be routinely frozen, are without protection and open to abuse and exploitation. Adequate protection for embryonic life from direct assault, abuse, and experimentation would have to be built into a remedial reproductive technology to ensure that it would be morally acceptable. I think this safeguarding can be done. Efficiency, cost, parental will, and medical desires to experiment should not overwhelm ethical respect for the rights and dignity of embryonic human life. Such moral safeguarding is equally important in determining which forms of genetic testing and interventions should be done.

The technologies which regulate and limit birth can also serve the wellbeing of individuals, marital partners, and the family as a whole. Technologies for limiting and regulating births should also aim at strengthening the bond between sexual partners, strengthening the ties of the family as a whole, and ensuring moral responsibility in the use of one's reproductive potential to create new life. When the human conceptus is counted as a member of the greater human family and a member of the family of its progenitors, then methods which kill prenatal human life would be forbidden. If in the family equal justice is owed women, children, the sick, the handicapped, and the dependent old, then stages of development or other forms of power do not sanction abuses of power for the ends of the more powerful.

However, technological methods of birth control and sterilization which are not abortifacients do not destroy embryonic life or destroy bonding. Indeed, since sterility is more "natural" over a female lifespan than intermittent fertility, a decision for female sterilization does little but speed up what is the inevitable cessation of fertility. Contraception and sterilization should be morally acceptable when used for good ends and in good contexts.

These technologies should be seen as a neutral category. They are used for good purposes when they are used for protecting life and health; for example, when they are used to execute responsible decisions to limit the number of children for the good of the family as a whole. Contraception and sterilization are particularly valuable when they can strengthen marital sexual bonding by allaying anxiety, avoiding sexual abstinence, and increasing the frequency of sexual intercourse. Marital sexuality is a calling, and contrary to some celibate concerns over unbridled lust it can be a creative endeavor to keep sexual desire alive and well in the midst of stressful modern marriages.

Marital sexuality is a good means to increase psychological unity, and its cultivation should be encouraged. The reasons given for a ban upon contraception seem too narrowly focused upon biologically concrete details of each single act.[19] To insist upon an analysis of each sexual encounter seems misguided; the relevant unit of analysis should be the whole bond, the whole relationship as it exists in and endures through time. To judge a person's sexual act within a marriage only by isolating its physiological characteristics repeats the worst features of the dehumanizing depersonalization inherent in a technological deformation of life. Christians should be the last people who would want to view the human body as a mindless reproductive machine separated from subjective human consciousness and interpersonal purposes. Is it not better to see that the psycho-social good of the whole person and the good of the whole family are more important than the functioning of a part?

And so the arguments and discussions go on. I have only skimmed the surface of many difficult questions here in order to initiate and stimulate reflection for the future.

LAST THOUGHTS

Many complex and difficult moral challenges exist and will continue to emerge as science and technology progress. Moral discernment and prudence will be required by all responsible segments of society. The church for its part will seek to teach and learn as it grows in its understanding of the good news and its mission to create a civilization of love. Slowly Christians have begun to realize and fully understand that human technology, like sexuality, marriage, and the family, is a gift of God. Christians will continue to struggle for wisdom and prudent exercises of their moral responsibilities in the world, aspiring always to develop work and communities worthy of our Maker. Reproductive technologies can be assessed, regulated, and selectively used for the enrichment of human life.

NOTES

1. See Kathleen Gough, "The Origin of the Family," *Journal of Marriage and the Family* (November 1971), pp. 760-68; see also Peter J. Wison, *Man the Promising*

Primate: The Conditions of Human Evolution (New Haven: Yale University Press, 1980).

2. See Peter Caws, "Praxis and Techne," in *The History and Philosophy of Technology,* ed. George Bugliarello and Dean B. Doner (Urbana: University of Illinois Press, 1979), pp. 227-37.

3. One of the most helpful and astute discussions of technology is that by Hans Jonas, "Toward a Philosophy of Technology: Knowledge, Power and the Biological Revolution," *The Hastings Center Report,* vol. 9, No. 1 (February 1979), pp. 34-43; a historical approach to the specific American scene can be found in Harold G. Vatter, "Technological Innovation and Social Change in the United States, 1870-1980" in *Technology, the Economy, and Society: The American Experience,* ed. Joel Colton and Stuart Bruchey (New York: Columbia University Press, 1987), pp. 19-56.

4. These ideas of agency and making are creatively developed in Elaine Scarry, *The Body in Pain: The Making and Unmaking of the World* (New York: Oxford University Press, 1985).

5. A most pessimistic view of technology is given by Jacques Ellul, *The Technological Society* (New York: Vintage Books, 1964).

6. See Daniel Callahan, *What Kind of Life: The Limits of Medical Progress* (New York: Simon and Schuster, 1990).

7. See Jane B. Lancaster and Chet S. Lancaster, "The Watershed: Change in Parental-Investment and Family-Formation Strategies in the Course of Human Evolution," in *Parenting across the Life Span: Biosocial Dimensions,* ed. Jane B. Lancaster, Jeanne Altmann, Alice S. Rossi, Lonnie R. Sherrod (New York: Aldine de Gruyter, 1990), pp. 187-205.

8. Robert A. LeVine and Merry White, "Parenthood in Social Transformation," in *Parenting Across The Life Span: Biosocial Dimensions,* ed. Jane B. Lancaster, Jeanne Altmann, Alice S. Rossi, Lonnie R. Sherrod (New York: Aldine de Gruyter, 1990), pp. 271-93.

9. See Alice S. Rossi and Peter H. Rossi, *Of Human Bonding: Parent-Child Relations Across the Life Course* (New York: Aldine de Gruyter, 1990); see also E. E. LeMasters and John DeFrain, *Parents in Contemporary America: A Sympathetic View* (Belmont, California: Wadsworth Publishing Company, 1989).

10. See Lori B. Andrews, J.D. and Lisa Douglass, M.A., *Alternative Reproduction,* Technical Paper 14; see also Lori Andrews, *Between Strangers: Surrogate Mothers, Expectant Fathers and Brave New Babies* (New York: Harper and Row, 1989).

11. See, for example, The New York State Task Force on Life and the Law, *Surrogate Parenting: Analysis and Recommendations for Public Policy* (May 1988).

12. For one Catholic response, see The Catholic Health Association of the United States, *Human Genetics: Ethical Issues in Genetic Testing, Counseling, and Therapy* (St. Louis: CHA, 1990).

13. These core affirmations appear in significant and much-noted church documents of very different times and places such as the Vatican Council statements on marriage and the family and the recent Vatican Instruction on Respect for Human Life. See *Pastoral Constitution on the Church in the Modern World,* Part 2, chap. 1, "Fostering the Nobility of Marriage and the Family," pp. 248-58; Preface and Part 1, chap. 1, "The Dignity of the Human Person," pp. 199-222; *The Documents of Vatican II,* ed. Walter M. Abbott, S.J. (New York: New Century Publishers, 1966); see also, Congregation for the Doctrine of the Faith, *Instruction on RESPECT*

FOR HUMAN LIFE in Its Origin and on the DIGNITY OF PROCREATION, Replies to Certain Questions of the Day, Vatican Translation (Boston: Daughters of St. Paul, 1987).

14. See, for instance, the contrast between viewpoints in documents gathered by the Catholic Health Association and documents appearing in a publication of the Pope John XXIII Medical-Moral Research Center. See The Catholic Health Association of the United States, *Responses to the Vatican Document on Reproductive Technologies* and, by contrast, articles by Ralph M. McInerny, John M. Haas, and William E. May in *Reproductive Technologies, Marriage and the Church: The Pope John Center* (Braintree, Massachusetts: The Pope John XXIII Medical-Moral Research and Education Center, 1988).

15. A fuller statement of the points made here can be found in Sidney Callahan, "The Ethical Challenge of the New Reproductive Technology," in *Medical Ethics: A Guide for Health Professionals*, ed. John F. Monagle and David C. Thomasma (Rockville, Maryland: Aspen Publications, 1988), pp. 26-37; see also Sidney Callahan, *In Good Conscience: Reason, Emotion and Intuition in Moral Decisionmaking* (San Francisco: Harper Collins, 1991).

16. See, for instance, as a representative sample, Carolyn Merchant, "Mining the Earth's Womb," in *Machina Ex Dea: Feminist Perspectives on Technology*, ed. Joan Rothschild (New York: Pergamon Press, 1983), pp. 99-117; Barbara Katz Rothman, *The Tentative Pregnancy* (New York: Viking Press, 1986); and Norma Juliet Wikler, "Society's Response to the New Reproductive Technologies: The Feminist Perspectives," *Southern California Law Review*, vol. 59, no. 5 (July 1986), pp. 1043-57.

17. For a gripping personal account complete with interesting reflections and references to other feminist literature, see Paul Lauritzen, "What Price Parenthood?" in *The Hastings Center Report*, vol. 20, no. 2 (March/April 1990), pp. 38-46.

18. See the best seller by feminist Margaret Atwood, *The Handmaid's Tale* (New York: Ballantine, 1986).

19. For a defense of *Humanae Vitae*, John Paul II's approach to contraception, see John M. Haas, Ph.D., "The Inseparability of the Two Meanings of the Marriage Act," in *Reproductive Technologies, Marriage and the Church: The Pope John Center*, pp. 89-106.

12

HUMAN SEXUALITY

Toward a Consistent Ethical Method

RICHARD A. McCORMICK, S.J.

The first half of 1990 produced two interesting episcopal happenings. The first was the employment by the American bishops of a public relations firm (Hill and Knowlton) and a pollster to get across more effectively their teaching on abortion. The second was a series of listening sessions on abortion conducted by Archbishop Rembert Weakland with the women of his archdiocese (Milwaukee). These may seem to be unrelated events; indeed, they probably are. But I see them as profoundly significant and contrasting metaphors.

The employment of a public relations firm to shore up the episcopal teaching effort suggests a great deal about the teacher, the taught, and the teaching. I do not believe it is unduly straining matters to say that the public relations metaphor suggests that the teacher has done all that is necessary to be in possession of the truth, that the teaching is indeed sound and complete in all respects, but that those to be taught—at least significant segments of them—have not understood this truth or have not been persuaded by it. More sophisticated packaging may succeed where preachment has not. If various pro-choice groups use such professional packaging to their advantage, why should the bishops be chastised for doing so?

Weakland may agree with that or he may not. But his own procedure took a different direction. Because the unequivocal teaching of the Catholic church has not gained the full support of many Catholics, especially women, Weakland wanted to find out why. As he worded it: "Listening is also an important part of any teaching process; the Church's need to listen is no exception." Weakland went on to say of the faithful women of his archdiocese: "I have faith and trust in their wisdom and honesty. I knew I had much to learn from them that I had not heard yet. Listening seemed absolutely necessary to me." And learn he did: "Not only did I learn much, but most of the participants said they did too."[1]

I find Weakland's statements extremely interesting. His assertion that "listening is also an important part of any teaching process" can be understood in two ways, both of which are true and germane to my topic. First, listening as a part of teaching can refer to the inescapable need to consult all sources of knowledge and wisdom before one draws normative conclusions. This would seem to be obvious to anyone who rejects a quasi-magical notion of the church's magisterium. As Weakland words it: "The Church's need to listen is no exception."

The second understanding of listening as a part of teaching is that one teaches *by* listening. The very act of listening is itself instructive and enlightening, and indeed about the very matters that constitute the concern of listening. What I have in mind, of course, is that the teacher who sincerely and genuinely listens communicates many things: a sense of the dignity, worth, and importance of those listened to; a sense of the honesty, openness, and humanity of the teacher; a sense of the realism, importance, and limitations of the teaching itself. These "senses" render us much more docile and favorably disposed to what is ultimately concluded. We might say that such "senses" help us to see more clearly. Thus it is that Weakland can conclude that "not only did I learn much, but most of the participants said they did too."

My subject is concerned with a consistent ethical method. The use of "toward" in the title implies that no such consistency exists where official teaching is concerned. In his stimulating book *An Inconsistent Ethic? Teachings of the American Catholic Bishops*,[2] Kenneth R. Overberg, S.J., has richly documented the difference in approach of the bishops to social and so-called personal morality. In the first instance their teachings amply reflect the characteristics of sound moral reasoning: biblical, communal, dynamic, personal. Thus the teachings are empirically oriented, tentative, open to change, collaborative, and so on. By contrast, matters of personal morality are deductive, nontentative, authoritarian, noncollaborative, heavily reliant on past statements, and so forth. A kind of double standard prevails. The same observations are generally valid with regard to documents of the Holy See. On the one hand, we have *Octagesima Adveniens, Populorum Progressio* and *Laborum Exercens*; on the other, there is *Persona Humana, Humanae Vitae, Donum Vitae, Inter Insigniores*, and the C.D.F.'s instruction on homosexuality. I do not believe it is unfair to apply to these latter documents the characteristics just noted (deductive, nontentative, authoritarian, noncollaborative, heavily reliant on past statements). The upshot is that these documents by and large do not teach if by that term we refer to the personal engagement of individuals in a way that opens their eyes, sharpens their sensitivities, and enlightens their minds. That means that they fail in their primary and most basic mission.

What has gone wrong? There are probably many dimensions to an adequate answer. But one key dimension that cannot be overlooked is that church authorities have not listened adequately. If "listening is also an important part of any teaching process," as the astute Rembert Weakland rightly contends, it is no wonder that the church's sexual teaching is not effective.

If the church's authoritative teachers engaged in genuine listening in the sexual sphere, what would their sexual teaching look like? I believe it would have precisely those characteristics whose absence is now lamented. These traits touch above all the way the church goes about building and communicating her teaching. Several years ago in the Nash Lecture, I listed ten characteristics I hoped to find in moral theology in the year 2000. With one or two modifications these are precisely the characteristics I believe genuine listening would produce in the area of human sexuality. These may look like wishful thinking given the present posture, proclivities, and procedures of some Roman authorities. But even wishful thinking can serve a useful purpose. I will list eight characteristics that I would hope to find in sexual tutelage.

PERSONALIST

I use this term in a specific sense and in a quite restrictive context. The context is the determination of the morally right and morally wrong of human actions. The specific sense is that it is the human person in all facets and dimensions who is the criterion of this moral rightfulness and wrongfulness. That formulation is meant to contrast with an approach that employs an isolated dimension of the human person as criterion.

I do not think it is unfair to say that some earlier Catholic approaches fell into this trap. John Courtney Murray referred to this as the "biologist interpretation" and argued that it confused the "primordial," in a biological sense, with the natural.[3] Thus we find Franciscus Hürth, S.J., an influential advisor to Pius XI and Pius XII, laying heavy stress on biological facticity. "The will of nature," he says, "was inscribed in the organs and their functions." He concluded: "Man only has disposal of the use of his organs and faculties with respect to the end which the Creator, in His formation of them, has intended. This end for man, then, is both the biological law and the moral law, such that the latter obliges him to live according to the biological law."[4] For this reason, John C. Ford, S.J., and Gerald Kelly, S.J., wrote in 1963: "One cannot exaggerate the importance attached to the physical integrity of the act itself both in papal documents and in Catholic theology generally."[5]

For example, there are repeated references in *Humanae Vitae* to *naturales leges* (n.11) and *biologicas leges* (n.10). The same is true of *Familiaris Consortio*.

Vatican II moved beyond such "physical integrity" when it proposed as criterion "the person integrally and adequately considered." As Louis Janssens words it: "From a personalist standpoint what must be examined is what the intervention as a whole means for the promotion of the human persons who are involved and for their relationships."[6]

I mention this personalism because, while it is explicitly honored in some recent official documents (for example, *Donum Vitae*, the C.D.F.'s document on reproductive technology, explicitly refers to the integral good of the human person as the key criterion), many of us believe that an older biologism reappears when (indeed, whenever) there is a question of specific conclusions and applications.

INDUCTIVE

This follows from the personalism I noted above. Whether our actions or policies are supportive of persons or detrimental to them cannot be deduced from general principles. It takes time and experience. And the church must have the patience to provide for this maturation process. In the decades prior to Vatican II a much more deductive approach was in evidence.

This is clear in the gradual transformation of social teaching in the church. As the Jesuit editors of *Civiltà cattolica* point out, this teaching evolved through stages.[7] *Rerum Novarum* represents the first stage. It was dominated by "Christian philosophy" and a "rigidly deductive" method. This had two shortcomings. First, it left no room for the relevance of the sciences (economics, sociology, political science). Second, and as a consequence, doctrinal elaboration was seen as an exclusively hierarchical task, lay persons being merely "faithful executors."

The second stage covers the pontificates of Pius XI and Pius XII and may be called the stage of "social doctrine." *Quadragesimo Anno* used this term for the first time. It referred to an organic corpus of universal principles still rigidly deduced from social ethics. However, there is greater emphasis on the historical moment and applications of principles to practice, hence the beginnings of a reevaluation of the place of lay persons in the process.

The third stage began with John XXIII. John moved from the deductive to the inductive method, his point of departure being the "historical moment," to be viewed in light of the gospel. This led to a complete reevaluation of the place of lay persons vis-à-vis social teaching, a reevaluation completed by Vatican II. Lay persons do not simply apply the church's social teaching; they must share in its very construction.

This is an interesting development. One thing seems clear: a similar development has not occurred in all areas of Catholic moral theology, for instance, familial and sexual morality. If a clearly deductive method, one that left little room for the sciences and lay experience, prevailed in the elaboration of social teaching, it is reasonable to think that the same thing occurred in familial and sexual morality. And if this social method has evolved since John XXIII, it is reasonable to think that the same thing ought to happen in all areas of church teaching.

ECUMENICAL

Vatican II acknowledged the ecclesial reality of other Christian churches, the presence of the Spirit to their members, and the grace-inspired character of their lives. It encouraged ecumenical dialogue and work, and it relaxed its discipline on common worship. Pointedly it stated:

> Nor should we forget that whatever is wrought by the grace of the Holy Spirit in the hearts of our separated brethren can contribute to our own edification.[8]

The Council took this with utter seriousness and stated:

> In fidelity to conscience, Christians are joined with the rest of men in the search for truth, and for the genuine solution to the numerous problems which arise in the life of individuals and from social relationships.[9]

In our times one would think that ecumenism in moral discourse would be a given. Yet let me share a sneaking suspicion. It is this: ecumenical procedure is honored *except where the Holy See has taken an authoritative position in the past.* In those areas — and we all know what they are — consultants are chosen only if and because they agree with past formulations. Others, even and especially Catholics, are positively excluded. That this is a threat to ecumenical dialogue is clear. It is also clear that threats to such dialogue are threats to the church's credibility as well as its growth in understanding and witness.

What will the Catholic church learn from ecumenism of method on sexual questions? That is, of course, hard to say in advance. It is also difficult to predict what other Christian groups might learn from the Catholic church. But let me offer one possibly fruitful area of discussion — the relation of the unitive and procreative.

In *Donum Vitae* the C.D.F. states:

> The Church's teaching on marriage and human procreation affirms the "inseparable connection, willed by God and unable to be broken by man on his own initiative, between the two meanings of the conjugal act: The unitive meaning and the procreative meaning."[10]

The quote within the quote is taken from *Humanae Vitae.* But this encyclical and the C.D.F.'s instruction understand this inseparability as applying to each conjugal act. It is interesting to note that other Christian groups have supported a similar principle but understood it differently. They have asserted that the unitive and procreative dimensions should indeed be held together, that married love should be generously life-giving, and that pro-creation should occur in the context of covenanted love. But they have viewed such inseparability as something to be realized in the relationship, not in the individual act. Is there in this view something that could instruct the magisterium?

MODESTY AND TENTATIVENESS

Karl Rahner once composed a "Dream of the Church." He imagined the pope speaking to an ecumenical group and saying:

> The ordinary magisterium of the pope in authentic doctrinal decisions at least in the past and up to very recent times was often involved in error and, on the other hand, Rome was accustomed to put forward and insist on such decisions as if there could be no doubt about their ultimate correctness and as if any further discussion of them was unbecoming for a Catholic theologian.[11]

This is not just the *stylus curiae*. It seems to be a perennial temptation of those to whom there attaches both jurisdictional and teaching authority. There is the seemingly irresistible penchant to prescribe and proscribe *urbi et orbi* with utter certainty and forever. It is as if teaching would not be taken seriously unless it is proposed for all ages.

Thus, for example, in the C.D.F.'s *Inter Insigniores* (1976) the norm of not ordaining women to the priesthood is said to be observed "because it is considered to conform to God's plan for his church."[12] That is a theological lock-in. It is quite possible, I believe, to oppose ordination of women (I hasten to say that I do not) for reasons and with analyses other than that.

In this connection it would be dishonest to overlook what has been referred to as "the dogmatization of *Humanae Vitae*." That phrase refers to the way the present pope connects the central concrete conclusion of *Humanae Vitae* with doctrinal truths. Thus, those who deny that every contraceptive act is intrinsically evil are said to deny God's goodness and providence. The Cologne Declaration[13] protested such escalatory moves. I agree with the protest. Not only do such moves involve a thinly veiled coercion; more important, they are at odds with centuries of Catholic tradition which refused to view concrete moral imperatives as emanating from mystery.

PLURALISTIC AND COLLABORATIVE

I put these two together because I believe that official Catholicism has yet to learn how to view and use pluralism in a positive way. Open and honest collaboration could go a long way toward solving this problem.

There is something in the Catholic spirit that seems to feel the need for absolute agreement and conformity, even to the most detailed applications of moral principles. I think I know what that something is. It is a past authoritative teaching and practice that thought it possible to dot every "i" and cross every "t" on very detailed matters and imposed such certainties in a quite forceful and vigorous way. Public questioning of such conclusions was simply unacceptable. Such imposed uniformity created expectations about Catholic unity that were intolerant of pluralism. There is still a rather noisy but tiny minority that believes we cannot disagree about, for example, in vitro fertilization between husband and wife, or about withdrawing artificial nutrition and hydration from persistently vegetative patients without forfeiting our basic Catholic unity.

In the United States these attitudes are concretely symbolized in the case of Charles Curran. Curran has repeatedly stated that his differences with authoritative pronouncements have three characteristics: 1) They concern matters remote from the core of the faith; 2) they are matters heavily dependent on support from human reason; 3) they are involved in such complexity and specificity that logically we cannot claim absolute certitude in their regard.

I do not want to rehearse this issue here. Nor do I want to *promote* pluralism. Pluralism in these matters is a fact, not dominantly a value. But it is a fact that we should come to expect and accept peacefully, especially in a church second to none in its reliance on the presence of the Spirit to its members. Yet we have not. Among the examples of unfair exercise of church authority, Alain Woodrow listed the "elaboration of Catholic moral doctrine by a Roman teaching authority which ignores or contradicts the opinion of experts, specialists, commissions and local moral and pastoral theologians, particularly in the field of human sexuality."[14]

ASPIRATIONAL

Moral theology will continue to be concerned with practical problems and problem-solving in the domain of sexuality. And it should be. Rightfulness and wrongfulness of conduct, while secondary, remain important. But a too-exclusive concern can diminish other extremely important aspects of morality and collapse morality into moralism.

To make this point let me distinguish between an ethics of minimal duty and an ethics of aspiration. The former is by and large minimalist, concerned with the negative, with uniform standards and legislative sanctions. Of it we may say what John Courtney Murray stated of the notion of natural law:

It does not show the individual the way to sainthood, but only to manhood. It does not promise to transform society into the City of God on earth, but only to prescribe, for the purpose of law and social custom, that minimum of morality which must be observed by the members of a society, if the social environment is to be human and habitable.[15]

If I read the signs of the times correctly, there are very many people who, while by no means denying the importance of the "human and habitable," want more. They want an ethics of aspiration — one that is demanding, positive, aesthetic, centered on who they might become. This is particularly true in the sexual sphere where the most fundamental challenge is to mature to the point where sexual expression can be the language of profound friendship and other-concern.

COMPASSIONATE

Very little need be said here. The point should be fairly obvious. St. Paul wrote: "For I do not do the good I want, but the evil I do not want is what I do. Now if I do what I do not want, it is no longer I that do it, but sin which dwells within me. So I find it to be a law that when I want to do right, evil lies close at hand" (Rom 7:15-17). We live in a broken world and share its brokenness. The jar of our ancient fall profoundly dislocated our whole being and threw us out of harmony, and even as redeemed we must daily die if we are to live. Our brokenness will appear in our sexuality in many ways, above all perhaps in exploitative conduct.

The church's sexual tutelage, if it is to succeed in enlightening us at various stages of our lives, must never forget our brokenness. What institutional forms this compassion and reconciling function will take is still to be worked out in several important areas (for example, the divorced and remarried, the homosexual community).

FEMINIST

I mention this as a characteristic of sexual teaching because I think it true to say that the woman's perspective has been notably absent in the formulation of Catholic sexual morality. Daniel Maguire pointed out some time ago that the experience of women gives them certain advantages in moral perceptivity (for example, at-homeness with bodily existence, integration of affect in moral judgment, association with children).[16] By contrast, the experience of macho-masculine culture has in varying ways impeded male sensitivity (for example, by proneness to violent modes of power, anticommunitarian tendencies, disabling abstractionism, consequentialist bias, fear and even hatred of women).

If sexual ethics in the Catholic community is affected by the above characteristics, it will be en route toward consistency with the development of social ethics. Possible? Yes, but only with a conversion of attitudes in high places.

NOTES

1. Weakland's "Response" plus a "Summary Report" of the hearings are in *The Catholic Herald*, May 24, 1990.

2. Kenneth R. Overberg, *An Inconsistent Ethic? Teachings of the American Catholic Bishops* (University Press of America, 1980).

3. John Courtney Murray, S.J., *We Hold These Truths* (Kansas City: Sheed and Ward, 1960), p. 296.

4. F. Hürth, S.J., "La fécondation artificielle: Sa valuer morale et juridique," *Nouvelle revue théologique* 68 (1946), p. 416.

5. John C. Ford, S.J., and Gerald Kelly, S.J., *Contemporary Moral Theology: Marriage Questions* (Westminster, Maryland: Newman, 1963), p. 288.

6. Louis Janssens, "Artificial Insemination: Ethical Considerations," *Louvain Studies* 8 (1980), p. 24.

7. "Dalla 'Rerum novarum' ad oggi," *Civiltà cattolica* 132 (1981), pp. 345-57.

8. *Documents of Vatican II* (New York: America Press, 1966), p. 349.

9. Ibid., p. 214.

10. "Instruction on Respect for Human Life in Its Origin and on the Dignity of Procreation" (Vatican City: Vatican Polyglot Press, 1987), p. 26.

11. Karl Rahner, "Dream of the Church," *Tablet* 180 (1981), pp. 52-55.

12. Austin Flannery, ed., *Vatican Council II: More Post-conciliar Documents* (Northport, New York: Costello Publishing Co., 1982), p. 338.

13. *Tablet* 243 (February 4, 1989), pp. 140-42.

14. Alain Woodrow, "The Rights of the Christian," *Tablet* 243 (February 4, 1989), pp. 776-77.

15. Murray, p. 297.

16. Daniel C. Maguire, "The Feminization of God and Ethics," *The Annual* (Society of Christian Ethics, 1982), pp. 1-24.

PART III

WORK IN
CATHOLIC SOCIAL THOUGHT

13

THE ECONOMIC PASTORAL LETTER REVISITED

ARCHBISHOP REMBERT G. WEAKLAND, O.S.B.

Since the time of Pope Leo XIII Catholic social teaching has become an integral part of the church's self-consciousness. The body of that teaching has grown most rapidly in recent years for two reasons. First, the document of Vatican Council II on *The Church in the Modern World* has brought social issues more clearly into the light of the gospel and its practical application to our times. Second, many nations have taken up the challenge of Pope Paul VI in *Populorum Progressio* to make an analysis of the applications of the teaching necessary to an ever-changing situation in every nation. In doing so, new problems have been faced and thus new plateaus reached.

The economic pastoral letter of the bishops of the United States, *Economic Justice for All: Catholic Social Teaching and the U.S. Economy*, passed overwhelmingly by the United States bishops in November 1986, is perhaps the most extensive of these national reflections. By now the immediate impact of the document has ceased and it is time to assess some of its strengths and weaknesses in the light of a constantly changing economic scene. In fact, one could easily say that the document would not be written in the same way if it were written today. Changing times demand a fresh look. In this essay I would like to examine just a few of the areas that were not treated at great length or were treated inadequately in that pastoral letter—items that may be of more importance for the future.

SYSTEMIC CONSIDERATION

As the East bloc moves from its Marxist approach to economic issues to a more capitalist stance, many questions about the very systemic nature of

201

capitalism arise. These were already being asked earlier but were avoided in the bishops' letter, lest it turn out to be an academic treatise rather than a pastoral document. It is inevitable that a comparison must be made today between the United States approach to capitalism, which is deeply rooted in Enlightenment philosophy, and the present practice of such countries as Japan and Korea, which have not known in their history an Enlightenment and have a different mix of the private and public sectors as well as a different societal makeup that is less individualistic. Many are posing again questions about the very nature of capitalism and what happens to it in a culture that has sprung from a different philosophical matrix.

The economic pastoral avoided an in-depth analysis of these questions. It was agreed upon at the outset by the writing committee that the approach would not be theoretical but phenomenological.

The short paragraphs in the letter that treat the systemic questions are found in the middle of the document, almost buried there, and seldom cited (par. 128-31). Here the bishops try to be evenhanded, but in reality accept that the system as such is not immoral and then proceed to point out ways in which it must be improved. The debate over the essentially immoral nature of capitalism that has raged for decades in Latin America was thus avoided. On the other hand, all know that it has not been solved to the satisfaction of most participants.

Since the publication of the first draft of the economic pastoral letter in 1984 the contributions to this debate in the theological sphere have not been numerous. It should not be surprising that most of this type of discussion has taken place outside of the United States. I would like to cite here two noteworthy contributions.

In November of 1985 Cardinal Ratzinger gave a talk in Rome to a group of assembled German industrialists. His talk was entitled "Market Economy and Ethics."[1] The cardinal framed his remarks around four sets of questions. Given his general theological positions, so contrary to the whole Enlightenment project, it was not surprising that he raised some of the most critical questions about the free market and its philosophical roots.

His first set of questions emphasized the contradiction between the claims of freedom and the deterministic nature of the market system. "Deterministic in its core (*in ihrem eigentlichen Kern deterministisch*)," was his description. Thus, he stated, the system can, but does not necessarily work for the common good. The development of the spiritual powers of the human person must also be a part of the economic agenda and here the capitalist system has nothing to contribute. He sums up these first observations by saying that the "market rules function only when a moral consensus exists and sustains them."

In his second set of questions Ratzinger brings forth the inability of the market to help those nations where the inequality is so large that they find themselves outside the competitive arena and thus seek centralized economic controls as the only answer for themselves. Although these attempts have not born the fruit some may have hoped for, the author does not a priori dismiss them as morally unfounded.

Third, the cardinal questions the ability of the Marxist approach to solve the question of inequality, since it too is deterministic, more radically so than even liberalism. Here he sees points in common in the deeper philosophical presuppositions of the two systems. One would expect that the cardinal would reject this Marxist approach because of its reduction of ethics to history and party strategy.

The fourth set of questions the author raises in terms of a dialogue between church and economy are those that the bishops of the United States totally avoided. In their crassest form they are summed up in a quote from Theodore Roosevelt, made in 1912, that Cardinal Ratzinger cites: "I believe that the assimilation of the Latin-American countries to the United States will be long and difficult as long as these countries remain Catholic." He also quotes a 1969 lecture of Rockefeller in Rome where the latter recommended replacing Catholics in Latin America with other Christians, an undertaking, Ratzinger asserts, that is in full swing. It is not surprising that Ratzinger recalls the thesis of Max Weber that certain Christian denominations have a closer affinity to the capitalist agenda than others.

Ratzinger here shows a certain negativism with regard to post-World War II economic development and the role of the United States. He said in that lecture in 1985: "On the other hand, we can no longer regard so naively the liberal capitalistic system (even with all the corrections it has since received) as the salvation of the world. We are no longer in the Kennedy-era, with the Peace Corps optimism; the Third World's questions about the system may be partial, but they are not groundless." Here the cardinal opened up again the old controversies about capitalism being more congenial to some denominations than to others, an argument that most have intentionally avoided in the past decades, at least since the writings of Max Weber on the Presbyterians and capitalism. Should it be opened again? The cardinal certainly thinks so.

These ambiguous statements by the cardinal, not taken to their ultimate conclusions, show nevertheless a deep distrust of the capitalist system, especially as manifested in the United States. By phrasing his concerns more in the realm of questions, he does not have to find an alternative solution. He comes the closest to doing this when he states that the subjective and the objective in ethics in the economic system must meet and specifically in those handling the system itself. "It is becoming an increasingly obvious fact of economic history," he remarks, "that the development of economic systems which concentrate on the common good depends on a determined ethical system, which in turn can be born and sustained only by strong religious convictions."

Ratzinger does not openly condemn capitalism as intrinsically evil, but he does come close to it in the many questions he raises. Perhaps this is why his lecture, given to a conservative group of capitalist industrialists, has not been much quoted by the neo-conservative economists or political writers. He makes the point quite clearly that the former discussions on this point are not finished. It is disappointing that Ratzinger does not go further into the area of objective ethics, as he called it, in the economic realm. It would have led him into the kind of systemic analysis that is needed from an ethical point of view. Nevertheless, his conference raises some of the most serious objections to capitalism and its determinism that can be found in Catholic literature today. Theologians of liberation theology might be surprised by his defense of their criticisms of capitalism.

But the most extensive and comprehensive critique of the bishops' economic pastoral letter comes from Brazil from the pens of Clodovis and Leonardo Boff. Writing in the *Revista Eclesiastica Brasileira* in 1987 these two authors make a lengthy and minute examination of the economic pastoral letter under the title, "A Igreja perante a economia nos EUA – Un olhar a partir da periferia."[2] I omit here the words of praise that are raised about the letter to get at the substance of the most severe criticisms they launch against it. The tone, by the way, of the response is clear and friendly, even when it is basically critical.

They object to the fact that the capitalist system itself was not called into question. "Without doubt the American bishops strike vigorously at the apparatus; yet, they do so only to repair it and not to replace it." The reason why they sense the American bishops are not capable of tackling the system as such is that the basic presuppositions of their socio-analytic tools do not permit them to do so. One could say that the basic difference here is that the two authors do not perceive of any middle class in their analysis of society. They see only the rich and the poor, even when they approach the American phenomenon. They are correct when they state that in the United States the "option for the poor" is not an adversarial slogan that pits one group or class against another. Class conflict is not the type of analysis used by the American bishops and this, in the mind of the Brazilian authors, vitiates the analysis used.

Perhaps, however, a deeper division in approach is evident in that the American bishops did not accept the economic dependency theories that make the poverty of the Third World the result of exploitation on the part of the capitalists of our First World. This causal relationship is nowhere accepted in the economic pastoral letter, but it is presupposed by many Latin American authors.[3]

It must be asserted that these theories were examined by the bishops' committee drafting the letter, but never accepted as proven. Other elements, such as corruption in Latin American governments, had to be factored into the equation, as well as the enormous amount of capital flight taking place from Latin America to the United States. Nevertheless, the lack of clear analysis of the position that the American bishops were taking on these points, so crucial to Latin American authors, diminished the enthusiasm with which the letter was read and accepted by other areas of the world.

The two strongest criticisms from this sector are focused on the fact that the bishops did not have a clear and enunciated social theory to accompany their economic analysis, nor did they answer the question raised by Latin Americans and that is based on the dependency theories: Is poverty, or is it not, an integral component of the capitalist system? Is the capitalist system intrinsically evil? Does it exploit the poor to fill the coffers of the rich?

They criticize the letter as being a functional analysis of capitalism and not a systemic one. They do not believe that the system can be repaired and fixed, because it is systemically flawed. They also criticize the letter as taking only an ethical and never a political approach to economic issues. That is why such words as *exploitation* or *domination* do not exist in the letter, they say. This criticism joins that of some other critics in the United States who found the letter totally lacking in a perception of the relationship between economics and political power.

For all these reasons the authors find the document of the United States bishops flawed, even though they praise its worthwhile attempt and openness.

These two approaches to the systemic questions, that of Cardinal Ratzinger and that of the Boff brothers, which were for the most part omitted in the economic pastoral letter, are cited because they do point out an agenda that is not finished. Because the American bishops did approach the subject in a functional manner and not in a theoretical and systemic way, they have left themselves open to criticism that the basic philosophical foundation from the Enlightenment upon which capitalism and free market economies are based has not been carefully scrutinized for its ethical content. This task remains as yet undone.

There seems to be a need to do so today, not just because of the third-world analysis and experience, but because of the new kinds of approaches to capitalism from Japan, Korea, and now the East bloc. How much of the Enlightenment roots are left in those new phenomena?

Another reason for pursuing this examination comes from the large number of scandals in the United States economy in the last decade that are of much concern, namely, the Wall Street abuses and the pathetic and tragic situation of the Savings and Loans. Not to examine how these may be indigenous in the system because of greed and the tendency to monopolize would be a lack of objective research. It seems that we can never get away from the whole theory of what greed is and when good self-interest turns into pernicious greed. Does the system make such distinctions between the subjective and the objective almost impossible?

ETHICAL *VS.* BIBLICAL CATEGORIES

The drafting committee of the bishops made the decision that the presentation of principles that should be used to judge an economic system would proceed on two parallel tracks. The first would be a biblical analysis; the second would be ethical, in the sense that it would come out of the Catholic tradition of using the natural law and more philosophical approach. It was hoped that in this way the debate in the public forum could take place on specifically Christian grounds, that is, from the biblical perspective, and then also from the philosophical point of view to engage those who did not share our biblically grounded faith.

Probably this approach mirrors the state of moral theology in the Catholic church today. Nevertheless, it was soon seen in the discussion that followed the issuing of the pastoral letter that this sharp distinction was not necessary. There was a need to bring these two approaches together into a single synthesis. Most readers who shared our values but not their biblical basis did not see a need to separate the two categories. Most Catholics would have liked to have seen the two joined; they wanted to see the philosophical supported by the biblical vision.

This project of joining the two visions is a necessary one. Such a composite vision would gain more support for the convictions that derive mostly from natural-law theories. Perhaps the one area where the joining of the two would be most difficult is in the whole question of subsidiarity. To my knowledge there has not been a moralist who has shown how that concept, as proposed by Pope Pius XI and used by every subsequent pope, fits into a biblical perspective. Even its derivation from natural law is not clear. It is just stated as a fact or a principle by Pope Pius XI and not rationally based in scripture or in any traditional philosophical system. Its historical roots are evident from what it is fighting against, namely, state corporatism, but its source in Catholic tradition is not clear.

This question has a certain importance since it serves as a link to so many other Catholic approaches to society, government, and economics. Does it inevitably lead to the principle that small is beautiful? Even in its original formulation and in the way it has been repeated by papal documents it admits that some issues are of such a nature that they can only be decided by the larger national or international bodies.

Many of the questions and some of the terminology of the classical writers on capitalism should also be examined in the light of the biblical vision. So, for example, as already cited, the question of self-interest and its excess in greed has not been analyzed carefully. I am not sure that the terminology is good. Perhaps one should rephrase the whole issue, today in particular, not in the light of greed or self-interest, but in the light of the obligation, personal and communal, to take care of one's responsibilities. Even the accumulation of wealth, not just its creation, must be seen in such a light. There should be a way of seeing the creation of wealth as having as its first purpose the common good and then as its second aim that of helping the individual take care of personal and communal responsibilities.

The fear exists that these issues will continue to haunt the discussion if they are not faced squarely and correctly. The pastoral letter of the United States bishops treats economic questions in a positive way; that is, it tries to see how the system should function, what aims it should have, who should be affected by it, and how all should participate in it. These are all admirable aims. But the letter does not treat of the dark side, the dangers and pitfalls, so explicitly. These questions are not analyzed as minutely as the goals that should be there because they have traditionally been seen as more in the realm of private morality. But the issue remains of how private or subjective morality affects the whole question of the functioning of the system itself.

Perhaps this is the perspective that Cardinal Ratzinger raises when he says that the objective and the subjective aspects of the ethical discourse in economics should be joined. Greed is a subjective aspect that influences the running of the system. Exploitation of workers is a subjective ethical question that affects the outcome of the system. One could name many more of these subjective issues. Their biblical roots should be evident.

The objective questions, on the other hand, deal with the whole issue of the built-in qualities of the system itself, which tend to cause the system to malfunction or function in a way that is harmful to society or the individuals in it. For example, monopolies have always plagued capitalism. Since the system is based on competition, monopolies endanger the system as such. From this perception arose the need for clear governmental regulations so that competition, being essential to the system, can function in a way that benefits all and respects the rights of all. The economic pastoral letter does not treat explicitly the whole question of monopolies and how in the history of the capitalist system, if some outside regulatory force is not present, monopolies prevent the system from working for the good of all. This systemic question is most important today when there is no international force that can regulate monopolies in an economy that is already international and interdependent. Perhaps no other systemic question will be so urgent for capitalism in the future than that of monopolies.

Questions about chronic recessions and the resultant unemployment are systemic issues. The whole area of inequities and the manner in which the rich seem to get richer in the system as the poor seem to have so little access to the capital needed to enter the system is another systemic problem. This problem is more talked about today than even when the economic pastoral was issued. Such inequalities in society where the gap between rich and poor continues to grow at such a rapid pace is a systemic issue since it derives from the way the system functions. The "have's" have more to invest and, thus, their wealth grows at a faster rate. Taxing was usually seen as one of the principal ways of equalizing such growing gaps. But taxing is outside the system and acts as a corrective to the system itself.

Government has become for capitalism the great regulator. But the role of government can also be positive in stimulating the economy, in providing funds for research, and the like. This role of government is crucial to any analysis of economic theories and practice. It is not clear in the pastoral letter how government and the economic factors intersect. In the hearings we heard from those on the more libertarian side of the scale, who held that least government is best and that the market would by itself regulate all, to those who were inclined to socialistic solutions that involved government at all levels. These issues that center around the role of government and the economy are still unsolved, but they are of extreme importance if one looks at the new scene today. The rising capitalist nations have a different perspective on the relationship between the state and the private sector than does the United States. In this respect our history is unique.

The church in its social teaching has had a positive attitude toward government, more positive than that of many current political groups in the United States, but it has not tried to ground that view—taken, for the most part, from natural-law tradition—into its biblical vision.

In this same area of concern, many rightly criticized the economic pastoral letter as naive, in that it did not treat of the relationship between power and the accumulation of wealth. The Latin American critics used the categories of money and politics quite freely in their critique. There is no doubt that this lacuna does pose a problem in the letter. Perhaps it would have entailed a keener analysis of the role of economic entities in the United States and their influence on the political system. I am sure the bishops thought this would have taken them far afield from the original intent of the letter. On the other hand, one cannot omit the fact that there is a close relationship between government and the power that comes from money and its use. The Bible has much to say about this latter question, but to my knowledge no one has asked similar questions concerning power and its proper use in biblical terms.

These questions become ever more real to us as we see the power of international financial entities in comparison to the financial, political, and social power of many nations. Some businesses are more powerful than the nations they function in.

In this connection the discussion of economic power enters into the whole question of the role of nations, the rights of nations, the sovereignty of nations. Since our economy is now international and interdependent in its scope, and since the boundaries of nations in this regard have become less clear, the whole question of the concept of nation is now being brought into question. This issue will grow as one of the most important in our contemporary history. We see so many areas of Africa, Asia, and especially now the Eastern bloc assert their historical national roots—based on racial and ethnic diversities—at a time when, economically speaking, the question of nations is posed in a serious way with regard to viability in the future.

The economic letter seemed to ignore these larger questions, even though it was aware of the need to confront the new economic situation that is one of interconnectedness around the globe. Questions of government and its role, questions of monopolies in an interdependent economy that defy national boundaries, the effects of monopolies on economically weaker nations, questions of national sovereignty in the light of multinational corporations that are bigger and more powerful than the nation itself—these issues go beyond the biblical and ethical vision that is presented in the letter and demand a new look in a new world.

In this respect one could also say that environmental issues were not faced in the letter. The section on agriculture in the original plan was to treat natural resources in general. The drafting committee had already proceeded to hearings, for example, on coal and like resources. All of this involved the future of this planet as such. This plan was not followed because of the urgency of the farm situation, but that does not mean that the issues of natural resources and ecology were unimportant for an analysis of economic structures and will disappear. They must also be treated from the biblical perspective.

BIBLICAL SPIRITUALITY AND THE ECONOMY

Although many commented favorably on the final chapter of the economic pastoral letter as being practical and helpful, there was still some feeling that it was not helpful enough. It was not clear to priests how to preach the abundance of material found in the document. It was also not clear to many of the laity how to apply these principles in their daily lives and in the workplace. They appreciated the role of liturgy and the fact that the church itself must be just in its economic relationships, but they wished more of a blueprint for themselves.

Perhaps the most difficult pastoral task that is yet to be accomplished is to make people aware of the communal nature of their vocation both as a human person and as a baptized member of the church. This is a question of attitudes that must be faced if the contents of the letter are to be put into practice. So many sociologists point out the nature of our society and the Lockean individualism that permeates it. These fundamental influences, which go back to the founding of this nation, have been recently reinforced by psychological concerns about the self that can reach the point of a kind of collective narcissism. Combating such extreme individualism but coupling it with a wholesome respect for self and one's identity and worth will not be easy. The best way to help the economy, however, is to alter some of the selfish attitudes that pervade the society. In this way the goals of society change and the aims of the economic system are broadened.

Simultaneously, people must become more aware of their societal duties. We have used frequently the phrase "common good" in Catholic social teaching in the past, but it is not an active concept in the lives of so many. The church's approach to economic issues is very much connected with this term. Other modes of expression, such as solidarity and participation, are helpful and useful.

Perhaps the most difficult attitude is one of moving from charity to advocacy. Charity is a necessary Christian virtue, but it is not an economic solution to any problem. It is easy to preach charity and thus to alleviate the signs of a problem at once. But the ultimate solution must be to help people to participate in the life of society by being able to make their contribution and not to become wards of society. To this day I cannot understand those who criticized the economic pastoral letter of the bishops as being a proponent of a large welfare state. This was to distort the very message of the letter, which was one of participation. In the opening paragraphs that was made clear as one of the marks upon which an economic system would be judged.

Nevertheless, people do need more help in sorting out in their daily lives how they should respond to our economic system. They also want to know how they should live in a society that is market-driven and where they are bombarded daily by so much advertising and forced to consider so many things they do not need or want. These perennial questions are now joined with those of ecological concern on both a micro and macro level.

Such problems of living a good Christian life in this day and age are compounded by the international, intercultural, and interracial aspect of our world. We now relate also to those who live thousands of miles away from us. Here the contrasts of rich and poor are even more startling and seem even more hopeless.

Perhaps one of the principal duties of the church today should be to continue to give everyone a sense of his or her individual worth, while at the same time trying to create for all the incentives that are needed to take care of one's own responsibilities and then to contribute also to society. The church did well in the past in this area, and there is every reason to feel that it can continue to do so now.

Catholic social teaching, and in particular the economic pastoral letter of the United States bishops, is not an economic plan for the future, but the values in them are indeed valid for building a better and more just future for all on the planet. The times we live in are constantly asking for new reflections on how we can and should build a more equitable future for all. The values are not outmoded even when the practical solutions demanded seem to change with the times. Catholic social teaching gives a vision of the human person that functions in an economic society according to the intrinsic worth of each. It does not neglect that the aim and destiny of the person, however, goes beyond this earth, so that all economic systems will have their deficiencies and human limitations.

The next decades will be crucial for this planet and for the welfare and human dignity of each person who lives on it. These same decades will pose a special challenge for Catholic social teaching. It is only at the beginning of the important reflections begun one hundred years ago by Leo XIII.

NOTES

1. *L'Osservatore Romano*, German ed. (November 29, 1985); *L'Osservatore Romano*, English ed. (December 23, 1985).

2. *Revista Eclesiastica Brasileira* 47 (June 1987), pp. 356-77.

3. A fine and balanced analysis of this question can be found in Arthur F. McGovern, S.J., "Latin America and Dependency Theory," *This World* (Spring-Summer 1986), pp. 104-23.

14

INCENTIVES AND THE ORGANIZATION OF WORK

Moral Hazards and Trust

CHARLES K. WILBER

Traditional economists argue that the best way to solve economic problems is to rely on the economic growth generated by each individual's pursuit of self-interest in a free market regulated by the forces of market competition. In pursuit of income each person provides something (product, service, or labor) others want and are willing to pay for. Through a process of voluntary market exchange, over-all production is maximized while at the same time individual freedom is protected. Since self-interest is the motor that drives the economy, incentives are all-important. The incentive of potential profit leads some people to take the risks involved in producing and marketing a new product, investing in new technologies, or lending their savings to others to do so. Other people respond to the incentive of wage differentials and undertake the training required to become a plumber, an accountant, or an engineer. Thus incentives are the key to productivity, and productivity is the key to economic growth. It is efficiency, not justice, that concerns traditional economists.

In contrast, Catholic social thought has focused on the injustices created by reliance on the free market while at the same time warning of the dangers of state socialism. In 1891 Pope Leo XIII wrote, "The present age handed over the workers, each alone and defenseless, to the inhumanity of employers and the unbridled greed of competitors" (*Rerum Novarum*, par. 6). In 1931 Pope Pius XI wrote, "The ultimate consequences of the individualist spirit in economic life are ... : Free competition has destroyed itself; economic dictatorship has supplanted the free market; unbridled ambition for power has likewise succeeded greed for gain; all economic life has become tragically hard, inexorable, and cruel" (*Quadragesimo Anno*, par. 109). In 1961 Pope John XXIII wrote, "Work, inasmuch as it is an expression of the human person, can by no means be regarded as a mere commodity. . . . Its remuneration is not to be thought of in terms of merchandise, but rather according to the laws of justice and equity" (*Mater et Magistra*, par. 18).

In 1981 Pope John Paul II wrote, "The fact that the one who, while being God, became like us in all things devoted most of the years of his life on earth to manual work at the carpenter's bench . . . constitutes in itself the most eloquent 'gospel of work,' showing that the basis for determining the value of human work is not primarily the kind of work being done, but the fact that the one who is doing it is a person" (*Laborum Exercens*). This encyclical was written because despite the fact that "From the beginning of the industrial age, the Christian truth about work had to oppose the various trends of materialistic and economistic thought . . . the danger of treating work as a special kind of 'merchandise' or as an impersonal 'force' needed for production . . . always exists, especially when the whole way of looking at the question of economics is marked by the premises of materialistic economism." John Paul II argues that "The principle of the priority of labor over capital is a postulate of the order of social morality. . . . When a man works, using all the means of production, he also wishes the fruit of this work to be used by himself and others, and he wishes to be able to take part in the very work process as a sharer in responsibility and creativity at the workbench to which he applies himself." He argues that the subjective aspect of work — its effect on the dignity of the worker — takes precedence over the objective aspect of work.

In the light of traditional economists' claims about the importance of incentives for the operation of markets, is the treatment of work in Catholic social thought viable? This "humanization" of work may be impossible because of: a) the way markets create a bifurcation of people as consumers/workers, coupled with the competitive pressures that force business firms to become ever more efficient; and b) the consumerism rooted in human greed *and* the workings of the business system.

Because of competition one firm cannot improve working conditions, raise wages, or democratize the workplace if the result is an increase in production costs. Competition from other firms will keep the costs from being passed on in higher prices and, thus, profits will decline. The bifurcation of people into consumers/workers means that what they prefer as consumers — lower prices — makes what they prefer as workers — better working conditions and wages — less obtainable. Reliance on the market as the primary decision-making mechanism bifurcates the decision into separate areas. What people want as workers will not be ratified by those same people as consumers. Since competition is now worldwide, even a whole country faces difficulties in mandating workplace improvements that raise costs.

The problem is reinforced both by human greed and the constant effort of business to promote consumption as the ultimate end of life. This creates constant pressure to reduce labor costs, undercutting attempts to improve the quality of work life. The only hope may be to change work organization in ways that are both humanizing *and* efficient.

I argue in this paper that subordination of short-run interests to long-run interests and moral behavior that constrains free riding (taking advantage of benefits without paying the cost), in addition to being good in themselves, are essential for the efficient operation of the economy. Traditional economists are wrong when they claim that individual self-interest is sufficient to achieve efficient market outcomes. In fact, the "humanization" of work called for in Catholic social thought can be more efficient than the present organization of work. The next section of the chapter outlines the theory underlying this claim. The remainder applies the theory to the organization of work.

IMPERFECT INFORMATION, INTERDEPENDENCE, AND MORAL HAZARDS

Scholarly work in economics over the past fifteen years demonstrates that, under conditions of interdependence and imperfect information, rational self-interest frequently leads to socially irrational results. Traditional economic theory assumes independence of economic actors and perfect information. However, the more realistic assumptions that one person's behavior affects another's and that each has less than perfect knowledge of the other's likely behavior, give rise to strategic behavior, or what game theorists call moral hazards. An example will be helpful.

A classic example of moral hazard, known as the Parable of Distrust, is the situation where both the employer and worker suspect that the other one cannot be trusted to honor the explicit or implicit contract. For example, the employer thinks the worker will take too many coffee breaks, spend too much time talking with other workers, and generally work less than the employer thinks is owed. The worker, on the other hand, thinks the employer will try to speed up the pace of work, fire him or her unjustly if given the chance, and generally behave arbitrarily. When this is the case, the worker will tend to shirk and the employer will increase supervision to stop the expected shirking. If the worker would self-supervise, production costs would be lower. Thus distrust between employer and worker reduces efficiency.

In this case the pursuit of individual self-interest results in the worker and the employer as individuals and as a group becoming worse off than if they had been able to cooperate, that is, not shirk and not supervise. The problem is simple and common. The employer and worker are interdependent and do not have perfect knowledge of what the other will do, and the resulting lack of trust leads to behavior that is self-defeating. This outcome is made worse if distrust is accompanied with feelings of injustice. For example, if the worker feels that the contract is unfair (low wages, poor grievance machinery, and so on), the tendency to shirk will be increased.

There are numerous other cases, for example, inflation. A labor union fights for a wage increase only to find that others also have done so and thus the wage increase is offset by rising consumer prices. No one union alone can restrain its wage demands and maintain the support of its members. Business firms are caught in the same dilemma. They raise prices to compensate for increased labor and other costs only to discover that costs have increased again. Distrust among unions, among firms, and between unions and firms makes impossible a cooperative agreement on price and wage increases.

The case of recession is similar. As aggregate demand in the economy declines, each company attempts to cope with its resulting cash-flow difficulties through employee layoffs. However, if all companies pursue this strategy, aggregate demand will decline further, making more layoffs necessary. Most companies agree that the result is undesirable for each company and for the whole economy, but no one company on its own can maintain its work force. In effect each company says it will not lay off its employees if all the others also do not lay off their employees. Yet, again, no agreement is concluded.

These cases have two things in common. They all have a group (in these cases, workers and their employers) with a common interest in the outcome of a particular situation. And, second, while each attempts to choose the best available course of action, the result is not what any member of the group desires. In these cases the individual motives lead to undesired social and individual results. Adam Smith's "invisible hand" not only fails to yield the common good, but in fact works malevolently.

Why is it so difficult for the individuals involved to cooperate and make an agreement? The reason is that exit is cheap, but voice is expensive.[1] Exit means to withdraw from a situation, person, or organization and depends on the availability of choice, competition, and well-functioning markets. It is usually inexpensive and easy to buy or not, sell or not, hire or fire, and quit or shirk on your own. Voice means to communicate explicitly your concern to another individual or organization. The cost to an individual in time and effort to persuade, argue, and negotiate will often exceed any prospective individual benefit.[2]

In addition, the potential success of voice depends on the possibility of all members joining for collective action. But then there arises the "free rider" problem. If someone cannot be excluded from the benefits of collective action, he or she has no incentive to join the group agreement. Self-interest will tempt people to take the benefits without paying the costs; for example, watching educational television without becoming a subscriber.

This free riding explains why union organizing is next to impossible in states that prohibit union shops (where a majority of the workers voting for a union means all workers must join and pay dues).

The problem is further complicated by the possibility that what started simply as a self-interested or even benevolent relationship will become malevolent. Face-to-face strategic bargaining may irritate the parties involved if the other side is perceived as violating the spirit of fair play. This can result in a response of hatred rather than mere selfishness. Collective action is even more unlikely if the members of the group are hateful and distrustful of one another.

These moral hazards are situations where there is some act under the individual's unilateral control that promises to produce a welfare improvement for that individual that is not consistent with what individuals who share a common preference want to obtain as a long-run result. The alternative line of action that would be consistent with the more preferred long-run result is marked by the fact that no matter how hard the individual tries, alone he or she can produce no net benefits or fewer than in the unilateral activity. So the moral hazard exists because the alternative line of action requires some level of trust that can lead all to engage in the process necessary to reach group agreement.

A common consciousness of one's interdependence with others is required for an individual or organization to overcome moral hazards. Collective action requires a degree of mutual trust. If malevolence arises, the moral hazard will be strengthened. In addition, morally constrained behavior is necessary to control free riding. Thus self-interested individualism fails, for moral hazards are ubiquitous in our economy.

Could not a traditional economist construct an "enriched" notion of self-interested behavior that would overcome moral hazards without the need for moral values? I think the answer is a qualified yes. An enriched concept of self-interest could encompass the foregoing of short-run interests for long-run interests, but moral commitment makes this much easier. Furthermore, this would leave the free-rider problem unresolved.

The argument might proceed like this. A self-interested person, recognizing the reality of interdependencies and imperfect information, is willing to cooperate with others if it increases his or her personal welfare. Thus cooperation becomes one more means to maximize one's self-interest.

However, the flaw in the argument is the failure to account for the likelihood of cooperative behavior based only on self-interest to degenerate into individuals cheating on the collective agreement. Free riding must be accounted for. Pushed to its logical extreme, individual self-interest suggests that faced with interdependence and imperfect information, it is usually in the interest of an individual to evade the rules by which other players are guided.

This problem can be illustrated by the case of OPEC. The member countries can be considered to be acting out of enlightened self-interest.

They have many fundamental differences—political, economic, religious, geo-political. At times two of the members—Iran and Iraq—have been in such disagreement as to be in a declared state of war. Nevertheless, OPEC has survived because each member realizes that its own well-being is closely connected with that of the others. OPEC tries to maintain high prices and profit levels by setting production quotas. However, since 1973, their biggest problem has been evasion of the quotas by individual member countries. Enlightened economic actors do cheat. Each member country has an incentive to cheat on the cooperative agreement because, with the production quota holding up prices, if one member expands its output it makes even greater profits. However, if one country violates the agreement, the others usually follow. The result is that the increased output from all the member countries drives down the price and every member is worse off than before. Thus, enlightened self-interest results in a cooperation that is inherently unstable.

Traditional economists could respond with the claim that establishing enforcement mechanisms is the answer to cheating on collective agreements. As an example, OPEC sets up committees to determine production quotas and verification groups to ensure compliance. However, even with a great amount of resources expended on collective enforcement, cheating continues. Not only is cheating a major problem for OPEC but the costs of policing collective agreements is substantially more than the costs of maintaining those agreements through internalized moral commitments.

How then can we overcome the moral hazards generated by interdependence and imperfect information? The resolution of the problem is not easy, for they are persistent and intractable. There are at least three possibilities: government intervention, group self-regulation, and institutional reinforcement of those moral values that constrain self-interested behavior.

Market failures such as pollution or monopoly have generally been seen as warrants for government intervention. However, there are ubiquitous market failures of the moral hazards variety in everyday economic life. In these cases private economic actors can also benefit from government measures for their protection, because interdependence and imperfect information generate distrust and lead the parties to self-defeating behavior. Certain kinds of government regulation—from truth-in-advertising to food-and-drug laws—can reduce distrust and thus economic inefficiency, providing gains for all concerned. However, government regulation has its limits. Where the regulated have concentrated power (i.e., electric companies) the regulators may end up serving the industry more than the public. In addition, there are clearly situations in which government operates to serve the self-interest of the members of its bureaucratic apparatus. Free-market economists would have us believe that such is always the case. This is an exaggeration. Government can serve the common good, but it has clear limits. One major limitation on the ability of government to regulate is the willingness of people to be regulated.

The Kennedy administration's wage-price guidelines were a partially successful attempt to control inflation through public encouragement of labor and management cooperation to limit wage increases to productivity increases. The cooperation broke down because of the growing struggle among social classes and occupational groups for larger shares of the GNP. More formal cooperation between labor and management, monitored by government, might reduce the distrust that cripples their relationship. In order to do so government would have to be accepted by all sides as above the fray and willing to encourage agreements that would benefit society. The experience of the 1970s, in which government activity delivered less than it promised, and of the 1980s, when it was used to serve the agenda of bureaucrats and to facilitate the goals of the powerful, both imply a diminished capacity of government to play this role.

The second way to overcome moral hazards is self-regulation. Sellers could voluntarily discipline themselves not to exploit their superior information. This is the basis of professional ethics. Surgeons, for example, take on the obligation, as a condition for the exercise of their profession, to avoid performing unnecessary operations, placing the interest of the patient first. The danger is that their professional association will end up protecting its members at the expense of others.

This leads us to the final possibility — developing institutions to heighten group consciousness and reinforce moral values that constrain self-interested behavior so that the pursuit of short-run rewards and free riding can be controlled. Is it possible to rebuild institutional mechanisms so that long-run interests and moral values become more important in directing economic behavior? Yes, but we must rethink our view of people as simply self-interested maximizers. Economists have made a major mistake in treating love, benevolence, and particularly public spirit as scarce resources that must be economized lest they be depleted. This is a faulty analogy because, unlike material factors of production, the supply of love, benevolence, and public spirit is not fixed or limited. These are resources whose supply may increase rather than decrease through use. Also they do not remain intact if they stay unused.[3] These moral resources respond positively to practice, in a learning-by-doing manner, and negatively to non-practice. Obviously if overused they become ineffective.

A good example is a comparison of the system of blood collection for medical purposes in the United States and in England.[4] In the U.S. we gradually replaced donated blood with purchased blood. As the campaigns for donated blood declined, because purchased blood was sufficient, the amount of donations declined. In effect, our internalized benevolence toward those unknown to us, who need blood, began to atrophy from non-use. In contrast, blood donations remained high in England where each citizen's obligation to others was constantly emphasized.

People learn their values from their families, their religious faith, and from their society. In fact, a principal objective of publicly proclaimed laws and regulations is to stigmatize certain types of behavior and to reward others, thereby influencing individual values and behavior codes. Aristotle understood this: "Lawgivers make the citizen good by inculcating habits in them, and this is the aim of every lawgiver; if he does not succeed in doing that, his legislation is a failure. It is in this that a good constitution differs from a bad one" (*Nicomachean Ethics*, 1103b).

Habits of benevolence and civic spirit, in addition to heightened group consciousness, can be furthered by bringing groups together to solve common problems. Growth of worker participation in management, consultation between local communities and business firms to negotiate plant closings and relocations, establishment of advisory boards on employment policy that represent labor, business, and the public; all are steps toward a recognition that individual self-interest alone is insufficient, that mutual responsibilities are necessary in a world where interdependence and imperfect information generate distrust and tempt individuals into strategic behavior that, in turn, results in less than optimal outcomes.

THE ORGANIZATION OF WORK

Distrust between workers and employers leads to inefficient results if neither side trusts the other to live up to the contract. As a result the worker has an incentive to shirk and the employer has to increase supervision costs to counter the possibility. If somehow workers would self-supervise — not shirk — productivity would be higher and all could benefit.

Changing the institutional environment from a purely competitive one by adding cooperative mechanisms might enable the trust to grow that is necessary for people to alter their behavior. The most likely approach is encouragement of workers' self-management and worker ownership. Of course, most firms and their managers believe that efficiency and discipline require one absolute center of control over work — their control. Nevertheless, in some cases managers are exploring ways to change the organization of production to increase their workers' job satisfaction. Quality-control circles and profit sharing are becoming common management responses to encourage employees to make their work contribution through the social group in the factory.[5]

The reason for these new management initiatives is clear — under the old system many workers expressed their boredom, anger, and despair by working as slowly as possible, by appearing at work irregularly, by doing poor quality work, by occasional acts of sabotage, and by frequent job changes. The "efficient" system of authoritarian discipline and minute division of labor has been a contributing factor to lagging productivity in the United States economy. These managers see profit sharing and other worker-participation devices as a means of establishing the more cooperative relationship with their employees that is necessary to compete in the economic world aborning.

It is useful to look at some ways workers have tried to gain control over their work situations. I summarize a particular form of cooperation, worker management, and two specific instances, the Employee Stock Ownership Plan (ESOP) at Weirton Steel in the United States and the industrial cooperatives of Mondragon in the Basque region of Spain.

Worker Management

Worker-owned and managed firms are relatively new on the national scene in the United States, though some have existed at the local level for many years.[6] They have become important for several reasons. It is becoming clear that profitable plants are being closed, not just unprofitable ones, and this is more common when the plant is a small part of a conglomerate holding company. The plant may be closed because higher profits can be earned if it is moved to a lower wage area, for a tax write-off, or for a variety of other non-production-related reasons.[7] In these situations purchase of the plant by the present employees preserves jobs, which makes it an attractive possibility. In addition, there is now a legal mechanism, ESOP, to facilitate employee ownership; it provides significant tax incentives to firms.[8]

There is increasing evidence that worker-owned firms incorporating employee participation and workplace democracy have rates of productivity at least as high and frequently higher than traditional firms.[9] Thus worker-owned firms have been used to maintain employment at plants that otherwise would have closed *and* have been used to maintain and improve productivity as well as the quality of work life. In fact, they all appear to be linked. As employees become owners and managers, the old distrust that led to shirking and excessive supervision can often be reduced. The new environment enables workers to see that the short-run advantage of shirking is outweighed by the negative impact on long-run productivity and profits that they share in. Free riding is still possible, of course, if the employees never develop the moral commitments to coalesce as a group.[10]

A 1988 report[11] published in England indicates that stock ownership and profit-sharing schemes actually stimulate worker performance. It analyzed the results of 414 companies in the period 1977-85 and showed that those with such programs did consistently, and in some cases spectacularly, better than the others. Also, the smaller the firm, the more direct the impact.

Weirton Steel

An interesting case in the United States is Weirton Steel. Since 1984, the employees have owned the company under an ESOP and have operated the plant profitably. Management and labor attribute this success—under the previous ownership of National Steel the company was on the edge of bankruptcy—to the implementation of the ESOP. In the face of general decline in the steel industry, Weirton has expanded its employment from seventy-eight hundred when the ESOP began to eighty-four hundred. The company has paid out about one-third of its profits each year — $15-20 million — while reinvesting the remainder in plant modernization. R. Alan Prosswimmer, company vice-president and chief financial officer, attributes the company's turnaround to the ESOP: "Over $10 million in savings last year alone were attributable to our employee programs." Walter Bish, president of the Independent Steelworkers Union, added that the workers, since becoming owners, "are much more aware of the fact that quality is important." Rank-and-file workers speak similarly saying that the ESOP has resulted in "a lot of attitude changes," because previously workers "were working for National Steel and the profits went there. Now the profits are staying here."[12]

Mondragon

Of particular interest as a model for employee-owned-and-managed firms are the industrial cooperatives of Mondragon in the Basque region of Spain.[13] Their achievements are quite impressive. The first of the Mondragon cooperatives was established in 1958. Twenty years later the one hundred cooperatives together had sales close to $1 billion, one-fifth of which was exported to other countries. Among the many goods produced are refrigerators and other home appliances, heavy machinery, hydraulic presses, steel, semi-conductors, and selenium rectifiers. Among the cooperatives are the largest refrigerator manufacturer in Spain, a bank with over $500 million in assets, a technological research center, a technical high school and engineering college, and an extensive social security system with health clinics and other social services.

The ownership and management structure of the Mondragon cooperatives is of particular interest. Every new member must invest a specified amount in the firm where he or she is employed. At the end of each year a portion of the firm's surplus or profit is allocated to each worker's capital account in proportion to the number of hours worked and the job rating. The job-rating schedule allows for a quite narrow 3:1 ratio between the highest and lowest paid workers. The result is a pay scale quite different from that prevailing in private industry. In comparison, lower-paid workers earn more in the cooperatives, middle-level workers and managers earn the same, and top managers earn considerably less. Each cooperative's board of directors is selected by all the members and, in turn, the board appoints the managers. There is a social council made up of elected representatives of the lowest-paid workers, which negotiates with the board over worker grievances and other issues of interest.

The purely economic results are impressive. When both capital and labor inputs are accounted for, the Mondragon cooperatives are far more productive in their use of resources than private firms in Spain. One compar-

222   *Charles K. Wilber*

ison with the five hundred largest firms in Spain found that in the 1970s the average cooperative used only twenty-five percent as much capital equipment per worker but worker productivity reached eighty percent of that in private industry.[14]

How might we explain this highly efficient labor force in the Mondragon cooperatives? Clearly worker motivation plays a major part. As workers became owners and participated in management decisions the incentives to shirk were lessened. The structural environment made it easier for trust to develop. Thus strategic behavior declined as workers saw that their short-term individual interests could conflict with their long-term interests. Shirking might benefit them here and now but productivity would benefit them over the long haul.

The free-rider problem was controlled by moral commitment to group solidarity. Basque nationalism clearly has been the foundation for this moral commitment, which makes it difficult to transfer the Mondragon experience whole. However, this may be a chicken-egg problem. Must the moral commitment to group solidarity exist first or will the experience of ownership and management help create it? I do not know but the continued deterioration of our industrial structure is creating the conditions for worker buyouts.

Other factors also inhibit the transferability of the Mondragon experiment. Ties with local communities and limited labor mobility appear important to the success of the cooperatives. In the United States, where there is more labor mobility and weaker ties of community, the moral commitment to group solidarity may be more difficult to generate.

Fostering subordination of short-run interests to long-run interests and moral constraints to free riding are our most important challenges. To realize the vision of human work contained in Catholic social thought, changes in work organization must not decrease productivity. Thus building institutional mechanisms, such as worker management structures, that overcome moral hazards and create trust is essential to provide the necessary incentives.

NOTES

1. See George A. Akerlof, *An Economist's Book of Tales* (Cambridge: Cambridge University Press, 1984); Kenneth E. Boulding, *The Economy of Love and Fear* (Belmont, California: Wadsworth Publishing Company, 1973); Fred Hirsch, *Social Limits to Growth* (Cambridge, Massachusetts: Harvard University Press, 1978); Albert O. Hirschman, *Exit, Voice, and Loyalty: Responses to Decline in Firms, Organizations, and States* (Cambridge, Massachusetts: Harvard University Press, 1970); Andrew Schotter, *Free Market Economics: A Critical Appraisal* (New York: St. Martin's Press, 1985), pp. 47-88; A. Allan Schmid, *Property, Power, and Public Choice: An Inquiry into Law and Economics* (New York: Praeger, 1978).

2. Exit is more difficult in Japan where the Confucian tradition is much more binding. As a result, with much greater emphasis on harmony and consensus at all

levels, voice is more appreciated and cultivated. See Hirschman; also idem, *Rival Views of Market Society* (New York: Viking Press, 1986), pp. 77-101.

3. See Hirschman, *Rival Views of Market Society*, p. 155.

4. See Richard M. Titmuss, *The Gift Relationship* (London: Allen and Unwin, 1970).

5. Michael J. Piore, "A Critique of Reagan's Labor Policy," *Challenge* 29:1 (March/April, 1986), pp. 48-54.

6. The best-known and most studied of these firms are the plywood cooperatives in Oregon and Washington. See K. Berman, *Worker-Owned Plywood Companies* (Pullman, Washington: Washington State University Press, 1967).

7. Barry Bluestone and Bennett Harrison, *The Deindustrialization of America* (New York: Basic Books, 1982).

8. U.S. Congress, Joint Economic Committee, *Broadening the Ownership of New Capital: ESOPs and Other Alternatives*, 94th Congress, 2d session (Washington, D.C.: Government Printing Office, 1976).

9. Henry M. Levin, "Issues in Assessing the Comparative Productivity of Worker-Managed and Participatory Firms in Capitalist Societies," in *Participatory and Self-Managed Firms*, ed. D. Jones and J. Svejnar (Lexington, Massachusetts: D.C. Heath, 1982); R. Oakeshott, *The Case for Workers' Coops* (London: Routledge and Kegan Paul, 1978); K. Friden, *Workplace Democracy and Productivity* (Washington, D.C.: National Center for Economic Alternatives, 1980).

10. See B. Thurston, "South Bend Lathe, E.S.O.P. on Strike Against Itself?," *Self-Management* 8 (Fall 1980), pp. 19-20.

11. *Profit Sharing and Profitability* (London: Kogan Page/IPM, 1988). Also see the news report, "Letting Workers in on the Share-Out," *The Sunday Times*, January 22, 1989, p. E1.

12. Pete Sheehan, "A New Model of Economic Democracy: The Workers of Weirton Steel," *New Oxford Review* 50, 10 (December 1987), pp. 13-17.

13. See Henry M. Levin, "The Workplace: Employment and Business Intervention," in *Handbook of Social Intervention*, ed. E. Seidman (Beverly Hills, California: Sage Publications, 1983); A. G. Johnson and W. F. Whyte, "The Mondragon System of Worker Production Cooperatives," *Industrial and Labor Relations Review* 31, 1 (1977), pp. 18-30; H. Thomas and C. Logan, *Mondragon: An Economic Analysis* (Boston: Allen and Unwin, 1982); and William and Kathleen Whyte, *Making Mondragon: The Growth and Dynamics of the Worker Cooperative Complex* (Cornell: ILR Press, 1988).

14. Henry M. Levin, "Raising Employment and Productivity with Producer Cooperatives," in *Human Resources, Employment and Development*, vol. 2, ed. P. Streeten and H. Maier (New York: St. Martins's Press, 1983).

15

WORKER RIGHTS AND RESPONSIBILITIES IN A CHANGED COMPETITIVE CONTEXT

ROBERT L. KUTTNER

American workers are now competing in a globalized economy. As a number of writers have observed,[1] they can compete either by "working cheaper" or by "working smarter." That is, in a unified world market, Americans can hold on to market-share either by competing directly against the hundreds of millions of underemployed and desperately poor workers of the Third World—by working at third-world wages—or by increasing the capital-productivity that justifies premium wages. If American workers expect ten times the wages of workers in Bangladesh, then they need to generate ten times the hourly output per worker. For the most part, that doesn't simply mean better worker motivation. It means smarter capital, smarter industrial organization, and an entirely different conception of the worker's role.

In this competition to retain a significant share of "high-value-added" production, the United States has not been doing very well. A growing literature emphasizes a series of structural differences between the American workplace, and those of our advanced industrial competitors such as Japan and the nations of the European community. The several differences really boil down to a single difference—the contingent nature of relationships in the American ultra-market economy.

In pure laissez-faire economics, every relationship is a price-auction in miniature—a one-night stand. In laissez-faire theory, economic actors need to be free to choose a better supplier, a better worker, a better employer, a better investment, and on a moment's notice. Thus the hallmark of the American economy is contingent relationships between suppliers and producers, between producers and customers, between investors and entre-preneurs, and of course between managers and employees. This approach to capitalism is at the heart of what has become a cliché about what ails America—the "short time horizon" that afflicts everyone from portfolio managers to product designers to corporate chief executives.

Japan, Germany, France, and Sweden, among others, have a much more social conception of capitalism;[2] owners of capital stick with investments for the long term and don't demand high performance every quarter. In return, entrepreneurs can plan for the longer term. The hostile takeover is not permitted in Japan and is far less frequent in Europe. Japanese and German corporations cultivate long-term relationships with suppliers. That, in turn, makes it rational for the supplier to invest in expensive, long-lived equipment and process-technology. And virtually every other advanced industrial economy has public policies to compensate for the market's notorious tendency to under-invest in human capital.

At the root of this institutional difference is a different conception of what makes for an efficient, socially sustainable economy. European corporatism and the Japanese blend of Confucism, Buddhism, and Shinto, each in its own way tempers laissez faire—but in a fashion that enhances economic performance as well as social solidarity. In standard Anglo-Saxon economics the prevailing assumption is that egalitarian preferences may be necessary to comport with ethical norms held by citizens in their noneconomic capacity, but that egalitarian policies necessarily come at the expense of economic efficiency. In reality, as Japan and Europe have demonstrated, the opposite is true. There are strategies which enrich social comity, and by so doing, improve economic performance. Far from compromising economic efficiency, the ethical imperative can complement the economic imperative. I have surveyed these in my 1984 book, *The Economic Illusion: False Choices Between Prosperity and Social Justice.*[3]

CATHOLIC SOCIAL TEACHING AND LAISSEZ-FAIRE INDIVIDUALISM

As a non-Catholic, I am extremely respectful of the role of Catholic social teaching as one counterweight among many to the utopian claims of extreme laissez-faire individualism as necessary economics. In general, the forces that call for a more social conception of capitalism are weaker in the United States than in other nations. In Japan the combination of a feudal history, a very strong, competent and prestigious state bureaucracy, and the religious teachings on the question of reciprocal social obligation, all reinforce Japan's famous group consciousness. In Europe corporatism draws strength from a variety of factors—the greater class consciousness of workers, the greater strength of trade unions, the history of relatively stronger unitary states, the fact that small exporting states, say Sweden or Austria,[4] can't afford the luxury of social strife, the Burkean tradition of noblesse oblige conservatism which respected the value of established social structures and feared pure capitalism, and of course the influence of the Roman Catholic Church and of Christian Democratic parties that made the social market economy respectable to conservatives.

In secular, liberal America, the prevailing ethic is more individualist than that of Europe or Asia. Redistributive policies are held by conservatives to reward laggards and to hold back the most enterprising; the race is to the swift. The secular ideologies that challenge this conception are far weaker in America, and religious social teaching is not as influential in the society as a whole. Our traditional conception of the separation of church and state further fragments the coalition that favors a social market economy. Federal aid to education, for example, was retarded for over a generation by disputes over aid to parochial schools. Disputes over reproductive choice further split what ought to be a coalition on broader questions of the social market. In Europe, where the ideal of anticlericalism is less absolute, and where there is a more finely tuned cynicism on both sides of the debate, practical accommodations are simply made. The church is accorded a larger social role, even though the polity makes sure it retains ample running room to preside over an essentially secular society. There are the usual fierce battles over budgets—but the battles over first principles have faded.

Nonetheless, Catholic social teaching in America is immensely important as one of the few available and potent counterweights to the prevailing claims on behalf of pure capitalism. There is also a secular tradition, in the writings of such social critics as John Maynard Keynes, Thorstein Veblen, Richard Titmuss, Karl Polanyi, Robert Heilbroner, among many others, holding that a social market economy is necessary economics, quite independent of any religious or ethical framework. As Polanyi demonstrated in his masterwork, *The Great Transformation,* which was his history of the attempt of market forces to achieve primacy over others, "The idea of a self-adjusting market implied a stark utopia. Such an institution could not exist for any length of time without annihilating the human and material substance of society. ... To allow the market mechanism to be the sole director of the fate of human beings and their natural environment, indeed, even of the amount and use of purchasing power, would result in the demolition of society."[5] Or as Heilbroner observed more recently in *The Nature and Logic of Capitalism,* a pure market economy is not only amoral but tends to drive out pre-capitalist or extra-capitalist values that are the necessary source of the morality and comity on which capitalism itself depends.[6] The logic of social cohesion and economic efficiency in these writers is largely secular, yet it seems to me that these two traditions have much in common and can draw strength from each other.

LABOR MARKET POLICY

One could write a lengthy treatise on the different realms of a capitalist economy which require extra-capitalist values and associations for the sake of capitalist efficiency as well as of a social ethic. My subject here is labor market policy, which serves both as an instructive case in point and as metaphor for the larger problem. One central inefficiency of a pure market economy is that when labor-management relations are contingent, neither the manager nor the worker is likely to attain a sufficient commitment to the other and to the larger enterprise, and neither is likely to invest adequately in training.

Moreover, when labor is cheap and expendable, the manager will prefer cheap labor to smart capital. In the short run cheap labor may produce cost advantages, but over the long term cheap labor does not increase the productivity of the enterprise. Paradoxically, the more expensive labor is, the more it is likely to be replaced with capital, which over time makes the entire economy more efficient and the wage earners better off. Paradoxically, too, the weaker trade unions are, the more likely they are to define security in terms of a particular job classification, which retards the dynamic flexibility of the economy as a whole. In order for this alternative approach to benefit particular workers (who are at risk of losing particular jobs), the entire strategy needs to be anchored in a commitment to full employment, worker employment security, lifetime learning, and labor mobility.

In short, we need nothing less than a new social contract between labor and management, in which workers get employment security, influence, and the prospect of steady upgrading, and management gets a more highly skilled and flexible work force. A labor market policy in a social market economy should include the following elements:
- Government should help create co-determination in corporate governance, both to improve the efficiency of the enterprise and to help give birth to a more effective form of trade unionism.
- Pension funds should be immune from management raids and should be a source of capital for new corporate forms.
- Unemployment compensation as a form of social labor market subsidy should give way to lifetime learning and retraining.
- Wage subsidy to breadwinners should be used to ensure that a worker with a full-time job earns enough to keep a family out of poverty.
- Government should systematically seek to convert low-wage, dead-end jobs into para-professional jobs with career ladders.

In the 1980s government became more hostile both to trade unions and to the idea that public policy needs to pay attention to labor markets, to the quality of the labor force, or to labor's constructive influence upon productivity. These realms are linked, both as substance and as politics. Politically, in virtually every industrial democracy trade unions provide the most reliable key electoral constituency for political parties that believe in a mixed economy. There is a close correlation between the strength of organized labor and the ability of progressive administrations to govern successfully. In nations with weak or fractious labor movements, the right is the usual majority party. In nations with strong, unified labor movements, the center-left party begins with a powerful ally. In the United States a hostile national administration and a turbulent climate of industrial transition have combined to weaken trade unionism in this decade.

Substantively, labor's enthusiastic support for industrial transitions depends on some social guarantee that such transitions will benefit the work force, rather than take place at labor's expense. A society grows more productive by substituting capital for labor and by applying new technologies. When workers have reason to view those transitions as a source of increased living standards and improved opportunity, rather than as threats to their livelihood, positive sum gains result.

Therefore, a labor agenda for the 1990s in the United States ought to include several mutually reinforcing elements. Government needs to help the labor movement reinvent itself—both as a valid policy goal per se, and to revive a political constituency for progressive politics and government. An authentic brand of co-determination can help accomplish that; traditional "business unionism" probably cannot. Second, government ought to reform radically the structure of pension funds, their governance, their influence on both capital markets and their role in worker ownership. The present system is perverse. Not only are most pensions beyond the control of workers, but the practice of tying pensions to individual firms allows pension assets to be raided in takeover attempts, often at the expense of workers. In capital markets, pension funds, which logically ought to be a source of stable, patient capital, are managed instead in the interest of short-term performance, which paradoxically fuels the very takeover game that harms workers. Many workers find themselves displaced by capital which represents their own deferred savings. Instead, pension fund capital could help underwrite restructurings that truly benefit and empower workers. Finally, government needs to devise an active labor market policy that would provide opportunities for lifetime learning, retraining sabbaticals, and job upgrading, as industrial transitions occurred—and to guarantee that work pays a living wage. All three of these issues are of course closely linked.

AMERICAN LABOR AND CO-DETERMINATION

Consider first the question of co-determination. The idea that more collaborative labor-management relations would be good for the United States economy has long been a tantalizing concept, floating just at the margins of serious economic debate.

Micro-economically, less adversarial labor-management relations could lead to gains in productivity and competitiveness. Macro-economically it could encourage workers to accept other benefits than higher wages, such as job security or retraining opportunities, which would allow the economy to "cheat the Phillips curve" and enjoy tight labor markets with less inflationary pressure. The usual tradeoff between inflation and unemployment is not an iron law of economics. Rather, it results primarily because we lack institutions of constructive social bargaining. In a laissez-faire economy, low unemployment gives workers the bargaining power to demand wage increases in excess of real productivity gains. Fearing inflation, the authorities then keep the money supply too tight and public spending too low.

But with a serious social compact, we could run a high-growth, full-employment economy without wage-driven inflation. Workers could be assured job opportunities and lifelong training and retraining; industry would be assured a high-quality work force and labor peace. Government would invest in substantial upgrading of worker skills and restructuring of industry.

The broad and idealized appeal of this approach, however, tends to blind many advocates of quality-of-worklife strategies to the central question of power. The idea seems to be that all moves in this direction are to be encouraged, regardless of who is ultimately in charge and regardless of how much authority is genuinely handed over to workers. In a highly competitive economy, where firms are under ruthless cost-cutting pressure, benign bargains tend to be scrapped as soon as the going gets rough and one side — management — retains all the power. Unions, consequently, have tended to resist the conventional version of an incomes policy, viewing such proposals, in power terms, as a one-way street.

The conservative or neo-liberal version of this approach includes the "Tax-based Incomes Policy" (TIP), which was in vogue in the late 1970s; this would give workers and firms tax incentives for restraining wages. A variation on the same theme is Martin Weitzman's proposal for a "Share Economy," in which pay packets would be partly based on a share of the firm's total earnings rather than on a fixed wage.[7]

Weitzman's model claims, as a matter of technical economics, that by helping labor markets to clear and making firms operate with the marginal cost of labor lower than the average cost, this novel compensation system would reduce unemployment. And perhaps it would. But the Share Economy strategy, like the TIP strategy, fails to change the governance of the firm. In fact, it gives workers another downside risk associated with entrepreneurship — the opportunity to take pay cuts during downturns — without offering workers the control that usually belongs to the entrepreneur. The progressive version of co-determination looks to enhance the institutional standing of workers and of trade unions, and not just to induce wage restraint for its own sake.

Co-determination turns out to embrace contradictory practical meanings. Many enthusiasts of labor management collaboration innocently hope to attain productivity gains and to move beyond "adversarial" relationships without the need for substantial institutional change. To some in management, the goal is lower wage costs, more docile workers, and weaker unions. To others, it means genuine sharing of responsibility and authority.

As we begin to think seriously about what a more collaborative system

230 Robert L. Kuttner

of industrial relations really implies, and how it would look institutionally, several paradoxes become evident: The move toward more collaboration comes during a period of intensified competition, both globally and domestically. As a result, the same pressures that impel us to invent a more constructive system leave us with far less slack in the system to facilitate the necessary transitions. A firm faced with ruthless cost-cutting pressures is hard-pressed to guarantee that workers who accept greater flexibility will not be laid off. A manager whose competitors are underpricing him cannot guarantee that a bargain exchanging flexibility for job security will necessarily stick. Ironically, it would have been much easier to invent a system of more collaborative industrial relations back in the 1950s, when our economy was insulated from global pressures, when there was money in the system for wage and pension increases, and when unions had more industrial penetration and more power. But the very stability of that system undermined any incentive for such change.

The old system, which lasted roughly from the late 1930s to the late 1970s, is often called business unionism. It offered a kind of crude social contract in which government guaranteed workers' rights to bargain collectively for wages and working conditions, and in turn most large companies reluctantly tolerated unions. The unions refrained from challenging management prerogatives. Employees sought security in industry-wide master contracts and in an elaborate set of job classifications and work rules. The old industrial relations system was a kind of armed truce, balanced and undergirded by labor's ability to inflict damage, by industry's ability to live in a predictable competitive environment, and by government's willingness to enforce the ground rules.

The ability of American trade unions to deliver benefits to their members and the ability of government to broker a generation of social peace were covertly dependent on American economic preeminence internationally, and on tacit toleration of oligopoly at home. We did not have ruthless price competition in the basic industries, and that created an umbrella where unions could bargain for master contracts and regular raises, and industry could pass the cost along to customers. But an interdependent global economy, based on an imperfect mix of open trade and national industrial strategies, leaves industry with far less of a cushion.

The postwar period of industrial stability is now history, and so is the old basis for labor power. The century-old slogan, Take wages out of competition, which has been the rock-solid principle of traditional trade unionism, is a dead letter in many industries. On the contrary, wages are back in competition, not only between firms, but between different plants within the same firm, and even, under "two-tier" arrangements, between different generations of workers doing identical jobs in the same plant. Industrywide master contracts, the basic instrument of postwar labor solidarity in the United States, have all but vanished.

Thus all the major preconditions of the old social contract have dissolved.

Global competition and deregulation have ended oligopoly; the strike no longer has the force that it once did; many companies are much more anti-union; and, if one more assault were required, the National Labor Relations Board (NLRB) is no longer impartial.

The power balance between labor and management has shifted — except in one dramatic respect. Management may have more power today to weaken unions, but at the same time management needs labor's cooperation more than ever. At one time in the history of mass production, it may have been possible to design machines to be idiot-proof and to deploy human drones as one more interchangeable part. However, the very nature of the new technology demands smart, flexible, inventive human workers who can respond creatively to situations not anticipated in manuals or programmed into assembly lines. It is not enough to have brilliant engineers and dumb workers, if in fact it ever was.

But while the new economy cries out for more collaborative labor-management culture, the traditional social organization of the corporation resists it. And this suggests a related paradox: the current weakness of organized labor makes it easier for management to resist sharing authority in a meaningful way. A great many quality-of-worklife experiments (QWL) seem to show great promise, but when a crunch comes, management usually retains the real power. And next time, workers are far more wary of QWL. Employee Stock Ownership Plans are gaining popularity, but only a small fraction of them have produced real participatory management and power sharing as well as profit sharing. In short, given the impact of heightened competition on industrial relations, genuine collaboration is all the more imperative — and all the more difficult to accomplish.

A further paradox involves the mismatch between skills and jobs. As a whole, the United States needs a more highly skilled, better trained work force. But too many of the available jobs still demand only minimal skills. Too many employers seem bent on reducing labor costs in the short run rather than creating high-wage, high-skill jobs for the long run. Society has no mechanism for steadily upgrading the quality of work and of the work force. Corporate personnel officers in the service sector commonly complain that they can't find high school graduates competent to read instructions or to do basic arithmetic, or to show up on time, or to take five-dollar-an-hour jobs — not that they have advanced training programs going begging.

It is a staple of the labor economics literature that firms generally under-invest in training — for the perfectly rational reason that a worker newly trained at company expense is entirely free to go to work for a competitor. This is a classic case of an "externality": The person called on to make the decision doesn't get the full benefit or suffer the full cost. So optimal social decisions are not always made by private actors. Society does have real shortages of workers in certain highly skilled craft occupations, such as machinists, but we have far too few mechanisms to train them. There is, of course, the obvious need for schools to do a better job equipping new workers with basic skills, but also the more subtle need for systematic upgrading of the work force throughout one's productive life.

In order to help labor and management break out of this trap, which serves neither, government must play a very different role. The old industrial relations system offered a very limited three-way social contract, in which government was a player, but only as arbiter of collective bargaining under the Wagner Act framework, not as an active party helping labor and management to invent new ways of collaborating. Rather, government's function was to allow labor and management to bargain for shares of a growing pie in an economy whose institutions were, in retrospect, remarkably stable.

Today, the economy is undergoing radical restructuring, as it must. But the benefits and costs are very unequally distributed; the few mechanisms available to ease the pain are minimal and defensive; and there are even fewer mechanisms or resources to convert the turbulence into broadly based opportunity. The principal engine of restructuring today is the hostile corporate takeover, which forces firms to engage in a degree of radical reorganization, either defensively or under new management, that the old stable system would never have accepted.

Economists can debate whether the outcome is beneficial in the long run—my own view is that the effect is mixed at best—but it is clear that neither workers nor society have a seat at that bargaining table, and that the financial climate in which a large number of companies are bent out of shape either executing or resisting takeovers makes long-term workplace collaboration all but impossible. The added financial and institutional turbulence of a takeover economy only intensifies the underlying industrial turbulence. As a result, innovative social contracts between labor and management that might be devised are usually stillborn.

This is most vividly illustrated in industries experiencing the most dramatic shake-ups. Consider, for example, airlines and steel. In the case of Eastern Airlines, the prospect of bankruptcy brought both labor and management to the very brink of a radically new form of social contract, in which management gave workers partial ownership and shared authority both on the shop floor and boardroom, and workers departed from the adversarial tradition, began thinking like profit-maximizing managers, and agreed to a more flexible form of compensation in which wages were reduced and part of their pay was based on gross earnings. In its first year, the new approach saved tens of millions of dollars, and Eastern was able to run in the black for the first time in years.

But the competitive pressures of deregulation, the old habits of traditional management, the inability of Eastern's several unions to pursue a common strategy, the fact that labor still was only a minority owner, and management's option to sell out to a new owner or to declare bankruptcy, all snuffed out this new bargain before it had time to mature.

In the steel industry, the integrated mills are in the midst of a long-term restructuring that will leave the United States with fewer mills, reduced production capacity, a fraction of the workers it once had, but a far more productive and dynamic industry in what remains. Along the way, a much more collaborative industrial relations culture is struggling to be born.

For example, at LTV Steel, labor and management agreed to an experimental arrangement (at one plant in Cleveland) of the sort long advocated by industrial relations experts. The old book of job categories would be thrown out; workers would be paid according to one of three skill levels, and made available to perform any of several jobs; most workers would be salaried; there would be job-security guarantees and new shop floor authority for the work force.

Shortly after that agreement was struck, LTV went into bankruptcy—in part because the cost of pensioning off its workers exceeded the savings it achieved from closing excess capacity. The only institution we have for socializing some of this cost is the Pension Benefit Guarantee Corporation (PBGC), which has become a kind of backdoor Ministry of Industrial Restructuring in a society that does not believe government ought to be in that business at all. So, instead of facilitating collaboration, or spending public money to lubricate new bargains, taxpayer money goes only to mop up the cost of private failure and to ease a little of the pain inflicted on workers.

In cases such as Eastern or LTV, where government plays the passive role of offering the protection of the bankruptcy law, or the bail-out of pension liabilities, or the temporary shelter of trade injury protection, the federal government needs to play a far more affirmative role in bringing about co-determination and restructuring arrangements, both as guarantor of the bargain and as supplier of technical assistance and sometimes of public capital.

If government contributed capital to the deal by buying some stock with full voting shares, government, as a part-owner, could insist to management that its long-term interest was in seeing whether this novel, productivity-enhancing bargain between labor and management be given more time to prove itself, rather than subjected to a fire sale when the going got rough. Eastern might then have been able to surmount a period of difficult market conditions; the several unions might have worked together more constructively; and the new social contract would have had a chance to prove itself. At minimum, management would have been denied the unilateral option of selling out to a third party.

This approach seems socialistic, for it amounts to an agency of government selectively buying preferred stock and voting shares. But it is no more socialistic than a series of measures highly prized by American capitalists, such as the Pension Benefit Guarantee Corporation, the Chrysler bailout, the Air Force subsidy of development of numerically controlled machine tools, and state laws preventing shareholders from maximizing their gain by tendering shares to corporate raiders. The difference is that our version of a mixed economy is far more likely than the current one to produce equitably shared, dynamic gains.

Today's global economy, with its intensified global competition and industrial transition, requires new forms of corporate governance. If a firm wants society to shelter it from the risk of hostile takeovers or give it subsidies, it must offer some alternative form of accountability to the usual sorts of market discipline. One could imagine an alternative corporate form. The corporation would not be vulnerable to hostile takeovers—but in return it would have authentic power sharing and worker co-determination at every level from the shop floor to the boardroom.

Plugging into a long, well-established legal and financial tradition, which holds that shareholders are owners and owners are decision-makers, is probably far better strategically and philosophically than inventing a new regulatory overlay at odds with that tradition. It makes more sense to devise a system in which workers and public officials receive stock in exchange for a special market preference, and vote their shares to demand a collaborative mode of management.

It may well be that government should begin this effort experimentally, on a moderate scale, in a few companies at a time. Worker buyouts and public sector involvement should no longer be limited to the basket cases. Government should create a new framework where contributions of public capital translate into shares of ownership and influence, and that influence is used to produce positive sum gains for worker, firm, and society. A firm that lives by the free market risks perishing in the free market.

PENSION FUNDS

This raises the second issue—the role of pension-fund capital. Pension funds are of course deferred wages. The present regulatory schema fails workers on several counts, even on the narrow test of providing income for their retirement. Workers who change jobs lose benefits. Pension savings are often available to be raided, based on the fiction that they are "overfunded." And a firm with a generous pool of pension assets often finds itself the target of either a hostile raid or a preemptive raid by its own management. ERISA—the Employee Retirement Income Security Act—creates a labyrinth of regulation, but it fails to give workers the most elementary protections against the raiding or termination of pension funds.

There is a need for nothing less than radical pension-fund reform. Ideally, private pension funds should be collapsed into a second, earning-based second tier of social security. The present system of social security would continue as a pay-as-you-go system. The second tier would be based on earnings histories and paid-in contributions, but funds would no longer be under control of corporate trustees and the accrual of funds would follow workers wherever they went. Only this degree of reform would permit full portability and full protection against either raiding or spurious or authentic bankruptcies. Failing that, there should be a drastic overhaul of the regulations permitting raiding and termination and far tougher conflict-of-interest strictures to prohibit managers from using pension assets in corporate takeover contests. All firms should be required either to have pension plans that meet a minimum standard, or to pay into a pool for workers in small firms without such plans.

A fully funded, socialized, earnings-related pension system would also provide a large pool of capital under social control. Some of this capital could be used to finance restructurings or worker buyouts. Even if the present system of company-based pension plans were continued, further reform is needed both to curb abuses and to assure that when pension-fund capital, or ESOP capital, is used in restructurings, it results in authentic worker control or co-determination.

TOWARD AN ACTIVE LABOR MARKET POLICY

Traditional trade unionism and the traditional welfare state, comprised of pension funds, unemployment compensation, and the like, were efforts to socialize some of the gain and some of the pain of pure capitalism during a period when the American economy was enjoying both steady growth and institutional stability. As Gosta Esping-Andersen has observed,[8] the original welfare state, of the sort imagined in the two wartime Beveridge Reports, was intended to sustain people during periods of their lives when they were involuntarily unable to be gainfully employed—Beveridge called them "interruptions." But as Esping-Andersen observes, the more recent inventions of the welfare state are necessarily intended to better integrate work and non-work aspects of human life, to facilitate necessary transitions, and to reconcile management's desire for a dynamic, adaptable work force with the individual's desire for flexibility and security. Thus, rather than being the antithesis of work, the modern welfare state is its partner. By supporting child care and parental leaves, it makes it possible for parents to also be workers without sacrificing their dedication to either pursuit. By supporting career transitions, the welfare state makes it possible for the work force to become steadily more productive. By supporting a more flexible and staged conception of "retirement," the welfare state makes it possible for older workers to work less strenuously while still contributing productively to society.

It virtually goes without saying that each one of these innovative areas of a work-and-welfare state is least highly developed in the United States— because of the peculiarly American conception of capitalism as radically individualist and social.

Elsewhere in the industrialized world, public policy socializes some of the cost of necessary labor market transitions—retraining and reemploying those with inadequate or superceded skills. Often, as the Eastern and LTV cases suggest, the invention of collaborative labor-management bargains during periods of rapid industrial transition and restructuring founders on the very real problem that there is no place to put the excess labor. Productivity gains literally mean more output for less labor input; unless the industry happens to be a rapidly expanding one, it is all but impossible to negotiate collaborative bargains in one company. Even forward-looking bargains like the last round of auto contracts cannot quite guarantee full job security for all workers because they cannot predict market conditions. And of course workers without strong unions have no such protection at all. The traditional system we have for separating employment security from job security—namely, unemployment insurance—costs society a lot of money but doesn't buy very much besides a short-term dole. Trade Adjustment Assistance was essentially a more adequately paid version of the unemployment compensation for selected workers.

Therefore, it is necessary to drastically overhaul the system we have for socializing the costs of labor market transitions and in the process use those outlays to upgrade continuously the skills of the entire work force. When a worker is laid off because of a restructuring, or a downturn in the business cycle, the choice ought not be short-term unemployment compensation versus a lower paid job elsewhere. If the worker is 58, perhaps an early retirement plan makes sense; but if the worker is 38, he or she should be a candidate for a retraining sabbatical.

At present, we have small programs for helping to train disadvantaged young workers and for reemploying workers displaced by industrial transition. But about eighty percent of our total labor market outlays go for unemployment compensation. Other industrial nations invest much more heavily in subsidizing labor market transitions. Sweden's ratio of outlays is the reverse of ours: less than twenty percent of manpower outlays go to pay the cost of idleness and more than eighty percent go to subsidize retraining and reemployment.

The Swedish system continuously upgrades the work force and allows workers to welcome rather than resist industrial restructurings that improve productivity in the long run. When the Swedish unemployment rate rises, the national labor market board can declare that funds are now available for workers to take paid sabbaticals, to learn new skills. This opens up jobs for other workers, reducing the over-all unemployment rate, and upgrading the productivity of the entire work force at the same time. The labor market board can also use labor market subsidies as tools of regional or sectoral industrial policies.

For example, if a town has lost a major employer, say a shipbuilder, a local ad hoc tripartite committee of business leaders, labor representatives, and local government can get funds to conduct a study and determine what kind of new industry might be suitable, given the local labor force. The local committee can then submit a proposal to the national labor market board, which in turn can offer a prospective employer subsidies to pay the cost of retraining and part of a few years' wages.

This system, in effect, uses a labor subsidy as a capital subsidy, and as a delicate tool of planning. Unlike the caricatures of economic planning, which invariably feature some heavy-handed bureaucratic czar attempting to "pick winners and losers," this approach is locally based and relies on entrepreneurs to identify opportunities. It allows government and trade unions to play a constructive role, with the additional benefit of targeting development to localities with high unemployment, and continuously upgrading worker skills. It is far better than our characteristic system of enticing new development by means of bargaining away a needed local tax base.

Changing the emphasis of our labor market subsidies from subsidizing unemployment to subsidizing reemployment would accomplish several other goals that serve the broader objective of a more collaborative and competitive economy. First, an approach like the Swedish system of labor market boards encourages firms to focus on their internal labor markets. By socializing part of the cost of training, it compensates for the tendency of managers to under-invest in upgrading the skills of their workers. It also can be part of a national strategy of constantly working to create good, high skill, well-paid jobs, rather than cheap ones.

Most important for our goal of a new social contract between industry, government, and labor, the existence of an active labor market policy makes it possible to negotiate new productivity-enhancing agreements, because it creates a temporary place to put excess labor. This not only has direct payoffs in terms of the productivity of the labor force as a whole, but it also facilitates more collaborative management by making it possible for labor to operate more flexibly. Retraining sabbaticals and reemployment subsidies are one more element of the bargain for government to bring to the table, and one more benefit that can substitute for wage inflation.

A further important challenge is the systematic upgrading of low-wage service-sector work. Service-sector work, on average, pays lower and more maldistributed wages than the manufacturing work it is replacing. Most of the new jobs will be service-sector jobs, but roughly half of the jobs created during the 1980s pay an annual wage of less than $11,000. There are essentially two possible strategies for upgrading service-sector work—wage subsidy, and professionalization.

A number of academic experts, such as Robert Lerman of Brandeis University, David Ellwood of Harvard's Kennedy School, and Harvard sociologist Theda Skocpol,[9] have urged that the present welfare system be converted to a system of wage subsidy, using a revised version of the earned income tax credit (EITC). For example, if the head of a household earned $200 a week as a fast-food cashier, the Labor Department would make up the difference between that wage and the poverty level for that worker's family. There would have to be experiment and refinement of this approach, to make certain that employers did not lower prevailing wages in order to have the government make up the difference. Moreover, the fact of working would trigger a variety of social fringe benefits, such as child care, the opportunity for retraining sabbaticals, and comprehensive health insurance. This strategy represents a substantial improvement over traditional welfare approaches because it rewards the holding of a job with a higher standard of living.

There is also a need for the Labor Department to initiate pilot programs aimed at the systematic upgrading of work in the human services, which is expected to be a major growth area. For example, home health care is both a more cost-effective and a more dignified alternative to nursing-home care for the elderly. Yet home health-care services are available only sporadically and are notoriously underfunded. As a consequence, the work is a typically "secondary labor market" job—low paid, without fringe benefits or career ladders, and subject to predictably high turnover. The system treats home health-care workers as comparable to housemaids.

A home health-care worker, however, could just as logically be a paraprofessional, analogous to a visiting nurse. This would require greater training, higher pay, and the creation of career paths. But for society, the greater expense would be well worth the cost if it kept more people out of nursing homes. There are dozens of other service occupations where professionalization would be an avenue both to more productive provision of the service and better-paid careers.

A very good co-determination model was devised under Labor Secretary Ray Marshall's leadership during the Carter Administration—the COSH Group. With a modest amount of public funding and Labor Department encouragement, in-plant Committees on Occupational Safety and Health began involving themselves intimately in plant safety. This gave workers and unions a new systematic capacity to protect the labor force, but it also led ineluctably to areas of "management prerogative"—questions of capital investment and the organization of production—that have been conventionally off-limits in the American system of labor relations. This role did not come easily to some unions. But at a time when labor is in a defensive role, trade unions need to recoup by involving themselves far more directly in the process of corporate governance, and not just by devising such new services as credit cards.

Labor-management collaboration during a period of heightened competition, technological change, and corporate restructuring, requires more than better labor laws or training in participatory management. It requires a new conception of the governance of the corporation, of the corporation as a social creature, of workers as stakeholders in that corporation, and of government as guarantor of an effective social contract. That, in turn, requires a very different conception of what it means to have an "efficient" capitalist society. It requires new institutions and new imagination. The payoff is immense: a more productive and competitive economy, a much better prospect of high growth macro-economics without inflation. That the payoff is also a more decent, defensible society should not blind us to the fact that it is also sounder economics. The principles and the mechanisms sound a lot like ideas that can be inferred from Catholic social teaching. But just as you don't have to be Jewish, as the commercial went, to love Levy's Jewish Rye Bread, you don't have to be Catholic to appreciate that a social conception of the market also makes for a more sustainable and dynamic capitalism.

NOTES

1. See Barry Bluestone and Bennett Harrison, *The Great U-Turn* (New York: Basic Books, 1987); also Robert B. Reich, *Tales of a New America* (New York: Times Books, 1987).

2. See Ronald Dore, *Flexible Rigidity* (Stanford: Stanford University Press, 1986). See also Peter Gourevitch, *Politics in Hard Times* (Ithaca: Cornell University Press, 1986.)

3. Robert Kuttner, *The Economic Illusion* (Boston: Houghton Mifflin, 1984).

4. Peter Katzenstein, *Small States in World Markets* (Ithaca: Cornell University Press, 1985).

5. Karl Polanyi, *The Great Transformation: The Political and Economic Origins of Our Time* (Boston: Beacon Press, 1957 [first published 1944]), p. 73.

6. Robert Heilbroner, *The Nature and Logic of Capitalism* (New York: W. W. Norton Company, 1985), especially pp. 84-85.

7. Martin Weitzman, *The Share Economy* (Cambridge, Massachusetts: Harvard University Press, 1984).

8. Gosta Esping-Andersen, "The Work and Welfare State," forthcoming in *The American Prospect.*

9. For a summary, see Theda Skocpol, "Sustainable Social Policy: Fighting Poverty Without Poverty Programs," in *The American Prospect* (Summer 1990), pp. 58-70.

16

CAPITALISM AFTER COMMUNISM

Now Comes the Hard Part

THOMAS S. JOHNSON

Large numbers of people around the world have been opting for capitalism over communism as their chosen method for economic organization. They are abandoning command economies, in which governments make all the decisions about production and distribution, and are setting up new, enterprise-based economies, in which most decisions are made in the market on the basis of price, quality, and profits.

Their choice is not surprising. Capitalism, despite its shortcomings, has done a demonstrably far better job than communism when it comes to expanding aggregate production, boosting wealth and income, and distributing the output to greater numbers of people, thereby reducing poverty and raising individual standards of living.

Capitalism's relative success in these areas generally has been the case throughout the eighty years in which formal systems of communism have been in place. What probably is most different now is that the Information Age has succeeded in shrinking the globe, allowing people to share quite graphically each other's experiences, desires, and expectations. No longer in the dark about what is happening elsewhere, masses of people are now making the choice for contemporary capitalism, or what is called the modern mixed economy.

These recent and breathtakingly rapid developments have provided an opportunity to take a fresh look at capitalism. This time, however, we can do so unencumbered by the ideological baggage of the past. The examination need no longer involve the issue of capitalism versus communism. Instead, the examination can sharpen its focus on ways to make market-based economies work even better in terms of meeting broad human needs, both material and spiritual.

In a sense, communism had been a rather convenient thing to have around. Its existence served to simplify debate, narrow the options, and discourage rigorous examination. Subtleties were frequently not allowed. Attempts at meaningful discourse were often enfeebled by a hardening of the categories. We saw that as recently as 1986 in some of the dogmatic reaction to the United States bishops' pastoral on the economy—although, in fairness, the bishops too exhibited their own share of rigidity.

Today we can move beyond all that. We have the opportunity to get beyond a debate that was both oversimplified and at the same time over-complicated by its association with national and political rivalries. We can work now to identify the best features of the modern mixed economy and build upon them and expand the benefits they bring to a maximum number of human beings.

In short, with one debate seemingly resolved, we can now focus our energy and attention on eliminating the significant faults and inadequacies of capitalism that we know to exist, while at the same time preserving those special properties that imbue the markets with their special genius. As I suggest in the title of this essay, this will not be an easy task, but it is an urgent challenge and one that must engage the very best thinking of business leaders, political leaders, educational leaders, and religious leaders alike.

NEW YORK CITY: THE CHALLENGE IN MICROCOSM

New York City, where the bank I work for has its headquarters, starkly reveals the best and worst of our free-enterprise economy. On the one hand, there is probably not a place in the world where the fruits of a competitively ignited human spirit are so much in evidence. The products of free, competitive urges abound. The city is literally charged with energy. The atmosphere is dynamic, resulting in the best there is to offer, not only in the areas of business and commerce but also in the arts, entertainment, education, and scholarship.

On the other hand, there is New York's devastating problem of home-lessness, high unemployment (particularly among minority youth), rampant drug abuse, and a terrifying crime rate. Perhaps most discouraging is the existence of large numbers of what we now refer to as the structurally unemployed—people without the basic skills to qualify for jobs in the modern economy. This situation has led to the creation of large groups of people whose spirits have been crushed and who live literally without hope. They are the people who have been left out of the process—the very poor in a city of enormous wealth.

On a perhaps less immediate level, but no less important if the fruits of the market are to continue to ripen for more and more people, there is the problem of an old and decaying infrastructure. Bridges are crumbling. The public transportation system is in dire need of repair. A lot of things just don't work anymore. The seed corn for future growth and prosperity is being allowed to rot, and what is worse, not being planted at all due to severe municipal budget constraints.

It goes without saying that all of these problems are of great practical concern for those in leadership positions in corporations and banks. It is axiomatic that the health of the community has much to do with the health of one's business. But these problems should also concern business leaders for a far loftier reason: they violate basic standards of ethics and morality. Joining together with leaders in politics, religion, and academia, we need to evolve a new set of standards against which our economic system can be judged moving forward and then work at finding ways to meet those standards.

STANDARDS AND CONFLICTS

Setting standards is the easy part. We can probably all agree to organize our thoughts around such simple premises as: 1) the desire for a just distribution of goods and the meeting of fundamental human needs, 2) the need for effective means of increasing the aggregate production of goods, 3) the mandate to conserve resources for those not yet born, and 4) the protection of human dignity and the opportunity for goodness.

The far more difficult challenge will be in dealing with the conflicts that necessarily will arise. We all need to recognize that tradeoffs will be required and that reaching a maximum standard in any of the four areas is not achievable. This may be hard to accept, but unless we can find a way to both reinvent human nature and turn finite natural resources into unlimited wellsprings, accept it we must.

For example, there is a fundamental conflict between increasing the aggregate production of goods and conserving resources for the future. There is also a conflict between achieving a just distribution of goods and maintaining the maximum level of competition. This latter conflict has always been a major issue dividing political conservatives and liberals. We need to find a way to get beyond doctrinaire rhetoric.

In addition, we will all need to possess a clear understanding of the design elements of the modern mixed economy and how they vary from country to country. This is the subject of the first part of this chapter. In the second part I will suggest some principles that may be useful in assessing those tradeoffs that necessarily will be part of the examination process.

DESIGN ELEMENTS OF A MARKET-BASED ECONOMIC STRUCTURE

There are important distinctions within the capitalist world. Three distinct aspects that are referred to when we talk about an economic system may be stated as questions: Who owns it? How does the system function to create productivity, efficiency, and growth? and What is government's role, not only in the functioning of the system but in dealing with the economic inequities that may result from a market mechanism? These three questions are of course interrelated, but only by separating them can a firm analytical foundation be established for purposes of evolving Catholic social thought.

Ownership

Ownership is very broad within the Japanese, European, and American systems, certainly in comparison with precapitalist patterns. There is significant concentration of wealth, particularly in Europe and the United States, especially if it is measured only in terms of direct ownership. By direct ownership I mean assets that would show up on an individual person's accounting balance sheet. If we include in the definition of ownership, however, indirect ownership, it is much more widespread. Indirect ownership would include, in the United States for example, the ownership of enterprise by pension funds, charitable foundations, educational endowments, and so on. These are known collectively as institutional investors. They represent a broad base of beneficial owners, for example, the workers for whom pension funds will provide future income security. A proper economic (as opposed to standard accounting) balance sheet would show less wealth distribution inequality in the United States than the more common view supposes.

The importance of understanding the patterns of ownership is not to justify the inequalities of wealth that remain, but to emphasize that there can be, within the general context of what are considered to be capitalist systems, varieties in ownership patterns. The Japanese model, for example, differs from the United States model because much ownership is inter-institutional. Ultimate owners are individual Japanese shareholders, perhaps even more so than in the United States, but the authority that goes with ownership is exercised among companies that have cross holdings in each other. European ownership patterns resemble the Japanese model.

While there can be different models of ownership within a so-called capitalist system, all of them differ in important respects from statist systems that have prevailed in the communist world and to an extent in Latin America. Decision-making by owners or their representatives in capitalist systems is aimed, importantly, at measurable performance in terms of profits, productivity, and growth, while performance in the statist models is less oriented to these factors and more oriented to bureaucratic choices aimed at the deliberate accomplishment of a state-defined objective. The objective may be stated in terms very similar to the objectives of investors in Western economies, but it functions in a political context rather than in a competitive profit-seeking context. Thus, decisions on where savings will be put to work are not limited to infrastructure, the public minimum good, and so forth, but to the totality of what will be produced, by whom, with what technology, and so on. Because of the monopoly of state power, there is less self-correction of errors, because "owners" cannot opt out of investments to seek better returns elsewhere.

The ownership differences between the capitalist and non-capitalist models are blurred in two important respects. First, there is considerable variety in the definition of the scope of productive enterprise that is properly state-owned within the so-called capitalist nations. Even in Germany, for example, a country certainly associated with the capitalist pattern, state ownership goes much further than it does in the United States. It was only recently, within the last ten years, that more than fifty percent of German gross national product was produced by non-state enterprises.

A second way in which ownership is blurred is most evident in certain of the developing countries, particularly in Latin America. In these areas there is frequently an implicit partnership between the state and hereditary concentrations of private wealth that operate to protect a historic hegemony. Such a hybrid system is neither totally statist nor is it in any meaningful way capitalist. If a definition of capitalism is that the capital stock is allocated largely on the basis of decision rules oriented to profitability, productivity, and growth, the Latin American patterns, at least up to the most recent reform movements in those countries, do not fit it.

Market Functioning

The second area where there are profound differences within capitalist countries has to do with the question, How does the system function to create productivity, efficiency, growth, and so on? Here there are obvious differences in the rules of business, for example, between the United States and Japan. These differences relate to how open these economies are to cross-border transactions, to what degree companies are allowed/prohibited from working together for their mutual benefit, patent protection for physical and intellectual goods, and the like. There are also tremendous differences in how the companies operating in these countries coordinate with other institutions of the society and their governments. In Japan, and to a great extent in the European countries as well, there is a high degree of coordination of economic policies, including active participation of affected industry groups with the government. In the United States, on the other hand, there is a much more antagonistic relationship between the government and business organizations.

The most important characteristic of successful economic systems is that businesses operate largely within a competitive open-market context. There may be some protection from foreign competition, but the most successful economic regimes are those in which business is conducted in a highly competitive setting. This is not surprising, for it is competition that imbues the markets with their special genius. Thus, while the Japanese may legitimately be criticized for having markets that are less open to foreign competition, industry by industry there is lively competition among Japanese companies within Japan. The same is true throughout Europe and in the United States.

A profound question that is now facing the central European economies, which are liberalizing and privatizing the ownership of state enterprise, is the degree of competition that will be promoted. If, for example, the Russian state airline, Aeroflot, becomes privatized—that is, ownership is either distributed or sold to private parties—but it remains officially sanctioned as the only airline allowed to operate in Russia, the outcome will be profoundly different from what it would be if competition is encouraged.

One of the reasons large economies tend to do better than small economies is that there is a large enough market to allow large-scale production, while still allowing room for enough firms to provide the competition that leads to productivity, innovation, and growth. Smaller countries, particularly if they are isolated geographically and therefore not subject to competition across borders, tend either to have companies that are too small to be efficient or large companies that are protected from competition and therefore do not perform as well. It is interesting to contrast experience in Europe with that of Latin America. In Europe there are large companies headquartered in small countries, and even though there might be only one in a country in a given industry, the relatively free trade across national borders and the proximity of the other countries produce a competitive discipline that enables very large companies to be highly productive and highly competitive even though they are headquartered in small countries. In Latin America, with physically larger countries and many more barriers to cross-border trade, even privately owned companies do not tend to be very efficient; they are not subjected to the degree of competition that exists in the European context.

The importance of distinguishing between who owns the capital resources and how companies operate cannot be overstated. Disparate patterns are observed in ownership, but successful, productive, innovative, growth-oriented performance only occurs in settings in which lively competition is the rule.

The Role of Government

A third distinction within the capitalist world involves the role of government, although all systems recognize that government does have some role to play. Nowhere does there exist a totally unfettered free-market system. Be it in Sweden, which has a high level of redistributive taxation, or Hong Kong, which has what is generally regarded as the most government-free approach, what is found is some form of the modern mixed economy. Even in the most laissez faire of places, we see government functioning in some way to create and maintain the proper conditions for economic progress, as well as social stability and fairness.

Anti-trust laws, for example, seek to prevent the creation of monopolies that would undermine competition and lead to market inefficiencies. Monetary and fiscal policies are employed to counteract inflation and to reduce the ups and downs of the business cycle. Regulations are promulgated to set rules and standards for a broad range of activities. Economic infrastructure projects like building roads, bridges, and dams are generally financed by government.

Another accepted, albeit controversial, function of government is to address in some degree the issue of economic inequality. This role has less to do with how a market-based economy functions and more to do with how it may fail to function in terms of meeting the basic human needs of all members of society. Under this category fall such "safety net" programs as welfare, food stamps, and other types of minimum income maintenance schemes. Also embraced by this heading are such efforts as affirmative action and special programs to assist the structurally unemployed.

The issue of the proper role of government in a free enterprise economy is, of course, at least as old as *The Wealth of Nations*. Adam Smith suggested that a government should limit itself to three areas: defense against "the violence and invasion of other independent societies"; protecting society from "the injustice or oppression of every other member of it"; and supporting "certain public works and certain public institutions, which it can never be for the interest of any individual, or small number of individuals, to erect and maintain."

No one disagrees with the appropriateness of the first two roles, and few would reject the notion that government needs to get involved if roads and bridges and other forms of economic infrastructure are to get built. Two hundred years after Smith's death, however, public opinion continues to vacillate with respect to how much further governments should go, particularly in smoothing out what might be described as capitalism's rough edges. As the United States bishops made clear in the 1986 pastoral, however, this issue is an essential area for Catholic inquiry.

These are the three important design characteristics of a modern, market-based economic system. First, despite variations in the patterns of ownership, it is essentially private and/or exercised in reference to private considerations of profit, growth, and so forth. Second, for these systems to succeed there must be lively competition so that resource allocation and pricing, buying, and other decisions are made largely according to the actual needs and desires of consumers and the factors of production, rather than the calculated (even if well-meaning) judgments of bureaucrats. And third, though the ingredients of the modern mixed economy differ from country to country, there is a recognition that government has an appropriate role to play both in the efficient functioning of the markets and in addressing in some form the issue of inequality. The world is in the process of making a decision to adopt such systems virtually everywhere. There will be variations in how the systems work, but the argument over decision-making by bureaucrats versus an open marketplace has been settled.

THE FUTURE—MAKING ECONOMIC INSTITUTIONS FUNCTION ACCORDING TO CHRISTIAN PRIORITIES

Deliberation and teaching on the work, wealth, income, consumption, and savings aspects of human life can now proceed within a narrower, less ideological context. The question can no longer be, Does one accept or reject the capitalist or socialist model? because most of the world has made its choice, rejecting statist decision-making in the economic realm.

Careful thought can now be devoted to how our existing and evolving modern economic systems can be made more sensitive to Christian principles. The rest of this chapter is devoted to my suggestions about the avenues that will be most fruitful for our future decisions and that we need to think about now.

In proceeding to a new stage of thinking about economic systems and institutions, we can bypass the arid arguments about capitalism versus some radically different form of productive enterprise, and we can stop attempting to force choices between a radical distribution-of-wealth view and a radical production-of-goods view. We can now get to the real issues and the more meaningful distinctions.

Since there are conflicting elements in any reasonable set of principles upon which one might judge how modern economic systems work, there needs to be real analysis and deliberation over how to resolve the conflicts. It is in this area that Catholic social teaching can now make a new contribution. In essence, Catholic social teaching has been freed from political ideology and it can now be devoted to the most important questions by which the detailed design of political/economic systems can be judged.

For starters, we need to reject forcefully the suggestion that has been made, including by some Catholics, that the church has no business venturing into economic issues. We saw this in 1984, when the first draft of the bishops' pastoral was circulated. Some critics argued that in emphasizing the need for creative and more effective social programs, the bishops might compromise the integrity of free markets and the initiatives of free people. That was a legitimate concern, but some went further and argued that the bishops had neither the competence nor the mandate to address something as far afield from religion as economics. Indeed, *Forbes* in an editorial even offered up a mock prayer: "From sermonizing prelates, making up in presumption what they lack in knowledge of economic affairs, O Lord, deliver us." Six years later, we need to get beyond that.

Minimum Participation for Each Person

The first question, and the one that will be most difficult to answer, is the one so profoundly raised by the bishops in their pastoral letter. It is the question of how to set minimum standards of material goods that an economic system should provide to all of its people. Our deliberations should no longer start with an abstract principle of redistribution, but rather with how well we are providing housing, food, education, and health care for every member of society. This will be a difficult discussion, because there will be disagreements about the relative importance of different elements of human welfare. It will be doubly difficult because the discussion must respect cultural differences, historical factors, and the practical gaps in expectations between the rich societies and the poor societies in the world today. The bishops' letter raised—but only just raised—the profound question of whether a minimum that is appropriate for the United States, for example, can be used as a target for the entire world. Any minimum that could be acceptable for the population of the Western world will be extremely difficult to achieve in a short time for the impoverished nations whose population so greatly outnumbers us. Yet the moral issue remains: our consumption of goods, and particularly our consumption of irreplaceable resources from the earth, is in some respects at the expense of others who do not have or will not have access to these goods.

Throughout the discussion of a minimum, religious leaders must go beyond material calculations. They must help in determining and promulgating a measurement that, perhaps uniquely for each society and for each stage of societies' growth, allows human beings the freedom to live a life in which they can choose to follow God's will. At the least, this measure must assure that human beings are removed from bondage—either literal bondage imposed by a political system or the de facto bondage that results from such a low level of sharing in the wealth that does exist that all hope for progress is extinguished and individual work is always seen as inadequately rewarded.

There are many areas in which this discussion must consider differences in approach and result among the Western nations. The minimum level of health care and housing that is provided by European countries, for example, is measurably greater, and arguably fairer, than what is provided in the United States. The result, in terms of homelessness and infant mortality is a moral issue, and it is an economic issue as well. In comparing the European approach with the United States approach, it seems clear that one does not need to compromise aggregate economic growth to have a fairer distribution of goods. European growth, since the mid-'70s at least, has been greater than the growth that has been experienced in the United States on average. Here, therefore, is an example of where today's discussion can be much more constructive. We must discuss, within the context of each society perhaps, objectives for minimum standards of goods and services that ought to be available to all people, and then we must determine, in practical terms, how best to meet these objectives.

Saving and Investing for Growth and Productivity

A second area for discussion is the need to invest for growth in the future. Here also, Catholic social teaching can play an important role. The allocation of public and private investment resources will produce the wealth of tomorrow that can elevate the minimums enjoyed by each person. The allocations are in two dimensions. First, we make decisions on how much to save out of current consumption in order to provide for future growth. Second, we make decisions about economic infrastructures and what productive enterprises we wish to be involved in.

These are not purely economic choices. They obviously involve moral questions as well. The most fundamental question, particularly applicable to the taxing power of the state, is how much to invest when any investment at all may result in limiting the resources available for current goods and services that are already at minimal levels. This is the question that is so frequently voiced today in the Third World, and it is a question of profound moral importance.

Catholic social teaching can help to clarify this question. There should be discussion, for example, of whether individual human beings can truly be considered as participants in any system if they do not contribute to its future growth when they have the capability to do so. Certainly every human being has some responsibility to conserve resources and provide for the future. No human being would deny responsibility, for example, to attempt to provide for the future of his or her children. If that is true we all, as members of the human family, have a social responsibility to do the same.

Another perspective is the responsibility of those who have relatively greater wealth to save and invest more, so that others will be given the opportunity, with the use of capital provided from the wealthy, to raise their participation in the economic system in the future. The history of economic development in the United States, for example, is that we relied heavily on imported capital for all of the nineteenth century. In the twentieth century the expansion of the United States westward and later the economic development that occurred in the southern part of the country relied on capital imported from the Northeast, where development had occurred much earlier.

When a moral discussion takes place on the subject of responsible investment to provide for the future and for development in other parts of the world, the United States' record in the last fifteen or so years should be judged deficient. The United States, still the wealthiest nation in the world, has relied during this period on imported capital to balance its books. Our huge federal government budget deficits have forced us to compete for scarce capital in the international markets, and this has pushed up the cost, and reduced the availability, of capital to poorer parts of the world. Catholic social teaching needs to get into the discussion of the rights and wrongs of macro-economic policy as well as private decision-making, and the discussion can start with an examination of this most recent period.

A third area in which moral discussion should take place is related to the process of community or social decision-making. The complexity of the decisions that need to be made, particularly when they relate to ecological questions, has frequently led to a near breakdown of our ability to arrive at voluntary consensus. Where there is not voluntary consensus we are reduced to a status of alienation, and resources that could be used for constructive purposes are wasted in an endless process of unconstructive debate.

The development of single-issue politics in the United States is an example of breakdown of social dialogue. This is a moral issue if it results in wasted resources. It is a profound moral issue when it results in apathy and alienation. The same difficulties seem evident in Japan, for example, in the long-lived debate about Tokyo's new international airport and the resulting removal of acreage from agricultural production. It is also obviously seen throughout Europe in the Green Movement. When advocacy of a point of view is driven to the extent that it fails to recognize any merit in an opposing point of view, and particularly when it results in the breakdown of society's ability to get on with its task of doing better for the future, this becomes a profound moral issue.

Catholic social teaching should address itself to the process of decision-making as well as to the actual decisions that are made. The process of decision-making has a lot to do with the ability of each individual human being to feel that he or she has some real influence on social decisions. It is inevitable that there will be differences in emphasis on how resources should be allocated. The process itself has moral value if it teaches human beings how to listen, accommodate themselves to the views of others, and express their own beliefs in a constructive way.

The torts crisis in the United States is an example of the alienation of individual human beings from each other. A developing feeling that it is fine to attempt to garner huge resources from impersonal organizations, with little recognition of the undeniable fact that those resources are appropriated from other human beings through those organizations, is an issue that has moral consequences. A judicial system that goes beyond protecting society and its individual members from abuse and facilitates enrichment at the expense of other human beings is a morally deficient system.

Another example of a flawed social decision-making process was the debate that occurred in New York City about whether to build a proposed road system to be known as Westway. From about 1970 to 1980 there was rancorous disagreement about this question. The debate found its way through multiple layers of courts. The opposing sides would give no ground; there was no vehicle for arriving at consensus; and after ten years government officials simply abandoned the effort. A political/legal decision-making process that can keep an issue like that unresolved for more than ten years, resulting in estimated legal expenses of well over $1 billion, and fails to produce a social consensus, is not a good system. The $1 billion spent on legal expenses to support the arguments of the opposing sides could have built a lot of housing or it could have provided a lot of health care.

Study of the variety of ways in which social consensus is arrived at in different parts of the world could perhaps result in ways to improve the genuine participation of individuals in decision-making about their welfare and about the future. The process of arriving at consensus about infrastructure and investment decisions in Japan, for example, might be worthy of study. That process has created opportunities for tremendous growth in wealth and employment, which in turn have created opportunities for self-fulfillment for great numbers of the Japanese people.

On the other hand, study of Japan's system would need to inquire whether the whole society, rather than just its business, intellectual, and governmental leaders, participates in arriving at the consensus. There are early apparent signs of some alienation of ordinary workers in Japan that might indicate a system that makes "good" economic decisions, but does not provide as well for individual participation and fulfillment.

There are many other examples of effective and ineffective decision-making, and Catholic social teaching can contribute greatly if it addresses how decisions can be arrived at more efficiently, with a maximum of involvement by the greatest number of individuals in the process.

Our Responsibility to Those Who Will Live in the Future

A third area in which Catholic social teaching can contribute is in how we make sure that we are providing for the future of our planet and for those who are not yet born. Questions relating to the destruction of natural eco-systems and the use of irreplaceable resources, as well as whether we are investing enough to provide for an acceptable life for those who will inhabit our world in the future, are moral issues. The responsibility to save and the responsibility to conserve are difficult questions and they relate not just to the next generation and not just to our own children. We are all children of God and therefore everyone's children are brothers and sisters, and we need to think about how best we can leave the world in good condition and more productive for them.

How our descendants live will depend in a major way on how much we save and invest. Different societies, even at radically different levels of present wealth, save different amounts; those who save more provide better for the future. Much can be learned from discussion of how best to encourage individuals and institutions to accept responsibility for providing for a better future. Demanding that institutions, and particularly governments, build now the structures that will be needed in the future and avoid spending resources for consumption now that will deprive the future is a moral responsibility. The deteriorating transportation and education infrastructure in the United States, for example, is evidence of a usurpation of resources for current consumption that ought to be preserved and enhanced for future people. Discussion of the intersection of our moral responsibilities to those who are not yet born and a pattern of fiscal management in our country that results in using up resources that they will need can help produce a better consensus on how to use today's resources. Such a discussion should demand an accounting from public officials for how they use resources. This accounting must be in terms not only of the needs of the present population, but it must also, to be consistent with Christian principles, reflect our responsibilities to the future.

Work and the Individual

A fourth and final suggestion for discussion in the context of Catholic social teaching relates to work. Catholic social teaching already argues that work is fulfilling and that every human being has the right to have the opportunity for fruitful participation in productive work. Much of that work in the future will be done in large corporate organizations. Increasingly, as the world opts for market-based economies oriented to productivity and growth, large organizations will continue to emerge in the pursuit of cost advantages. The economies of large-scale production have long been accepted. In fact, this is not even a principle limited to capitalism, because within the failed socialist economies large-scale production was pursued for the same reason.

There are many moral and social implications of work within large organizations. If work is to be fulfilling to human beings, it must be conducted in a setting that is respectful of human needs and of moral values. The large organizations in which work is done must therefore be designed not merely according to theoretical engineering or economic formulations, but in a way that adequately considers the impact that work in these organizations has on the individuals who work there.

There are special opportunities and responsibilities inherent in business and professional leadership. Making the enterprise successful and at the same time trying to accomplish as many socially desirable objectives beyond efficiency and profitability as possible, would make work truly good and morally fulfilling. Additionally, styles of leadership that try to bring out the best in others help to make work a positive moral force.

The opportunity for ministry to our fellow human beings at work is likewise important. We spend more than half of our waking hours for most of our lives at work, and it is therefore extremely important that the way in which we spend those hours be assessed from the perspective of human and spiritual values. If enjoyment and fulfillment come only from non-work activities, then work is not being conducted according to God's plan.

Catholic social teaching has over the last one hundred years addressed many aspects of work, including the right to a just wage, the right of labor to organize into unions, and so on. With expanding areas of the world entering the era of modern industrial production, and with increasingly complex technologies, it is now more than ever important for Catholic social teaching to address how work is organized and how work, particularly in very large organizations, can be fulfilling and moral. People at all levels of modern enterprises have a desire for their work to be not only productive, but meaningful in their personal lives. Work must be human if it is to be fulfilling, and it must be moral if it is to be consistent with God's plan. Much thought therefore should be devoted to systems of organization and management, communications methodologies, compensation patterns, and ways to include workers as full members of an enterprise, including empowering them to participate genuinely in decision-making.

Beyond work, the modern economy has led to changes in living patterns. With more opportunities for women to work, for example, the distribution of domestic work at home is affected. Likewise, intergenerational living patterns have changed. There is much to be gained from study and careful reflection on alternative models for preserving the best of family values in the modern setting. There are differences in approach, for example, in providing living arrangements for elderly people. In many European countries, facilities are provided in the immediate neighborhoods in which they spent the earlier parts of their lives. In this way the tendency toward a separation between older people and other age groups can be minimized and the solidarity of families and of society as a whole insured. There are many other aspects of work patterns and living arrangements that can benefit from careful study and discussion.

IN CONCLUSION

To sum up, we are presently entering an exciting period in which there are many challenges, but far better opportunities for constructive dialogue on how Christian principles can be brought to bear on economic decisions, and on how those decisions can be made more responsive to the needs of all of God's children whether now living or to be born in the future. Catholic social teaching now enters a new era in which the gross ideological divisions of the last century have receded, there are many successful and unsuccessful patterns of business and social organization to be studied, and there is a widespread solidarity of human beings throughout the world in pursuing a more meaningful and satisfying life.

The process that has emerged, particularly in the post-Vatican II era of constructive discussion involving not only religious leaders but all elements of society in searching for better answers for the moral dilemmas posed by the modern world can now be brought to bear even more pointedly on these questions. The premises of Catholic social teaching can be couched in many ways. I have argued here that they should be oriented to some very simple objectives such as:

1. a just distribution of goods and the meeting of basic human needs,
2. an effective means of increasing aggregate production and wealth,
3. conservation of resources for those who have not yet been born, and
4. the preservation and enhancement of human dignity and the opportunity for goodness.

These objectives would, I believe, command widespread, even universal assent in our society. At the same time we know that there is vigorous, often fierce disagreement about how they are to be achieved and about what programs and practices will most aid our society's efforts to achieve them. We face the paradox of continuing disagreement about social objectives that all of us claim to find attractive and morally compelling.

This is a situation that we cannot overcome altogether. As I have suggested, the four objectives may at times come into tension and conflict with each other. Increasing aggregate wealth and conserving resources are goals that often are likely to point us in opposite directions. Some ways of distributing goods to meet basic needs may infringe on human freedom and dignity. Just how we strike the right balance among these objectives can change with circumstances. The right balance is seen differently from different perspectives and cannot be settled by a fixed formula.

These are issues on which men and women of good will are likely to have differing opinions. In fact, such differences are to be welcomed as steps to the formation of a consensus for our society on how to achieve these morally urgent objectives. Particularly when they are put forward in a way that shows respect for experience, both our own and others, these differences should be evaluated positively and should be brought within the scope of Catholic social discussion and American public debate.

But there is also a darker side to our inability to get to these attractive but distant objectives. That is the tendency that can affect each one of us both as individuals and as members of groups and firms to put these objectives to one side and to pursue a private agenda of our own without regard to its impact on the common goods and objectives that are so central to our flourishing as a society. This tendency can show up in a wide variety of ways, ranging from negligence with regard to environmental risks to cheating on financial records, from the selfish pursuit of personal advancement to the various kinds of racial, ethnic, and religious prejudice.

What a theologian would want to call the sins of American corporate life and what lawyers would speak of as white-collar crime are to a very large extent actions that damage the four objectives I have set forth. The widespread occurrence of such acts shows how uneven and how intermittent our commitment to these objectives is and how corporate America, as well as each of us as an individual, needs to deepen its sense of how fundamentally important these objectives are. Attaining these objectives will often impose real costs and require real sacrifices. The effort to do this will push us to draw on our ethical and religious resources. It will require us to acknowledge that an effective orientation to these objectives is not something we can take for granted.

In conclusion, a world of greater solidarity among all peoples and in which patterns of economic organization have demonstrably produced dramatic improvements in peoples' lives, offers great possibilities for the new century. It will bring a tremendous expansion in the number of God's people who can participate meaningfully in economic production. With this will come greater opportunities for personal development according to God's plan and an existence truly free from economic and political enslavement.

For those already among the fortunate human beings who have benefitted from the explosive economic progress of the last two centuries, the new century promises opportunities to share their wealth for the benefit of future generations and for other parts of the world, and to enrich their lives with each other and at work each day. Perhaps above all, if Catholic social teaching can help us to develop a process through which human beings can together make decisions about the future of the world in a way that promotes human values and further solidarity, even when we make mistakes, we will be serving each other better and serving God.

17

WOMEN'S WAYS OF WORKING

CAROL COSTON, O.P.

What would happen if Maria Montessori and Virginia Woolf were to meet Leo XIII and Pius XI and dialogue with them about work? Could a feminist educator and writer find any common ground with Catholic social thought?

Who are these women and what do they have to say about the meaning of work? About women as workers? About values in the workplace?

What does the church's social tradition say in response? Are there convergence points? If there are areas of agreement between Catholic social thought and feminism, how have contemporary Catholic women tried to integrate both perspectives into their worklives? And finally, what guidance can this give to Catholic social thought in the future?

DEFINING WORK THROUGH WOMEN'S EXPERIENCE

In the United States bishops' pastoral, *Economic Justice for All*, work has a threefold significance for people: 1) a way to meet their material needs, 2) a way to exercise self-expression and self-realization, 3) a way to contribute to the well-being of the larger community (no. 97).[1]

In my experience of women's organizations, this definition is consistent with "women's ways of working." Women particularly contribute to the well-being of the community in that the majority of teachers, social-service workers, health-care providers and volunteers in non-profit organizations are women. "Well-being of the community" is another way to express a key element in Catholic social tradition—the common good. Some goals of the common good, as articulated in *Mater et Magistra* and applicable to this essay, are "to make accessible the goods and services for a better life to as many persons as possible . . . to provide employment for as many workers

256

as possible ... that harmony in economic affairs and a friendly and beneficial cooperation be fostered" (nos. 79-80).

Women have traditionally been the volunteer or underpaid backbone of
innumerable organizations dedicated to the common good and through this
have often exercised creative self-expression. Some women are able to do
this and also meet their material needs, but millions more must work in
mind-numbing and back-breaking jobs which are not forms of creative self-
expression.

This chapter focuses on ways in which four women-led organizations—
two from the early 1900s, two from the 1970s—reflect the common good
in their purpose or mission and incorporate other principles and values
contained in Catholic social thought within their internal processes. The
Montessori "Children's Houses" and Rachel's Women's Center provide
direct services in ways which help participants empower themselves to grow
and change. The Women's Cooperative Guild and NETWORK work for
systemic change within the social-justice tradition. Each of these four models of women's organizations will be expanded upon.

MARIA MONTESSORI MEETS LEO XIII

Pope Leo XIII and Maria Montessori were both in Rome in 1891. I do
not know if they ever met personally, but if they did they may have discussed
women's proper role in the workplace. While Leo was preparing for *Rerum
Novarum*, Maria was struggling to enter the University of Rome Medical
School.

The medical school refused her first application, and her father was
unalterably opposed to Maria's chosen career. Maria, however, was determined not to accept a woman's traditional role and was finally admitted in
1892.

In 1896, after earning scholarships each year and making extra money
through private tutoring, Maria, rising above individual and institutional
sexism, became the first woman to graduate from a medical school in Italy.

Curiously, although Leo's most specific reference to women (which, inci-
dentally, appeared in the "Child Labor" section of *Rerum Novarum*) would
indicate a definite bias toward keeping women in the home, there is some
evidence that, in response to Montessori's admittance to the medical college, he later opined that medicine was an acceptable profession for a
woman.[2]

A few months after graduating, at age 26, Dr. Montessori represented
Italy at an international women's congress in Berlin and gave a speech on
the conditions of working women in Italy. Excerpts from Dr. Montessori's
speech and Pope Leo's encyclical—where he consistently referred to
"man's labor" and "workmen"—give us a hint of what their conversation
about the role of women in the workplace might have been like.

LEO: "Women, again, are not suited to certain trades; for a
                  woman is by nature fitted for home-work, and it is that
                  which is best adapted at once to preserve her modesty, and
                  to promote the good bringing up of children and the well-
                  being of the family" (no. 33).

MARIA: "I speak for the six million Italian women who work in
                  factories and on farms as long as eighteen hours a day for
                  pay that is often half of what men earn for the same work
                  and sometimes even less."

Afterward, she asked the delegates to approve a proposal for equal pay
for equal work by women, beginning with those working in state-owned
factories. They did so unanimously.[3]

Following a stint working with children in Rome's insane asylums, Dr.
Montessori directed a day-care center in a slum area housing project.
Through her work with these sixty 3- to 7-year-old children (whose parents
were illiterate), she began to develop a unique approach to education which
culminated in the world-renowned Montessori Method. It is beyond the
scope of this essay to describe her organizational model in detail, but many
of her insights on children at work and the values learned are relevant to
this discussion on women's ways of working and will be referred to later.

VIRGINIA WOOLF MEETS PIUS XI

In 1931, when Pius XI wrote *Quadragesimo Anno*, he referred almost
entirely to "workingmen," only briefly expressing concern about the "virtue
of girls and women" in modern factories. Although the pope does suggest
(in the section on "Support of the Workingman and His Family") that it
is acceptable for women, as part of the family, to contribute to "common
maintenance" in a rural home or that of artisans or small shopkeepers, he
clearly does not approve of women working elsewhere.

Ironically, that same year Virginia Woolf published *Life as We Have
Known It*, a book by members of the Women's Cooperative Guild in England, in which they described their jobs, families, and political awakening.
Woolf admires and supports these working women who had no choice about
whether or not to be wage-earners. In her "Introductory Letter" to the
book, Woolf recalls her impressions of them at one of their Cooperative
Congresses as "humorous and vigorous and thoroughly independent." She
was impressed with the dignity and determination with which each of the
"delegates" represented the concerns of her particular constituency.[4]

Excerpts from Pope Pius XI's encyclical *Quadragesimo Anno* and Virginia Woolf's "Introductory Letter" give us a hint of what a conversation
between them about the role of women in the workplace might have been
like.

PIUS: "Mothers will above all devote their work to the home
               and the things connected with it; intolerable, and to be
               opposed with all Our strength, is the abuse whereby
               mothers of families, are forced to engage in gainful
               occupations outside the domestic wall to the neglect of
               their own proper cares and duties" (no. 71).

VIRGINIA: "Most of the women had started work at seven or eight,
               earning a penny on Saturday for washing a doorstep.
               . . . They had gone into factories when they were four-
               teen. They had worked from seven in the morning till
               eight or nine at night and had made thirteen or fifteen
               shillings a week. . . . They had seen half-starved women
               standing in rows to be paid for their match-boxes while
               they snuffed the roast meat of their employer's dinner
               cooking within."[5]

Pius XI apparently saw no good coming from women working outside
the home, nor did he refer to them in sections on "Workingmen's Unions."
On the other hand, Woolf praised the Women's Cooperative Guild for
providing these working-class women with multiple opportunities to
improve their educational, job training, social and organizational skills.

MODEL #1: "CHILDREN'S HOUSES"

In 1907 Dr. Montessori officially opened the first Children's House in a
slum area housing project. A group of wealthy bankers invited her to direct
a day nursery for the tenants of their newly renovated buildings. These
builders wanted to protect their investment from the fifty children of poor
working parents who "ran wild throughout the building, defacing the newly
whitewashed walls and . . . other petty acts of vandalism."[6]

For her part, Dr. Montessori saw this as an opportunity to test some of
her educational ideas on normal children. The child care was free to those
working parents who agreed to send the children there on time, "clean in
body and clothing, and provided with a suitable apron." She also invited
the mothers to be actively involved in this education process: "Once a week,
at least, the mothers may talk with the Directress, giving her information
concerning the home life of the child, and receiving helpful advice from
her."[7]

Dr. Montessori stressed the importance of freedom for students and of
providing them choices for "auto-education" activities. Further, she felt
that no child could be free unless he or she were independent. Discipline
was developed through opportunities for constructive work. Work became
its own reward and artificially induced competitions or rewards and pun-
ishments were banned.

Both community life and personal initiative were developed because the children felt a sense of ownership and responsibility for the classroom. They maintained daily order by returning materials to shelves, polishing the tables, and caring for the animals and plants. The children also felt and demonstrated responsibility for each other. For example, they took turns distributing the noon meal, which they ate in common.

Montessori and Leo XIII's Approach to Women Workers

In his encyclical Pope Leo did not discuss what happened to children when women had to become wage-earners. Montessori, however, assumed that poor women had to work outside the home. So she focused her energies on setting up Children's Houses to provide for the education, health, moral and physical development of their children. These became the forerunners of today's head start and full-service child-care centers.

MODEL #2: WOMEN'S COOPERATIVE GUILD

The Women's Cooperative Guild was established in 1883 as a way for women in local Cooperative Societies to become a more powerful force in the Cooperative Movement, to share in its administration and to strengthen its impact on public policy. By 1930 the Guild had sixty-seven thousand members and nearly fourteen hundred branches.

The experience of being part of the Guild encouraged the women to identify social problems — long hours, little pay, and a lack of running water and electricity — and provided forums to develop strategies for change. The Guild Annual Meeting also helped stretch the women's concerns to broader public policy issues. Woolf noted that the delegates expressed positions on the taxation of land values, reform of the divorce laws, the minimum wage, care of maternity, education of children over 14 years of age, and adult suffrage. The women learned "to speak out, boldly and authoritatively, about every question of civic life ... [including] peace and disarmament and the spread of Cooperative principles ... among the nations of the world."[8]

The Guild experience also helped empower women workers. Virginia Woolf, as a writer and publisher, must have been pleased to publish the seventeen "Extracts from Letters Written in 1927" in which the women describe the influence of their Guild experience on their reading. One woman wrote: "I have, of course, to keep well abreast of current topics and for that I have to read the daily papers or such parts as may be of value. ... But I must admit that everything I can get hold of relating to International matters have a keen interest for me." Another wrote: "My reading, of course, is done in time stolen from my sleeping hours, and, I am bound to confess, any meal times when alone or with my little son, who also reads."[9]

Points of Convergence between the Popes and the Feminist Models

Popes Leo XIII and Pius XI shared with the Guild a definition of work as a way to meet material needs and each actively supported the value of just wages for the worker. However, the encyclicals focused almost exclusively on the male worker and his needs, while Montessori, Woolf, and the Guild recognized and supported women wage-earners.

These two popes did not refer specifically to work as creative self-expression or self-realization. This, however, was an important second definition of work for Montessori and members of the Guild. Montessori set up her Children's Houses to facilitate this value. The Guild women held that their organizational work was creative, educational, and empowering.

A third definition of work, as contributing to the well-being of the larger community, was affirmed by the popes as well as the Guild, Montessori, and Woolf through their support for workers associations.

The popes encouraged associations that directed "the activities of the group to the common good," although the references were generally to men's associations. Using a more inclusive approach, Montessori viewed the associations formed around the Children's Houses as ways not only to care for the children and provide services for working women, but also to serve as models for other tenement-clubs, which could provide alternatives to gambling-houses and saloons.

The Women's Cooperative Guild, which was founded in 1883 and thus preceded both encyclicals, worked for the common good by voicing the neglected needs of married working women. "They supported vigorously the establishment of School Clinics. They brought forward a National Scheme for the care of Maternity . . . for the inclusion of Maternity Benefit in the Insurance Act."[10]

Whereas Pius XI worried about women's virtue in the workplace, the Guild offered protections and support systems. It not only provided work opportunities for women, but through its nearly fourteen hundred branches the Guild offered safe spaces for women to meet, a workshop wherein they "could remodel their lives, could beat out this reform or that."

The Guild also took the concern for the common good in the workplace beyond national boundaries through its International Cooperative Women's Guild. For example, in 1930, at its Congress in Vienna, 250 delegates from twenty countries discussed "whether the economic position of women should be best solved by State family allowances or factory work." In addition, the International Guild "has steadfastly stood for Peace, and has laid before the League of Nations the strong demand of its members for Disarmament."[11]

MODEL #3: RACHEL'S WOMEN'S CENTER

Rachel's, begun in 1979, provides direct services to homeless women as a contribution to the common good—a service in the church's charity tradition of responding directly to the needs of the poor. Rachel's current director, Mary Ann Luby, is a Catholic sister and the bulk of financial, board, and staff support comes through the efforts of Catholic women.

Mary Ann Luby's basic approach is to value the women's human dignity and to offer them all the opportunity "to get their lives together." Mary Ann believes that every human has the potential for change and that change largely occurs through human relationships.

As a day shelter for homeless women in the District of Columbia, the Center tries to implement these values by offering a broad range of services which provides a holistic and integrated approach similar in concept to that designed by Maria Montessori for poor women and children in Italy.

These services address physical needs through food programs, drug and alcohol addiction sessions, and health assessments; spiritual needs through bible studies and structured discussions on women's issues; social needs through cultural workshops, outings, and knitting classes; emotional needs through assertion training, general problem solving, and support group sessions; and educational needs through job-training skills.

Mary Ann believes in addressing more than just the primary human needs. Her philosophy in operating the center goes beyond providing food and shelter to include a belief in the importance of helping the women build self-esteem. Without self-esteem it is almost impossible to get out of the shelter system and into independent living.

Participation is another important value at Rachel's and the high degree of participation by its occupants makes it unique among local shelters. Through weekly house meetings, the women are consulted on almost all program development. Mary Ann believes that the women know better than anybody else what they need, so she spends a lot of time listening to them. Several of the women who were drug addicts, for example, came to ask for a weekly drug and alcoholics anonymous meeting. Together they wrote a grant proposal and a set of goals and have continued to meet ever since.

The women also participate in planning celebrations such as holidays and birthday parties. Because the women are involved in the initial planning, they feel more ownership of and responsibility for the events. Mary Ann acknowledges that these events are "more profound when the women have done them."

Similarly, the women participate in the cleaning of Rachel's by signing up for a chore each morning when they come in. Thus they become active participants in shaping their environment and develop a sense of responsibility for "their space," just as the Italian students did in the Children's Houses.

A final example of their active participation is the women's involvement in advocacy on issues that affect the homeless. Rachel's women are encouraged to attend congressional and local hearings, give testimony, and lobby on their own behalf—rather than always having others speak for them.[12]

MODEL #4: NETWORK, A CATHOLIC SOCIAL-JUSTICE LOBBY

NETWORK, begun in 1971, works for the common good by seeking systemic change through the legislative and political process. This advocacy is in the justice tradition of Catholic social thought, particularly emphasized since Vatican Council II. NETWORK was started by forty-seven Catholic sisters and from its inception has been women-led.

What Rachel's and NETWORK have in common is that they try to integrate their vision of the common good into the organization's mission, in the goods or services it produces, and into their internal processes. They particularly try to integrate the values of participation, empowerment, and cooperation. In doing this they follow in the footsteps of Montessori, the feminist educator, and the Guild—a feminist organization.

Just as Rachel's somewhat echoes a Montessori organization, so too does NETWORK echo the Women's Cooperative Guild; both were started by women, kept women in leadership positions, and organized themselves to influence public policy. Both groups developed ways for poor women at a local level to articulate their needs to policy makers at a national level.

NETWORK has a Washington office, which does research and lobbying on national legislation. Information and action suggestions are then sent to the thousands of members, who are organized by congressional districts.

NETWORK is rooted in Catholic social justice teachings and, as such, perceives its mission as seeking the common good in public policy, especially for the economically poor. This is done through supporting legislation which provides: 1) just access to economic resources, 2) fairness in national funding, and 3) justice in global relationships.

Just as the Guild convened regular forums for its members to provide mutual support and to give direction to its advocacy work, so too does NETWORK. The membership is consulted regularly through the publication, in phone conversations with state coordinators and congressional district contacts, in regional workshops, and national legislative seminars.

Through its "Bridge Building Project," NETWORK attempts to insure that its advocacy positions are rooted in the experience of those who suffer most from unjust policies. This year NETWORK convened two groups of women to assist in shaping its policy positions. The first were Catholic sisters in direct ministry with the economically poor, along with women who themselves suffer from poverty; the second were housing advocates, including women who were formerly homeless. This second group drafted a position paper on housing, which NETWORK distributed to all members of Congress. NETWORK also organized a major lobbying campaign around the statement involving its local membership and the media.

In addition to its legislative goals, NETWORK is committed to creating an alternative organizational model from a feminist perspective. A goal of the NETWORK staff and board is that the organization mirrors internally the same principles and values it advocates in national legislation. Thus, *how* things are done is as important as *what* is done.

Some elements of this alternative model are the following:

1. Co-responsibility for the goals of the organization
2. Participatory decision-making
3. Equality of persons
4. Commitment to reflection on shared values
5. Emphasis on cooperation rather than competition
6. Integration of professional activities with spiritual, personal, and communal life.

Because of space limitations, only a few of the operational ramifications of these elements are highlighted.

Participatory Decision-Making and Equality of Persons

NETWORK functions with a participatory management style at both the staff and board level. The guiding assumption is that people should be involved in all major decisions that affect their individual work lives and the health and direction of the organization. All staff participate in key decisions such as budget setting, salary scale, large capital expenditures, new programs or staff positions, and public policy positions. All staff attend and participate in board meetings and committees.

In deliberating on the salary issues, NETWORK agreed with the definition of work as a means for workers to meet their material needs; but it also had to operate under the financial constraints facing most non-profit advocacy groups. In addition, the NETWORK women realized how undervalued women's work had been traditionally, especially "support staff" positions such as secretarial work. Thus, the decision to have everyone on the staff receive the same salary was based on the underlying belief that all persons are inherently equal, though differently gifted, and of different experience and competencies. It is the fundamentally equal dignity of the person as worker that gives each person and her role in the organization equal value.

The actual salary level assumes a modest standard of living and a high commitment to NETWORK's mission. It reflects Pius XI's definition of a just wage as "sufficient to meet adequately ordinary domestic needs" (no. 71).

But NETWORK would probably find Virginia Woolf's definition of poverty more appropriate to its salary decision: "By poverty is meant enough money to live upon. That is, you must earn enough to be independent of any other human being and to buy that modicum of health, leisure, knowledge and so on that is needed for the full development of body and mind. But no more."[13]

NETWORK Strives for Integration in the Workplace

The women at NETWORK recognize that a healthy approach to political ministry is to integrate their professional activities with their spiritual, personal, and communal lives. To help achieve this, NETWORK sets aside several days each year for a reflection process on political ministry. These days help the women discover the relationship between faith values and work on legislative issues. The reflection culminates with symbol, ritual, and prayer, which help express a deepening commitment to their ministry for justice.

NETWORK staff members also take time to create and celebrate rituals that develop the organization's communal life. The staff year begins with a commitment ritual around contract signing and, at an Epiphany ritual, each staff member is affirmed for her particular contributions to NETWORK. Rituals are an important part of all NETWORK-directed seminars and workshops. These activities recall the ritualized procedures of the Guild's Annual Congress, the birthday celebrations at Rachel's, and the many seasonal rituals within the Catholic tradition.[14]

CAN FEMINISM IN THE WORKPLACE GUIDE CATHOLIC SOCIAL THOUGHT?

These four women-led organizations have lived out a definition of work as self-expression, a means of meeting material needs, and a way to contribute to the common good. Each group and its leadership has also sought consistency between its outward mission and its internal processes. I believe the ways in which they have done this can be useful to the institutional church in any future articulation of Catholic social thought.

What might these women emphasize if consulted? Or as Virginia Woolf asked in *The Three Guineas*: What are the lessons "educated men" can learn from "daughters of uneducated women"?

Montessori Would Speak Up for Women Wage-Earners

Maria Montessori and the working women benefiting from the Children's Houses would ask the popes and their advisors to accept the fact that millions of women have no choice: they *must* work for wages outside the home. Therefore, lecturing them about their "proper role" in the home is not helpful; they know full well their maternal responsibilities and carry them through the days—some, literally, on their backs—or in their anxious hearts.

A majority of the women in the world work more hours daily than men and in most cases carry a double load. For example, women do agricultural, domestic, or professional work for ten or more hours daily, and then add several hours more for their own household work, while the men relax under the trees, in the pubs, or in front of television sets.

Maria Montessori would suggest that the encyclicals focus more on articulating what support systems and wages are needed by working women and whose responsibility it is to provide them.

The Women's Guild Would Urge Participation

The Women's Cooperative Guild would probably emphasize women's representation and broad participation in the workplace. They recognized how an organization is strengthened when each member feels she has a *real role* in shaping its direction and setting its financial and programmatic priorities. The Guild women empowered themselves through participation in local, national, and international gatherings, through self-education programs and through political advocacy.

The institutional church, by contrast, does not yet really seek women's broad participation or welcome their active involvement in decision-making. As a result, women are walking away in droves and finding their personal sense of religious commitment more fulfilled in other institutions, such as the Guild. For example, a 70-year-old Guild member, writing in 1920, describes her retirement setting "along a ditch":

> There is a railway bank at the end of the path covered with grass and beautiful dandelions. I can sit outside the little shed and see the church tower of old Hampstead Church and think of all the good work that has been done in the Guild Office. I go there all day on a Sunday, and am sure there is as much spiritual feeling going along a ditch as there is in hearing a sermon . . . thank God that I became a Guild member for more reasons than I can explain.[15]

The Guild might also suggest that the popes could use some women writers such as Virginia Woolf. Woolf's spirited descriptions of the "humorous and vigorous and thoroughly independent" Guild women and her keen observations of Guild meetings make for livelier reading than the ponderous prose of *Quadragesimo Anno* on the "uplifting of the proletariat."

Rachel's Women's Center Would Recommend Listening to Women

Both the staff and the women served at Rachel's would recommend: "Listen to the women." Just as homeless women were best able to advise on their particular needs and to help set appropriate policies and procedures for running their Center, so too should the teaching church listen to women from many countries, lifestyles, and educational backgrounds. It is fairly clear that Leo XIII and Pius XI listened primarily, if not entirely, to men in drafting these first encyclicals. As a result, women and their needs as wage-earners were not taken seriously, nor was attention given to their child-care concerns.

Similarly, in contemporary Catholic social teachings, women's ongoing childcare needs are not given enough serious and thoughtful attention, nor are women's concerns and dilemmas around child-bearing. The predominant focus in church statements on public policy and in allocation of church resources continues to be on the abortion issue. So once again, in an area they know the most about, women are made passive recipients of church policies and magisterial pronouncements, rather than active participants in shaping them.

NETWORK Would Counsel Consistency between Theory and Practice

As a political lobby group founded in the early 1970s, NETWORK studied and supported John XXIII's encyclicals, the Vatican II documents, Paul VI's *Call to Action,* and the Synod statement on *Justice in the World.* The group was influenced by the teachings' emphases on participation, cooperation, need to move to political action, justice as a constitutive element of preaching the gospel, listening to the experiences of the poor, just wages and the common good described in broad terms as in *Mater et Magistra* — "the sum total of those conditions of social living."

NETWORK staff saw the power of challenging others, religious and lay, to become involved in political ministry, to integrate their faith commitment with their public lives as citizens. But the staff also knew that the values they advocated in public had to be reflected in their internal structure as well. Nancy Sylvester, I.H.M., NETWORK's National Coordinator, explains:

> It is one thing to testify and lobby on minimun wage or urge that local people should be involved in decisions that affect their lives, but if you don't also advocate for this in your own organization, the public soon sees the inconsistency and you lose credibility.

To the extent that the official church carries social-justice values forward in political actions, public statements, and use of church resources, the teachings can be motivational and directional. However, when church workers and the public at large observe huge disparities between theory and practice, the teachings lose their moral force.

PERSONAL REFLECTION ON PAST AND FUTURE SOCIAL JUSTICE TEACHINGS

For twenty-five years my work has been in the social-justice arena: first in educating against racism and the Vietnam War, then as a political lobbyist and activist with NETWORK, and now in the area of alternative investments. I view this work as a ministry for the common good, and in the 1960s and 1970s I felt supported by the theory and practice of Catholic social teachings, which I read and studied. I was proud of what Catholicism stood for, especially when it advocated for the needs of the world's poorest, encouraged broad-based participation in both politics and the church, and spoke out fearlessly for all human rights. However, since then I have been keenly disappointed and disillusioned by inconsistencies between theory and practice. I often find it difficult to believe that the institutional church takes its own teachings seriously. The following examples illustrate this.

Inconsistent Messages Regarding Political Activity

Paul VI's encyclical *Call to Action*, which described politics as a way to live out the Christian commitment, inspired many women religious to take up political ministry. Several even felt called to public office—both elected and appointed. These women worked directly with the poor and offered constituents a fresh perspective on the role of public servants. Yet John Paul II forced several United States religious to choose between their political ministry and their congregations because he declared it was unacceptable for religious to hold political office.[16] This directive against political activity seems to run counter to his own well-publicized meetings with politicians and heads of state and his statements during public appearances—all highly political acts.

Common Good More Than Abortion

John XXIII taught in *Mater et Magistra* that the common good includes all the conditions of social living and urged national governments to create employment, care for the less privileged, and provide for the future. In *Pacem in Terris* he outlined a whole series of rights and duties within a well-ordered society; yet, many in the United States hierarchy continue to use the abortion issue as the single litmus test for political candidates.

Moreover, in 1984, when twenty-four United States women religious, prompted by an over-all concern for the common good, joined others in publicly asking for a dialogue on the issue of abortion in an ad in the *New York Times*, these women and their communities bore the brunt of an authoritarian and disproportionate reaction from the Vatican.

WOMEN'S WAYS OF WORKING AND THE FUTURE OF CATHOLIC SOCIAL THOUGHT

Women's organizations, such as the four described in this essay, can offer future church documents rich experiences in creating alternative workplaces. Their voices need to be heard during the formulation of church teaching, not after the fact. Women need to participate fully in evaluating the effect of past teachings and suggesting future changes.

If not, Catholic social teaching and the world will be the poorer for it.

And women's productivity, creativity, spirituality, and thought will find other outlets that give meaning and expression to their lives and values.

If the churches then become more empty on Sunday, look for the women gathered "along a ditch" by a dandelion-covered railway bank. They'll be there finding that "spiritual feeling" and giving thanks for women's ways of working.

NOTES

1. Since the encyclicals are easily available in many editions, I will simply reference in parentheses the number of the section quoted.

2. Rita Kramer, *Maria Montessori* (New York: G. P. Putnam, 1976), p. 35.

3. Ibid., p. 55.

4. Virginia Woolf, "Introductory Letter," *Life as We Have Known It,* ed. Margaret Llewelyn Davies (New York: W. W. Norton Company, 1975), p. xxvii.

5. Ibid., p. xxxi.

6. Kramer, p. 110.

7. Maria Montessori, *The Montessori Method* (New York: Schocken Books, 1964), pp. 70-71.

8. Woolf, pp. xvii-xxxvi.

9. Ibid., pp. 116-20.

10. Margaret Llewelyn Davies, "Notes on the Women's Co-operative Guild," in Woolf, p. xii.

11. Ibid., p. xiii.

12. The information and quotations regarding Rachel's Women's Center are taken from an interview by Nancy Chupp with Mary Ann Luby on May 14, 1990.

13. Virginia Woolf, *Three Guineas* (New York: Harcourt Brace and Company, 1938), p. 122.

14. Information on NETWORK is taken from materials and oral interviews provided by Nancy Sylvester, current national coordinator of NETWORK, and from my own experience as NETWORK's director for eleven years.

15. Woolf, *Life as We Have Known It,* p. 55.

16. The women religious were Sisters of Mercy Agnes Mary Mansour, Elizabeth Morancy, and Arlene Violet. Each made the painful choice to withdraw from formal membership in the congregation in order to pursue her personal sense of ministry in public office. Jesuit priest Robert Drinan was also forced to choose between remaining in the United States Congress or in the Jesuits. He chose to remain a Jesuit.

PART IV

PEACE IN
CATHOLIC SOCIAL THOUGHT

18

THE CHALLENGE OF PEACE
REVISITED

JOSEPH CARDINAL BERNARDIN

I am very pleased to have this opportunity to reflect on the United States Catholic bishops' 1983 pastoral letter, *The Challenge of Peace: God's Promise and Our Response*. I find it especially gratifying to offer these reflections one hundred years after Pope Leo XIII's great encyclical, *Rerum Novarum*.

Pope Leo XIII's name is synonymous with the church's social teaching. However, "the church's social teaching" is a complex phrase encompassing three distinct forms of magisterial teaching, and Pope Leo's contribution to each varied considerably.

The first strand of this body of teaching pertains to *church-state relations*, and Pope Leo played a particularly significant role in this regard. He began a gradual move away from the teaching of Pope Gregory XVI and Pope Pius IX, initiating a fundamental shift in thinking which Pope Pius XII and Pope John XXIII developed more substantially in the middle of the twentieth century. In turn, these two popes laid the groundwork for Vatican II's epochal *Declaration on Religious Liberty*, which further transformed our fundamental understanding of the relationship between church and state.

The second strand deals with Catholic teaching on *church and society*. This is the social encyclical tradition, which Pope Leo XIII directly inaugurated with *Rerum Novarum*: the tradition of systematic reflection on modern socio-economic issues in the light of Catholic social philosophy. He played a decisive role in setting the direction of this teaching, which has unfolded in the works of his successors through Pope John Paul II. It is this particular contribution we especially celebrate in this centennial year.

This initiative of Pope Leo provided us with the first articulation of the church's views on the socio-economic organization of society in the Industrial Age. By proclaiming the dignity of work and defending the rights of workers, he focused on a theme that would recur in ecclesial teaching throughout the following century. Changed conditions in society have precipitated continued development of this tradition to keep current this aspect of the church's teaching. But Pope Leo XIII will forever be remembered for his courageous and insightful beginning of this body of modern Catholic teaching on church and society.

The third strand of the church's social teaching involves the *church and international relations*, the area least affected by Pope Leo XIII but most relevant to *The Challenge of Peace*. Although he was very active in diplomatic affairs, his contribution to the church's teaching on international relations does not stand out like his work in the first two areas.

Instead, Pope Pius XII provided the decisive impetus for this part of Catholic social tradition. During World War II he foresaw the postwar importance of organizing the world's first truly interdependent order. After Hiroshima and Nagasaki the creation of an international order that could ensure the security of nations in the Nuclear Age assumed a dramatic new urgency. Accordingly, Pope Pius and his successors found themselves increasingly concerned about dimensions of Catholic social teaching that were often quite unlike that in *Rerum Novarum*.

As I have intimated, the foundation of the United States bishops' pastoral letter on war and peace lies in this third strand of Catholic social teaching, which, after Pope Pius XII, underwent substantial development by Pope John XXIII, Pope Paul VI, Vatican II, and Pope John Paul II. The pastoral letter is also a contribution to the church's universal teaching by a local church, which carries out its mission in one of the world's superpowers. The letter seeks to answer a question of global significance — how to keep the peace in the nuclear age.

I will explore the contribution of *The Challenge of Peace* in three ways:

1. I will briefly summarize the *character* of the international teaching of the church from Pope Pius XII through Pope John Paul II.

2. I will then analyze the *role* of *The Challenge of Peace* in the light of this Catholic teaching on war and peace.

3. Finally, I will propose some *directions* for the future.

THE CHARACTER OF THE CHURCH'S TEACHING

The moral problem of warfare has been a perennial question from the time of the New Testament and the patristic age. However, the development of nuclear weapons provoked a necessary reassessment of what the church had said and taught prior to World War II. This new type of weapon brought about a significant shift in the church's perspective on international relationships.

In several of his addresses, especially in his Christmas messages, Pope Pius XII began to articulate the need for new structures to resolve disputes and find alternatives to the use of force. He was convinced that war was no longer an appropriate means of resolving international conflicts. The convergence of scientific advances, social and political upheaval, as well as economic changes, presented an unprecedented challenge to organize the world's first truly international order. The Holy Father envisioned an international authority to coordinate the interaction of sovereign states in an increasingly interdependent world.

As I said earlier, this theme of international relations has remained a central thread in postwar papal teaching and has primarily focused on issues of economic justice, human rights, and the use of force. In a world of limited resources and a growing division between the "haves" and the "have nots," economic justice is an essential element in developing authentic peace. With the experience of the Holocaust, the political victimization of countless people throughout the world, and the trivialization and exploitation of the dignity of the individual, papal teaching has also pointed to respect for human rights as a key element in the quest for peace. So, too, the development and stockpiling of sophisticated weapons capable of massive and indiscriminate destruction — a looming threat to world peace — evoked a strong, but nuanced response from both the popes and the Second Vatican Council.

Economic Justice

Papal teaching sees economic justice in a wider perspective than the relationship between employer and workers. It includes the role of the state in securing just social and economic structures. It brings a moral dimension to the various economic theories which help shape our modern world. Moreover, papal social teaching offers a critique of the economic relationships among nations in an increasingly interdependent world. Popes from Leo XIII through John Paul II have spoken out on these various aspects of economic justice. In their pronouncements after World War II it became increasingly clear that, to maintain authentic global peace, it is necessary to construct a social order which works justly for all nations, regions, and peoples of the world.

In *Mater et Magistra* (nos. 157ff) Pope John XXIII began to address the growing economic gap between developed and developing countries. Pope Paul VI further addressed that concern and wrote that "excessive economic, social, and cultural inequalities among peoples arouse tensions and conflicts, and are a danger to the peace" (*Populorum Progressio*, no. 76). To confront these inequalities is to promote peace. But this requires international cooperation based on the recognition and respect for the dignity and worth of every human person.

Pope John Paul II developed this idea of economic justice even further in his encyclical *Sollicitudo Rei Socialis* when he spoke of the chilling economic effects East/West tensions have had on developing countries:

Today, the reality is that these resources are used to enable each of the two blocs to overtake the other and thus guarantee its own security. Nations which historically, economically, and politically have the possibility of playing a leadership role, are prevented by this fundamentally flawed distortion from adequately fulfilling their duty of solidarity for the benefit of peoples which aspire to full development (no. 23).

As the Holy Father stated, this expenditure of very limited resources in underdeveloped countries for weapons is a great tragedy. It not only contributes to the possibilities for violence internally as well as conflicts between and among nations, it also robs a country of the capital it needs for development.

Economic justice is essential in building a lasting peace. In *The Challenge of Peace*, an often neglected section in the third chapter, "Shaping a Peaceful World," focuses on this issue. Today as never before, economic justice deserves a great deal of attention in our quest to develop an authentic and lasting peace throughout the world.

Human Rights

The memory of the Holocaust haunts the modern world. Compounding the nightmare, the image of suffering and death brought by war, political expediency, and even natural disaster is permanently etched on the modern conscience.

Respecting basic human rights has been a traditional value in Western society and the Judeo-Christian heritage. After World War II the understanding and appreciation of human rights became even more compelling. Human rights are values derived from natural law as well as our theological tradition. Papal teaching during the last century has recognized this natural-law foundation for human rights. One of its finest articulations can be found in *Pacem in Terris*, where Pope John XXIII wrote:

> Beginning our discussion of the rights of man, we see that every man has the right to life, to bodily integrity, and to the means which are necessary and suitable for the proper development of life. These means are primarily food, clothing, shelter, rest, medical care, and finally the necessary social services. Therefore, a human being also has the right to security in cases of sickness, inability to work, widowhood, old age, unemployment, or in any other case in which he is deprived of the means of subsistence through no fault of his own (no. 11).

> By the natural law, every human being has the right to respect for his person, to his good reputation, to freedom in searching for truth and — within the limits laid down by the moral order and the common good — in expressing and communicating his opinions, and in pursuit of art. He has the right, finally, to be informed truthfully about public events (no. 12).

The natural law also gives man the right to share in the benefits of culture, and therefore the right to a basic education or to technical or professional training in keeping with the stage of educational development in the country to which he belongs (no. 13).

In addition to these philosophical and natural-law aspects church teaching has also recognized the theological dimension of human rights. Every human being is made in the image and likeness of God according to this teaching. The rights of every human being to life, freedom, and justice are grounded, therefore, not only in natural law, but also in the theology of creation and redemption.

In papal teaching these same human rights guide the relationship between individuals and the public authorities within a single state, as well as the relations between and among states. Human rights are innate and universal. Therefore, each of us has the duty to protect them, and the international community has an interest and responsibility in guaranteeing them. Much of the papal social teaching over the past century has been an eloquent witness to these rights and a continuing call to nurture and secure them, both individually and universally.

In a special way the subject of human rights has framed papal social teaching on international relations. Pope John Paul II, in his encyclical *Laborem Exercens*, wrote:

> Respect for this broad range of human rights constitutes the fundamental condition of peace in the modern world: peace both within individual countries and societies and in international relations, as the Church's magisterium has several times noted, especially since the encyclical "Pacem in Terris" (no. 16).

Human rights, therefore, are at the very foundation of an authentic peace. Every human being has a right to life. Every person deserves to live in an atmosphere of security, free from anxiety and violence, free to grow and develop, to express self and choose the mode of governance. Human rights were part of the basic principles on which the United States bishops relied in developing *The Challenge of Peace*.

The Use of Force

The church's teaching on the use of force was also an essential part of the background for the pastoral letter on war and peace. The use of force in Catholic social teaching embraces a body of thought which can be traced back to the very earliest days of the church. Because of its importance, I will examine certain of its aspects in greater detail.

Albert Einstein's famous observation about the development of nuclear weapons sums up the problem quite well: "Everything has been changed except our way of thinking." The past fifty years has seen an unprecedented development of new and more powerful weapons capable of indiscriminate destruction. Pope John Paul II stated it well in his address at Hiroshima on February 25, 1981:

> In the past, it was possible to destroy a village, a town, a region, even a country. Now it is the whole planet that has come under threat. This fact should finally compel everyone to face a basic moral consideration: From now on, it is only through a conscious choice, and through a deliberate policy that humanity can survive.

Pope Pius XII was the first pope of the nuclear age. His pronouncements regarding this new development in weaponry had a significant impact on subsequent church teaching. He began by situating his considerations regarding nuclear weapons within the context of the traditional just-war framework. Moreover, he refused to provide moral justification for a Catholic position supporting conscientious objection. The just-war theory was also the point of departure for our pastoral letter. However, the tensions between the just-war theory and pacifism, with its consequent support for conscientious objection, moved us to a deeper appreciation of the richness and diversity of the church's tradition. But more about that later.

While Pope Pius XII did not rule out in principle the use of nuclear weapons, he assessed their moral significance in terms of the principle of proportionality. If their effects could not be contained, he argued, they could not be used. Moreover, he felt that the magnitude of their destructive capacity demanded a diminishing of the legitimate causes of war from the traditional three (self-defense, avenging evil, and restoring violated rights) to a single one—self-defense. And even self-defense does not permit the uncontrolled use of nuclear weapons, if it leads to the annihilation of the human race (cf. Address of Pope Pius XII, September 30, 1954).

A significant development of church teaching on the use of force emerged in Pope John XXIII's encyclical *Pacem in Terris*. There he decried the growing stockpile of weapons. He sharply criticized the arms race between the East and the West, with its extraordinary human and economic costs, and condemned the balance of terror maintained through the monstrous power of nuclear weapons.

In many ways *Pacem in Terris* set the stage for the work of Vatican II, especially the fifth chapter of *Gaudium et Spes*, which represents a significant development in church teaching regarding war and peace. The Council Fathers questioned the stockpiling of weapons and the strategy of deterrence (no. 81). They defined peace as more than the mere absence of war and laid the foundation for the right to conscientious objection in the same section (no. 78). Most significantly, the only condemnation or anathema offered by the Council is found in the following declaration in *Gaudium et Spes*:

Any act of war aimed indiscriminately at the destruction of entire cities or of extensive areas along with their populations is a crime against God and man himself. It merits unequivocal and unhesitating condemnation (no. 80).

Pope Paul VI played a significant role in articulating this issue at the Council as well as in the post-conciliar debate on peace and the use of force. His commitment to a ministry of peace was one of the most visible dimensions of his papacy. Surprisingly, however, he did not issue a major teaching document on this subject in the style of Pope Pius XII or Pope John XXIII. His major contribution is found in his eloquent address to the United Nations in 1965 and the inauguration of an annual Day of Peace throughout the church, a practice which continues to the present.

The United Nations address was a dramatic appeal to banish war from human affairs: "No more war, war never again!" At the same time the Holy Father made a careful case for affirming a limited but real right of self-defense. In a more pastoral tone, his World Day of Peace messages continued this same plea for peace and the acknowledgment of legitimate defense.

Pope John Paul II has continued this tradition in his discourses on the topic at the United Nations, at Drogheda in Ireland, and at Hiroshima. Moreover, his World Day of Peace addresses and the message to scientists associated with the Pontifical Academy of Sciences (whom he sent to meet with world leaders) greatly influenced our work on *The Challenge of Peace*.

From this tradition of church teachings on the use of force, certain questions and themes emerged as we began to draft the pastoral letter; in particular, the tension between the Christian traditions of pacifism and just war, as well as the concept of deterrence as a legitimate option in a world armed with fifty thousand nuclear weapons.

I will now explore these themes and questions in greater detail. I will also reflect on the Catholic tradition as it specifically influenced our development of *The Challenge of Peace* as a document reflecting the church's teaching in the context of one of the two great superpowers of the day.

THE CHURCH'S TEACHING ON WAR AND PEACE AND *THE CHALLENGE OF PEACE*

The Challenge of Peace reflects the rich character of this extensive body of church teaching on international relations. It attends to the three concerns of economic justice, human rights, and the use of force within the encompassing framework of the present global order and nuclear context. As such, the letter exemplifies the application of the Catholic social tradition by a local church.

Given the empirical context within which we framed the document, the letter treats the issues and policy questions of the early 1980s. Most notable to the media were issues with political implications. Many still recall the

280 Joseph Cardinal Bernardin

public attention the third draft's use of the word *curb* in place of *halt* received in our recommendation on the testing, production, and deployment of new nuclear weapons systems. Pastoral and theological issues, however, were the central focus of *The Challenge of Peace*.

As the introduction stated, "Apprehension about nuclear war is almost tangible and visible today." Bringing the resources of the Catholic tradition to bear on the debate on public policy had a corollary purpose of articulating clearly and convincingly the substance of this tradition and the manner in which the church should bear witness to it.

An analysis of *The Challenge of Peace* in the light of the church's tradition on war and peace must consequently address both the political and the pastoral dimensions of the issues. I will comment on two issues discussed in the pastoral: our approach to nuclear weapons, and our consideration of the pacifist and just-war strands of our tradition.

In regard to our approach to nuclear weapons, the pastoral letter clearly stated our intentions:

> The task before us is not simply to repeat what we have said before; it is first to consider anew whether and how our religious-moral tradition can assess, direct, contain, and we hope, help to eliminate the threat posed to the human family by the nuclear arsenals of the world (no. 122).

With this in mind, *The Challenge of Peace* scrutinized the questions raised for the church in one of the two nuclear superpowers.

The pastoral letter's framework for the consideration of the issues surrounding nuclear weapons received its shape from the church's tradition. Besides employing categories of moral analysis found in papal teaching, it also incorporated two characteristic strands of it. On the one hand, the letter offered a prophetic critique of the nuclear arms race, inveighing against it because of the threat it poses to the world as well as the cost it exacts even if the weapons are never used. On the other hand, the letter mirrored the Holy See's cautious and carefully drawn approach to arms control and disarmament. This led to the careful consideration of nuclear policy.

In evaluating policy *The Challenge of Peace* applied appropriate elements of the tradition to questions of the use of nuclear weapons and the policy of deterrence. Just-war criteria directly and categorically ruled out counterpopulation warfare, determined that no situation legitimating the initiation of nuclear war could be perceived, and questioned whether limited nuclear war could really be waged.

The question of deterrence, however, was not so easily resolved. The pastoral letter concluded that deterrence can be accorded only a "strictly conditioned moral acceptance." In other words, deterrence must be seen, as Pope John Paul II has said, "not as an end in itself but as a step on the way toward progressive disarmament." Proposals for a nuclear arsenal that are based on strategies of prolonged nuclear war or on winning a nuclear war are unacceptable, as are efforts to establish superiority in nuclear capacity. These conclusions led to prudential judgments that have a level of specificity that papal and conciliar teachings appropriately do not have.

While papal teaching does not discuss specific public policies, it does provide certain procedural criteria with respect to disarmament questions. The pastoral letter considered its policy options within the framework of these criteria. In its recommendations to halt the development of new nuclear weapons systems, to support deep bilateral cuts in nuclear arsenals, and to enhance control over deployed weapons, the letter scrupulously abides by the criteria that disarmament be gradual, controlled, guaranteed, and bilateral. *The Challenge of Peace* thus follows the logic of the tradition and takes it to a level appropriate for the local church.

In constructing the framework for the consideration of these policy questions, *The Challenge of Peace* had to handle a pastoral question that re-emerged incisively in the nuclear age: specifically, the relationship between the pacifist and the just-war strands of the church's tradition.

The historical context in which *The Challenge of Peace* was written demanded greater clarity in the ethical constructs needed to face the contemporary issues of war and peace. For some, the horrible destructiveness of modern warfare raised questions about the adequacy of traditional moral categories in guiding ethical reflection. The church's teaching itself had expanded to affirm the right of individuals to opt for conscientious objection. With *Gaudium et Spes* as a point of departure, the United States bishops' reflection on the Vietnam War led many to the conclusion that Catholics could claim conscientious objector status, both generally and selectively. Change, both in the church and in the world, precipitated a new appraisal not only of war itself, but also of our manner of reflecting on it.

The Challenge of Peace sought to articulate the church's teaching on war and peace in order to respond to this pastoral need. It concluded that "the new moment" in which we find ourselves sees the just-war teaching and nonviolence as distinct but interdependent methods of evaluating warfare. They diverge on some specific conclusions, but they share a common presumption against the use of force as a means of settling disputes (no. 120). These two approaches may relate paradoxically to each other, but they represent two streams in the tradition which are needed to inform ethical reflection on the current reality.

The melding of pacifism and the just-war teaching emphasizes the Christian obligation to defend peace. They differ, not in intent, but in method. *The Challenge of Peace* makes clear that sovereign states do maintain the right to resort to military force for the purpose of self-defense of their own nation or of another nation unable to defend itself against an aggressor. Nevertheless, in an age of advanced technological warfare, the analyses of just-war and pacifist moralists often converge in their opposition to deadly methods of warfare. They also join in the insistence that humankind must find nonviolent means to resolve international conflicts.

Accordingly, the pastoral letter stressed the importance of diplomacy and encouraged fuller study of nonviolent means of resistance to evil. More specifically, it urged the establishment of the U.S. Academy of Peace. These recommendations acknowledge, as the pastoral letter stated, "non-violent means of fending off aggression and resolving conflict best reflect the call of Jesus both to love and to justice" (no. 77).

The Challenge of Peace concludes that both the pacifist and the just-war approaches are essential for reflection on war and peace in our time. While there is a tension between the two, this tension holds forth the hope for peace. Accordingly, the bishops said, "We believe the two perspectives support and complement each other, each preserving the other from distortion" (no. 121). As we anticipate future world events, we can expect that these two essential dimensions of the church's teaching on war and peace will help us respond faithfully to our Christian responsibility to defend peace.

Developments Since The Challenge of Peace

In the years since the National Conference of Catholic Bishops adopted *The Challenge of Peace*, changes unforeseen in 1983 have swept over the globe. New questions have emerged, and new challenges now confront us. Even before the transformations in Eastern Europe and the Soviet Union began, the United States bishops acknowledged that we must be prepared to update the analysis in the pastoral letter in the light of new international developments. Of particular concern was the assessment of deterrence and the extent to which the conditions set by the pastoral letter were being met.

The need for such a review was apparent soon after the letter was published. The early to mid 1980s were a period of continued escalation in the arms race. Some people called for a total condemnation of deterrence on the grounds that this trend revealed the failure of the deterrence policy to meet the pastoral letter's "strictly conditioned moral acceptance" of the policy. Moreover, just weeks before *The Challenge of Peace* was adopted, President Reagan announced plans for the Strategic Defense Initiative (SDI), which its advocates said would transcend deterrence.

An ad hoc committee of bishops was appointed in November 1985 to reassess the positions of the pastoral letter. The committee's examination of nuclear policy from 1983 to 1988 reviewed both the troubling developments and promising aspects of the issue.

The most surprising development during this period was the changed climate in regard to arms control. Possibilities not visible when *The Challenge of Peace* was drafted became realities that resulted in the 1987 Intermediate Nuclear Forces (INF) Treaty. This represented a welcome breakthrough in what had been the moribund arms-control process and resulted in a relatively small reduction of nuclear weapons. The new impetus in arms control and the bilateral treaty were very much in accord with the criteria of the pastoral letter.

The Strategic Defense Initiative, meanwhile, significantly changed the terms of the debate on United States nuclear policy. Besides altering the climate for arms-control talks with the Soviet Union, it presented the ad hoc committee with a new set of questions.

The assessment of SDI was difficult because the stated intention of this weaponry system and its possible consequences were quite different. Its advocates presented SDI as a program that would take us beyond deterrence to a system of nuclear defense. But others charged that this seemingly moral "advance" would, in fact, be a costly destabilizing factor of dubious feasibility and would make nuclear war more likely. The ad hoc committee concluded that, in the final analysis, risks seriously outweighed benefits, and the deployment of SDI would not meet the moral criteria of the pastoral letter.

The committee's report, however, continued to acknowledge the "strictly conditioned moral acceptance" of deterrence. In doing so, the committee neither endorsed the status quo nor suggested that progress in arms control and disarmament had been fully satisfactory. On the contrary, it argued that even stronger steps needed to be taken in order to meet the moral criteria of *The Challenge of Peace*.

The rapid changes that made it necessary to reassess the pastoral letter for the period of 1983 through 1988 have been outpaced by more recent events. If no one could predict in 1983 that progress in arms control would occur in the late 1980s, even less could one have foreseen the dramatic transformation that has occurred in Eastern Europe and in East-West relations since Mikhail Gorbachev came to power in the Soviet Union. One of the dilemmas which ethicists face in the contemporary world is the difficulty of keeping up with technological change. Global political change presents a similar problem for those who seek to apply moral reasoning to international political questions.

DIRECTIONS FOR THE FUTURE

From the perspective of 1991 the bishops' two documents look very much like texts produced in the 1980s. I find that altogether appropriate, and I will use the concluding section of this essay to indicate why the texts of the 1980s took the form they did, and why it will be necessary to go beyond these arguments in the 1990s.

Both *The Challenge of Peace* (1983) and *The Report* (1988) were essays on the ethics of "means." This style of analysis is very typical of Catholic moral teaching, which has always had a concern for *how* human affairs were conducted as well as *what* purposes were being pursued. The 1986 Vatican Instruction, *Donum Vitae*, was an example of an ethic of means, as indeed are significant parts of social, sexual, and medical ethics in the Catholic tradition.

While this point locates the analysis of the bishops' documents within a broader framework, it does not fully account for why the documents of the 1980s were so explicitly focused on the means question. This was due in great part to the character of the nuclear debate. The dilemma of the nuclear age, as *The Challenge of Peace* observed, was composed of two elements: a profound political competition between two major states (each representing a composite worldview), *and* an ability of each state to use vast nuclear arsenals to defend their interests.

From the mid-1940s through the late 1980s the prevailing political conviction in the West—supported by ample empirical data—was that little if any fundamental progress could be made in reconciling the political divisions of the superpowers. The focus of politics and strategy, therefore, was on the *means* of the conflict. Specifically, the focus was on joining a conception of *strategic doctrine and arms control* in policy which would produce "stability." Stability here primarily meant avoiding nuclear war without sacrificing essential political values; it also meant reducing the possibilities of war by accident or miscalculation; finally, it meant seeking to control (not eliminate) nuclear weapons through negotiations. The 1983 and 1988 documents were—in the policy sections—an effort to contribute to the political-strategic dialogue on means from the perspective of Catholic moral theology.

The two documents look like texts of the 1980s, not the 1990s, because the changes within the Soviet Union, in Eastern Europe, and between the United States and the Soviet Union have produced the consensus view among analysts, diplomats, and citizens that the Cold War is over. More technically, this means that possibility for shaping *fundamental* political change is now present for the first time in almost fifty years. This possibility is, in turn, reshaping the political, strategic, and moral agenda between the United States and the Soviet Union.

The new agenda, in outline form, works something like this. First, political ethics should precede strategic ethics; relations between the superpowers and their relations with others should be cast in terms of a framework of order, justice, and change in world politics. It is the kind of framework found in *Pacem in Terris* and *Sollicitudo Rei Socialis*; the empirical political circumstances of the past made the moral vision seem unreachable. Today, this kind of conception of order is the precondition for addressing more specific issues of politics, strategy, and economics.

Second, within the primacy of a political ethic, the politics and ethics of means must be pursued with new intensity through arms control; arms control should include nuclear, chemical, and conventional arsenals.

Third, beyond the superpower and European agenda, two specific measures need more attention: the conventional arms trade with and among developing nations, and the issue of proliferation—again understood as proliferation of nuclear and chemical weapons, as well as ballistic missiles. This third step would be one way of following Pope John Paul II's call to join traditional East-West issues with North-South questions. Finally, both the proliferation and arms-trade issues open the way beyond political-strategic concerns to the political-economic agenda now equally important to any discussion of world order.

The texts of the 1980s, especially Part Three of *The Challenge of Peace*, give us a starting point for the agenda of the 1990s. But it is not sufficient simply to amend the texts of the last decade. They spoke to the questions of the moment; the transition between the 1980s and the 1990s has not been organic. A profound and potentially very hopeful change has occurred. The 1990s is not a time for amending past conceptions; it is a decade which will require fundamental assessments — politically and morally — of how we can use the transition to the millennium creatively in pursuit of the values which the social tradition has taught us: peace, justice, truth, love, and freedom.

19

PEACE AND PLURALISM

Church and Churches

MARY EVELYN JEGEN, S.N.D.

Beginning with definitions of negative and positive peace, the first part of this essay reviews notions of peace in Catholic social thought and then discusses cultural influences that help explain the pluralism in the ideas of peace operating in culture today. The second part of the chapter looks at pluralism in the understanding of peace within the Catholic church, among Christian churches, and among people of other living faiths. The third part of the essay discusses four conclusions about the future of peace in Catholic social thought and practice.

THE HISTORY OF THE IDEA OF PEACE

Negative Peace and Positive Peace

Negative peace is commonly understood as the absence of war, or more properly, as the absence of violence. In this essay, the focus will be on the societal context; therefore, negative peace refers to the absence of war or structural violence.[1] As such, negative peace is a positive value. Positive peace on the societal level is less easy to define. I use throughout this chapter the definition of Michael Nagler: "[Peace is] that state in which all parties spontaneously desire one another's welfare."[2] "Spontaneously" in this definition I take to mean freely and willingly, without the coercion of law; it does not mean that there are no pressures against the desire. In this sense, for example, we can say that we spontaneously try to rescue people in emergencies. We do not rely on the city code to tell us that we should try to save a child from a burning building even at great risk to ourselves.

Nagler, who draws on such diverse sources as St. Augustine and Gandhi in coming to his definition of positive peace, argues that most human energy for peace today is mobilized by negative peace, which is inadequate to set in motion the dynamisms needed to create a peaceful social order. Those familiar with Catholic social thought will recognize in Nagler's definition of positive peace a remarkable similarity to the notion of the common good that is foundational in Catholic social teaching. Those familiar with biblical theology will see immediately the harmony between Nagler's definition and the biblical notion of justice as fidelity to the demands of a relationship.[3] Nagler's definition has the important advantage of going beyond such sayings as Peace is not merely the absence of war, or Peace is the presence of justice.

Peace in Catholic Social Thought

St. Augustine's "peace is the tranquillity of order" underlines all subsequent notions of positive peace in Catholic social thought; the just-war teaching, for which he shares a major responsibility, serves as a foundation for negative peace or at least for issues immediately germane to it. There is a considerable body of teaching on war and peace in the addresses of Pope Pius XII, and a major advance in a systematic treatment of both positive and negative peace in Pope John XXIII's encyclical *Pacem in Terris*, where peace is treated within the framework of human rights. The notion of development as the new name for peace in Pope Paul VI's encyclical *Populorum Progressio* builds on this relationship with particular attention to the relationship of peace to economic and social rights. In Pope John Paul II's encyclical *Sollicitudo Rei Socialis* the absence of peace is seen as directly related to structural sin.

In tracing the line of papal teaching, it is important not to neglect the conceptual developments in the annual messages for the World Day of Peace since 1967. Two of these call for special attention here: the message for 1990, which deals with environmental issues as a dimension of the human quest for peace, and the first message of Pope John Paul, in 1979, "To Reach Peace, Teach Peace," which is particularly important for the development of the idea of positive peace and even more important for ways to turn this idea into a cultural value.

At the level of episcopal conferences, the section on peace in the Medellín documents is of special importance as a harbinger of what was to come in the pastoral letters of at least eight conferences of bishops, following the letter of the United States bishops in 1983. Medellín's treatment of peace is important also because of the inductive method used, beginning with an analysis of the specific factors of injustice that add up to a negation of peace. If *Populorum Progressio* gave us development as the new name for peace, Medellín made clear the relationship among peace, justice, and liberation.

Cultural Roots of Ideas of Peace in Western Thought

It is at the cultural level that social change for justice and peace must be sought, in the attitudes and beliefs and values that are the underpinnings of all systems and policies. For this reason it is important to know where our attitudes and beliefs about peace, war, and violence come from. Some historical understanding improves our possibility of contributing to the kind of cultural transformation that is called for if people are to live in societies in which all parties spontaneously desire each other's welfare.

According to Pope John Paul II, we need a revisionist history of peace.

> Let us ... learn to reread the history of peoples and of mankind, following outlines that are truer than those of the series of wars and revolutions. Admittedly the din of battle dominates history. But it is the respites from violence that have made possible the production of those lasting cultural works which give honor to mankind. Furthermore, any factors of life and progress that may have been found even in wars and revolutions were derived from aspirations of an order other than that of violence.[4]

Our contemporary culture sees war as a constitutive dimension of society. Evidence is in the maintenance of the military-industrial complex and the size of the defense budget of every state in the world for which we have records.[5] There is a tacit assumption that this is an adversarial world, built as surely from actual or potential enemies as it is built of the physical elements of nature. This goes far beyond a belief in the wounded condition of human nature that we know as original sin. The question raised by Michael Nagler in *The Bulletin of the Atomic Scientists*, "Is 'security' dominating one's enemies, or learning to live so that one does not have enemies?" would hardly be seen by many as a realistic question on the political level. Our culture believes in diplomacy, but also in the necessity of peace through strength, that is, through military strength that is able, when needed, to prove superiority over the similar strength of an opponent. Within this set of beliefs we cherish peace as the absence of war, and military defense as a right and duty. In *The Challenge of Peace* we read:

> The council and the popes have stated clearly that governments threatened by armed, unjust aggression must defend their people. This includes defense by armed force if necessary as a last resort. We shall discuss below the conditions and limits imposed on such defense (par. 75).

This set of beliefs comes to us from our Greco-Roman heritage. *"Si vis pacem, para bellum,"* has been handed down to us from Homer, Herodotus, Thucydides, from Julius Caesar, Livy, and Vergil. The implications for our faith, particularly for a performative faith, of the tacit assumption that war is inevitable and somehow normal, should not be overlooked. What does such an assumption do to our beliefs about human nature, about grace and freedom, about the nature of God? Our faith, or at least our understanding of our faith, is culturally conditioned. It is very difficult to reread a history of peoples as Pope John Paul urges, within our cultural heritage, because the history may have been lived, but it has not yet been written. Today, the tools of historiography make such an enterprise possible.

An examination of that formative period of our culture we call medieval reveals the influence of Judeo-Christian values as transmitted through popular culture. Notions of noncombatant immunity, of limitations in kinds of weaponry, of stipulation of times and places that were off limits for war, such as the Truce of God and the Peace of God, all these developed alongside other elements, such as the use of war to vindicate what were perceived as God's own rights, as in the case of the Crusades.

On balance, it is clear that the Greco-Roman elements in our heritage of theory and practice of war and peace have overshadowed the elements that come to us from our Judeo-Christian heritage, and further, that some parts of our Judeo-Christian heritage are based on inadequate and distorted understandings of that heritage. The warrior god is perhaps the best example, and the one with the most serious implications. A consequence of this is that our culture has much stronger and socially controlling ideas of negative peace than of positive peace. A simpler way of saying this is that we know a lot more about war and the absence of war than we do about the construction of peace on the societal level. Any poll, casual or scientific, will show that people overwhelmingly want peace, and that they aspire to it as realizable on the intrapersonal and interpersonal levels but as hardly more than an important ideal on the societal level. History, in this view, will remain a chronicle of intermittent periods of peace set between wars. The twentieth century, in this history, will be known as the century of total war, not as the century of the beginning of the United Nations.

There are distinctive parts of our cultural notions about positive peace that also come to us from the Judeo-Christian tradition: shalom, love of enemies which demands forgiveness rather than retaliation, preferential concern for the poor, in short, love raised to the level of a political dynamism. These notions are developed further later in this chapter.

There are also new elements affecting our understanding of peace and its opposites that come from the seventeenth century forward. Important among these ideas are the sovereign national state, and later, the citizen army, national war efforts, total victory, and unconditional surrender. This is the cultural world into which we were born, and many of these ideas were not questioned by our teachers and are not questioned even now by most people who sincerely want peace.

Other new elements that cannot be ignored today are the insertion of environmental issues into the problem of peace, and also the influence of women's movements. Concerning the latter, on the one hand, the claim to social equality is doubling the number of those who can now claim the right to engage in lethal combat when the government declares a war or fights one undeclared. On the other hand, the women's movement insists on the possibility, and the need, to devise alternative ways other than the military for assuring security, for defending the widow and the orphan.

In summary, peace is an historicized idea. Only in a particular context does it have social significance, and therefore significance for social teaching, including Catholic social teaching. To work constructively with the notion of peace, to find our way as peacemakers, it is necessary to understand and analyze our own societies, the political, economic, and also the cultural elements, and also to understand the rich and complex history of both negative and positive peace.

PEACE AND PLURALISM IN PRACTICE

Pluralism within the Catholic Church

In 1981, when only the chairman of the committee to write the pastoral letter on peace had been appointed, some twenty bishops signed an open letter to Archbishop Bernardin specifying a list of questions they thought needed to be addressed by all the bishops in the forthcoming letter. This open letter, which gained wide circulation by being printed in *Origins*, was drafted during a two-day meeting by three bishop-members of Pax Christi, with the help of two scripture scholars, a theologian, and Pax Christi's national coordinator.[6] The meeting had been called at the insistence of Bishop Carroll Dozier of Memphis. His great concern was that the developing American Catholic social teaching on peace should be constructed in the context of the best scripture scholarship available.

Popular concern was an important factor in bringing the bishops of the United States to write their celebrated pastoral letter, *The Challenge of Peace*, which had such a considerable effect on other bishops' conferences. The complexity of the cultural factors operating within this concern is reflected in the pluralism of positions represented in *The Challenge of Peace*.

This growing pluralism in positions on peace is both a reflection of and an influence on the pluralism in theology in the church today. In general, it is accurate to say that a theology of positive peace, as distinct from moral theology dealing with guidance about participation in war, resonates with an ascending Christology, a Christology from below, that puts the accent on the humanity of Jesus and his historical experience without prejudice to the mystery of his divinity, whatever the difficulties of expressing that mystery in human language. Likewise, theories of positive peace find compatibility with ecclesiologies that stress the communitarian over the institutional dimensions of the church.

Those involved directly in efforts to influence public policy in ways they see as consistent with their vision of a just and peaceful society will often be members of intentional communities or of some adaptation of the small

Christian base communities. This phenomenon can be attributed partly to the inner coherence between the ends sought, the means used, and the structure and style of the small faith-sharing group in any of its forms or even its partial realizations. A faith that grapples with the issues of peace in our century, a century characterized by violence and threats to peace that have no precedents, needs the support that can come only from sharing that faith in a context that is of human dimensions, a context that honors the essential need for interpersonal ways of sharing faith and its consequences in the social arena.

Until fairly recently it has been war and the moral issues immediately related to entering and participating in war that have most engaged theologians, and specifically moral theologians, and also for the most part social activists. This is reflected in *The Challenge of Peace*, which has as subtitle, *A Pastoral Letter on War and Peace*. The order of terms is significant. Vatican II's *Pastoral Constitution on the Church in the Modern World* urges the church to undertake the evaluation of war with an entirely new attitude. Coming to this new attitude is difficult because there is so little theological literature that adequately relates a teaching on war and peace to the developments of Christology and ecclesiology.

The pluralism of views on peace and war is brought into clear focus in *The Challenge of Peace*, where different views are explicitly recognized and even used as an organizing principle for one part of the letter. The letter distinguishes between the just-war teaching and nonviolence as "distinct but interdependent methods of evaluating warfare." This description is useful, it seems to me, only as a sociological description. The two positions are interdependent only in the sense that they should prevent their adherents from arrogant absolutism and oversimplification of the complex realities with which they deal. The two methods are incompatible at another level, however, and recognition of this is a necessary presupposition to a more adequate development of the position that, for want of a better terminology, is called nonviolence.

It has been well said that where one stands on a social issue depends on where one sits. Certainly this is true in the case of the just-war teaching, where judgment in a concrete case is influenced by social identification more than by explicit theologizing. Anything approximating a theory of peace will have one set of characteristics if it is written by the military in an adversarial framework, and quite another if it is produced by the victims. Until recently, most formal theology dealing with peace and violence, as distinct from some theological wisdom captured in literature and the arts, has been written by those protected by custom and law from engaging directly in combat in war. Important recent linguistic studies are showing how theorizing on war from the safety of distance constructs a terminology that enables one to evade the concrete reality as far as possible. Killing human persons becomes "the use of force," and the dead persons themselves are "casualties." The examples can be multiplied.[7]

Although there has always been literature sensitive to the victim's experience of war and institutionalized violence, as distinct from the analysis and description by academicians of various disciplines, today the victim's view has a greater cultural role, through authors such as Elie Wiesel, and through television, which has brought not only ideas, but the sights and sounds of war and almost a kinetic experience of violence into the privacy of one's home. This, perhaps more than any other single factor, is making possible the evaluation of war with an entirely new attitude. The vicarious experience of the victim, including the soldier as victim of policy that is misguided or immoral, is helping to establish a social climate for a new kind of reflection and analysis that will make possible new kinds of public policy. Eventually, all this may issue in a new kind of law, including a new respect for international law as absolutely necessary and as important as national law. In short, attention is leading to a new level of understanding, which in turn is giving rise to fresh judgments calling for new responsibilities. For the Christian, all this is in the ambience of the distinctive love that is poured into our hearts by the Holy Spirit given us in Christ (Rom 5:5).

To balance all this, there is also an increase in individual violence, provoked by visual and emotional stimulation, and even more by the structural violence of poverty.[8]

The pluralism of positions on peace issues has a great value even if the positions themselves are incompatible. The pluralism sets up a creative tension and a dialectic from which emerge fresh insights. Reasoning about peace and war has theological, political, juridical, and the ethical dimensions. That kind of multidimensional reasoning is sometimes found in academic circles, but it is also found in the crucible of the social-political struggle for changes in public policy, thanks especially to those we correctly call the radicals of the peace movement.

A case in point is that of the Plowshares Eight, which has a ten-year history in the courts, including a final appeal to the United States Supreme Court. This legal case provides a rich mine, still largely untapped, of theological, political, juridical, and ethical reasoning that is a ready source for students of law and others.[9] In our day peace and justice are symbols of pluralism and also of tension within the church. Peace and justice are also the best symbols of the basic tension between Judeo-Christian values and social realities that is one of the distinctive marks of our culture. This tension expresses itself not only in speculative efforts and in the social and political behavior of individuals, but also in peace and justice movements that become effectively organized locally, nationally, internationally, and also at the highest level of the church, where the Pontifical Commission on Justice and Peace was instituted to carry out a mandate of the *Pastoral Constitution on the Church in the Modern World* (chap. 5, art. 90). This chapter will limit itself to a consideration of religiously based peace and justice movements, although it recognizes the importance of the many peace and justice movements that have no explicit religious reference.

In the United States, the Catholic Association for International Peace, which advocated the application of the just-war teaching to the new situation of warfare ushered in during World War II, no longer exists. At the opposite end of the spectrum, the Catholic Peace Fellowship, an affiliate of the interfaith Fellowship of Reconciliation, has remained small. The Fellowship of Reconciliation requires pacifism as a condition of membership. A third Catholic peace movement, Pax Christi USA, which is a section of the only international Catholic peace movement that aspires to membership throughout the world, has grown steadily since 1975. One reason for its appeal is that it explicitly embraces a pluralism of positions on peace issues among its members. There has been from the beginning a strong and articulate pacifist membership in Pax Christi USA, and more recently, a concerted effort to teach nonviolence as a way of engaging in conflict, a way that flows from an adherence to values central to the life and teaching of Jesus. However, espousing pacifism is not and, according to the statutes of the movement, cannot be a condition of membership.

Pax Christi International was founded near the end of World War II to foster reconciliation among Catholics who found themselves on opposite sides of that devastating conflict. In 1952 Pope Pius XII gave the movement its status as an international peace movement. Today, Pax Christi is organized as a federation with national sections in Europe, the United States, Canada, and Australia. The movement is currently being organized in a number of countries in Asia and the Pacific, and hopes to find its way in Africa as well.

Pax Christi works on the grassroots level, and also as an organization to influence public opinion and opinion within the church on matters of peace, justice, and human rights. Its professed aim is "to work for peace for all people, as the fruit of justice, while always witnessing to the peace of Christ." It does this by carefully planned programs of prayer, study, and action. The "prayer, study, and action" formula was given to Pax Christi in the '50s by Cardinal Feltin of Paris, the movement's first international president.

The movement was founded by lay people, and although Pax Christi has always elected a bishop as its international president, a practice followed by most national sections, lay people continue to form the majority of the movement, including a majority on the international executive committee, which is democratically elected.

Pax Christi looks to the gospel and Catholic social teaching as the foundation of its work. In 1963 the movement adopted the encyclical *Pacem in Terris* as its charter, enabling it to develop a very broad and consistent concept of positive peace as founded on the four pillars of truth, love, justice, and freedom. Unlike many other single-issue peace movements, Pax Christi has the strength that comes from fostering the spiritual and theological development of its own members along with its work on social issues.

The movement has consultative status with the Economic and Social Council of the United Nations, and in 1983 was awarded the Unesco Peace Education Prize for its work in stimulating the growth of an international peace climate. The organization regularly makes interventions in the UN Commission on Human Rights in Geneva, and also has organized fact-finding missions and visits of solidarity to Central America, Haiti, and Brazil.

Peace and Pluralism: Church and Churches

Any consideration of the religious pluralism of the peace movement must take into account the historic peace churches: the Mennonites, founded in the sixteenth century, the Society of Friends or Quakers, in the seventeenth, and the Church of the Brethren in the eighteenth. These churches continue to play a significant role today. In the United States this is perhaps most widely recognized at times of military conscription, because members of these three pacifist churches are exempt from military service, at least from combat duty, on religious grounds. One effect of this has been to help sharpen the arguments for selective conscientious objection on the basis of the just-war teaching that has guided the consciences of most Catholics and mainline Protestants when faced with the obligation of military service.

For years the Quakers have taken international leadership in United Nations circles in promoting the right to conscientious objection as a universal human right. The Quaker office in Geneva has acted as resource and coordinator for other groups, including Pax Christi, in their efforts on this issue. This long and painstaking work is now bearing fruit. The right of conscientious objection as a universal human right, and the right to alternative service that is not punitive, are now being addressed in the UN General Assembly and in national parliaments and legislatures partly, at least, because of the work of Quakers and their allies. Another issue which is under international scrutiny, thanks to the Quakers, is the use of minors as combat soldiers, a practice challenged as a violation of the international declaration on the rights of the child.

Among the mainline Protestant churches in the United States, the Methodist pastoral letter *In Defense of Creation* is the outstanding example of a public theological effort akin to the United States bishops' 1983 letter on war and peace. Compared to *The Challenge of Peace*, the Methodist letter takes a position clearly opposed to deterrence in a way that is less accommodating to the present political reality, or in a way that is less nuanced, depending on one's point of view on this issue. In a longer historical perspective, *In Defense of Creation* may be remembered less for what it says about deterrence than for the constructive way it includes environmental issues.

The Russian Orthodox Church has participated ecumenically in peace efforts through the World Council of Churches, but also through a program of bilateral conversations with Pax Christi International. This program began in 1972 when Metropolitan Nikodim met with Cardinal Alfrink of Utrecht, then president of Pax Christi. This meeting was followed by formal meetings in Vienna in 1974 and in Leningrad in 1976, a pattern that was continued even during the most difficult periods of East-West relations. Topics discussed at these biennial seminars have included such issues as security and disarmament, and relations with the Third World. The main emphasis has always been on the specific role of the churches in these matters. More important than the formal discussions themselves has been the climate of confidence and trust established, and the mutual understanding and friendships engendered. Russian Orthodox participation in these bilateral conversations has always included metropolitans, archbishops, and theological experts; the Pax Christi side has had comparable participation.

Mention should be made of the churches in China, in discussing peace and pluralism, because of their singular situation in a nation whose geopolitical importance can hardly be overestimated. The delicate and difficult situation of the Catholic church vis-à-vis the government of China has created a need for reconciliation within the Catholic church in China itself. This is an area that calls for careful attention and investment of time and energy now. The program of bilateral conversations between Pax Christi and the Russian Orthodox Church suggests one kind of program that, with modifications, could be undertaken with some partners in China.

On the level of ecumenical movements and organizations that focus on a peace agenda, there is here space to mention only a few of those that have more than local participation. In 1968 the World Council of Churches and the Pontifical Commission on Justice and Peace jointly organized Sodepax, a body to act together on promoting social justice, development, and peace. In the almost twenty years of its existence, Sodepax broke new ground in several of its high-level international conferences on issues of international economic justice, and on peace as the fruit of justice. At one of these early conferences Gustavo Gutiérrez read a paper that was to become, several years later, the heart of his book *A Theology of Liberation.*

The justice/development line developed more vigorously than the peace line of both the Pontifical Commission and Sodepax, partly because of the talents of people like Louis LeBret, O.P., Vincent Cosmao, O.P., Barbara Ward, and Philip Land, S.J., who were active in the early days, and whose expertise was more closely related to issues of economic development than to peace issues. But there were institutional reasons as well for a more muted approach to matters of peace. Inevitably peace discussions touched on political issues in which the Vatican had its own more diplomatic approach.

Sodepax was not destined to have a long life, but the kind of work it inspired went on in other forums, if not at the highest levels of the churches. In 1984 and again in 1987 there were international conferences in Budapest titled *Towards a Theology of Peace.* Participants came from Catholic and

Protestant churches throughout Europe, from the Russian Orthodox Church, and from Latin America, North America, Asia, and Africa. The 1987 conference had a larger number of theologians from the Third World. These two conferences were the result of the initiative of two individuals, a British layman, Stephen Tunnicliffe, and Bishop Karoly Toth of the Reformed Church in Hungary. The published proceedings of the 1987 conference reflect both the unity and remarkable pluralism of the Christian efforts for a more adequate theology and practice of peacemaking.

In 1989 in Basle Roman Catholics, Orthodox, and Protestants came together for a regional meeting on *Justice, Peace, and the Integrity of Creation*, or JPIC, as it is now familiarly known. The Basle meeting was in preparation for the major meeting of the JPIC program held in Seoul in March 1990. While the JPIC Seoul convocation is a program of the World Council of Churches, the Basle meeting was jointly sponsored by the European Bishops' Conference of the Catholic Church and the World Council of Churches.

In the United States in the early 1980s, five faith-based peace movements with national memberships joined together in the New Abolitionist Covenant, whose goal is to promote education and citizen action on the nuclear weapons threat and related issues. The five groups were Pax Christi, Fellowship of Reconciliation, Sojourners, World Peacemakers, and The New Call to Peacemaking, this last a joint program of the historic peace churches in the United States. Since that time the group has grown and meets annually for a retreat aimed at discerning the signs of the times and strengthening the bonds that unite these groups in their commitment to work for peace as the fruit of justice.

Peace and Pluralism: The Interfaith Dimension

The need for interreligious effort on peace issues flows immediately from contemporary geo-political realities. The major world religions are not to be studied only for personal interest nor to help clarify what is distinctive about our own faith and tradition; rather, as we grow in understanding the importance of the cultural dimension in the search for a just peace, we need to have an adequate understanding of the dynamic part different religions play in their cultures and societies. Equally important, we need to develop ways of dialogue that until now have been the domain of specialists.

Interreligious dialogue that deals with peace issues raises formidable problems. Nowhere are these greater than in Jewish-Christian dialogue. Here we are faced with the Judeo-Christian heritage of notions of the warrior God, not as peripheral, but as central to our foundational story in the Hebrew scriptures. This foundational history is also integral to our Christian faith. Though the problem of the warrior God has been dealt with well on the exegetical, historical, and theological levels, it is on the cultural level, on the level of popular religiosity, that the problem remains, and not only among fundamentalists. It has been pointed out that from the perspective of world history as we know it from written records, it is the civilizations of Judeo-Christian culture that have been, if not consistently the most aggressive, certainly the most devastating in their warring. The most conclusive evidence is from the twentieth century.

The close integration of religion and militarism is strikingly portrayed in the interdenominational chapel used by Jews, Catholics, and Protestants at Offut Air Force Base, home of the Strategic Air Command, near Omaha, Nebraska. The chapel sanctuary is dominated by a window showing a Moses-like air-force officer in a near ecstatic posture, listening to God speak from a light-filled cloud. The words from Isaiah engraved in the window are, "Here I am, Lord, send me." Smaller windows throughout the chapel show the mushroom cloud, the red telephone, and in one window, bombs falling through a starlit sky. None of this is meant to be social satire, but inspirational religious art. The fact that some people see in these windows something obscene is one more reminder of the depths of feeling on different sides of peace issues in a pluralist society. The point here, however, is to make a case for Jewish-Christian dialogue that may enable us to face together a troubling part of our heritage, a part that is very much alive, the myth of the warrior God that for centuries has been the source of the most powerful legitimation of the institution of war. To undertake seriously the injunction of Vatican II to evaluate war with an entirely new attitude, we will have to find ways to deal with the warrior God, ways that reach more than the world of scholars.

The notion of positive peace also has deep roots in the Judeo-Christian tradition, in the idea of *shalom*. This powerful symbol, which cannot be adequately translated by the conventional understanding of the word *peace*, has a long history and also a capacity for development that can contribute greatly to positive peace. Jewish-Christian dialogue can do what no amount of separate theologizing can do, that is, bring to an emerging world order that is in desperate need of new ways of thinking about peace, insights that are embedded in traditions that we hold in common, but that need to be reclaimed.

Muslim-Christian dialogue faces its own formidable obstacles, first of which, on the Christian side, is widespread ignorance of the riches of the Islamic tradition, of the Koran, and of Islamic religious literature. Added to this is the influence of recent and present political relationships, and the heritage of the Crusades. It is tempting to ask if it is even worth trying, if it is possible to transcend such a combination of hurdles to genuine dialogue. There is also the temptation to limit ourselves to addressing contemporary political issues. A recognition of the importance of religion in the formation of culture can help prevent the error of underestimating the crucial importance of genuine Muslim-Christian dialogue around issues of peace.

Buddhist-Christian dialogue also belongs on the agenda of today's and tomorrow's peacemakers. Here we have much to learn from a tradition that has a rich and original contribution to make to the universal human quest for peace. Apart from the riches of Buddhism itself in its various schools, there is the social reality that is its own argument. The Pacific rim is from some perspectives the most important center of geo-politics, and in many countries of the Pacific rim, Buddhism is a major element of the culture. In the name of peace, we dare not remain out of dialogue with it.

It is possible to point to some organized effort to promote interreligious understanding as it has an impact on the social agenda, and particularly questions of peace. In January 1989 the World Conference on Religion and Peace had its fifth international assembly in Melbourne, Australia. For more than twenty years the WCRP has been bringing together adherents of major and some minor world religions to address peace and justice issues. The Vatican was officially represented at the Melbourne Assembly. As a fraternal [sic] observer for Pax Christi, I experienced firsthand both the strengths and weaknesses of the WCRP. The broad range of participation prevented anything beyond the most general statements on any issue. Inter-religious dialogue to be fruitful must take place around specific topics with a more limited number of participants. In many cases the conversations must be bilateral for substantive inquiry to take place. The breadth of composition of WCRP has symbolic value, but it also exacts as its price the limitation to statements that have very little impact outside the circles of the organization itself. Having said this, it is only fair to add that what is often remarked about the United Nations can, with appropriate adjust-ments, be said abut the WCRP. For all its weaknesses, it is the best and the only organization of its kind that we have, and we would be poorer without it. The WCRP will grow in importance when there is more work of a similar kind going on at local and regional levels.

The Fellowship of Reconciliation, mentioned above, has a very active Jewish Peace Fellowship, which is an important pacifist voice within the Jewish community and beyond it. There is also a Buddhist Peace Fellowship affiliated to the American Fellowship of Reconciliation.

Pax Christi International has only recently formally embarked on inter-religious dialogue, using its years of experience of dialogue with the Russian Orthodox Church as one program model that can be adapted to new areas. Jewish-Christian dialogue was begun at a seminar in Berlin in 1989. A program in Muslim-Christian dialogue was initiated in Vienna in 1990 at the Pax Christi International Council. Both these programs owe much to the inspiring leadership of Franz Cardinal Koenig, president of Pax Christi International, 1984-90.

CONCLUSIONS

From the above I draw four conclusions about the possibilities for pro-moting positive peace.

First, the recovery and development of a biblical theology is having a profound, even a transforming influence on the understanding of peace. The work of developing a systematic or coherent biblical theology of peace has hardly begun, but it has moved beyond proof-texting, and it has made abundantly clear that peace belongs to every part of theology, not only moral theology. How great are the strides that have been made in method can be judged by comparing the passages on biblical foundations in *The Challenge of Peace* with similar passages in *Economic Justice for All*, written only three years later. These refinements in method now need to be applied to the study of peace.

A good example is in an essay commenting on the pastoral letter on peace by Sandra Schneiders.[10] She attempts to expose the challenge that the gospel presents to our present situation of cultural violence and particularly to its manifestation in the nuclear-weapons peril. The article identifies five aspects of the Christian mystery that are directly relevant to peace: the Christian vocation to peace, the Christian love commandment, the ministry of reconciliation, the preferential option for the poor, and the "reversal dynamic" of the gospel. Continuing this kind of biblical theology will insure that the development of Catholic social teaching is adequately grounded, and that it gives appropriate theological attention to positive peace.

In this way, and only in this way, will we come to an adequate understanding of what we call, for want of a more adequate term, nonviolence. Nonviolence is a way of engaging in conflict, not a way of removing oneself from it. It is a costly way that is expressed in the Hebrew scriptures in the Servant Songs of Isaiah and in the New Testament by the entire thrust of the life and teachings of Jesus.

Though the term *nonviolence* was not used in Catholic social teaching until recently, there are elements of nonviolence described in Catholic social teaching from John XXIII forward. There are striking examples in *Sollicitudo Rei Socialis* in the treatment of solidarity as the moral response to interdependence.

The contemporary search for nonviolent social structures and mechanisms has become an issue that crosses all religious and cultural barriers. Reasoning people of every culture recognize that collaborative efforts rather than competitive ones are essential for politics, especially international politics, as the price of human survival. Awareness of the magnitude of environmental problems is stimulating this new way of thinking. We cannot bring the riches of our own faith tradition to this search unless we root it in a continuing and disciplined scripture scholarship. Simply repeating what has already been achieved, or translating it into more effective educational materials, will not do.

Second, a history of peace is emerging, although more slowly or at least less systematically than a theology of peace. The church needs to support and foster this history. History is still, by and large, the child of nineteenth-century canons of historiography. This is why we remember our past as periodized by wars. We do not yet have commonly accepted frameworks for a history of positive peace, but we do have the tools and disciplines of a history of peace in intellectual history and in social and cultural history. One framework for a history of peace that deserves testing by researchers is in Pope John Paul II's 1979 message "To Reach Peace, Teach Peace." There we are urged to bring forward visions of peace, gestures of peace, and the language of peace. In introducing these categories, he says:

> An education worthy of its name must have as its first task, and produce as its first beneficent result, the ability to see beyond the unfortunate facts in the foreground, or rather to recognize, in the very midst of the raging of murderous violence, the quiet progress of peace, never giving in, untiringly healing wounds, and maintaining and advancing life. The movement toward peace will then be seen as possible and desirable, as strong and already victorious.

A history of peace can be greatly enriched by ecumenical and interreligious dialogue that makes peace its focus. Conversely, the interreligious dialogue can stimulate and help focus further research. Analysis of pressing social issues and refinement of ethical norms for participation in war, as well as research into the history of wars, should not obscure the need for this more basic kind of research into the history of peace.

Third, positive peace is above all a cultural enterprise. *Culture,* as the term is used by anthropologists, is a major preoccupation of Catholic social teaching, certainly since Vatican II, where an entire chapter of *Gaudium et Spes* is given to a treatment of the development of culture. The relationship of church and culture is one of the major themes of Pope John Paul II. It is positive peace that he has likened to a cathedral that must be built up day after day by works of peace. In *Pacem in Terris* peace is described as built on the four pillars of truth, justice, love or solidarity, and freedom. This essay has gone beyond description to a definition from a secular source: peace is the state in which all spontaneously desire one another's welfare. Whichever definition or description one prefers, it is important to recognize that it is the active pursuit of positive peace that offers hope for negative peace, that is, for the absence of war and of structural violence.

In the development of positive peace, the women's movement has an indispensable part to play. The intersection of the women's and peace movements can bring into focus ways of communication, of organization of power, of ways of dealing with conflict, of structures of mutuality that offer needed alternatives to structures of domination and subordination.

Another implication of the turn to culture as the theater for peacemaking is the need to pay much more attention to the victims of violence, both the victims of the organized violence of war who survive, and the victims of the no less real and lethal violence of structural poverty.

The emphasis on culture also requires that we make much more room for the affective dimension of human life in the social construction of peace.

Dr. Helen Caldicott, the pediatrician who became an internationally known antinuclear activist, was once asked on a television talk show, "Don't you think you are very emotional about this issue?" Caldicott blazed with emotion as she replied that she would hope so, that to be unemotional about issues of potential genocide and of the present dangers from the nuclear weapons enterprise would be inhuman. Stoicism, the stiff upper lip, is appropriate for making war; it is not appropriate for making peace. On the contrary, it is compassion that is the necessary and primary response that will characterize the peacemaker, and particularly the peacemaker who is a member of the community of disciples of Jesus.[11]

Attentiveness to the cultural dimension enables us to understand both the importance of, and also the limitations of, legal remedies for violence. An illustration is the present state of United States policy and practice in the matter of biological, chemical, and bacteriological weaponry. Research, and even production, proceed because there is no strong cultural abhorrence to these kinds of weaponry. To many they seem simply necessary as a means of deterrence, a means possibly more efficient and less expensive than other kinds of weaponry. The pope has written about this in the 1990 World Day of Peace message. We can ask ourselves if it is not equally important, even more important, that the United States hierarchy speak out forcefully and clearly to policy makers and also to their own people who need guidance. The fact that chemical weapons have had a comeback after a recess in their use after World War I demonstrates the power of culture to decide the limits of law. A longer historical perspective offers us positive examples as well. Practices like child abuse, incest, and torture are prevented more by cultural taboo, by a collective sense of moral abhorrence, than by any amount of legislation.

Fourth, the issue of work brings all this together. Here we come full circle, dealing with the same human and social reality that was the subject of the great encyclical whose centenary we are celebrating in 1991.

We do well to see peacemaking as a human work par excellence, a work to which we are all called. We can test the human worthiness of any enterprise by the norm of positive peace. Does this particular work contribute to that state in which all spontaneously desire one another's welfare? Does it promote human communion? Does it promote and support loyalties that transcend those of the immediate groups to which one belongs, including the nation, without abandoning those loyalties? Does it recognize the responsibility to care for the earth itself for this and future generations? These questions provide a reality test for the beatitude "Blessed are the peacemakers, for they will be called the children of God." They are questions that will decide the future direction of Catholic social teaching on peace and on the practice that flows from it.

NOTES

1. Violence is force used to injure; it may be physical or psychological, personal or structural. Especially useful at the structural level is Johan Galtung's definition

302   Mary Evelyn Jegen, S.N.D.

of violence as that which inhibits the fulfillment of a human being.

2. Michael Nagler, "Redefining Peace," *The Bulletin of the Atomic Scientists* (November 1984), p. 37.

3. John R. Donahue, "Biblical Perspectives on Justice," in *The Faith That Does Justice: Examining the Christian Sources for Social Change*, ed. John C. Haughey (New York: Paulist Press, 1977).

4. Pope John Paul II, "To Reach Peace, Teach Peace," Message for the World Day of Peace, 1979.

5. Ruth Leger Sivard, *World Military and Social Expenditures—1989*, 13th ed. (Washington, D.C.: World Priorities, 1989).

6. Bishop Carroll Dozier, Bishop P. Francis Murphy, Bishop Thomas Gumbleton, Carroll Stuhlmueller, C.P., Donald Senior, C.P., John Langan, S.J., Mary Evelyn Jegen, S.N.D.

7. Carol Cohn, "A Feminist Spy in the House of Death: Unravelling the Language of Strategic Analysis," in *Women and the Military System*, ed. Eva Isakssohn (London: Harvester-Wheatsheaf, 1988).

8. Michael Nagler, *America Without Violence: Why Violence Persists and How You Can Stop It* (Covelo, California: Island Press, 1982). See especially the material on violence on television.

9. Liane Ellision Norman, *Hammer of Justice: Molly Rush and the Plowshares Eight* (Pittsburgh: Pittsburgh Peace Institute Books, 1989). Especially telling are the arguments from necessity based on international law and the views of lawyers on both sides of the case. The case concerns eight persons who broke into a General Electric plant and damaged a nuclear weapons component.

10. Sandra M. Schneiders, "New Testament Reflections on Peace and Nuclear Arms," in *Catholics and Nuclear War*, ed. Philip J. Murnion (New York: Crossroad, 1983).

11. An important study is Monika Hellwig, *Jesus, the Compassion of God* (Wilmington, Delaware: Michael Glazier, 1983).

20

PEACEMAKING AS A WAY OF LIFE

BISHOP THOMAS J. GUMBLETON

Peacemaking is more than *a* way of life; for the believing Christian it should be accepted as the *only* way of life compatible with the message and life of Christ and his earliest followers. Whether it is the interpersonal peacemaking implied in the command to leave our gifts at the altar until we have reconciled with those we may have wronged and even, perhaps *especially*, those who have wronged us, or working on the peaceful resolution of the group antagonisms and hatreds which are reflected in the strife between races and classes and nations, our lives and actions should reflect the total commitment to love displayed by Jesus, ultimately, on the cross at Calvary.

On the other hand, to the extent that we Christians allow ourselves to be ruled by self-interest and pride, to jealously guard the advantages we have, or jealously envy the advantages possessed by others, and resort to various forms of violence against others to maintain our self-satisfaction, we deny Christ. It is as simple as that, as terribly simple as that. To speak for peace, to pray for peace, to teach peace, to work for peace, to do whatever we can whether great or small to *make* peace is our calling and must be put at the top of our priorities.

Given the essential role that peacemaking should play in the "way of life" for Christians and the duty of the leaders of the church to speak about the demands of peacemaking, it is gratifying that peacemaking has come to be a major theme in Catholic social teaching in the last few decades. It is perhaps discomfiting, however, to realize that the development of Catholic social teaching took so long when we consider the signs of the times of the past one hundred years. This has been a century, after all, which produced two world wars and innumerable smaller wars, with ever increasing numbers of noncombatant deaths, the use of weapons characterized by indiscriminate and massive killing capacity, all-too-nearly successful efforts to commit genocide, the systematic abuse of human rights, and a depressing array of other forms of social injustice and violence perpetrated against human beings (and, as we are becoming increasingly aware, against the planet itself). In an age when "crimes against humanity" became almost commonplace, the church seemed strangely silent. The *prophetic* word was not spoken in Nazi Germany or Hiroshima. At a historic moment when the world needed the clear call of denunciation against horrendous crimes and when individual Christians needed the strong, clear guidance of the teaching church, it was not there.

This failure of the church became very clear to me when I read an account by Robert McAfee Brown of an experience of his when he participated in a conference entitled "Facing the Twenty-first Century: Threats and Promises." This was a conference put together by Elie Wiesel, Nobel peace prize laureate. He had the inspiration to call together Nobel laureates from around the world from a variety of disciplines to gather with the singular purpose of discussing ways in which the world might reflect on the extreme barbarism of the twentieth century and perhaps help point the way that the world might avoid this same barbarism in the twenty-first century. The conference was to be formally convened on Monday, January 18, at the Elysee Palace. But since January 17 was the anniversary of the liberation of Auschwitz, it seemed appropriate to Wiesel, who was an inmate of Auschwitz during World War II, that conference participants make a pilgrimage to the concentration camp as a solemn beginning of their deliberations. He felt rightly that to visit Auschwitz—which will be the enduring symbol of the twentieth century as an age of barbarism— would provide an appropriate context for reflecting on the imperative need not to repeat such barbarism in the twenty-first century.

A charter flight was arranged to Crakow, and the group then visited Auschwitz and also Birkenau, the death camp for Auschwitz. It was here that the trip took on added meaning because Lech Walesa was able to join the group. Dr. Brown describes how two things happened during that brief visit that were for him very powerful symbols.

> The symbolic power of Wiesel and Walesa, Nobel Peace Laureates, one a Jew, the other a Pole, standing on a cold January morning in front of the monument at Birkenau and making mutual pledges to one another to create hope for children of the future, in the place where a million children were murdered, was a powerful symbol indeed.
>
> Another symbol, devastating to me as a Christian, was created during this visit. Although I do not know how many other members of the group sensed it, its impact will never leave me. We concluded our visit to Auschwitz close to the noon hour by entering one of the crematoria and standing silently in front of some of the furnaces with their tracks for the more "efficient" disposal of corpses. A Rabbi led some prayers, a Polish priest then read scripture—Psalm 130 ("Out of the depths"), I think—after which in the presence of these instruments of death, the Jews quite appropriately began to recite the Kaddish, the prayer for the dead.

And then it happened: interrupting the Kaddish and continuing in competition with its high solemnity at that special moment, the Church bells from outside the camp began to peel, celebrating the consecration of the host at the Mass in the parish church. My mind involuntarily and instantaneously took a leap back 45 years. I reflected that at that time real guards would have been in the room in which we were now standing, thrusting real corpses into real ovens heated to temperatures extreme enough to dispose of the corpses quickly and that those same guards who were burning those same bodies would have gone out of that same camp, traversed the few hundred yards to that same church, gone to Mass, received communion and returned that afternoon or the next day to continue that same grizzly occupation . . . quite unaware of any contradiction between receiving the Body and Blood of the Jew, Jesus, and destroying the body and blood of millions of other Jews.

The episode remains highly disquieting for it symbolizes so much the attitude of the Church in the presence of massive evil and suggests that if the Church in the 21st Century is going to help stem the tide of barbarism it will first of all have to deal a mortal blow to its own greatest institutional sin: indifference.[1]

PACEM IN TERRIS

Thank God we are beginning to overcome that sin. That is one of the reasons we celebrate these hundred years of Catholic social teaching. It is entirely right and proper that we acknowledge with gratitude the statements and declarations that now have begun to shape the fundamental commitment of the church to the quest for social justice and peace. But it is especially the last thirty years that we can celebrate most gratefully. We start very properly with Pope John XXIII's *Pacem in Terris*. It was acclaimed around the world for its insistence on the dignity of the human person, the rights and duties of individuals in societies, the imperative of halting the arms race and implementing a complete disarmament, and the sober reminder that

> Peace will be but an empty sounding word unless it is founded on . . . truth built according to justice, vivified and integrated by charity and put into practice in freedom (no. 167).

It was that document also that began for us within the church the development of what, later, the Vatican Council came to call "a whole new attitude toward war." John XXIII in one simple statement changed the whole framework for discussion of the use of violence in an atomic era. He insisted, "in this atomic era, it is irrational any longer to think of war as an apt means to vindicate violated rights" (no. 127). Such a statement — simple, concise, clear — calls us to give up violence even in the face of unjust aggression against us. We have not developed this thinking nearly far enough in my judgment, but at least we are brought to the beginning of a whole new way of thinking about war.

The work of John XXIII was truly the beginning of an outpouring of Catholic social teaching that continues even now and that builds on the previous teaching starting with Leo XIII. In recent years this teaching moved in quite extraordinary ways along new paths. In my judgment the single most significant development in this church teaching came during the synod of bishops called by Pope Paul VI in 1971 to discuss "Justice in the World." This teaching reached a new and profound understanding of how to overcome "indifference" and how to develop "peacemaking as a way of life."

It was clear that the bishops of that synod were troubled even as Robert McAfee Brown was troubled by the fact that Christians could be indifferent to massive evil, even to the point of participating in that massive evil and not seeing the contradiction with their own beliefs and commitments. In a document prepared for the synod workshops (par. 7) there is a synthesis of the general debate on world justice. The bishops asked themselves these hard questions:

> How is it that after 80 years of modern social teaching and 2000 years of the gospel of love that the Church has to admit her inability to make more impact upon the conscience of her people. This is not to say that Catholic works of mercy have not been immense nor that the flame of charity does not burn unquenchably in the breasts of thousands upon thousands of religious and laity who give their lives to the service of the poor, the aged, the sick, the orphaned, the forgotten. But it was stressed again and again that the faithful, particularly the more wealthy and comfortable among them simply do not see structural social injustice as sin. They simply feel no personal responsibility for it and simply feel no obligation to do anything about it. Sunday observance, the Church's rules on sex and marriage tend to enter the Catholic consciousness profoundly as sin. To live like Dives with Lazarus at the gate is not even perceived as sinful.

SOCIAL SIN

As the bishops discussed this failure on the part of the church their very strong reaction was that the whole social teaching of the church had to be removed from the high level of doctrinal pronouncement and forced into the consciences of the people of God.

And they developed a very key concept: *structured social injustice is sin.* In our own National Catechetical Directory we draw from this teaching to insist:

> Social justice focuses not only on personal relationships but on institutions, structures and systems of social organization (keeping in mind however that these are composed of persons) which foster or impede the common good at the local, national and international levels. Social justice is the concept by which one evaluates the organization and functioning of the political, eco-

nomic, social and cultural life of society. Positively the Church's social teaching seeks to apply the Gospel command of love to and within social systems, structures and institutions.[2]

This is a major step in the development of our thinking on questions of justice. Once we have begun to grasp and act on the concept of structured social injustice we begin to see clearly the profound contradiction in the life of the "Christian" who lives an exemplary personal life but participates in a society which perpetrates massive evil.

John Paul II in his encyclical *The Social Concern of the Church* also speaks about social sin:

> Moreover one must denounce the existence of economic, financial, social mechanisms which although they are manipulated by people, often function almost automatically, thus accentuating the situation of wealth for some and poverty for the rest. These mechanisms, which are maneuvered directly or indirectly by the more developed countries, by their very functioning favor the interests of the people manipulating them (par. 16).

A very helpful definition of social sin is provided by Bryan Hehir in an article published some years ago in *Chicago Studies*. "Social sin is a situation in which the very organization of some level of society systematically functions to the detriment of groups or individuals in the society." Clearly this is a new understanding of sin. It goes beyond the concept that sin is an individual act, something I might or might not do that would be contrary to God's law. My individual act is one part of a whole complex of actions that make up a situation, and it is the situation or that combination of the individual acts that does detriment to individuals or groups. And this, as the definition points out, can happen at any level of society. It could be within the society of a city, a nation, or within the community of nations. Wherever human society exists, it can be organized in such a way that it functions to the detriment of individuals or groups within that society.

A very clear example is the way our own nation was organized at the beginning with a Constitution that legally denied African-Americans full personhood and deprived them legally of their full human rights. Today we are much aware that the nation of South Africa is clearly organized in such a way that it works to the detriment of the majority of the people of that nation. Previously, I think we would not have seen this as a sin. Clearly, in the United States the church did not identify this grave injustice as sin. Personal morality was encouraged in our relations with African-Americans. But the very structure of our society was not described as sinful. No one was challenged to accept responsibility for the destruction and violence done to slaves by the system itself. The sinfulness, of course, isn't just in the structure. Sin doesn't exist in mechanisms. Hehir points out that the sinfulness lies in the way

social relationships are contrived or permitted to exist. People do organize
society or people do allow unjust structures to go on. The responsibility to
change the situation rests on all who participate in society: some are called
to assert their rights which are being systematically denied; others are called
to recognize their responsibility to change existing patterns of social relationships.

Anyone, of course, who helped to contrive an unjust situation and did
so knowingly would clearly be guilty of sin. But what happens much more
is that the situation has developed without an awareness on the part of
those who make up the society until after the fact. But then, if we continue
to "live like Dives with Lazarus at the gate" and do nothing about it, we
are guilty of sin.

I see development of the understanding of social sin as a key development because it also leads to quite a different understanding of how we
make peacemaking part of our everyday life, how we make peacemaking
actually a way of life. Social sin can help us to understand how violence
intrudes and destroys the lives of tens of thousands of people every day in
a way that is most cruel, in a way that could be called without exaggeration
an act of aggression against the poor, or even a war against the poor. Maybe
an example from the life of a Salvadoran peasant will help to emphasize
this reality:

> I worked on the hacienda over there and I would have to feed the dogs bowls
> of meat . . . and I could never put those on the table for my own children.
> When my children were ill they died with a nod of sympathy from the land
> owner but when those dogs were ill I took them to the veterinarian. . . . You
> will never understand violence or nonviolence until you understand the vio-
> lence to the spirit that happens from watching your children die of malnu-
> trition.

Just days before he was brutally murdered in November of 1989, Father
Ignacio Ellacuría, the former rector of the University of Central America
in San Salvador, spoke about this kind of violence in a talk in his Basque
homeland:

> You who live here in Europe have organized your lives around inhuman
> values. They are inhuman because they cannot be universalized. The *system*
> rests on a few using the majority of resources while the majority can't even
> cover their basic necessities. It is crucial to find a system of values and a
> norm of living that takes into account every human being.

The system—that is, the economic structure—in a country like El Salvador is organized in such a way that it works to the detriment of the
majority of the people there. It is a violent system that destroys and kills
innocent people. But it is not just *within* a country such as El Salvador. As

Father Ellacuría pointed out, the community of nations has been organized in such a way as to prevent the majority of people from getting basic necessities. It is a system that is doing violence to tens of thousands of people every day. John Paul II on his pilgrimage to Canada a few years ago spoke powerfully about this when he preached a homily on the twenty-fifth chapter of Matthew's gospel. Reflecting on the words "In as much as you have done it unto one of the least of these my brothers or sisters you have done it unto me," John Paul went on to say:

> Jesus is speaking of the whole universal dimension of injustice and evil. He is speaking of what today we are accustomed to call the North/South Contrast. Yes, South becoming always poorer and the North becoming always richer. In the light of Christ's words, this poor South will judge the rich North, and the poor people, and the poor nations, poor in different ways—not only lacking in food but also deprived of freedom and other human rights—will judge those people who take these goods away from them amassing to themselves the imperialistic monopoly of economic and political supremacy at the expense of others.

In 1971 the synod of bishops made it very clear that an essential part of the following of Christ, of the preaching of the gospel, of being a disciple, is to act against injustice. We no longer can be satisfied with statements. We must take up the cause of overcoming the sinful structures.

> Action on behalf of justice and participation in the transformation of the world fully appear to us as a constitutive dimension of the teaching of the Gospel, or in other words, of the Church's mission for the redemption of the human race and its liberation from every oppressive situation.

And this is peacemaking. In *Populorum Progressio* Pope Paul VI insisted that development is the new name for peace:

> To wage war on misery and to struggle against injustice is to promote, along with improved conditions, the human and spiritual progress of all men, and therefore the common good of humanity. Peace cannot be limited to a mere absence of war, the result of an ever precarious balance of forces. No, peace is something that is built up day after day, in the pursuit of an order intended by God, which implies a more perfect form of justice among men (par. 76).

This may seem an innocuous form of peacemaking, a way that might easily and readily be taken up by most Christians. But I warn you: it is not easy and it will not be taken up readily by very many.

Two articles by Ignacio Ellacuría make clear why this is so, and these same two articles provide a very helpful analysis of the way structured violence enters into human society and destroys peace. One was republished on the day after his brutal murder; it had been written three years earlier. This article drew from a previous and much longer article published in *Concilium*. The newspaper article was a response to a very harsh attack against him and the Jesuits at the University of Central America in San Salvador in an attack in the *Globe* written by Edward R.F. Sheehan. Mr. Sheehan charged that the Jesuits were "too utopian, too violent, too destructive." Father Ellacuría admitted:

His description that we are utopian comes closest to being accurate. . . . It is true that we aren't politicians and in that sense we are more utopian than pragmatic. We are a people of the Gospel, a Gospel that proclaims the kingdom of God and that calls us to transform this earth into as close a likeness of that kingdom as possible.

Then he went on:

Within such a perspective it is difficult to accept unbridled capitalism because the evils it has produced in history outweigh the good. As the Bishops of Latin America stated at their meeting in Puebla, Mexico in 1979, "We see the continuing operation of economic systems that do not regard the human being as the center of society and that are not carrying out the profound changes needed to move toward a just society."

For the Jesuits, Father Ellacuría stated,

It would be easier to accept systems that better confronted the problems of the poor and gave the poor the special place bestowed on them in a Gospel vision. Such a vision emphasizes the common good. It calls for liberation.

Father Ellacuría then goes on to point out that the Jesuits, in their teaching through liberation theology, through the formation of base communities in which people are made aware of their rights and of their obligation to assert those rights, do not promote violence. He says:

On the contrary, violence is what we are trying to overcome. But let us not deceive ourselves about where all this violence began. It started with what the Church calls institutionalized, legalized violence, whether in the form of economic exploitation, political domination or abuse of military might.[3]

He is describing a very concrete example of social sin: violent economic structures that kill the poor.

A VIOLENCE OF REPRESSION

But this is only the beginning of a pattern of violence that destroys peace. There is a second violence, a violence of repression. This begins to happen when those like the Jesuits and other liberation theologians in Latin America and in other parts of the world teach and encourage the poor to understand that God does not intend them to live in devastating, dehumanizing poverty, that God has indeed made this world for all and not for a few. In other words, when they teach, along with *Populorum Progressio*, that

> each man has therefore the right to find in the world what is necessary for himself. . . . All other rights whatsoever, including those of property and of free commerce are to be subordinated to this principle. . . . That is, private property does not constitute for anyone an absolute and unconditioned right. No one is justified in keeping for his exclusive use what he does not need, when others lack necessities (par. 22, 23).

When the poor hear this teaching and begin to act upon it by asserting their rights the second violence—the violence of repression—explodes against them. It is easy to document this. The bishops of Brazil many years ago called attention to this reality when they pointed out how a small minority of people have built socio-economic structures upon oppression and injustice and "are committed to maintain by all means possible a situation which was created in their favor."

How far this rich minority will go to maintain "a situation which was created in their favor" becomes starkly clear in El Salvador. Here the violence of repression has been extreme in the last decade. Father Ellacuría describes it:

> To call our position too violent and too destructive is to make an erroneous judgement and more. We have endured a good deal during these recent years. One of us, Reverend Rutilio Grande was murdered, and the rest of us received an ultimatum: Get out of the country or be killed. We decided to stay. Since then our home and our university have been bombed fourteen times. It doesn't take much to bring on further threats or worse. Since charges like Mr. Sheehan's legitimize all the worst impulses of the kind of people who have put up signs here saying "Be a patriot—kill a priest." In circumstances like these, Sheehan's judgement of us is more than simply erroneous; it is itself "too violent and too destructive."

The brutal death of Father Ellacuría and his colleagues from the University of Central America, as well as the two women who had stayed on the campus for protection on that night of November 16, 1989, brought worldwide attention to this violence of repression. But there have been tens of thousands of deaths in El Salvador. The violence against them has become so extreme that Archbishop Oscar Romero, himself a victim, described the situation of the poor.

> In El Salvador we all run the risk of death. . . . Christ invites us not to fear persecution because, you must believe me, my friends, whoever commits himself to the poor has to accept the same destiny as the poor. And in El Salvador we know the destiny of the poor: to be disappeared, to be tortured, to be killed, to reappear as cadavers.

REVOLUTIONARY VIOLENCE

This violence of repression, as it intensifies, will almost always result in the third phase of violence: revolutionary violence. Each form of violence is bad and destroys peace. But when we are faced with revolutionary violence, it is important to remember that the church has tolerated, though not encouraged, the resistance that is proportionate to the violence of an unjust aggressor. This tolerance may not seem in strict conformance with the gospel, but it is classical Catholic moral doctrine. Revolutionary violence can within that classical doctrine be justified when the necessary conditions are present. Pope Paul VI speaks of this in *Populorum Progressio*:

> There are certainly situations whose injustice cries to heaven. When whole populations destitute of necessities live in a state of dependence barring them from all initiative and responsibility, and all opportunity to advance culturally and share in social and political life, recourse to violence, as a means to right these wrongs to human dignity, is a grave temptation.
> We know, however, that a revolutionary uprising—save where there is manifest, long-standing tyranny which would do damage to fundamental personal rights and dangerous harm to the common good of the country—produces new injustices, throws more elements out of balance and brings on new disasters (par. 30, 31).

If we wish to talk about peacemaking as a way of life, we obviously must talk about overcoming violence, of preventing violence.

But where do we begin? My experience tells me that most often the church looks first to revolutionary violence. We condemn it and those who carry it out. Sometimes we try to give balance to our condemnation by talking about the extremes of the Right and the Left, as though violence would end and peace happen if only the revolutionaries would lay down their arms and those perpetrating repression would cease their repression.

Paul VI in *Populorum Progressio* pointed out a different beginning point:

> We want to be clearly understood: the present situation must be faced with courage and the injustices linked with it must be fought against and overcome. Development demands bold transformations, innovations that go deep. Urgent reforms should be undertaken without delay. It is for each one to take his share in them with generosity, particularly those whose education, position and opportunities afford them wide scope for action.

John Paul II made the same point even more forcefully when he cried out in behalf of the poor and oppressed:

> Social thinking and social practice inspired by the Gospel must always be marked by a special sensitivity towards those who are most in distress, those who are extremely poor, those suffering from all the physical, mental and

moral ills that afflict humanity including hunger, neglect, unemployment and despair. There are many poor people of this sort around the world. There are many in your own midst. On many occasions, your nation has gained a well-deserved reputation for generosity, both public and private. Be faithful to that tradition, in keeping with your vast possibilities and present responsibilities.

But this is not enough. Within the frame-work of your national institutions and in cooperation with all your compatriots, you will also want to seek out the structural reasons which foster or cause the different forms of poverty in the world and in your own country, so that you can apply the proper remedies.

... Neither will you recoil before the reforms—even profound ones—of attitudes and structures that may prove necessary in order to re-create over and over again the conditions needed by the disadvantaged if they are to have a fresh chance in the hard struggle of life.[4]

Where do we begin? Clearly it is the first violence that must be our overriding concern. Peacemaking as a way of life means above all action on behalf of justice. It means involving ourselves every day in the effort "to transform this earth into as close a likeness of the kingdom of God as possible."

BEING A PEACEMAKER TODAY

But I must be specific. What does this mean for the church in 1991 in the United States? I suggest that we must start with an awareness that our enormous wealth is a result of unjust structures in the international economic order. As John Paul II proclaimed in Canada, we have been "amassing to ourselves an imperialistic monopoly of economic and political supremacy at the expense of others."

And not only does our excessive wealth deprive the poor of their basic necessities, but it also brings about a kind of spiritual death within ourselves. Consider what John Paul II teaches in *The Social Concern of the Church*:

Side by side with the miseries of underdevelopment, themselves unacceptable, we find ourselves up against a form of superdevelopment. . . . This superdevelopment, which consists in an excessive availability of every kind of material goods for the benefit of certain social groups, easily makes people slaves of "possession" and of immediate gratification, with no other horizon than the multiplication or continual replacement of the things already owned with others still better. This is the so-called civilization of "consumption" or "consumerism." . . . All of us experience firsthand the sad effects of this blind submission to pure consumerism: in the first place a crass materialism, and at the same time a radical dissatisfaction because one quickly learns . . . that the more one possesses the more one wants, while deeper aspirations remain unsatisfied and perhaps even stifled (par. 28).

What Pope John Paul II is pointing out is that the existence of such massive wealth and superdevelopment together with the "miseries of underdevelopment" is an indication of cruel injustice against the poor and a loss of a sense of compassion on the part of the rich. If we address this problem of wealth first we will be able to bring healing to both the rich and the poor.

As the National Catechetical Directory makes clear, any group which ventures to speak to others about justice should itself be just, and should be seen as such. Thus we must first examine our own accumulation of institutional and personal wealth. Does the church in the United States — either in its leaders or the people as a whole — really meet the criterion set forth in *Populorum Progressio*? "No one has a right to keep what they do not need when others lack necessities" (par. 23).

And so, what does it mean to be a peacemaker in the United States in 1991? If you are a bishop it might mean refusing to live at an economic level where your household expenditures are two or three times the poverty level in the United States. Or it might mean refusing to allow parishes to build six, seven, or eight million dollar churches.

What does it mean to be a peacemaker in the United States in 1991? If you are in the military, it would obviously mean explicit refusal to fire any weapon of indiscriminate destructive capability. But even beyond the obvious it might well mean a refusal to participate in a system that includes a "strategic integrated operating plan" which integrates the use of nuclear weapons into the over-all plan. Or it might mean refusing to be part of a military system that includes carrying out "low intensity conflicts" in the Third World and a willingness to intervene militarily at any time in the Third World with the presumption that the resources in these areas belong to us.[5]

What does it mean to be a peacemaker in the United States in 1991? Maybe for most of us it will mean a profound realization that our wealth comes to us because there is that "first violence" in our socio-economic system both within our nation and within the community of nations: tax structures that take more money from the poor than from the rich; economic arrangements that bring commodities to us cheaply because people in poor nations are forced to work at fifty-five cents per hour or less. It will mean a willingness to denounce the policies of our own country, which structure this kind of violence. Over forty years ago basic United States policy goals were set forth by George Kennan, who at that time headed the State Department's planning staff:

> We have about 50% of the world's wealth, but only 6.3% of its population. . . . In this situation, we cannot fail to be the object of envy and resentment. Our real task in the coming period is to devise a pattern of relationships which will permit us to maintain this position of disparity without detriment to our national security. To do so we have to dispense with all sentimentality

and day-dreaming; and our attention will have to be concentrated everywhere on our immediate national objectives. We need not deceive ourselves that we can afford today the luxury of altruism and world-benefaction. . . . We should cease to talk about vague and . . . unreal objectives such as human rights, the raising of the living standards and democratization. The day is not far off when we are going to have to deal in straight power concepts. The less we are hampered by idealistic slogans, the better.[6]

It will mean that we advocate radical reforms and new structures that will include debt relief, fairer terms of trade, and a refusal to support any military intervention in the Third World aimed at preventing poor countries from maintaining control of their own resources. Maybe for most of us becoming peacemakers will require a conversion like that of Maria del Socorro Gutiérrez, former Secretary of Urban Housing in the government of Nicaragua:

> My story goes back many years. After Vatican II, my family, my friends, and I became involved in the Cursillo movement. For all of us this was a very exciting process. Before this, as Catholics, we recognized that faith is a gift from God. I was raised without ever reading the Bible, and worshipped without understanding, as all was in Latin. We learned to accept fear, guilt, sin, and an abiding sense of the devil. We operated not on love, but on guilt.
>
> In our twenties, we were exposed to the Cursillo — to the living presence of Christ. We read the Bible as though we were starved; we felt God was speaking to us through the Bible. We had new personal relationships, started a search for justice, and came to recognize God's presence in all. But something happened and we suddenly discovered that we were in a state of sin because of the shameful poverty all around us. We suddenly became aware. I'll tell you how that happened.
>
> In Holy Week, everyone in Nicaragua, who can, goes on vacation. We all decided to go to the beautiful tropical island of Grenada in Lake Nicaragua. We packed all the food and, of course, the Bible. Our only worry was whether we would get too fat! We arrived at 5 AM on Wednesday. Some campesinos came to us and asked if we could help their sick nephew. We said, of course, because my two brothers, who are doctors, were with us. The baby arrived all covered up in a blanket. When we removed the cloth we realized he was near death from starvation. We felt a great sense of sorrow and shame. This was like Biafra. My child was large and fat. Nothing could be done. The campesino baby died on Good Friday. And so, for us, the party was over.
>
> As soon as I returned to Managua, I started researching statistics on infant mortality. I came to realize that for most campesino women there was a terrible struggle for children to survive. We were educated, middle-class people, and when one lives surrounded by the poor, one becomes used to it. It is like those who pass by in the story of the Good Samaritan.[7]

To be a peacemaker in the United States in 1991 means we will open ourselves to conversion. To be a peacemaker in the United States in 1991 means we will refuse any longer to be like Dives with Lazarus at the gate or like those who pass by in the story of the Good Samaritan. It means we will take seriously the call of Pope Paul VI: "If you want peace, work for justice."[8] It means that we will fully accept the teaching of *The Challenge of Peace*: "Peacemaking is not an optional commitment. It is a requirement of our faith" (no. 333). It means that we will accept action for justice as a *daily* obligation so that in the deepest sense peacemaking is our way of life.

NOTES

1. Robert McAfee Brown, *Christianity and Crisis* (March 7, 1988).

2. National Catechetical Directory, *Sharing the Light of Faith* (Washington, D.C.: United States Catholic Conference, 1979), chap. 7.

3. *Boston Globe*, November 17, 1989.

4. John Paul II, speech at Yankee Stadium, 1979.

5. "Report of the Commission on Integrated Long-Term Strategy" (January 1988).

6. George Kennan, quoted in Michael Klare, "Low Intensity Conflict: The War of the 'Haves' Against the 'Have Nots,' " *Christianity and Crisis* (February 1, 1988), pp. 12-13.

7. Maria del Socorro Gutiérrez, *Commonweal* (February 12, 1988), p. 69.

8. Paul IV, World Day of Peace Message (1972).

21

THE CONTINUING PROBLEM OF DETERRENCE

WILLIAM V. O'BRIEN

The Cold War has ended. Cooperation has largely replaced competition and occasional confrontation in superpower relations. May we expect that the political, military, economic, and moral dilemmas of the delicate nuclear balance of terror have, therefore, been resolved? May we expect an era of arms control leading to the elimination of the threat of nuclear war?

I think not. Nuclear weapons exist and, indeed, proliferate. Many sources of conflict persist in a decentralized international system that shows little indication of developing effective international institutions sufficient to ensure international law and order. As long as there are multiple international actors, some willing to use force to protect and/or advance their perceived vital interests, and as long as there are nuclear weapons, there will be a need to deter recourse to those weapons. The basic practical and moral dilemmas of nuclear deterrence remain. They may not be faced by the same actors that have confronted them in the past but they will be faced by someone. Moreover, even the original nuclear powers may have to maintain nuclear deterrence postures, possibly against each other, but certainly against new nuclear powers that may not show the same restraint that the old ones demonstrated notwithstanding their conflicting aspirations and fears.

In this chapter I will review the problem of nuclear deterrence/defense as it developed from 1945 to 1989, the year of the great changes in the communist world. Following this, I will outline the principal moral positions taken with respect to nuclear deterrence and defense during this period. I will then discuss the future threats that may necessitate some form of nuclear deterrence and defense in the future. First, I will discuss the possibility of a continued threat from the Soviet Union. Then I will discuss possible new threats from emerging nuclear powers and the need to meet them with United States nuclear deterrent postures and/or local nuclear deterrence/defense.

I will conclude with a restatement of the practical and moral dilemmas of nuclear deterrence/defense, even in an age of beneficent change in the communist world, better superpower relations and resultant arms control progress.

THE PROBLEM OF NUCLEAR DETERRENCE/DEFENSE, 1945-89

From the Western point of view, nuclear deterrence/defense from the end of World War II until 1989 was necessary because of a twofold threat. First, there was the threat of nuclear attack or intimidation by the Soviet Union. Second, there was the threat of imposition of totalitarian communist rule on the defeated victims of Soviet military aggression and/or intimidation. It was believed in the West that this twofold threat justified the unprecedented maintenance of a nuclear deterrence/defense posture with all of its appalling risks and costs.

The United States nuclear deterrence/defense posture was viewed in two very different ways by those responsible for its maintenance, by strategic thinkers, and by the public. Probably the majority view was that of the *deterrence-only* school of thought. This understanding of nuclear deterrence emphasized the need to mount a deterrent so awesome in the magnitude of its capabilities that no aggressor would risk challenging it. If the "assured destruction" threatening "unacceptable damage" to an aggressor was manifestly disproportionate to any possible gain in a nuclear war, the potential aggressor would not dare to take actions that would trigger that damage. Deterrence-only strategies were epitomized by the classic mutual assured destruction doctrine (MAD) of the late 1960s. The unacceptable damage threatened was the destruction of hundreds of Soviet cities. The basic practical and moral justification for this posture—which was clearly based on the threat of disproportionate and indiscriminate destruction— was simply that it worked. If the threat of unacceptable damage remained credible it would never be challenged—and was, in fact, not challenged.[1]

A different approach was taken by those advocating a *deterrence-plus* strategy. This school of thought argued that it was not responsible to assume that the deterrent would unfailingly work. The contingency of a failure of deterrence, it was thought, should be faced and adequate doctrines and capabilities developed to fight a nuclear war if deterrence did indeed fail.[2] Deterrence-plus (nuclear deterrence plus nuclear war-fighting defense) strategies were reflected in efforts in the 1970s and 1980s to develop more flexible options.[3]

Understanding of these strategic debates and developments was hindered by the fact that the declaratory posture of the United States was not the same as the actual operational posture.[4] Not surprisingly, the declaratory posture might hold out more drastic threats of unacceptable damage than the operational posture. Nevertheless, two facts seemed to emerge. First, by the time of the debates over the drafting of the American Catholic bishops' 1983 pastoral, *The Challenge of Peace*, United States officials could say that the United States nuclear posture was not the classic MAD, in which massive countervalue countercity destruction was the threatened unacceptable damage. The United States government assured the bishops that the United States did not target cities "as such."[5]

However, the second fact was that, even with the introduction of greater flexibility in targeting, with an apparent trend in the direction of counterforce attacks on the enemies' military forces and their infrastructure, the deterrent threat still rested in substantial part on the willingness to countenance the great collateral damage that would inevitably be inflicted on noncombatants because of the problems of colocation of military and civilian targets in the Soviet Union and Warsaw Pact countries.[6]

The United States nuclear deterrence/defense posture seemed to be rather more of a neo-MAD than a limited nuclear-war posture. To establish a purely counterforce limited nuclear deterrence/defense posture would require very great progress in command, control, communication, and intelligence systems (C^3I) and development of effective counterforce weapons systems of high accuracy and penetrating capabilities.[7]

However, in the years following the 1983 pastoral the focus was not on the task of making possible a credible limited nuclear deterrent/defense posture. President Reagan's March 23, 1983 proposal to develop the Strategic Defense Initiative (SDI) challenged the monopoly of various forms of deterrence over strategic doctrine and practice. If SDI could protect cities, they could no longer be the total hostages required by MAD or the highly vulnerable components of mixed military-civilian targets threatened by counterforce nuclear deterrence/defense strategies.[8]

The entrenched dominance of some form of MAD was demonstrated in the great debate over permissive interpretations of the ABM Treaty needed to advance SDI. Beyond the technical arguments over treaty interpretation was the stark fact that the ABM Treaty is based on the assumption that MAD prevents nuclear war and must be preserved. SDI challenged fundamentally this axiom of the "theology of arms control." This, of course, was Reagan's intention.[9]

With Reagan's departure the United States government's commitment to SDI appears to have been significantly modified. Clearly some form of deterrence will continue to be required, and SDI is more likely to be judged on the basis of its relevance to future deterrence postures and to arms control than as an alternative to deterrence.

MORALITY AND NUCLEAR DETERRENCE/DEFENSE, 1945-89

The dilemmas of nuclear deterrence/defense confounded moralists throughout the nuclear age. The spectrum of efforts to resolve — or confirm the intractability of — these dilemmas is broad. I will simply outline three major moral positions: pacifism, conditional toleration of deterrence-only, and support for a just and limited deterrence-plus strategy.

To the ranks of pacifists, who held that no war was morally permissible, and those who believed that modern conventional war no longer met the requirements of just-war doctrine, were added nuclear pacifists. They concluded that, whatever the possibility of just-conventional-war, any war in which the use of nuclear weapons was likely was morally impermissible.[10]

Although pacifism in general and nuclear pacifism in particular were viewed more sympathetically by the Catholic church and the principal Protestant churches in the post–World War II era, the major Christian churches generally declined to move to a pacifist position on deterrence and defense. Instead, they tended to adopt some form of conditional acceptance of nuclear deterrence. The deterrence posture accepted by the American Catholic bishops in 1983 was a deterrence-only posture. The condition, inspired by the views of Pope John Paul II, was that deterrence would be a temporary posture that would be replaced by serious arms control measures leading to the complete elimination of nuclear weapons.[11] A 1988 review of the question by Cardinal Bernardin's committee led to a somewhat more cautious approach that seemed to concede that some form of nuclear deterrence would be necessary for some time.[12] The same review rejected the SDI as well-intentioned but not feasible and possibly subversive to deterrent stability and arms control progress.[13]

The third approach to nuclear deterrence/defense, taken by a minority of moralists and strategic thinkers, including myself, contended that nuclear deterrence and defense could be reconciled with modern just-war doctrine.[14] It was argued that a limited, counterforce nuclear deterrence/ defense posture of a deterrence-plus type could possibly meet just-war requirements. Proponents of this approach conceded that such a posture would require substantial improvement in C^{3}I and counterforce weaponry and that there was a serious risk of escalation in any recourse to nuclear weapons. On the other hand, proponents of a just and limited nuclear deterrence/defense posture argued that a deterrence-only posture based on the moral proposition that nuclear weapons could be deployed but never used was not credible.

The easing of East-West tensions appears to have provided a breathing space in which to reconsider these moral positions. With the relaxation of the principal threat of Soviet aggression and forcible imposition of totalitarian rule it would be easy to take the position that either no deterrent is necessary or that a sort of nominal deterrent of the deterrence-only variety will suffice. The just and limited nuclear deterrence-plus approach, always unpopular because it suggested the possibility of nuclear war, might seem to be irrelevant in the absence of plausible threats and scenarios for any kind of major war.

It should be said that I — and I daresay other proponents of just and limited nuclear deterrence/defense — never had any enthusiasm for this posture. We came to it by exclusion. We could not sacrifice all deterrence and defense as the pacifists did and we could not accept MAD because it threatened actions that were manifestly immoral. We recognized the great difficulties and risks inherent in any limited nuclear war posture but felt that such a posture was the least bad of very bad alternatives.

With this in mind, the strategic landscape will be reviewed to see if some form of just and limited nuclear-deterrence-plus may still be needed and morally justified or whether proponents of this approach can retire from the debate and enjoy the fruits of arms control and an improved international environment.

Effects of the End of the Cold War

If the Cold War is really over and Soviet and Soviet-bloc communism is now wholly or largely discredited, the mainsprings of East-West conflict would seem to have been removed. Superpower competition from 1945 to 1989 was always primarily based on the Western perceptions that the communist ideology engendered Soviet activities that far exceeded the natural scope of vital interests. To be sure, Soviet policies in regions adjacent to the U.S.S.R., obviously a vast and heterogeneous portion of the globe, were in part a reflection of traditional Russian imperialist interests and aspirations. But the overriding concern of the United States and the West was that communist ideology was insatiable, that it drove the Soviet Union to interventions and machinations through client states and movements that threatened parts of the so-called Free World. The universalist claims of communism encouraged fears that Soviet-dominated communist states and movements would build up a global revolutionary momentum and that this must be stopped, for example, through the Korean and Vietnam Wars.

Since the break-up of the Soviet-bloc in Eastern Europe in 1989 and the continuing apparent disintegration of the Soviet Union as a union of Socialist Republics and as a communist polity, it would appear that the old communist sources of aggressive foreign policies are dead or dying. Moreover, it certainly would seem that the Soviet Union has more than enough problems at home and is lacking in the incentive and resources to continue intervening in the Third World.[15]

If this proves to be the case, why do the United States and its allies need to mount a deterrence/defense posture against the Soviet Union? The answer appears to be that the West will continue to require a security insurance policy against changes in the Soviet Union that might bring new threats.[16]

In mid-1990, as this essay is prepared, the Soviet Union is apparently in very bad shape. The economy is in shambles and the population is unwilling to make the sacrifices necessary to reform it. The political leadership lacks the popular support and confidence necessary to effect fundamental political and economic changes. Nationalist and ethnic differences abound, and separatism threatens in many corners of the Soviet empire. The frustrations and antagonisms provoked by the state of affairs in the Soviet Union could very easily lead to drastic political developments. A different political leadership, very possibly more volatile and unstable than that of the Gorbachev regime, might emerge. Could a post-Gorbachev Soviet Union pose a new threat to the United States and its allies?

In mid-1990 there is little basis for an answer. Suffice it to say that projection of deterrence requirements for the United States and its allies cannot be made entirely on the assumption that the Gorbachev regime or something like it will prevail for a long time in the Soviet Union. Deterrence postures must be sufficiently flexible to deal with different Soviet regimes that may pose more of a threat or, on the contrary, even less of a threat.

Deterrence calculations and preparations must also anticipate technological developments that may alter the strategic nuclear balance. Although the Soviet Union may appear to be in disarray, it is one of the two leading nuclear powers. Indeed, the Soviet Union's status as a superpower has been primarily the result of its military power. While its conventional military power seems now to be less formidable than in the past its nuclear capabilities remain. Moreover, the momentum — or inertia — of its military-industrial complex may continue to develop new capabilities. These capabilities will be available to whoever rules the Soviet Union. If the rulers are less reasonable than Gorbachev's regime, a latent nuclear threat may still confront the United States and the Free World.

There is little reason to believe that the domestic problems in the Soviet Union and its erstwhile Soviet-bloc neighbors will be resolved soon. It is not to be assumed that their resolution will lead to a situation in which nuclear deterrence between the superpowers will be less needed. On the other hand, if Gorbachev or others like him prevail the deterrence requirement should be mitigated, but not entirely removed. Accordingly, notwithstanding arms control progress, the basic practical and moral dilemmas of nuclear deterrence will remain.

It should be remembered that arms control progress will continue *to be based* on a deterrence relationship. Even if there are dramatic quantitative and qualitative reductions in nuclear weapons systems, substantial systems will remain and as long as any remain the perennial problems of deterrence will remain.

Other Nuclear Threats

The Soviet threat and the superpower balance of terror have dominated thinking about nuclear deterrence and defense. As this threat diminishes, however, others may increase. In assessing new nuclear threats two things should be considered initially. First, a state's nuclear capabilities should be assessed. Second, a state's foreign and defense policy objectives should be analyzed. The Soviet Union has been a threat because it had major nuclear—as well as conventional—capabilities and because it had expansionist and interventionist foreign and defense policies. Among the emerging nuclear powers some may have significant nuclear capabilities, but they may have conservative, primarily defensive, foreign and defense policies. Others may have aggressive designs but only modest nuclear and conventional means.

To these two elements of means and ends must be added the relationships of individual nuclear states and their potential adversaries to the superpowers. It should not be forgotten that virtually all of the scenarios for superpower nuclear war have been based on attacks against the allies of a superpower, for example, a Soviet/Warsaw Pact attack on NATO countries. There has been no plausible *casus belli* for a war between the superpowers independent of the desire to attack or defend superpower allies.

Possible sources of new nuclear threats may be divided into two categories. The first is that of nuclear threats of an intercontinental magnitude comparable to those posed reciprocally by the Soviet Union and the United States. For now the only nuclear power that appears to pose such a threat is the Peoples Republic of China. The P.R.C. has the capability of hitting most of the Soviet Union and the United States with ICBMs. Moreover, it should be remembered that the P.R.C. is not committed to arms control agreements that would curb its nuclear weapons systems development. Any substantial qualitative and quantitative arms control reductions made by the U.S.S.R. and the United States will increase China's relative nuclear power.[17]

Of the present nuclear powers, two, Britain and France, do not pose an independent threat to anyone. They are part of the NATO deterrent force (notwithstanding France's independent posture). On the other hand, India and Pakistan, as regional nuclear powers, pose a threat to each other. Moreover, if the long-term links that they have with the U.S.S.R. and the P.R.C. respectively persist, there may be a danger of nuclear intervention in the event of nuclear war between the two subcontinent powers.

Israel is believed to have a nuclear military capability that can be quickly made operational.[18] It constitutes a deterrent not only to nuclear attacks by Arab states that develop nuclear weapons but also to missile attacks with chemical warfare (CW) which are emerging as a form of mass destruction that hitherto had only been potential threats.[19] Israel is an ally of the United States. A nuclear or even a strategic CW attack on Israel would confront the United States with a grave dilemma, namely the choice between acquiescing in the defeat or even the destruction of Israel and intervening, perhaps with nuclear weapons, in a Middle East war. A Soviet nuclear response in the event of an American nuclear defense of Israel would not seem as likely now as it has been in the past but the threat of superpower nuclear confrontation would be considerable.

It should be noted that in the contingencies just mentioned—Soviet or

P.R.C. intervention in an Indian-Pakistani nuclear war, or American or Soviet intervention in an Israel-Arab war—the possibilities of escalation from the level of military assistance to nuclear intervention, without necessarily involving the intermediate step of intervention with conventional force, would constitute a new and unwelcome threat.

Beyond these dangers there are the possibilities of radical states with aggressive goals acquiring nuclear weapons, for example, Iraq, Syria, and Libya. Thus far, nuclear powers have been reluctant to engage in nuclear saber-rattling, and none of them has ever used nuclear weapons. However, it cannot be assumed that some of the more radical states might not carry nuclear brinksmanship too far and trigger a nuclear war.

Finally, nuclear terrorism may someday be a reality rather than a part of the plot of a novel. As nuclear weapons proliferate, in some cases in unstable regimes, lax security and/or revolutionary actions may make nuclear weapons available to terrorists who by definition are indifferent to the deaths of the innocent and who usually are prepared to use any means to advance their causes.

The foregoing speculations may fairly be considered as worse-case scenarios. However, I would reiterate the point that the combination of nuclear capabilities and perceived vital interests, including self-preservation, could lead to nuclear war between regional powers. Moreover, the continuing links between regional powers and great powers such as the United States, the U.S.S.R., and perhaps, the P.R.C., could lead to wider wars in which the great powers might use nuclear weapons.

THE MORAL DILEMMAS OF NUCLEAR DETERRENCE/DEFENSE CONTINUE

Even with the relaxation of East-West sources of conflict and with arms control progress, some residual nuclear deterrence/defense postures will be necessary—in the United States and NATO, and in the Soviet Union. Moreover, states not directly affected by East-West developments will claim continuing and probably increasing requirements for nuclear deterrence/defense postures, for example, the Peoples Republic of China, India, Pakistan, Israel, and possibly some of Israel's Arab enemies.

Since the United States, the U.S.S.R., and the P.R.C. have security links with these regional nuclear powers, they will have to reconsider their commitments to them. Hitherto, support of regional powers has been limited to military and other assistance, including resupply of weapons and materiel in time of war, for example, the 1973 Yom Kippur War. Now, the possibility of regional nuclear war will raise the prospect of superpower nuclear intervention.

To the extent that such dangers will persist there will be a continuing necessity to develop nuclear strategies and capabilities appropriate to the challenge. All of the old questions of deterrence-only *vs.* deterrence-plus, of the reconciliation of credible deterrent postures with the limits of just war, will continue to confront us.

This may be very difficult. If arms control agreements make significant qualitative and quantitative cuts in the nuclear arsenals of the superpowers and United States-Soviet relations continue to be cooperative, it may be difficult for governments to justify nuclear deterrence/defense preparations that, in addition to serving as insurance in superpower relations, are now held out as necessary for contingencies outside of those relations.

A new debate over just cause may be necessary. In the Cold War era there was little dispute over the justice of defending the Free World, particularly Western Europe and Japan, from communist aggression. The main debate was over the deployment of nuclear deterrence systems, primarily countervalue in nature, as the means to the end of protecting the Free World. However, neither the Soviet Union, the Peoples Republic of China, nor the United States may be so dedicated to the putative just cause of protecting one of the regional powers mentioned above from nuclear aggression as to commit itself to nuclear intervention. However, in the case of Israel—faced with some of the most oppressive and aggressive regimes in the contemporary international system—the dilemmas of nuclear intervention would equal if not exceed those that have caused so many moral and practical debates with respect to the defense of NATO, South Korea, and Japan.

As the United States Catholic bishops conceded in their five-year review of *The Challenge of Peace*, nuclear weapons are a perennial fact of life and must be controlled.[20] They cannot be banished from the face of the earth. There is no foreseeable prospect for their control without the foundation of nuclear deterrence *by somebody* and that somebody must face the classical practical and moral dilemmas that have gone unsolved throughout the nuclear age.

The ultimate answer that is always given to these dilemmas is that the underlying conflicts that engender the perceived need for military force must be resolved, rendering military force superfluous. However, the magnitude of the task of eliminating *all* the mainsprings of conflict, thereby eliminating the threat of nuclear war and all other forms of war, is demonstrated by the present situation. Having seen the collapse of the long East-West political-military conflict, we now have major internal conflicts within the Soviet Union. These conflicts are so serious that the Soviets have been obliged to remove nuclear weapons from some of the regions affected.[21] Nuclear weapons in the hands of elements caught up in violent ethnic and civil strife take on a new, frightening dimension.

Throughout the third-world conflict continues in many places and new arms races to acquire weapons of mass destruction accelerate. In these circumstances the solution to nuclear threats by removing the underlying sources of conflict is not something that is in immediate prospect. Many of these conflicts may endure indefinitely, and they will endure in a world where it may be increasingly possible to acquire nuclear weapons. Every effort should be made to limit these trends while continuing efforts at arms control between the great nuclear powers. But, at the base of all of these efforts, there will have to be responsible states with credible nuclear deterrent/defense postures who will hold the line against recourse to nuclear war.

If this analysis is valid, the same fundamental moral issues concerning nuclear deterrence/defense will persist. The temptation to assure effective deterrence with deterrence-only postures will be challenged by those who argue for deterrence-plus postures based on war-fighting strategies and capabilities that might possibly conform to just-war standards. If the main threats of nuclear aggression come from regional nuclear powers the possibility of limited nuclear strikes to suppress them would seem to be greater than that of inflicting unacceptable counterforce damage on a power such as the Soviet Union. This leaves the problem of China, which is already more than a regional power.

So we may be in the process of trading the familiar Soviet/Warsaw Pact threat for a series of much lesser, more uncertain nuclear threats. The only thing that is sure is that nuclear weapons will continue to be developed, profound conflicts will continue to flare up around the world, and the need for moral and practical guidance in the maintenance of responsible deterrent/defense postures will continue to be great.

NOTES

1. On deterrence-only strategic doctrines and postures, see Donald M. Snow, *Nuclear Deterrence in a Dynamic World* (Tuscaloosa, Alabama: University of Alabama Press, 1981), pp. 5, 44, 69-73, 244; Klaus Knorr, *On the Uses of Military Power in the Nuclear Age* (Princeton, New Jersey: Princeton University Press, 1966), p. 89; Richard Smoke, *National Security and the Nuclear Dilemma* (Reading, Massachusetts: Addison-Wesley, 1984), p. 222.

2. On deterrence-plus doctrines and postures, see Snow, pp. 5-6; Richard Rosencrance, ed., *The Future of the International Strategic System* (San Francisco: Chandler, 1972), p. 6.

3. On efforts to develop deterrence-plus strategies and postures, see Snow, pp. 44-45, 69-73, 78-85; Smoke, pp. 220-23.

4. Aaron L. Friedberg, "A History of U.S. Strategic Doctrine — 1945 to 1980," *Journal of Strategic Studies* 3 (December 1980), pp. 37-71.

5. National Conference of Catholic Bishops, *The Challenge of Peace: God's Promise and Our Response*, A Pastoral Letter on War and Peace (Washington, D.C.: N.C.C.B., May 3, 1983), p. 56, n.81.

6. Ibid., sections 178-87, pp. 56-58.

7. I outline the requirements for a just and limited nuclear deterrence/defense posture in William V. O'Brien, "The Failure of Deterrence," in *The Nuclear Dilemmas and the Just War Tradition*, ed. William V. O'Brien and John Langan, S.J. (Lexington, Massachusetts: Lexington Books, 1986), pp. 153-97; "The Future of the Nuclear Debate," Ibid., pp. 240-44.

8. See James E. Dougherty's analysis of SDI's challenge to nuclear deterrence, "Technological Developments," in O'Brien and Langan, pp. 100-17.

9. See, e.g., Alan B. Sherr, "Sound Legal Reasoning or Policy Expedient? The 'New' Interpretation of the ABM Treaty," *International Security* 11 (Winter 1986-87), pp. 71-93; Michael J. Glennon, *Constitutional Diplomacy* (Princeton, New Jersey: Princeton University Press, 1990), pp. 134-45.

10. See Walter Stein, ed., *Nuclear Weapons and the Christian Conscience* (London: Merlin Press, 1961); Anthony Kenny, *The Logic of Deterrence* (Chicago: University of Chicago Press, 1985); John Finnis, Joseph M. Boyle, Jr., and Germain Grisez, *Nuclear Deterrence, Morality and Realism* (Oxford: Clarendon Press, 1987).

See the critique of the nuclear pacifist approach in J. Bryan Hehir, "Ethics and Strategy: The Views of Selected Strategists," in *Ethics in the Nuclear Age*, ed. Todd Whitmore (Dallas: Southern Methodist University Press, 1989), pp. 15-17.

11. *The Challenge of Peace*, sections 178-99, pp. 56-62.

12. "At the conclusion of its assessment of nuclear use, *The Challenge of Peace* has neither advocated any form of use nor has it condemned every conceivable use of nuclear weapons *a priori*. There is in the letter a narrow margin where use has been considered, not condemned but hardly commended. From this narrow margin the pastoral moves to an evaluation of deterrence" (National Council of Catholic Bishops, *Building Peace* [Washington, D.C.: N.C.C.B., 1988], section 40, p. 34). See the further discussion of deterrence, sections 41-54, pp. 35-43, and the concluding sections 111-87, pp. 76-87.

13. Ibid., pp. 57-76.

14. See Paul Ramsey, *The Just War: Force and Political Responsibility* (New York: Scribner's, 1968); James Turner Johnson, *Just War Tradition and Restraint of War* (Princeton, New Jersey: Princeton University Press, 1981); idem, *Can Modern War Be Just?* (New Haven: Yale University Press, 1984); William V. O'Brien, "Just War Doctrine in a Nuclear Context," *Theological Studies* 44 (1983): 191-220; idem, "The Failure of Deterrence and the Conduct of War," and "The Future of the Nuclear Debate," in O'Brien and Langan, pp. 153-97, 223-48.

See Hehir's critique of this approach in "Ethics and Strategy," in Whitmore, pp. 14-15.

15. On Gorbachev's foreign policy and its ideological implications, see David Holloway, "Gorbachev's New Thinking," *Foreign Affairs*, vol. 68 (America and the World, 1988/89), no. 1, pp. 66-81; Robert Legvold, "The Revolution in Soviet Foreign Policy," ibid., pp. 82-98.

16. For views of the possibility of major change in the Soviet Union, see Peter Reddaway, "Life After Gorbachev," *Washington Post*, November 26, 1989, p. C1, col. 4, p. 2, cols. 3-5; "Is the Soviet Union on the Way to Anarchy?" ibid., August 20, 1989, p. B1, col. 5, p. 2, cols. 1-5; Edward Luttwak, "Shape of Things to Come," *Commentary*, vol. 89 (June 1990), no. 6, esp. pp. 21-22; and Seweryn Bialer, "The Passing of the Soviet Order?" *Survival* 32 (1990), pp. 107-20.

17. See Chong-Pin Lin, *China's Nuclear Weapons Strategy* (Lexington, Massachusetts: Lexington Books, 1988).

18. The Harvard Study Group, *Living with Nuclear Weapons* (New York: Bantam, 1983), pp. 216, 222.

19. On April 3, 1990, Iraqi President Saddam Hussein, who had been developing great stores of mustard and nerve gas as well as intermediate range missiles capable of reaching Israel, threatened, "by God we will make fire eat up half of Israel if it

tried [to strike] against Iraq." "Iraqi Warns of Using Poison Gas," *Washington Post*, April 3, 1990, A1, col. 6; A16, col. 1.

20. "For living in the nuclear age means that we can condemn nuclear war, but we will still have to live with nuclear weapons" (N.C.C.B., *Building Peace*, p. 19).

See Robert Jervis, *The Meaning of the Nuclear Revolution* (Ithaca: Cornell University Press, 1989), for the implications of the nuclear revolution for deterrence and defense. Jervis considers all past nuclear deterrence/defense strategies to be outmoded. He argues that the role of nuclear weapons will be limited to providing threats of unacceptable escalation that will deter all reasonable actors from considering recourse to nuclear war. In this context he claims that traditional just-war doctrine precepts are also outmoded since they were based on the assumption that wars would be fought. In his view the nuclear revolution precludes major wars, certainly nuclear war, therefore the just-war concepts are no longer necessary. See his chapter, "Morality and International Strategy," ibid., pp. 107-35.

21. "Soviets Begin Moving Nuclear Warheads Out of Volatile Republics," *Wall Street Journal*, June 22, 1990, p. 1, cols. 1, p. 4, cols. 4-6.

22

PACIFISM AND THE JUST WAR TRADITION IN ROMAN CATHOLIC SOCIAL TEACHING

KENNETH R. HIMES, O.F.M.

Roman Catholicism has thought for a very long time about the moral issues that gather around the topic of war. Whether it has thought well about these issues can be and has been debated. In the remarks which follow I will make some clarifying comments about the two dominant ways of thinking about the morality of war, pacifism and just war. Then I will raise three questions about the Catholic church's present teaching: How did it come about? What is meant by just war and pacifism in Roman Catholicism? What is the relationship between the two approaches? I will conclude with a suggestion about the future of church teaching in this area.

TRADITIONS OF PACIFISM AND JUST WAR

Both the just war tradition and the pacifist tradition admit of a variety of interpretations. Within each tradition there are several theories of just war and pacifism. It is important to be clear, therefore, as to just what is meant by pacifism and just war.

Pacifism sometimes has been identified with nonviolence. No killing of any sort is permitted. Yet this view may be challenged since there are pacifists who do not exclude killing in personal self-defense or killing as a result of police action. For these people pacifism is not to be equated with the more inclusive term of nonviolence. The philosopher Jenny Teichman has noted that the word *pacifism* is a twentieth-century term; it is not found in the 1904 edition of the *Complete Oxford Dictionary*. The 1982 supplement to the dictionary records that the word was coined by a Frenchman in 1902 and was used to express "anti-warism."[1]

I will follow Teichman's suggestion that pacifism is best understood as being anti-warism and that this stance is properly seen as involving "a moral judgment and a personal commitment."[2] In other words, the opposition to war is based on ethical principle not simply pragmatic judgment, and the pacifist is one who personally opposes war and is not a person uninvolved in war due to some other condition, such as being part of a class of persons exempt from military service, for example, the clergy.

Historically, there is a close connection between pacifism and Christianity.[3] Yet the ethical norms followed by pacifists are neither uniform nor always reconcilable with each other. Just as there are different strands of thought within the one Christian tradition so, too, with pacifism. Pacifism is a set of theories, not any one theory, about why a person should oppose all war. We cannot assume, then, that because Roman Catholic social teaching approves of pacifism that any or all theories of pacifism are thereby approved.

What has been said above regarding pacifism might also be said about the just war tradition. As with pacifism, the just war tradition has close ties with Christian thought. Within the tradition there are many theories of what makes for a just war. Not all such theories are easily reconciled one to another. Nevertheless, despite the differences there is a moral basis in any argument for the just war tradition, not simply a pragmatic rationale. This common bond, the conviction that one can appeal to an ethical principle to legitimate a nation-state's decision to employ military force, unites the various just war theories.

Within Christianity it was Augustine who formulated the classic argument for why some war may be justified. War is seen as punishment in Augustine's vision. It was a practice used to correct the evil-doer who engaged in unjust behavior. Due to human sinfulness rulers act unjustly in their treatment of other rulers and peoples. When this occurs punishment and correction are required. War waged to correct the wrongful action of another nation is a permissible activity for Augustine.[4]

Something of Augustine's attitude continues to be found among those who subscribe to the just war tradition. War is a rational and moral activity when, like police action, it is governed by rules justifying the resort to violence and the nature of the violent force. Ideas about what the rules are, their grounding, and obligatory force vary and account for the fact that the just war tradition encompasses many theories of just war.

At present, ever since Vatican Council II, it can be said that the Catholic church accepts both pacifism and just war as possible interpretations by individual believers of the morality of war. This teaching of Vatican II has been developed since 1965 so that in 1983 the National Conference of Catholic Bishops stated: "We believe the two perspectives support and complement one another, each preserving the other from distortion."[5] What is meant by that claim and how we are to understand just war and pacifism within Roman Catholic social teaching will be examined later in this essay.

HOW DID THE PRESENT TEACHING COME ABOUT?[6]

Church teaching on war has always been influenced by a variety of factors — social, political, theological. With the rise of national industrial states in the nineteenth century war took on a different look. No longer was it a matter of small armies fighting face to face. The destruction left by the wars of the nineteenth century intensified the concern of civilized people. At Vatican I the bishops wrote:

> The present condition of the world has assuredly become intolerable on account of huge standing and conscript armies. The nations groan under the burden of the expense of maintaining them. The spirit of irreligion and forgetfulness of law in international affairs open an altogether readier way for the beginning of illegal and unjust wars, or rather hideous massacres spreading far and wide.[7]

Modern war's horrors led the church to a new sense of immediacy in the struggle to overcome war as a means of settling political and economic conflict. While his predecessors demonstrated concern, it was in the writing of Pius XII that the tension sharpened between the church's just war posture and the experience of war. World War II led Pius to enunciate two basic convictions. One was that all wars of aggression were to be prohibited, and the second was that defensive war to repel aggression was reluctantly necessary.[8]

As has been noted by commentators, Pius redefined the meaning of just cause in Catholic just war theory.[9] Classically, there were three appeals to a just cause: to vindicate rights, to repel unjust attack, to avenge injury. Pius, conscious of the grave nature of modern war, restricted the just war theory's appeal to but one cause — defense against aggression.

Even that one remaining cause of self-defense could not excuse any and all appeal to war. For Pius, the risks of war could outweigh the injustice done by the aggressor. If so, then a nation might simply have to endure the injustice rather than resort to war.[10] Evident in Pius XII's thought is the high regard Roman Catholicism has for order, in this case international order. The chaos of war might be worse than some measure of injustice in the existing social order.

Pius was committed to the need for nations to seek peaceful means of settling disputes, yet he could not give up on the idea of national self-defense, believing that "there can be verified in a nation the situation wherein, every effort to avoid war being expended in vain, war — for effective defense and with the hope of a favorable outcome against unjust attack — could not be considered unlawful."[11] So strongly did Pius believe this that in the same message the pope stated that a Roman Catholic could not in good conscience refuse to participate in a war declared by legitimate authority.[12]

Thus, even though the modern papacy was deeply disturbed by the fact of war and troubled by the massive destruction that war in the present age brought about, there was no fundamental abandonment of the just war tradition. Pius XII may have narrowed the category of just cause in church teaching on the just war, but the theory remained dominant in Roman Catholic discussion on the morality of war.

With John XXIII a new era began in Catholic reflection on just war and pacifism. The new era is characterized by a more searching challenge to the just war tradition's viability in the modern age. For John the emerging international order placed new demands upon all people to contribute to the "universal common good."[13] Just as individuals must regulate their activity so as to support and contribute to the common good of their society so, too, nation-states must regulate themselves so as not to violate the requirements of the universal common good. According to John the entire globe is constituted by a pattern of interrelatedness. In the papal view there is a genuine international order, which must be respected. Here the Johannine position is an extension of Pius XII's stance regarding the requirements of order in assessing the legitimacy of resort to war.[14]

John never explicitly denied the just war theory in *Pacem in Terris*, but his silence about the right of national self-defense coupled with his opposition to nuclear war created a mood of questioning on the topic of warfare.[15] The vagueness of John's support for the idea of a just war even led some to believe that he had ruled out the idea in his encyclical.[16] With his death it was left for the Council to take up the question in the ecclesial context of the papacy's growing disenchantment with the practice of war.

In *Gaudium et Spes* the bishops called for "an evaluation of war with an entirely new attitude."[17] In the text of the document the major reason cited for this new attitude is the manner whereby the "horror and perversity of war are immensely magnified by the multiplication of scientific weapons" (no. 80). It is the nuclear age which has forced the church to look at war in a new way. The scale of devastation threatened in any modern war is such that the faith community must reconsider the moral problematic of war. This historical context, the anxiety over whether modern war has ceased to be a politically rational enterprise, along with the ecclesial context mentioned above shaped the mood in which *Gaudium et Spes* was written.

When the bishops finished their work at the Council, it was clear they had not removed Roman Catholicism from the just war tradition. At the same time, however, the church was moving in a new direction as the Council declared that individual Catholics could refuse to take up arms on the basis of moral principle (*Gaudium et Spes*, nos. 78, 79). Ever since 1965, then, the Catholic church has officially accepted that a believer may subscribe to either the just war or pacifist traditions of moral evaluation. During the space of nine short years church teaching had undergone a dramatic change from Pius XII's opposition to conscientious objection to Vatican II's statement endorsing the idea.

WHAT IS MEANT BY JUST WAR AND PACIFISM IN ROMAN CATHOLICISM?

Given the fact that within both the traditions of just war and pacifism there are a variety of theories, it is important to be clear about just what the council said regarding pacifism and just war. Catholic teaching on just war and pacifism may be quite unlike other approaches to those traditions. The Council wrote in regard to just war:

> As long as the danger of war remains and there is no competent and suffi-ciently powerful authority at the international level, governments cannot be denied the right to legitimate defense once every means of peaceful settle-ment has been exhausted. Therefore, government authorities and others who share public responsibility have the duty to protect the welfare of the people entrusted to their care and to conduct such grave matters soberly.
>
> But it is one thing to undertake military action for the defense of the people, and something else again to seek the subjugation of other nations. Nor does the possession of war potential make every military or political use of it lawful. Neither does the mere fact that war has unhappily begun mean that all is fair between the warring parties (*Gaudium et Spes*, no. 79).

Several comments can be made about this text:

1. National self-defense is the only rationale given for resort to war. This follows the teaching of Pius XII narrowing the category of just cause. Even for a just cause the use of violent force is a last resort to be employed only after all other methods of resisting aggression have proved fruitless.

2. The right to take up arms in self-defense follows from the lack of an adequate international order, which might resolve disputes in other ways. Here the Council echoes John XXIII's words that the international com-mon good, which includes international peace, is best served by a supra-national structure that can serve to mediate disputes between nations. The right to self-defense is conditional, to be condoned only so long as other more appropriate methods of settling hostilities between nations are un-available.

3. For nation-states the *duty* of collective self-defense remains. It is quite clear in the conciliar decree that the leaders of a nation must exercise the right of collective self-defense. Pacifism is an option for the private citizen; it is not so for a nation or the leaders of a nation.

4. Even if there is a legitimate right of self-defense, there are limits to what can be done in the exercise of the right. Without spelling out in detail the restrictions on the means of warfare the Council accepted the premise of the *jus in bello* — the only justifiable force is controlled, measured force.

It can be safely presumed that the classic principles of noncombatant immunity and proportionality were on the minds of the bishops in this regard. One paragraph later in their condemnation of total war the bishops appealed to these principles without naming them as such (no. 80).

In regard to pacifism the Council wrote:

> We cannot fail to praise those who renounce the use of violence in the vindication of their rights and who resort to methods of defense which are otherwise available to weaker parties too, provided that this can be done without injury to the rights and duties of others or of the community itself (no. 78).

> And, it seems right that laws make humane provisions for the case of those who for reasons of conscience refuse to bear arms, provided that they accept some other form of service to the human community (no. 79).

Several points should be noted:

1. Earlier in *Gaudium et Spes* the bishops affirmed the dignity and liberty of conscience in moral matters (no. 16). When read in this context the approval of pacifism in the first quotation is on the level of subjective morality, the order of the good. A pacifist can be said to hold his or her views in good conscience. Nothing, however, is said by the bishops about the objective morality of pacifism, the order of the right. This is clear when one recalls the duty of collective self-defense.

2. The pacifist may forego resort to violent resistance before aggression but may not forego resistance completely. Pacifism within the Roman Catholic tradition must be placed in a setting of concern for justice and human rights. A pacifist cannot be indifferent to the "rights and duties of others or of the community itself." Thus, pacifism in the Catholic perspective cannot be equated with nonresistance. All believers must defend the cause of justice, must protect human rights, must resist evil. On the matter of how that is to be done, individuals may differ and the pacifist may seek methods other than war in order to resist evil.

3. The second quote from the conciliar text is addressed to those who make public policy. Here the question that arises is what legal provision should be made for pacifism. The *Pastoral Constitution on the Church in the Modern World* proposes that laws be passed which allow for conscientious objection to military service, but that the duty of the individual to serve the common good remains and ought be fulfilled in some other way.

Alternative service would appear to be a duty correlative with the right of the conscientious objector to dissent from the nation's decision to engage in war. René Coste comments:

> Good faith must always be respected, if it is genuine and rests on high motives. This raises the concrete problem of knowing how good faith can be recognized, and what suitable peaceful work for the community of a genuine

and arduous kind can be substituted for military service. States which have made legal provision for conscientious objectors generally establish two institutions, a court or commission to inquire into the conscientious objector's decision and a civilian service as substitute for the military service from which an objector is exempt. Vatican II emphatically endorses a general solution of this kind.[18]

The requirement of alternative service is to demonstrate that pacifism, within Roman Catholic social teaching, is not a higher or purer calling. Rather, it is a right granted to individual conscience which necessitates an expression of good faith on the part of the individual, a willingness to contribute to the nation's struggle against injustice in another way. The presumption is that the nation is just in resisting the evil of aggression and that all citizens have an obligation to contribute to that effort even if some are permitted not to bear arms.

Two themes serve as useful background for understanding Vatican II's teaching. The bishops at the Council accepted a view of peace based on the Augustinian idea, *"Pax omnium rerum tranquillitas ordinis."* While not directly quoting Augustine, *Gaudium et Spes* demonstrates the Catholic conviction that peace is more than the absence of war. It is "an inner force of justice and love."[19] The order that peace embodies is not the quietude accompanying tyranny but a social state achieved through justice when life is well-ordered and oriented to the dignity of persons and the common good of all.

Because peace is not simply the absence of war but entails a measure of justice and order, the Council had to consider whether in defense of a just order some violent means might actually foster true peace. This is most clearly evident in the statement that despite the grave harm of war there could be no simple dismissal of the argument that nations have a legitimate right of self-defense even though war is a last resort.

A second element of Catholic tradition at work in the minds of the bishops assembled at the Council was the centrality of conscience in the experience of human dignity. Ever since Thomas Aquinas there has been a certain undercutting of the role of individual conscience in just war theory. For Thomas and other scholastics it was not the individual citizen or soldier but the prince who was to determine the legitimacy of the decision for war. Such a belief reflected the medieval viewpoint that political authority could be assumed to have a concern and responsibility for the commonweal. This perspective encouraged deference toward political authority in general and toward the prince for determining the *jus ad bellum* in particular.

In the medieval world of Aquinas the paternalism of the prince was more readily accepted than the paternalism of the state could be in the post-Nuremberg world of Vatican II. In the first part of *Gaudium et Spes* there is profound concern for the dignity of individual conscience both in the religious and civil realms. With the rise of the limited constitutional state in the West and the sad experience of abusive state power in fascism, nazism, and communism the bishops were sensitive to the freedom of individual conscience before the state.

Nowhere was the tension between individual conscience and the authority of the state more deeply felt than within the pacifist community. For Catholic pacifists, "at the root of the moral collapse of modern society was an exaggerated idea of the authority of the state."[20] Pacifists saw the necessity of rescuing individual conscience from the overreaching claims of the modern state in regard to military service. Their agenda for defending the right of conscientious objection fit in well with Vatican II's emphasis on the dignity of the person and the rights of conscience. Thus, despite its support for the just war tradition's claim of a right to use force in self-defense, the Council, in deference to the rights of conscience, also supported the option of pacifists to refuse to participate in the military.

We can conclude this analysis of the conciliar teaching by suggesting that both pacifism and just war are treated as having the same end—the preservation of a just order, which is the foundation of true peace. Neither tradition is allowed to be indifferent to the struggle to attain and protect this good. True peace must be served by pacifists and just war advocates. Where the two groups diverge is on the question of means to the proper end. Both groups must engage in resistance against aggression, but one group refuses to permit war as a valid means of resistance. The other group is willing to consider the legitimacy of at least some wars in the struggle for the *tranquillitas ordinis*. The teaching of the Council allows pluralism to exist at the level of individual choice as to the means, but requires of all believers a devotion to the end.

Perhaps the most important gloss on the thought of *Gaudium et Spes* concerning just war and pacifism is the document *The Challenge of Peace*, issued in 1983 by the American episcopacy. The United States bishops state that the Catholic position "establishes a strong presumption against war which is binding on all; it then examines when this presumption may be overridden, precisely in the name of preserving the kind of peace which protects human dignity and human rights" (no. 70).

The episcopal letter demonstrates the importance of the idea of peace in Catholic moral reflection on just war and pacifism. Both traditions of ethical analysis oppose the too easy resort to warfare in human affairs. Note, however, that if war is to be permitted in Catholic teaching, it is on the basis of peace. Defensive war does not rupture peace in Catholic just war theory but is the means for restoring true peace, "the kind of peace which protects human dignity and human rights."

Augustine's notion of peace, supported by Vatican II, is found in the pastoral letter. Peace is more than the absence of war, it is *"tranquillitas ordinis."* The destruction of such a public order precedes the resort to war in Catholic theology. Peace has already been violated by the aggression of another before Catholic just war theory will consider any overriding of the presumption against war. It should be noted, however, that the pastoral letter is not as clear on this point as it should be. Later, in reference to the decision to override the presumption against war, the letter reads:

> Such a decision, especially today, requires extraordinarily strong reasons for overriding the presumption *in favor of peace* and *against* war (emphasis in original) (no. 83).

This is inconsistent with paragraph 70, cited above. As James Finn states:

> The traditional doctrine does not, therefore, override a presumption in favor of peace unless peace is understood merely as the absence of war, which has never been Catholic teaching. The just war doctrine recognizes that a defensive use of arms is sometimes required for the restoration of peace.[21]

The West German bishops were clearer in this regard. In their pastoral letter they considered the "limited function" of just war teaching "within a comprehensive peace ethic in the church."[22] The West German formulation captures the idea that just war theory in Roman Catholicism is seen as a means to peace and ought not to be contrasted with peace.

Before a nation decides to go to war it must weigh the consequences of the violence of war versus the reality of injustice due to aggression. Since Pius XII this is the sole rationale for going to war. When making the judgment about resort to warfare leaders of nations must decide whether there are other less evil methods of resisting aggression. In the modern era there is still a further element to be considered before going to war. In *The Challenge of Peace* the United States bishops state: "In today's interdependent world even a local conflict can affect people everywhere; this is particularly the case when the nuclear powers are involved. Hence a nation cannot justly go to war today without considering the effect of its action on others and on the international community" (no. 99). It was John XXIII who made concern for international order as well as a nation's domestic order a central factor in an assessment of the *jus ad bellum*. The growing emphasis on international order in Catholic social teaching has heightened the reluctance to approve of war. As a last resort, however, the force of arms cannot be denied a nation in the quest for restoring the peace.

A historical parallel can be cited. Traditionally, Roman Catholic teaching on domestic insurrection has demonstrated a greater hesitation to approve the resort to arms than has been the case within just war theory. The reason for this has been the Catholic concern for preserving social order. With the modern papacy we find discussion of the international community and war in a manner that recalls the medieval discussion of the domestic order when considering the possibility of insurrection. While insurrection is not absolutely ruled out in medieval political theory there is a willingness to countenance the continuation of some injustice for the sake of public order. So, too, with modern war the resort to arms is not absolutely proscribed but there is a growing reluctance to justify war. Some injustice may be endured for the sake of international order. *The Challenge of Peace* mentions the good of international order when it discusses the *jus ad bellum* criteria of proportionality (no. 99).

Pacifism in the American bishops' letter is viewed as a moral choice for persons committed to a genuine peace but who cannot accept that violent means may restore the peace (no. 73). Pacifism in Catholic theory remains committed not only to the abolition of warfare but the establishment of the *"tranquillitas ordinis."* Pacifism cannot be a sectarian withdrawal nor can it be a dismissal of the valid claims of the state to self-preservation. In this, Catholic pacifism may differ with certain Protestant theories of pacifism and radical countercultural movements that rely on elements of anarchical political theory.

When discussing pacifism the bishops are explicit in their repetition of the conciliar teaching; pacifism is a choice for the individual believer. Both "choice" and "individual" are key words. The pastoral letter only endorses pacifism as an option for individuals. It cannot be required of states or of individuals. It is not a duty but a choice (no. 75). Thus, those believers who maintain that pacifism is an essential aspect of Christian faith and therefore a duty rather than option do not find support in Catholic social teaching.[23]

Modern Catholic social teaching on just war and pacifism may be summarized as follows:

1. War may only be waged to restore peace after it has been destroyed by an act of aggression.

2. An effort must be made to find whether less evil means of restoring the peace are possible. War is a last resort as a means to establish the *"tranquillitas ordinis."* Still, in the end, a nation has the right to employ med force in self-defense.

3. In the decision to wage war consideration must be given to the overall proportionality of the evil of war versus the evil brought about by aggression. It may be necessary according to Catholic teaching to endure a measure of injustice for the sake of social goods like international order.

4. Within a just war there are specific and firm moral principles that govern any use of armed force.

5. Pacifism is an option individuals may choose. Both conscientious objection and selective conscientious objection are supported by Catholic teaching. The latter is premised on just war theory, while the former is derived from the legitimacy of pacifism (*The Challenge of Peace*, no. 233).

6. Pacifism requires a clear commitment to resist injustice and a desire to promote human rights and the common good. Sectarian withdrawal is not an option for Roman Catholics.

7. The pacifism approved by Catholic social teaching is based on the freedom of the person and the right of individual conscience. It is not a duty for all but an option for those who discern a moral call to oppose war.

THE RELATIONSHIP BETWEEN PACIFISM AND JUST WAR?

In an essay written after Vatican II, but before the American bishops' pastoral letter, Bryan Hehir posed a question regarding the teaching of Catholicism which approves both just war and pacifism. "In the new state of the question do we have moral complexity or simply contradiction in the two positions?"[24] The issue is one of coherence. Can Roman Catholicism plausibly hold the position that both just war and pacifism are acceptable positions? At Vatican II the answer of coherence was not pressed since pacifism was dealt with as a matter of individual conscience. Pacifism was approved in deference to freedom of conscience, not as an objectively correct theory.

Because of the church's respect for the freedom of the person there is a legitimate diversity allowed; the individual person acting in good conscience may choose between just war or pacifism. Freedom of conscience, however, must be coupled with responsibility for the formation of conscience. Sincerity is a necessary but insufficient condition for acting in good conscience according to Catholic teaching. The moral agent must make a reasonable effort to inform his or her conscience. Believers must make an honest attempt at finding out what is the morally right choice. Due to a variety of obstacles such knowledge may not be possible. Then the person is bound to act according to his or her best judgment, given what the person sincerely believes. The act may, in fact, be wrong but the person remains in good conscience if he or she acted on sincere conviction.

The position of the Council, while an important development in Catholic social teaching, could not be the final word. Inevitably believers were led to ask, What does the conscientious seeker find when he or she searches for the answer to the question of which stance is right, pacifism or just war? In 1983 the American bishops suggested one finds a complex reality which admits of a legitimate diversity. Thus the bishops opted for a stance of pluralism in regard to the moral evaluation of war; both just war and pacifism are approved.

In the pastoral letter the argument for pluralism is rooted theologically in the kingdom of God. Precisely because that reality has a twofold character, being both present and future, a single moral option is considered too restrictive as an adequate witness to the kingdom. Pacifism and just war are necessary options available to a church which must witness to both the present and future dimensions of God's kingdom. "In the 'already but not yet' of Christian existence, members of the church choose different paths to move toward the realization of the kingdom in history" (no. 62).

Pacifism is a path to be taken by those who remind the world of the fullness of God's promise of peace, while just war proponents choose on the basis of their recognition of the unrealized nature of the kingdom of God. Since both dimensions of God's message are true, it is present reality and future promise, those who live in the "in-between times" must develop an ethical stance toward war that encompasses both aspects of God's message. While this is obviously difficult for an individual, the community of believers, by allowing both pacifism and just war, is able to reflect something of the broad nature of human experience of the kingdom. It is in this sense that pluralism is necessary with regard to the morality of warfare.

Left at this, the pastoral letter does not really advance beyond the statement of Vatican II. What the American bishops have provided is a theological brief for vocational pacifism. Just as the church has always known some who by virtue of their chosen lifestyle refused to bear arms so today that option continues to remain open. In the past the church resolved the tension between the eschatological witness of pacifism versus the incarnational witness of just war by the divide between clerics or religious and laity. Now the divide is not so neat as Catholics of all canonical states in life are adherents of one or the other position, but the vocational nature of pacifism remains the same. It is still not a moral duty but a freely chosen option for some who are so called.[25]

After examining the relationship of pacifism and just war at the level of individual choice, one is still left with the question of whether at the level of theory the two approaches can be taught by the church. Once the question is put this way the issue becomes one of moral rightness. In *The Challenge of Peace* the reply is that both views are acceptable because they "support and complement one another, each preserving the other from distortion" (no. 121).

The suggestion that pacifism and just war "complement one another" is an interesting one given the seeming contradiction between just war and pacifist views. The basis for the complementarity is the argument that the two traditions share certain characteristics: 1) "they share a common presumption against the use of force as a means of settling disputes" (no. 120); 2) "both find their roots in the Christian theological tradition"; 3) in the present age just war and pacifism "often converge and agree in their opposition to methods of warfare" (no. 121).

Is this a sufficient basis for establishing complementarity between just war and pacifism? It is hard to see how it is so. While it is true that both just war and pacifism share the moral presumption against violence, they are very different in their understanding of the nature of the presumption. For pacifism the presumption makes war always and everywhere illegitimate. For the just war proponent the presumption places a burden of proof on those who would override the presumption but it can be overridden, even must be overridden in some cases.

If one applies the bishops' reasoning to another area the weakness of the claim of the pastoral becomes clear. Take the case of capital punishment. Those who are for and against capital punishment can be said to share a presumption against taking life. One side, however, justifies state execution for certain crimes, while the other side considers this judicial murder. Is it plausible to suggest that these two sides "support and complement one another"? Sharing a presumption against violence is not enough to establish complementarity when one side considers the presumption absolute and the other does not.

A second rationale for calling just war and pacifism complementary is that they both have roots in the Christian tradition. The difficulty, however, is that many opposing ideas have roots in the Christian tradition. One can find both opposition and support for religious liberty in Catholic teaching. The same can be said about taking interest on loans, baptism by force, slavery, the use of torture in interrogation, and many other examples. Roots in the Catholic tradition do not guarantee complementarity.[26]

Finally, as a third reason for asserting complementarity the pastoral letter observes that pacifism and just war often come to the same conclusion about specific methods of warfare. This is true, I believe, but not a very telling point. Since pacifism is bound to oppose all methods of warfare it is not surprising that there will be occasions when it can agree with just war theory's opposition to a method of warfare. Is that sufficient ground for calling the views complementary?

Again, if we transpose the claim to another context the weakness of the episcopal claim is clear. Suppose one person opposes all capital punishment for whatever reason and another person judges capital punishment to be morally licit but only by methods which prevent pain to the victim. For the second person a procedure which entails injection of a sleep-inducing drug followed by a lethal dose of morphine is admissible; electrocution, hanging, and firing squad are ruled out. Since the first person who is absolute in opposition to capital punishment and our second individual agree on their views about electrocution, should we consider their stances complementary? The common-sense view would oppose such language.

There seems to be a confusion in the pastoral whereby complementarity is equivalent to just war having something in common with pacifism. That is not sufficient, however, and obscures the real point, which is that pacifism and just war theory are in opposition to one another. They challenge each other, and they cannot both be right. Either war is sometimes permissible or it is not. There is no alternative. Either pacifism is right or just war theory is right. Vatican II did not deal with this point explicitly because it discussed the topic at another level, that of moral goodness. However, it is fair to say that Vatican II holds for the objective rightness of just war theory although the issue is not put in that way. The duty of state leaders to call people to arms, if necessary, in defense of the nation is an indication of the Council's view. A pacifist's moral goodness need not be challenged but any claim to objective rightness by the pacifist is countered by the Council's support for just war. The American bishops made an effort to move the question beyond the matter of moral goodness and personal conscience, but without success.

What we find, therefore, is some confusion about the nature of the relationship between pacifism and just war in church teaching. It is clear that individuals can opt for either pacifism or just war and find support in the documents. At the level of moral theory, however, it is more difficult to hold onto both pacifism and just war. Present church teaching indicates a clear preference for just war theory.[27] In the important statement by the American bishops there was an effort to press the question of the relationship between just war and pacifism. Ultimately, however, the episcopal letter does not break significant new ground. Its formulation of the relationship in terms of complementarity fails to explain how Catholicism might hold that both just war and pacifism are acceptable theories of moral evaluation.

CONCLUSION

A future concern for Catholic social teaching on war is to ask if pluralism at the level of moral theory or moral rightness is possible. Such a question forces one to explain how the church could endorse as possibly right theories which are odds with one another. Any future debate about the relation of just war theory and pacifism in Catholic social teaching will have to rethink the American bishops' approach, even while striving for the pluralism they desired.

To call pacifism and just war theory complementary too quickly resolves the question. At the level of moral rightness pacifism and just war cannot be complementary. It would be better to acknowledge the contradictory nature of the claims. Yet this contradiction need not drive Catholic teaching to endorse one theory and reject the other as at present.

What remains possible is for the church to talk about the ambiguity of moral reality and admit that the church as well as individuals must be modest about whether it is just war or pacifism that is right. Faced with ambiguity about the objective nature of war, the church ought to allow a legitimate pluralism at the level of theory. To opt for one or the other stance is to claim more knowledge of reality than is available.

Perhaps the church is not prepared to accept this limitation on its moral knowledge, but if pluralism is ever allowed to exist it will be because the reality of war is morally ambiguous, not because pacifism and just war are complementary. A future church teaching might frankly acknowledge that it must be modest in the conclusions it reaches about the complex choices as to how best to promote peace.

NOTES

1. Jenny Teichman, *Pacifism and the Just War* (Oxford: Basil Blackwell, 1986), p. 1. I have found Teichman's work a very useful essay for achieving terminological clarity.
2. Teichman, p. 3.

3. See Teichman, pp. 10-11.

4. See Frederick Russell, *The Just War in the Middle Ages* (Cambridge: Cambridge University Press, 1977), p. 16.

5. National Conference of Catholic Bishops (NCCB), *The Challenge of Peace* (Washington, D.C.: United States Catholic Conference, 1983), no. 121, p. 37.

6. Since the focus of this chapter is just war and pacifism in modern Catholic social teaching, I will not treat the history of earlier Christian reflection on these topics.

7. Cited in James T. Johnson, *Just War Tradition and the Restraint of War* (Princeton, New Jersey: Princeton University Press, 1981), p. 340. Johnson notes that this statement from the Postulata on war was presented in 1870 during the Franco-Prussian War and only five years after the American Civil War. The context, in other words, was one of great violence and bloodshed.

8. John Courtney Murray, *We Hold These Truths* (Garden City, New York: Doubleday, 1964), pp. 243, 246.

9. Ibid., pp. 244-45.

10. Pius XII, "War and Peace," an address to delegates to the Eighth Congress of the World Medical Association, 1954. In *Pattern for Peace: Catholic Statements on International Order*, ed. Harry Flannery (Westminster, Maryland: Newman, 1962), p. 237. I am grateful to Richard Miller of Indiana University for this citation. Dr. Miller graciously gave me a draft of a manuscript that examines many of the moral issues, including just war and pacifism, that surround modern warfare. His manuscript has been very helpful, although I have refrained from quoting his text directly in deference to its provisional state.

11. Pius XII, "Christmas Radio Message," December 23, 1956. In *Peace and Disarmament* (Rome: Pontifical Commission Iustitia et Pax, 1982), p. 137.

12. Ibid.

13. John XXIII, *Pacem in Terris*, no. 100. In *Seven Great Encyclicals*, ed. William Gibbons (New York: Paulist Press, 1963), p. 310.

14. Again, I am grateful to Richard Miller for pointing out the connection between Pius and John on this matter.

15. John XXIII, *Pacem in Terris*, nos. 126-27. In Gibbons, p. 315.

16. See James Douglass, *The Nonviolent Cross* (London: Macmillan, 1966), pp. 81-99.

17. *Pastoral Constitution on the Church in the Modern World*, no. 80. In *The Documents of Vatican II*, ed. Walter Abbott (Piscataway, New Jersey: New Century Publishers, 1966), p. 293.

18. René Coste, "Commentary on Part II, Chapter V," *Commentary on the Documents of Vatican II*, vol. 5, ed. Herbert Vorgrimler (New York: Herder and Herder, 1969), p. 354.

19. Ibid., p. 348.

20. William Au, "American Catholics and the Dilemma of War 1960-1980," *U.S. Catholic Historian* 3 (1984), pp. 49-79.

21. James Finn, "Pacifism and Just War: Either or Neither," *Catholics and Nuclear War*, ed. Philip Murnion (New York: Crossroad, 1983), p. 144.

22. *Out of Justice, Peace*, no. 107 (San Francisco: Ignatius Press, nd), p. 68.

23. Again, the pastoral letter is not always helpful in clarifying certain points. Among those it commends for their nonviolent witness is Dorothy Day. It is quite clear, however, that the pacifism of Dorothy Day goes beyond what the bishops

themselves support. For Day, pacifism was a moral duty generated by the teaching of the gospel. Whether her position will be accepted someday by Catholic social teaching is an open question. What is clear, though, is that Dorothy Day would not recognize her beliefs in the bishops' letter.

24. J. Bryan Hehir, "The Just War Ethic and Catholic Theology: Dynamics of Change and Continuity," *War or Peace?*, ed. Thomas Shannon (Maryknoll, New York: Orbis Books, 1980), p. 24.

25. It is clear that one of the forces contributing to the rise of pacifist sentiment in Roman Catholicism is the reform movements of lay Catholics who seek to live a more evangelical life than an older lay spirituality encouraged. Teichman remarks that "pacifism is a characteristic form of 'renewal' for Christianity" (Teichman, p.11). For the role that evangelic Catholic movements such as the Catholic Worker played in promoting pacifism with the church, see David O'Brien, "American Catholic Opposition to the Vietnam War: A Preliminary Assessment." In Shannon, pp. 119-50. See also, idem, *Public Catholicism* (New York: Macmillan, 1989).

26. A view similar to mine is Norbert Rigali, "Just War and Pacifism," *America* 150 (1984), pp. 233-36.

27. At a January 1983 meeting between a group representing the American bishops and members of the Vatican, it was clear that Vatican officials were uneasy with the idea of putting pacifism on equal footing with just war theory. See the official memo drawn up after the meeting, "A Vatican Synthesis," *Origins* 12 (1983), pp. 691-95.

23

CONDITIONS OF PEACE IN THE NEW INTERNATIONAL SYSTEM

Interdependence and Internationalization

ERIC O. HANSON

The meeting of Mikhail Gorbachev and John Paul II in December 1989 represented a new stage in the long tradition of European political-religious diplomacy, from the Emperor Constantine at the Council of Nicaea to the papal secretary of state Ercoli Consalvi at the Congress of Vienna. The Congress of Vienna restored the Papal States, with the result that the papacy supported the European consort of powers, even to discouraging Catholic Irish and Polish rebellions against Protestant Britain and Orthodox Russia. The Congress of Vienna also constituted the last European security system based on common values, structure, and procedures.[1] As later modified by Bismarck, that security system endured almost into the twentieth century. The rapid global political changes of 1989-90 mean that the world now faces the even greater challenge of constructing a new international security system based on common values, structure, and procedures that would both prevent war and institutionalize democratic rights. This international system would look to the European tradition in such documents as the United Nations Declaration of Human Rights.

The year 1989 witnessed momentous changes in various Eastern-bloc nations, from the first Polish postwar free elections in June to the execution of the Romanian dictator Nicolae Ceausescu on Christmas Day. Since scholars and commentators did not anticipate most of these cataclysmic events, there have been many recent hurried attempts at explanation. My general categorization of some of these general attempts uses the names of political actors: a) Mikhail Gorbachev, *perestroika* and Soviet foreign policy; b) Leonid Brezhnev, the complete stagnation of the Soviet economy; c) Ronald Reagan, the president's military buildup in his first term and willingness to negotiate in the second; d) Lech Walesa, peoples movements in the Eastern bloc; e) Karol Wojtyla, the Vatican's encouragement of human rights in Poland and Czechoslovakia; f) Dan Rather, Tom Brokaw, and Ted Koppel, international media coverage; g) Hans Genschler, Petra Kelly, and the Dutch Interreligious Peace Fellowship (IKV), European diplomacy and popular demonstrations during the period of Soviet-American crisis. As in most series of linked historical events, a complex causality blending these and other approaches most closely approximates the truth, guaranteeing employment for future social scientists and propagandists.

This chapter focuses on three pivotal events of 1989 to illustrate recent changes in the international system at international, regional, and national levels. All three events, with universal quasi-religious symbols like the Goddess of Democracy (half Statue of Liberty and half Buddhist Goddess of Mercy) received immediate comprehensive media exposure. People throughout the world, whatever their beliefs, experienced these events and their quasi-religious symbols at a very deep human level. In chronological order the three events are the Tiananmen Massacre in June, the opening of the Berlin Wall in November, and the December meeting of Wojtyla and Gorbachev. This chapter, however, presents them in reverse order. The meeting of the pope and the president signifies technological and ideological changes at the systemic level in international affairs. The opening of the Berlin Wall sets the discussion of the future of Europe, the most significant regional issue for global peace. The Tiananmen Massacre highlights the global role of third-world countries and the moral significance of North-South relations articulated in John Paul II's latest encyclical, *Sollicitudo Rei Socialis*. The final section of the chapter offers some thoughts on the current challenges facing the Catholic church in contributing to world peace. In short, this chapter constitutes a Catholic perspective on the signs of the times for world peace in our rapidly changing international system. As such, the author hopes it makes a small contribution to the continuing dialectic of Catholic social thought begun in *Rerum Novarum*.

POPE, PRESIDENT, AND THE NEW INTERNATIONAL SYSTEM

Soviet president and general secretary Mikhail Gorbachev met Pope John Paul II in Rome as a prelude to his talks in Malta with United States president George Bush. Thus, the military, political, and symbolic leader of the Warsaw Pact visited the two Western leaders who could most contribute to the long-term stability of East-West relations and the international system. While a single interlocuter sought to represent the East, the West must always be represented by at least two different types of leaders. The American president's job description does not include the kind of "spiritual" leadership demanded from the head of a Leninist party, notwithstanding whether or not the bland Mr. Bush can match the avuncular television charisma of his predecessor, Ronald Reagan. John Paul's legitimacy as Western symbolic leader results from the Catholic majorities and pluralities in many NATO states and from his campaign for individual and political rights in Eastern Europe, beginning with his inspirational first papal trip to Poland in 1979.

Both the Soviet president and the pope are media superstars. The day after their meeting, news photos of Gorbachev and John Paul II filled the international press. The front page of the *New York Times,* for example, highlighted a four-column photo of the pope exhorting his Soviet visitor. Both leaders, in contrast to Bush who has difficulty with "the vision thing," fit the new era of global politics with its emphasis on the public articulation of comprehensive political, economic, and cultural visions.

This is not just the end of the Cold War. This is the end of the postwar era. Compare the current situation with the period of Soviet-American hostility from the Soviet invasion of Afghanistan and the American failure to ratify SALT II in 1979 to the accession of Gorbachev and Reagan's second term in 1985. The two superpowers did not even attend each other's Olympics in Moscow (1980) and in Los Angeles (1984). Europeans became increasingly concerned about theater nuclear war as the time for the deployment of the Euromissiles in November 1983 approached.[2] Indeed, 1983 was the year of the Catholic peace pastoral. The hierarchies of West Germany, France, the Netherlands, Belgium, Ireland, Scotland, Austria, East Germany, Hungary, Japan, and the United States wrote national pastorals on war and peace. John Paul II expressed the urgency of the danger at Hiroshima in 1981 and set the parameters for the national episcopal positions on deterrence in his message, read by Cardinal Casaroli, to the United Nations Second Special Session on Disarmament in 1982.[3] In the Netherlands the ecumenical IKV, with Pax Christi as its largest member, effectively coordinated European public protest. It is in such global crises that religious institutions are called to exercise a more overt political role, serving both their members and all men and women who seek peace on earth. Final success, however, means the withdrawal of religious institutions from direct political roles. This is true at the international, regional, and national levels. For example, democratization has meant that the Polish church has become much less active politically.

The European arms debate did moderate with the signing of the Intermediate Nuclear Forces treaty at the Washington summit of November 1987. On strategic weapons, Bush and Gorbachev signed a statement of principles at the Washington summit in June 1990 that should result in a START treaty by the end of the year. Such a treaty would reduce the number of nuclear weapons held by both superpowers by roughly thirty percent. In the preparatory negotiations United States Secretary of State James Baker and Soviet foreign minister Eduard Shevardnadze finally broke the impasse on air-launched and sea-launched cruise missiles. The major remaining issues involve the Soviet SS-18s and the Backfire bomber. At the summit the two sides also agreed to eliminate most of their chemical weapons.

This new era in international politics has been fostered by the accelerating technological advances of the postwar period. Progress in electronics, communication, and weapons yield have promoted the internationalization of economics and the media, while greatly escalating the damage caused by even "limited" war. The Catholic church, therefore, as an expressive organization with a long tradition of reformist political activity and internationalization, has become more significant in world politics as the twentieth century has progressed.

The last thirty years have also witnessed the superpowers' discovery of the limits of military power in Vietnam and Afghanistan, the movement toward Western European integration, and the shift of economic power toward the Pacific region. The Sino-Soviet rapprochement, finalized in May 1989, has reduced tensions in East Asia and supported military reductions in both countries. This new era in international politics has three basic characteristics: 1) the rapid internationalization of cultural, political, and economic issues; 2) the increased political significance of the expressive politics of comprehensive political and ethical visions, articulated by both political and religious leaders, primarily through the international secular media; and 3) the increasing political significance of global economics, as the utility of large-scale war decreases. In the 1980s war meant political failure and obscene, mostly civilian, suffering in the Third World, in countries such as Iran, Iraq, El Salvador, Afghanistan, Lebanon, Cambodia, Sudan, Ethiopia, Angola, Mozambique, and Panama. In both NATO and the Warsaw Pact, even the preparations for war have exacerbated national and regional tensions, threatening to separate the superpowers from their allies.

THE BERLIN WALL AND THE FUTURE OF EUROPE

The opening of the Berlin Wall in November 1989 reminded many of the tense Soviet-American confrontations when Khrushchev ordered the wall built in 1961. John XXIII sought to involve the church more actively in the search for world peace. The pope even mediated between Kennedy and Khrushchev. The following year the Soviet leader received an advanced copy of the encyclical *Pacem in Terris* in Russian. The opening of the Berlin Wall thus symbolizes West German and Vatican *Ostpolitik*, the Christian Democratic vision of German and European reunification, the full establishment of the European Economic Community in 1992, and the possibility of further pan-European integration in East and West. No longer do Moscow and Washington determine Europe's fate. The future of Europe is the most important regional question for world peace. After all, this century's two world wars were predominately European wars, and nuclear and conventional firepower remains concentrated on that continent. How can the Catholic church contribute to a European consensus that will promote peace and democratization?

Both the international system and the Catholic church currently face "Eastern European moments." In the church this period follows the four-hundred-year "Italian era" from the Council of Trent to the death of the quintessentially Christian Democratic pope, Paul VI. The election of John Paul II brought to church leadership a man who had the Middle-European experience of the worst legacies of modern Europe, Auschwitz and the Gulag. The next Catholic era belongs to the Third World, especially Latin America. In the international political system, the "Eastern European moment" stands between the postwar Pax Americana and the coming triple hegemony of Europe, North America, and East Asia. These ecclesiastical and political "Eastern European moments" reinforce each other because they coincide.

When Gorbachev introduced the theme of "our common European home" in his visit to France in 1985, most observers dismissed it as shrewd propaganda. While analysts presently argue whether or not Gorbachev had another realistic choice, they do credit him with meaning what he says when he pledges that the Soviet Union will not intervene in the domestic politics of Warsaw Pact allies. Other Soviet politicians have expanded on Gorbachev's theme of a common Europe. Fyodor M. Burlatsky, a legislator with close ties to the leadership, has stressed that Europe is a cultural, not a geographical concept. As such, it could include even the United States with its European heritage. "In the end, it [our common European home] means the return to a single European civilization."[4] In both the Soviet and American cases, the ruling ethos of the nation derives from the European tradition, but the population includes an increasingly large minority of non-European descent. Certainly, the challenge of European political stability is primarily cultural and religious, only secondarily military. The devolution of the Soviet empire resulted from the failure of communist parties to maintain legitimacy, not from military or diplomatic debacle.

The pope would never include the United States in his concept of Europe. John Paul II's final meeting of his November 1982 visit to Spain focused on the Christian unity of the continent. In the cathedral of Santiago de Compostela, the great pan-European center of pilgrimage, King Juan Carlos opened this Vatican-designated "European act" before five thousand distinguished guests. The guests included several Nobel prize winners, the leaders of the European Common Market and the Council of Europe, and the presidents of the bishops' conferences of most European nations. The pope urged his listeners to reject "unnatural divisions" and "secularized ideologies" which threatened the traditional Christian moral virtues. Eleven months later John Paul II traveled to Vienna to again stress the common Christian heritage of Europe "from the Atlantic to the Urals." The fact that human beings are made in the image of God and redeemed by Jesus Christ, said the pope, has fostered human dignity and universal human rights. The pope also mentioned those "dark and terrifying traits" of European history, which have resulted in so much war and persecution. His host, Cardinal Franz Koenig, reminded his listeners that Austrian Catholics bear the cross of the banishment of Protestants during the Counter-Reformation and "above all the heavy cross of the persecution of the Jews."

In Wojtyla's vision Eastern Europeans have received through suffering a sacred "mission" to mediate the spiritual reunification of Europe, from the "ends of the earth" at Compostela to the many sources of Mother Volga. This vision stresses the strong faith and serious commitment of religious believers that has been manifested in the Marxist societies of Central and Eastern Europe. Although the pope would not deny that serious spiritual defects exist in Eastern Europe—he did call Poland a "mission" country on his last trip—the source of the vibrant spirituality for European renewal seems to him to exist in the East.

The pope realizes the enormity of the challenge facing the church in the new Europe. When he visited Czechoslovakia in April 1990 he announced a special synod of European bishops "at a not too distant date" to analyze the religious and social implications of the new situation. Both John Paul II and Gorbachev fear that religion can contribute to extreme ethnic nationalism, thus threatening to make the new Europe a Yugoslavia writ large. Such ethnic instability could well trigger Russian, French, and German military responses.

While the Marxist states' vacuum of moral values has served as a proto-religious experience leading to great spiritual heroism in some, many Central and Eastern European intellectuals have denounced the spiritual damage to their societies of the last forty years. These societies have suffered a terrible loss of language and communication, an erosion of ethical sensibility, and a subversion of the natural order. To steal from the Nazi or Communist authorities has been patriotic. The natural desire for the quiet, peaceful life has led to collaboration in and failure to protest heinous crimes. Czech president and playwright Vaclav Havel used his inaugural speech to call for a return to honesty, decency, and mutual respect. Although Czechoslovakia had suffered the worst environmental damage in Europe, he said, "the worst of it is that we live in a spoiled moral environment." This spoiled moral environment is not just the result of Soviet oppression, said Havel, but "something we have inflicted upon ourselves."

In response to what they perceive as undue euphoria about the future of Christianity in these countries, some Central and Eastern European theologians have stressed that many of their people could not find religion and its moral values in Marxist society. Most withdrew into the apolitical private worlds of their rural cottages, alcoholism, drugs, and general cynicism. The church exists not just for the great souls, they emphasize, but also for the population at large. Totalitarian states did not allow the churches to fulfill their general societal role. In contrast with the West, where religious asceticism challenges believers to transcend the multiple wonders of natural creation, the citizens of Central and Eastern Europe are emerging from forty years of physical and moral shabbiness, where rarely did they experience the Western temptation to spend money carelessly. In terms of personal moral choice, neither Marxist nor liberal democratic societies can be proud of their rates of alcoholism, drug abuse, and abortion.

Cynics might say that John Paul's vision reeks of the religion-dominated societies of neo-Christendom, but this is not necessarily so. The pope, like Polish prime minister Tadeusz Mazowiecki, comes from the Krakow intellectual circles that have advocated the secularization of politics and led the Polish-Jewish dialogue. But even this relatively enlightened Polish perspective needs the complimentary insights of the Dutch ecumenical tradition with its strong emphasis on interreligious dialogue, ecclesiastical human rights, arms control, protection of the environment, and European unification. The Dutch also show a healthy skepticism about the free-market economy as a moral panacea, however effective it may be at uprooting communist bureaucracies. Where the Vatican has most damaged the possibility of such a European religious dialogue has been in its attack on national episcopal conferences in Western Europe. This damage has been greatest in countries like the Netherlands, where curial action has fragmented the unity of these conferences and destroyed much of their legitimacy with the public, especially the young.

Commenting on John Paul II's third trip to Poland in 1987, I wrote in the *Los Angeles Times* that the pope believed that "the road between Washington and Moscow could lead through Krakow and Kiev." This road now extends through the Brandenburg Gate. The international Catholic church, by helping to focus a reunited Germany toward a reunited Europe and a reunited Europe toward global solidarity, can contribute toward the formulation of a comprehensive global vision of "justice, peace, and the integrity of creation"(European ecumenical theme).

THE TIANANMEN MASSACRE AND CURRENT THREATS TO WORLD PEACE

The Chinese 27th Army moved into Tiananmen Square on June 4, 1989. The third Chinese Democracy Movement ending in blood and smoke before an international television audience serves as an apt image for recent changes in third-world politics. Unlike the much bloodier Cultural Revolution two decades previous, Beijing could not hide its repression from the global community. Ironically, 1989 should have been Deng Xiaoping's year of triumph since Gorbachev, having satisfied Deng's "three demands" on Afghanistan, the Sino-Soviet border, and Kampuchea, was coming to renew Sino-Soviet relations. Instead, the Soviet president just brought more media coverage for the student demonstrations and hunger strikes.

Tiananmen receives primary emphasis in this chapter because of China's population and nuclear capability, but the basic issues of popular legitimacy, economic development, and national integration are relevant throughout the Third World. The focal comparison, for example, could be Iran under the Shah and Khomeini, or Peru and the Shining Path guerrillas. The six-part television series the Chinese government has blamed for the Democracy Movement, *River Elegy*, constitutes a marvelous visual expression of the third-world problematic of moving from tradition ("yellow river, yellow soil, yellow people") to "blue sky" modernization.

Third-world nations currently face three sets of particularly acute crises: national crises of cultural and political legitimacy; international economic crises; and international military crises. First, some national governments have lost any popular legitimacy they once possessed, thus threatening to set off an international chain reaction as they disintegrate into regionalism and even civil war and/or foreign intervention. If the Chinese government has suffered from a crisis of faith since the death of Lin Biao in 1971, the current situation among urban intellectuals and workers, the keys to economic modernization, is tragic ten thousand times over. Second, economic dislocations in one section of the world threaten the entire global economy. Latin American and Eastern European countries carry significant national debts. In the case of Eastern Europe, only internal bureaucratic reform and strong Western economic assistance can ensure that Finland, not Latin America, serves as the model for the devolution of the Soviet empire. Third, the primary present military danger comes from the disastrous combination of religious fundamentalism, intermediate-range delivery systems, and the proliferation of atomic, biological, and chemical weapons, especially in the Middle East and South Asia. The Middle East and South Asia offer a wide range of religious fundamentalism: Hindu, Jewish, Maronite Catholic, Shiite Islam, Sikh, Sunni Islam (in alphabetical order). The Chinese, among others, seem willing to supply missiles and some chemical arms.

THE CATHOLIC CHURCH IN THE NEW INTERNATIONAL SYSTEM

The international system is entering an era of triple hegemony by Europe, North America, and East Asia. The latter term includes primarily Japan, but also the Republic of Korea and the Republic of China (Taiwan). While the Catholic churches of all three regions have special opportunities and challenges in the service of world justice and peace, it is problematic that a comprehensive global political vision will come from either North America or East Asia. My first observation is that these two continents seem to function better than Europe without one. In the search for universal societal norms, Americans place a disproportionate stress on positive law, while Japanese rely more heavily on internalized cultural values. My second observation is that unless Europe can fashion a vision of its international vocation, it will be difficult for the continent to articulate the common values necessary for regional integration. Both social science and religion have demonstrated the utility of an outside "missionary" task in solidifying internal unity. If Europe were to focus totally on Europe, the continent would never find its soul. In this sense the murder of the six Jesuits and two women in El Salvador presents a challenge to the European soul as it does to the American one.

In their landmark book *Habits of the Heart*,[5] Robert Bellah, et al., criticized the exaggerated individualism of American culture and advocated the reappropriation of its earlier, more communal biblical and republican traditions. It is not just my long-range pessimism about such a reemphasis on collective responsibility that makes me pessimistic about an American articulation of a comprehensive global vision. The use of English as a world language and the United States educational atomization into locally-run school districts militates against general educational excellence, the teaching of foreign languages, and an international perspective.

There are immediate obstacles in American politics as well. Through his first year in office George Bush was unable to express any comprehensive vision for United States domestic or foreign policy. It is even questionable whether or not the country can attain the unity necessary to accomplish its own economic reconstruction so as to compete more effectively with Japan. And recent Bush foreign-policy initiatives toward Panama and China do not indicate increased emphasis on human rights and international law, two essential pillars of a future comprehensive vision. Bush's high approval ratings, popular support for the invasion of Panama, and the general disintegration of the Democratic Party at the national level do not presage any political changes during the next few years.

This pessimism about a comprehensive vision does not slight the current positive contributions of the Bush Administration, the people of the United States, and the American Catholic Church. Washington should continue to cooperate on arms control and democratization in Eastern Europe. The cultural emphasis on individualism and positive law seems to assist the United States in integrating political and economic refugees into its society. This is especially true of California, a high-technology and media-oriented Pacific Rim state with an increasingly third-world population and a GNP that would rank it sixth among the world's nations. The children of the Los Angeles city school system speak over one hundred different languages at home.

One friend, a Thai priest stationed in Rome, defends United States Catholicism to Western Europeans by pointing to the number of American families who regularly attend Mass. American Catholics can emphasize their international moral tradition by focusing on the physical, psychological, and spiritual health of the family. Current United States public policy and consumerist society have been particularly brutal toward children. The Catholic international spirit would help integrate immigrants within our nation and prepare Americans to play a constructive role in global peace and development. The current global crisis that cries for large-scale American Catholic participation is mediation of Israel and the Palestinians.

In summary, then, what national, regional, and international challenges does a comprehensive international Catholic vision of world peace face? In this "Eastern European moment," the first and primary challenge is national: to develop new structures of justice and human rights for the nations of Central and Eastern Europe within the constraints of national and regional politics of the Warsaw Pact. The necessity of a peaceful transition does not derive just from Catholic reformist politics or from the obvious military dangers of a radical solution. Rather, the requirements of economic development and symbolic politics mean that solutions necessitate the participation of all major sectors of the nation.

The complex challenges of rebuilding state legitimacy and the national economy require political and ecclesiastical policies different from those aimed at enduring as the opposition in a totalitarian state. In solving third-world economic problems, the Japanese experience seems more relevant than the American one. The Japanese model, extremely successful in both the late nineteenth and mid-twentieth centuries, was developed by a resource-poor non-white nation to attain parity with the North Atlantic powers. It stressed extremely high norms for the state bureaucracy, an area of weakness for Marxist regimes. It also emphasized the impact of cultural and political issues on national economic development. Recent Japanese foreign policy has emphasized economic aid for third-world development. In January 1990 prime minister Toshiki Kaifu spent eleven days visiting European leaders, including John Paul II. Kaifu brought economic aid for Central and Eastern Europe.

The international Catholic church must prepare for the coming of the era of third-world Catholicism. The transition could be facilitated because Eastern European and third-world nations have common experiences of international debt and authoritarian governments. They have suffered similar types of environmental damage as the side effects of their struggling economies. In fact, if we examine the conditions for core solutions to political legitimacy and economic development in Eastern European and third-world nations, they are remarkably similar. A core solution for political stability and economic progress, be it a center-right, centrist, or center-left coalition, must include approximately seventy percent of the political spectrum. Political representation from the urban middle class, which must not fragment for ideological reasons or out of personal loyalties, is necessary for all solutions. Any solutions will require at least the neutrality of the "primary ethical broker,"[6] the military, and the relevant superpower(s).

In both third-world and Eastern European countries the public debate over governmental legitimacy has given prominence to "primary ethical brokers," institutions recognized by the majority of the population as articulating the ethical sense of that society, for example, the Lutheran Federation of Evangelical Churches in the German Democratic Republic, the Catholic episcopal conferences in Poland and Chile, the ecumenical Christian alliance in South Korea, and the Protestant South African Council of Churches. As in international affairs, the more crucial the national political crisis, the more overtly political must be the activities of these "primary ethical brokers."

The Japanese model mentioned above does have many advantages in solving national cultural, political, and economic crises. It also has one glaring weakness: its insularity fostered by a national perception of uniqueness so strong that it vitiates much of the content of the constantly trumpeted *kokusai-ka* (internationalism).[7] Christianity, by contrast, offers the strong universalist orientation of the communion of saints: "There is neither Jew nor Greek." In *Pacem in Terris* Pope John XXIII devoted the entire fourth part to a moral argument for a worldwide public authority, the absence of which, he said, constitutes a "structural defect" in the international system. In a world whose primary characteristic is the rapid internationalization of all national cultural, political, and economic challenges, we Catholics should be known for the universal breadth of our vision and the international efficacy of our love.

NOTES

1. Gordon A. Craig and Alexander L. George, *Force and Statecraft: Diplomatic Problems in Our Time* (New York: Oxford University Press, 1983), p. x.

2. For the arms-control negotiations of this period, see Strobe Talbot, *Endgame: The Inside Story of SALT II* (New York: Harper and Row, 1979); idem, *Deadly Gambits: The Reagan Administration and the Stalemate in Arms Control* (New York: Alfred A. Knopf, 1985).

3. See Chapter Eight, "Arms Control as a Catholic Political Issue," in Eric O. Hanson, *The Catholic Church in World Politics* (Princeton, New Jersey: Princeton University Press, 1987), pp. 281-322.

4. Fyodor M. Burlatsky, interview in *New York Times,* November 30, 1989.

5. Berkeley: University of California Press, 1985.

6. Hanson, chaps. 7, 9.

7. Edwin O. Reischauer, *The Japanese Today: Change and Continuity* (Cambridge: Harvard University Press, 1988). The Japanese "postwar comprehensive settlement of accounts" remains in the future. Ellen L. Frost, *For Richer, For Poorer: The New U.S.-Japan Relationship* (New York: Council on Foreign Relations, 1987), mentions four possible dominant Japanese world-views: residual pacifism, martial nationalism, material nationalism, and liberal internationalism.

CONTRIBUTORS

Joseph Cardinal Bernardin has been the Archbishop of Chicago since 1982. For four years (1968-1972) he served as General Secretary of the National Conference of Catholic Bishops and the United States Catholic Conference. He was named Archbishop of Cincinnati in 1972 and from November 1974 until November 1977 he served as President of the U.S. Bishops' Conference. Cardinal Bernardin has been an elected delegate to the World Synod of Bishops in 1974, 1977, 1980, 1983, 1987, and 1990. Bernardin served as chairman of the U.S. Bishops' Committee which prepared the pastoral letter, *The Challenge of Peace.*

Lisa Sowle Cahill is Associate Professor of Theology, Boston College. Professor Cahill is President-elect of the Catholic Theological Society of America. She serves as editor for *The Religious Studies Review, The Journal of Religious Ethics, The Journal of Medicine and Philosophy* and *Concilium.* Among her books are *Between the Sexes: Toward a Christian Ethics of Sexuality* (1985) and, with Thomas Shannon, *Religion and Artificial Reproduction* (1988).

Sidney Callahan is Professor of Psychology, Mercy College, Dobbs Ferry, New York. Callahan has published nine books including the award-winning *With All Our Heart and Mind: The Spiritual Works of Mercy in a Psychological Age* (1988). She has served as a consultant or member of the Hastings Center, the Catholic Health Association Project on Genetics and Reproductive Technologies, and the National Science Foundation Advisory Committee for Science and Society. Callahan serves as columnist for perspectives on ethics in *Health Progress*, the official journal of the Catholic Health Association of the United States. She also serves on the national board of the Association of Rights in the Church.

John A. Coleman, S.J. is Professor of Religion and Society, The Jesuit School of Theology and the Graduate Theological Union, Berkeley, California. Author or editor of over ten books, including *An American Strategic Theology* (1982) and *Sport* (1989), Coleman serves on the national board of the Association of Rights in the Church and on the foundation and editorial board of the international Catholic journal, *Concilium.* He serves as an associate editor of *The Ecumenist.*

Ernie Cortes is a member of the national staff of the Industrial Area Foundation. He was instrumental in organizing the San Antonio Communities Organized for Public Service (COPS), the El Paso Inter-religious Sponsoring Organization (EPISO) and the United Neighborhood Organization (UNO) in Los Angeles. He was named a McArthur fellow in 1984.

Carol Coston, O.P. is Director, Partners for the Common Good Loan Fund. She has served ten years as Executive Director of *Network*, a Catholic social justice lobby in Washington, D.C. In recent years, Coston has done extensive research and writing on worker-owned cooperatives, small businesses and on alternative investments.

Charles E. Curran is presently visiting Professor of Ethics at Auburn University. He is a distinguished Catholic moral theologian, former President of the Catholic Theological Society of America, of the Society for Christian Ethics and the American Theological Society. Among his most recent books are *Faithful Dissent* (1986) and *Toward An American Catholic Moral Theology* (1987).

Bishop Thomas J. Gumbleton is the Auxiliary Bishop, the Archdiocese of Detroit. He has served as President of Pax Christi-USA and also of Bread for the World. He served on the committee which drafted the U.S. Bishops' pastoral, *The Challenge of Peace.*

Eric O. Hanson is Professor, Department of Political Science, Santa Clara University, and member, Center for International Security and Arms Control, Stanford University. He is author of the award-winning *Catholic Politics in China and Korea* (1980) and *The Catholic Church in World Politics* (1987).

J. Bryan Hehir is Senior Research Scholar at the Kennedy Institute of Ethics and Research, Professor of Ethics and International Politics, the School of Foreign Service, Georgetown University, Washington, D. C. Hehir serves as counselor for social policy, U.S. Catholic Conference. A widely published author, he has contributed many chapters to books and articles to *America, Commonweal, Theological Studies*, and *Worldview*. As secretary, Department of Social Development and World Peace, U.S. Catholic Conference, Hehir played a major role in drafting the two main social pastorals of the U.S. bishops in the 1980s. In 1984 he was a recipient of the McArthur fellowship.

Kenneth R. Himes, O.F.M. is Associate Professor, Department of Moral Theology, Washington Theological Union, Silver Springs, Maryland. He is an associate editor of *New Theology Review*. His essays have appeared in *America, Sojourners, Commonweal* and *The Ecumenist.*

Mary Evelyn Jegen, S.N.D. is Vice-President of Pax Christi International and also is an adjunct faculty member in the department of Graduate Religious Studies, Mundelein College, Chicago. Among her many books are *How You Can Be a Peacemaker: Catholic Teachings and Practical Suggestions* (1985).

S. Ryan Johansson is visiting Lecturer in the Ethics and Society program, Stanford University. Previously, she served as Associate Research Demographer and Lecturer in demography in the Graduate Group in Demography, University of California, Berkeley. Her scholarly articles in demography, stressing the ethical and humanistic implications of the field, have appeared in *Population Studies, The Journal of Family History* and *The American Journal of Physical Anthropology*.

Thomas S. Johnson is President of Manufacturers Hanover Bank. He has taught finance at the Graduate School of Business at the Ateneo de Manila University in the Philippines and served as special assistant to the Comptroller, the United States Department of Defense. Johnson is chairman of the Board of Directors, Union Theological Seminary, New York City.

Robert L. Kuttner is economics correspondent for *The New Republic*. He is one of four contributing columnists to *Business Week's* "economic viewpoint" and writes a weekly, syndicated, editorial column originating in *The Boston Globe*. Kuttner has been a Kennedy Fellow at Harvard University's Kennedy School of Government and served as chief investigator for the U.S. Senate Committee on Banking, Housing and Urban Affairs. Among his books are *The Economic Illusion* (1984) and *Revolt of the Haves* (1980).

Bishop Raymond A. Lucker is the bishop of New Ulm, Minnesota. A pioneer in the American catechetical renewal, Bishop Lucker has spent a lifetime devoted to renewal of the church in religious education, catechesis, evangelization and theology. His most recent book, *My Experience: Reflections on Pastoring,* appeared in 1988. Bishop Lucker was elected by his fellow American bishops to the World Synod of Bishops in 1977.

Richard A. McCormick, S.J. is John A. O'Brien Professor of Christian Ethics, University of Notre Dame. From 1974 to 1986 he was Rose F. Kennedy Professor of Christian Ethics at the Kennedy Institute of Ethics, Georgetown University. McCormick is a former president of the Catholic Theological Society of America. Among his many books are *The Critical Calling: Moral Dilemmas Since Vatican II* (1989). McCormick's much regarded yearly notes on moral theology for *Theological Studies* have made him the most esteemed Catholic moral theologian in the English-speaking world.

James and Kathleen McGinnis are the founders and coordinators of the Parenting for Peace and Justice Network (an international Catholic group). James McGinnis is Director, the Institute of Peace and Justice, St. Louis. Authors of numerous books and popular lecturers, their best-known book on family ministry and social justice is *Parenting for Peace and Justice* (1981; 1990).

David J. O'Brien is Professor of History, Holy Cross College, Worcester, Massachusetts. A prolific author, he has written *Public Catholicism* (1989) and edited, with Thomas A. Shannon, *Renewing the Earth: Catholic Documents on Peace, Justice and Liberation* (1977). Active for many years in many peace and justice movements in the American church, O'Brien chaired the 1976 Call to Action Conference for the American bishops.

William V. O'Brien is Professor of Government, Georgetown University where he specializes in International Law and Relations, with emphasis on legal and moral issues of war. He has twice served as President of the Catholic Association for International Peace. Among his many books are *The Nuclear Dilemma and the Just War Tradition* (co-authored with John Langan, S.J., 1986) and *The Conduct of Just and Limited War* (1981).

Archbishop Rembert G. Weakland, O.S.B. is Archbishop of Milwaukee. He studied music at the Julliard School of Music and Columbia University. He was Archabbot of St. Vincent's Archabbey, Latrobe, Pennsylvania and served two terms as Abbot Primate of the Benedictine Confederation. Archbishop Weakland chaired the National Bishops' Committee drafting the pastoral letter, *Catholic Social Thought and the U.S. Economy.*

Charles K. Wilber is Professor of Economics at the University of Notre Dame. Among his eleven published books are *An Inquiry Into The Poverty of Economics* (1983) and *Capitalism and Democracy: Schumpeter Revisited* (1985). Wilber served as consultant to the U.S. Bishops' drafting committee on *Catholic Social Thought and the U.S. Economy.*

Gordon C. Zahn is Professor emeritus in sociology at the University of Massachusetts and serves as the national director of the Center on Conscience and War in Charlestown, Massachusetts. Among his best-known books are: *In Solitary Witness: The Life and Death of Franz Jaegerstaetter* (1964) and *German Catholics and Hitler's Wars* (1962).

INDEX OF NAMES AND TITLES